Our Country!

A Panorama of American Life in the 70's

With brilliant, sensitive photographs and eloquent text, this superb volume captures the enthusiastic spirit of Americans at work and at play, learning and creating, helping one another, and contributing to a more livable world for today and tomorrow. Through its penetrating focus, *OUR COUNTRY!* will awaken in every reader the pride and thrill of living in these 50 states. Oversized at 9¾" x 11½", 288 pages, 450 illustrations with 150 in vivid full color.

Gift Price for U.S.News Subscribers Only: Standard Edition: **$14.50,** plus shipping.

See Other Side for Companion Book to *OUR COUNTRY!*

200 YEARS

A Bicentennial Illustrated History of the United States

*A memorable gift for friends . . .
business associates . . .
young people . . .
from the Book Division of
U.S.News & World Report.*

Two magnificent volumes bring to life the fire, passion, and drama of two centuries of American history—a fitting tribute to the nation's Bicentennial. *200 YEARS* includes four full-color picture portfolios, a one-of-a-kind Presidential Portrait Gallery, and two unique reading portfolios of original and historic letters, diaries, and journals. Oversized at 9½" x 12½", enclosed in a decorative and durable slipcase, more than 700 pages, 800 illustrations with 234 in brilliant full color.

**Gift Price for
U.S.News Subscribers** Only:
$29.95, plus shipping.
*(Suggested Bookstore
Price is $45.)*

See Other Side of This Card for Companion Book to *200 YEARS*

ENDSHEET: By 1883, when William Walker painted this scene at New Orleans, steamboats were giving way to railroads.

FRONTISPIECE: The 1864 Republican campaign parades in New York featured the Lincoln lantern borne high on a pole.

TITLE PAGE: Twenty-six of his generals ride with Grant in this stirring, symbolic painting by Ole P. H. Balling.

200 YEARS

A Bicentennial Illustrated History of the United States

BOOKS by U.S.NEWS & WORLD REPORT

Books by
U.S.News & World Report
A Division of U.S.News & World Report, Inc.

Directing Editor
Joseph Newman

❂

Contents

Volume Two

Introduction

To "form a more perfect Union"; to "insure domestic tranquility"; to "secure the blessings of liberty"—these were the fond hopes of the Founding Fathers when, in 1787, they wrote a Constitution for an American federal government. During the next seven decades the political institutions they had fashioned worked with reasonable success and, for the most part, maintained the always delicate balance between individual liberty and social order. But in 1861 the American political experiment seemed on the verge of collapse when eleven southern states, as a climax to an intense sectional conflict, attempted to dissolve the Union. The attempt brought on a bitter four-year Civil War, in which a half million Americans lost their lives. All knew, said Lincoln, that 250 years of black slavery had somehow caused the crisis; and he, for one, would not doubt God's justice if "this mighty scourge of war" brought slavery to an end.

Peace came in the spring of 1865 with American nationality vindicated, for the Union had survived its severest test. Equally important, 4 million black slaves were delivered from bondage, and the American commitment to liberty and equality might now be given a new and deeper meaning.

Though the postwar years of Reconstruction had their tragic aspects, the action of Congress in behalf of the freedmen was an impressive achievement: some limited relief and educational assistance; the Fourteenth Amendment, which granted citizenship and extended "the equal protection of the laws" to black Americans; the Fifteenth Amendment, which prohibited political disenfranchisement based on race or color; even several experiments with civil-rights legis-

The basically serious business of Americans electing a leader has been a democratic production ranging from high drama to farce. In 1892 one of the most amusing scenes was a Republican loser pulling a victorious Democrat through Chicago in a cart.

lation. However, enforcement was another matter, for the interest of most northern white voters in the welfare of the freedmen was short-lived. During the 1870s, when the abandonment of racial justice seemed to be the price of sectional reconciliation, northerners were quite ready to pay the price; and in the last years of the nineteenth century the condition of black Americans reached its nadir. They, like the American Indians who had been defeated and pushed onto bleak and arid reservations, entered the twentieth century with equality still a remote and shadowy dream.

Meanwhile, in the decades following the Civil War, an economic, social, and demographic revolution was transforming the country and profoundly affecting American life. The organization of the eastern railroads into networks and the building of the great transcontinentals sped the settlement of the West and, by facilitating interregional trade, encouraged the nationalizing of American business. A group of talented but ruthless entrepreneurs, by their technological and organizational innovations, pioneered the American industrial revolution, united railroads and manufacturing corporations into vast economic empires, and in the process turned the United States into one of the world's foremost industrial powers. Much of the labor for the mills, mines, and railroads came from millions of immigrants who poured into the country—a growing proportion from southern and eastern Europe. Whereas in 1860 America was still predominantly agricultural and rural, by 1900 the products of its factories exceeded in value the products of its farms, and by 1920 the majority of the people lived in cities.

These social and economic changes, though holding out the ultimate promise of greater material comfort for all, presented in their immediate effect a bewildering array of novel problems. Southern and western farmers complained bitterly that their needs and interests were being neglected in this new urban age. Industrial workers protested angrily, sometimes violently, against low wages, long hours, and the dehumanizing tendencies of a raw industrial society. New ethnic minorities among the immigrants felt the scorn and suffered the discrimination of native-born white Anglo-Saxon Protestants. Many social critics asked whether democratic institutions could survive in a society which permitted great industrial combinations to exercise so much uncontrolled economic and political power. Could the federal government, they asked, operating under a Constitution framed for the needs of a simple agricultural society, find the means to restore economic order and social justice? Could the government continue to "secure the blessings of liberty" for all the people?

The history of the twentieth century is in large part the story of how these questions were answered. During the Progressive Era before World War I, the public mood was optimistic and from a later perspective naive: if the people could be shown what was "right" they would act in the general interest. Progressives sought to make government more responsive to the majority will. They believed that corporate power could be checked, either by breaking up the giant trusts or by regulating their activities closely. Their view of social problems was mechanical: decide what was wrong, explain to the citizenry what should be done, then, presto—all would be well.

World War I marked the crest of this wave of optimism; it would make the whole world "safe" for the progressive brand of democracy. When it failed to do so, the progressive faith received a harsh setback; the twenties saw a conservative reaction, a renewed desire to limit the sphere of government, and a revived faith in every-man-for-himself and in the useful and essentially benign function of private business in the social order. But when the Great Depression struck the nation in the 1930s, a progressive resurgence, symbolized by Franklin Roosevelt's New Deal, produced a new confidence in democracy and in the need for government manipulation of the economy and even of the social structure of the country.

Once again, this new confidence in the possibility of reform reached a climax in war. Again the United States joined in what seemed to be a crusade to make the world a better place. And this time a combination of factors made the huge cost in lives and money seem worthwhile: fascism had been a real threat to humane values and it had been destroyed; atomic energy (while posing grave moral problems when used for destructive purposes) heralded a new age of material comfort; other technological advances reinforced this belief.

The Communist threat led to the cold war and delayed the expected millennium, but it, too, kept the progressive spirit alive: Americans seemed determined to demonstrate the virtues of freedom. They set out to right the wrong of centuries of racial discrimination in their own house and to wipe out tyranny, poverty, and ignorance throughout the world through a massive program of military and economic aid to the European democracies and to the underdeveloped nations of the other continents.

Although youthful confidence yielded to mature self-doubt during the sixth and seventh decades of the twentieth century, the American experience remained the world's best hope; no one could review the nation's history since 1776 without pride in its enormous accomplishments.

It is from our past that we can learn to create our future. With its narrative style and pertinent illustrations, this book is intended to make American history more available for readers of today. This awareness of the lessons of our past is vital as our nation enters the third century of its existence—the most challenging human experiment ever attempted on this earth.

PART ONE

Forging of the Union   1861-1897

Chronology:

The Winds of War

February 1861	Confederacy formed
April 1861	Civil War begins at Fort Sumter
July 1861	First Battle of Bull Run
March 1862	*Monitor* vs. *Merrimac*
September 1862	Battle of Antietam
January 1863	Emancipation Proclamation
July 1863	Battles of Gettysburg, Vicksburg
April 1865	Lee surrenders at Appomattox
April 1865	Lincoln assassinated

One Country Indivisible

1866	Freedmen's Bureau strengthened
1867	Alaska bought from Russia
1868	Johnson impeached and acquitted
1869	Transcontinental railroad finished
1872	Amnesty for Confederates
1873	Financial panic
1876	Custer's last stand

The Technological Giant

1879	Edison produces electric light bulb
1881	Garfield assassinated
1883	Civil service reformed
1886	American Federation of Labor founded
1890	Sherman Antitrust Act
1892	People's (Populist) party formed
1893	Financial panic
1894	"Coxey's Army" marches to Washington

10

Guns of Sumter

In the early spring weather of February 10, 1861, a messenger rode through the Mississippi countryside to the plantation Brierfield, bearing a telegram for former Senator Jefferson Davis. Davis, who was in the garden with his wife pruning a rose bush, read the message at once:

> We are directed to inform you that you are this day unanimously elected President of the Provisional Government of the Confederate States of America, and to request you to come to Montgomery immediately.

Mrs. Davis saw a grim change on her husband's face when he spoke, "as a man might speak of a sentence of death." Three weeks earlier he had resigned his Senate seat in Washington in an emotional address, weeping at an ovation from Southern sympathizers in the gallery. He hoped, he said, that he would be arrested, so that the right of a state's secession might be tested in the courts. On February 18, when he was inaugurated as president of the Confederacy in Montgomery, Alabama, six states had already left the Union—South Carolina, Mississippi, Florida, Alabama, Georgia, and Louisiana—and Texas was soon to follow.

In the but recently completed 1860 election, Abraham Lincoln, the first Republican President of the United States, had not received a single electoral vote from the South, and in five Southern states he drew no popular ballots, even from cranks. Thus the lawyer from Illinois had defeated Stephen A. Douglas, of the divided Democrats, by a mere half a million votes—a minority President. Lincoln and Davis had been born in Kentucky log cabins within 100 miles of each other.

The son of a revolutionary soldier, the future Southern president was born Jefferson Finis Davis, the last of ten children. He grew up on the old frontier, attended college and then West Point, became a hero of the Mexican War and a wealthy planter. In twenty years in Washington—in Congress and as secretary of war—Davis had become the leading Southern spokesman in the bitter struggle over the expansion of slavery and the sovereignty of states.

Though Brierfield was worked by slaves, Davis hired a black overseer, and no Negro was punished unless convicted by an all-black jury. Oddly enough, Davis made no mention of slavery as he took office as chief of the Confederacy. He was now fifty-two, an upright, unbending man who had refused to play at conventional Washington politics.

Davis was thin, almost gaunt, with a tuft of gray beard on his chin and one weak eye clouded by some ailment—neuralgia, it was said. Beneath his stern reserve lay a violent temper; he once fought a fellow senator with fists, and had come near fighting two duels. Sam Houston said out of intimate knowledge of Davis, "He is as ambitious as Lucifer and cold as a lizard."

Sectional strife, though almost as old as the republic, was now reaching a new climax. Davis had been in the midst of these constitutional quarrels for almost twenty years. He and his cohorts were persuasive. Their talk of secession had been echoed by sympathizers in California, Oregon, and New Jersey, and even in New York City.

In his inaugural address Lincoln put the situation plainly to Davis and the Southern rebels: "In your hands, my dissatisfied fellow countrymen, and not in mine, is the momentous issue of civil war. The government will not assail you. . . . We must not be enemies. Though passion may have strained, it must not break our bonds of affection."

Lincoln spoke from a base of potential power, for

Target of the opening shots of the Civil War on April 12, 1861, Fort Sumter in Charleston harbor twice traded hands: after its Federal defenders surrendered, the fort was held by the South for four years. In the painting opposite, the Confederate flag still flies over the ramparts after 22 months of Union shelling.

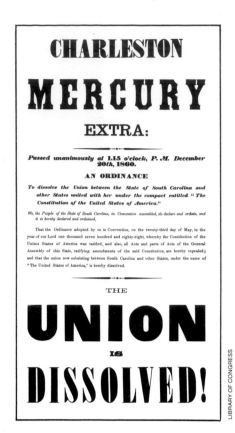

The "good news" announced to the people of South Carolina was joyously received in the state. But one citizen remarked, "South Carolina is too small for a republic and too big for a lunatic asylum."

ing the war—the first Battle of Bull Run, or Manassas—was fought in July, 1861, when Federals advanced on Beauregard.

In suffocating heat on July 21 the largest American armies ever assembled met along the banks of Bull Run. Hundreds of carriages crowded the Union rear, bearing U.S. officials, politicians, and women who had driven from Washington to see McDowell's victory. Picnic parties were scattered over the rolling fields within sight of the front lines. McDowell's men crossed Bull Run against dug-in Confederates, and Louisiana and South Carolina regiments fell back before the first assaults. A string of small, isolated battles erupted along Bull Run. By noon, fighting centered on the slope of Henry House Hill, where a small South Carolina brigade, supported by Virginians under T.J. Jackson, now a general, fired on the enemy. Jackson moved calmly among his artillerymen as they drove back several assaults, and for an hour or more 9,800 Confederates held the hill against almost 25,000 Federals.

At this moment Colonel J.E.B. Stuart's Virginia cavalry blundered into a scattered band of Federal Zouaves, who fled. One of Jackson's regiments charged from a pine grove and fought for a battery of Federal guns, and near three o'clock, in an unaccountable turn of the tide, the Union lines drifted rearward, retreating across Bull Run. As men began to run, panic seized McDowell's army and some of the first rebel yells of the war echoed over the smoky fields as Confederates pursued. Federal soldiers overran the carriages of frightened civilians.

When the shattered Union army filed into Washington the next day, McDowell had lost 3,000 men, about half of them prisoners; the Confederates had lost 2,000.

On Henry House Hill the saws of the surgeons whined all night, until huge piles of amputated limbs, Northern and Southern, grew outside the makeshift hospitals.

The Confederacy celebrated its first heroes, among them Jackson, now known as Stonewall for his stalwart stand on the hillside. But Confederate weaknesses were already revealed in criticism of Davis: Why had he not destroyed the enemy and taken Washington? Why had he forbidden Beauregard to pursue? Mrs. James Chesnut, wife of a Confederate official, wrote in her diary: "Many here already hate Jeff Davis." The Confederate congress probed the army's shortage of food and transport.

There was terror in the North. Horace Greeley of the *New York Tribune*, who had urged an invasion, wrote Lincoln: "If it is best for the country and for mankind that we make peace with the rebels at once and on their own terms, do not shirk even from that." William Tecumseh Sherman, whose brigade had been shattered, despaired of his troops: "Nobody, no man, can save the country. Our men are not good soldiers. They brag, but don't perform, complain sadly if they don't get everything they want, and a march of a few miles uses them up." Lincoln responded to this gloomy chorus by calling for 400,000 more troops.

The President also called a new general to command, George B. McClellan, a Democrat given to resounding oratory who was known to his troops as "The Little Napoleon." McClellan replaced the aging Winfield Scott as general in chief of the armies, reorganized the regiments around Washington, cleared out the city's bars and bordellos, staged numerous parades, and said, "I flatter myself that Beauregard had gained his last victory. . . . I shall . . . crush the rebels in one

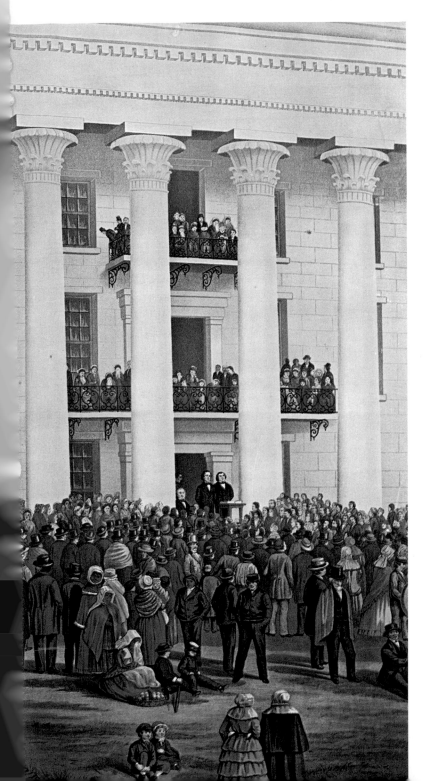

A crowd gathers (below) at the portico of the state capitol in Montgomery, Alabama, on February 18, 1861, for the ceremony during which Jefferson Davis became provisional president of the Confederacy. The shorter man at his side is Howell Cobb of Georgia, owner of a thousand slaves, who resigned as Buchanan's secretary of the treasury to agitate for secession. Cobb had presided over the establishment of an interim Confederate government in 1861.

campaign." Controversy hovered about the new commander, but Lincoln said, "I will hold McClellan's horse if he will only bring us success."

The President took the first steps in the gigantic blockade of the South, the "Anaconda" campaign, proposed by General Scott. Expeditions took Fort Hatteras and Roanoke Island on the North Carolina coast, seized Port Royal Sound in South Carolina, and occupied Ship Island in the Gulf of Mexico, a base from which New Orleans might be taken. By now, more than 40,000 men were joining the Federal armies each month.

New names were heard in early 1862 from Federal victories in the west, in the Mississippi basin—U. S. Grant at Fort Henry and Fort Donelson, in Tennessee, and George Thomas at Mill Springs, Kentucky. Within an incredibly few weeks, the western troops, with the aid of new ironclad gunboats, had opened a route of invasion that reached from Ohio into Alabama. There was ominous meaning for the Confederacy in the firm words of Grant's report: "Fort Henry is ours. The flag of the Union is reestablished on the soil of Tennessee. It will never be removed." Nashville fell. Tennessee's legislature fled to Memphis. Albert Sidney Johnston, the Confederate commander in the west, fell back to Decatur, Alabama, but retained the confidence of Jefferson Davis: "If Sidney Johnston is not a general, we had better give up the war, for we have no general."

The war was fought by boys. Some were as young as ten, and the majority were under twenty-one. The officers, too, were young—some generals in their mid-twenties. Many of the military leaders adopted outward signs of their individuality—long hair, whiskers, fancy clothing. The Confederacy awarded no medals, and the Northerners scorned to wear any. Chivalry was apparent on both sides when enemies met, and a Confederate officer who lived for many years after the conflict said, "This was the last gentlemen's war."

A Confederate soldier stands guard in a frozen field to warn nearby troops of possible attack. Cold, lonely duty such as this, alternating with the terrible heat of battle, soon destroyed illusions about the glory of war. The idyllic scene opposite, of the rebel camp at Corinth, Mississippi, fails to indicate that disease was rampant there, killing 10,000 men within two months after Shiloh—as many as were killed in the battle itself.

it difficult for other nations to recognize a Confederacy which purported to fight for freedom while enslaving many of its people. "All the revolutionary vigor is with the enemy," complained one citizen of the Confederacy, recognizing the irony that the Southern rebels were conservatives who looked to the past rather than the future.

Davis's government made desperate efforts to overcome the agricultural South's disadvantage in producing war materiel. They established war plants and subsidized private plants, but were short of raw materials and skilled labor. By 1862, arsenals in the North could turn out 5,000 rifles a day while the best the South could do was 300 a day. In order to clothe its troops, the South, lacking machines, had to employ thousands of women to make uniforms and shoes by hand.

During the early months of 1862, the adversaries grew stronger. Davis argued with Joseph Johnston, and Lincoln with McClellan, each capital wracked by controversies over grandiose schemes of battles and campaigns. In Hampton Roads, a menacing Confederate ironclad, the *Virginia* (also called the *Merrimac*), ripped apart a Federal fleet—only to be defeated soon afterward by a superior Yankee invention, the *Monitor*, whose guns fired rapidly from a revolving turret.

McClellan shipped an army of more than 100,000 to Fortress Monroe and in the spring of 1862 began a push toward Richmond. The rebel lines fell back stubbornly before him, but in May the Federal outposts were within sight of Richmond, and McClellan's aviators peered into the city from observation balloons. Abruptly, the Confederacy seemed to be crumbling,

with the capital under siege and costly failures in the west.

Federal General John Pope had won easy victories along the Mississippi, one of them with the aid of the Navy over a Confederate stronghold at Island Number Ten, a victory which threatened the major east-west railroad in the Confederacy. Albert S. Johnston, now with Beauregard as his lieutenant, marched into Ten-

The South's abiding heroes, Generals Robert E. Lee (left) and Stonewall Jackson plan the battle of Chancellorsville, where the Confederacy's dazzling victory in May, 1863, was shadowed by Jackson's death after being accidentally shot by his own troops.

20

nessee with 40,000 men to challenge an invasion force of 37,000 under U. S. Grant, camped at Pittsburg Landing on the banks of the Tennessee River near a little church called Shiloh.

The rebels struck unexpectedly at sunrise on Sunday, April 5, 1862, despite Beauregard's fears that the enemy had been heavily reinforced, and almost drove the divided Federals into the river. Waves of Confederate infantry broke against W. T. Sherman's line and the fifth assault poured over the position, and pushed on, leaving the valley littered with bodies. Fleeing Federal troops hid under a 100-foot river bluff. Sherman was hit twice by bullets but remained in command until Grant came belatedly from his headquarters and calmly called up reserves, formed a new line, and put cannon into position to check the next rebel charge. The day was long and chaotic as the amateur armies flailed at each other.

Albert Sidney Johnston was killed and Beauregard took the Confederate command. In the night, Grant was reinforced by General Don Carlos Buell's Army of the Ohio, and after long and bloody fighting the next day, the rebels withdrew. Bloody Shiloh was the greatest battle yet fought in America, with over 13,000 Federal and 10,000 Confederate casualties.

Amid these gloomy reports from the west, the threatened Confederate capital was cheered by dazzling victories of Stonewall Jackson in the Shenandoah Valley. The obscure and eccentric professor from Virginia Military Institute, who knew the valley so intimately, used its rolling terrain as an enormous military chess board to confuse his enemies. In the first six months of 1862, with an army never larger than 20,000, he isolated and defeated four Union armies with a combined strength of some 60,000, drove them from the valley, and threatened Washington itself. His valley campaign was to emerge as the war's classic example of skilled military tactics, and it would be studied by soldiers throughout the world for a century to come.

President Davis had ordered Richmond evacuated, and government records were ready to be moved southward for safety. U.S. warships could be seen in the James, and George McClellan's huge army had attacked on May 31, 1862, through woodlands at Seven Pines, just east of Richmond. The armies tore at each other savagely until nightfall, both suffering heavy casualties, the most fateful of them General Joseph E. Johnston, who was severely wounded. President Davis replaced him with Robert E. Lee, who was to command the Army of Northern Virginia to the end.

Since his failure in a minor campaign in western Virginia, Lee had been derided as "Granny Lee" and "Evacuating Lee," and now, when he began the apparently impossible task of driving the Union army from the gates of Richmond by digging more trenches, newspapers branded him "The King of Spades." Lee wrote his family, "I wish that mantle had fallen upon an abler man," and methodically prepared for an assault on McClellan. He strengthened the city's defenses, drilled his troops, and secretly called Jackson's army across Virginia to join an offensive. The country was soon to learn that Lee was one of the most audacious commanders in American history.

At the outbreak of the war, Lincoln had offered West Pointer Lee field command of the Union armies, but Lee chose to serve Virginia and the Confederacy, saying, "I cannot raise my hand against my birthplace, my home, my children." Davis trusted Lee, and for a while it seemed that Lee might be appointed secretary of war, but Davis decided to name him "commander" to be posted at Richmond "under the direction of the President," which allowed Davis to retain full authority. This move came after Davis vetoed a bill that would have given Lee full authority in the field. About all this, Lee wrote his wife, "I do not see either advantage or pleasure in my duties. But I will not complain, but do my best."

Lee began his drive on June 25 at Mechanicsville, opening The Seven Days, a storm of battle that drove McClellan southeastward to a beachhead on the banks of the James. Both North and South were stunned by the casualty rolls as the armies fought through the overgrown country in engagements at Gaines Mill, Savage Station, and Malvern Hill, where the brief campaign ended. McClellan lost almost 16,000 men and the Confederates more than 20,000, but Richmond had been saved.

Lee was not content to fend off McClellan, and when General John Pope, fresh from victories in the west, invaded northern Virginia, Confederates hurried to meet him. In August, as Pope's army lay near Warrenton, Lee sent Jackson in a flank march around Pope to seize the Federal supply base at Manassas. Pope turned furiously upon Jackson at the battle of Groveton on August 28, and the following day, when Lee had concentrated his army, the Confederates defeated Pope at the battle of Second Manassas/Bull Run, and drove his army from Virginia. Lee then invaded Maryland, though he left behind him about 30,000 stragglers—men who protested that they had enlisted to protect the Confederacy and not to invade the North.

A young boy watching from the Maryland bank wrote of the rebel troops who waded the Potomac: "They were the dirtiest men I ever saw, a most ragged, lean and hungry set of wolves. Yet there was a dash about them that the Northern men lacked. They rode like circus riders . . . and spoke a dialect I could scarcely understand. They were profane beyond belief and talked incessantly."

Lee camped at Frederick for a few days, tried in vain to persuade Marylanders to join the rebellion, then boldly divided his army into four divisions, recaptured Harpers Ferry and began a move northward to Harrisburg, Pennsylvania. But the usually hesitant George McClellan, who followed with a large army, had the luck to find a copy of Lee's orders, which had been used as a cigar wrapper and discarded in a Frederick camp. Union troops were soon pressing the Confederate rear.

Lee entrenched a few miles to the west, at the village of Sharpsburg on Antietam Creek, where the armies locked in battle on September 17, 1862, the bloodiest single day of the war. Some 26,000 men fell, nearly 5,000 of them killed. McClellan pressed attacks all day, each of them beaten off by Lee, who concentrated his army at the last moment. David Thompson, a young New Yorker in Ambrose Burnside's command, had a lifelong memory of the battle's climax:

"The firing grew more rapid . . . there burst forth . . . the most vehement, terrible swearing I have ever heard. . . . I only remember that as we rose and started, all the fire that had been held back so long was loosened. In a second the air was full of the hiss of bullets and the hurtle of grapeshot.

"The regiment . . . had gone in on the run, what there was left of it, and had disappeared in the cornfield . . . there was nothing to do but lie there."

The Confederates held Sharpsburg the next day, awaiting further attacks, but both armies were exhausted, and after nightfall Lee recrossed the Potomac into Virginia, his first invasion of the North a costly failure.

Lee was candid in his dispatches to Davis, and in September, 1862, although his army was in a good military position, he wrote to the president, proposing that the Confederacy make a peace offer based on recognition of Southern independence. He argued that seeking peace would win the respect of other nations and shift guilt for the war to the North. "The proposal of peace," he wrote, "would enable the people of the United States to determine at their coming elections

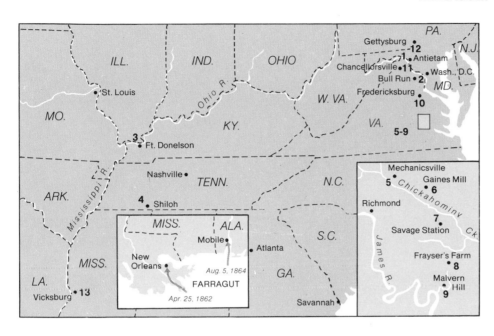

The key Union victory at Antietam came after hand-to-hand fighting such as shown in Alfred R. Waud's drawing above, and after the crucial charge by Union forces across the "Burnside bridge," in Edwin Forbes's drawing below.

Before bloody Antietam (1) in September, 1862, forces of the North and South had see-sawed in numerous battles: Bull Run (2), won by the Confederates; Fort Donelson (3), a Union victory; Shiloh (4), won by the Union; "The Seven Days" at Mechanicsville (5), Gaines Mill (6), Savage Station (7), Frayser's Farm (8), and Malvern Hill (9), all of which were drawn contests; and Second Bull Run, a Confederate win.

After Antietam, the rebel forces scored a victory at Fredericksburg (10) and again at Chancellorsville (11). Then came Gettysburg (12) and Vicksburg (13).

whether they will support those who favor a prolongation of the war, or those who wish to bring it to a termination."

In purely military matters, Lee was equally honest with his chief. Although he praised his troops after the unsuccessful invasion of the North, he wrote to Davis on September 21, "A great many men belonging to the army never entered Maryland at all; many returned after getting there, while others who crossed the river kept aloof. . . . Some immediate legislation, in my opinion, is required, and the most summary punishment should be authorized." He saw both the internal and external weaknesses of the thus far successful Confederacy.

Davis's government continued to hope for recognition from Britain and France, but the slavery issue prevented them from granting it. Although the laws of the U.S. and of most Western nations regarded the slave trade as piracy, punishable by death, civilization's rules had not been enforced. The only force actively seeking to suppress the slave trade was the British navy, but the U.S. had for years refused permission to the British to search American ships.

In 1860, the Republican party, which nominated Lincoln, established as one of its platform planks that there would be no interference with slavery in the states. Because of this, abolitionists denounced the Republicans, saying they were as bad as Cotton Whigs

On the morning of March 9, 1862, the victorious Confederate ironclad *Merrimac* (right) and the Union's challenger, *Monitor*, fought at close quarters for four hours in Hampton Roads until the *Merrimac* withdrew. The classic duel is depicted in the painting below by Xanthus Smith.

and calling Lincoln "the slave-hound of Illinois." In his inaugural address in March, 1861, Lincoln reiterated his party's pledge to respect slavery in the states, and in August, 1862, he wrote to Horace Greeley, "My paramount object in this struggle is to save the Union, and is not either to save or to destroy slavery."

But the Northern troops' performance at Antietam gave Lincoln the climate of victory he had been waiting for to broaden the basis for the war. To gain more vigorous support of the war effort among the Northern abolitionists, on September 22, 1862, he issued a proclamation stating that on January 1, 1863, slaves held in a state or in a portion of a state that was still in rebellion against the federal government would be "then, thenceforward, and forever free." For Lincoln, "the moment came when I felt that slavery must die that the nation might live," and he told his cabinet that he had made a covenant with God to free the slaves when the rebels were forced out of Maryland; God's decision had been given at Antietam. The Emancipation Proclamation was hailed by many in Europe, dashing the Confederacy's hopes that Britain and France would become its allies.

After the proclamation, the North began to organize Negro regiments, but the pay of a white private was almost twice that of his black counterpart. The Confederates were highly insulted by having to fight with or against Negro troops. Even though the Southern

Guns on the bluffs of Vicksburg fire on Union ships (above) as they steam down the Mississippi under the command of Rear Adm. David D. Porter (right) to supply transports for Grant's troops. After this feat, Union soldiers were able to cross the river and eventually attack Vicksburg from the rear, where they were repelled by the city's defenders (left). Grant's men laid siege to the city, which surrendered on July 4, 1863, one day after Lee's defeat at Gettysburg. Vicksburg's fall opened the entire river to the Union.

army had used slaves and free blacks as servants and laborers, the Confederacy would not allow Negroes to bear arms until 1865.

When the war began, there were only about 16,000 men in the U.S. regular army, but the states also had militia regiments which were sent into battle. They wore fancy uniforms and had fancy names, among them Rough-and-Ready Grays, Susquehanna Blues, Frontier Guards, Tigers, Invincibles, Game Cocks, Zouaves, and Rangers. Among the gaudier fighting units on the Confederate side were the three Zouave regiments from Louisiana. When the Zouaves fought the enemy, they made excellent targets in their bright red, baggy trousers and red fezzes.

Because the motley costumes had created considerable confusion on the battlefields, the opposing forces eventually adopted official uniforms—blue for the North and gray for the South, considered more practical than the Arabian Nights outfits some had previously worn. The official Confederate uniform of cadet gray coat and light blue trousers was in fact rarely worn by the soldiers, who garbed themselves in homespun jackets and trousers dyed a butternut shade of yellowish-brown and in other non-regulation clothing, including captured dark blue Union uniforms. The rebels frequently wore a wide-brimmed slouch hat instead of the prescribed kepi. Those who didn't go barefoot found that shoes were better than boots for marching.

In the fall of 1862, Confederates who had deserted flocked to Lee's camp in northern Virginia, but there were signs of hard days ahead. Rations, already short, were reduced by Richmond, and Lee's men searched the woods for roots and buds to prevent scurvy during the winter. "Jeb" Stuart's cavalrymen made a spectacular raid on Chambersburg, Pennsylvania, to burn a key railroad bridge, only to discover that it was iron. By

now, rebel cavalry horses were becoming scarcer, and thousands of them were, like Lee's soldiers, without shoes. Meanwhile, the Union's cavalry, like its infantry, grew ever-stronger.

In November, 1862, McClellan was dismissed by Lincoln, who explained, "I said I would remove him if he let Lee's army get away from him, and I must do so. He has got the slows."

Lee wrote, "I hate to part with McClellan, for we always understood each other so well. I fear they may continue to make these changes until they find someone I don't understand."

Lincoln, who had replaced McClellan with Major General Ambrose E. Burnside, urged his new commander to attack, and in the bitter December weather of 1862, Burnside crossed the Rappahannock at Fredericksburg. He threw most of his 125,000 troops into suicidal attacks against Lee's 78,000, who waited in an impregnable position on the heights above the river. Confederate fire ripped apart the assault waves and rebel marksmen took a deadly toll as the Federal regiments charged time after time. Lee told staff officers as he watched the slaughter, "It is well that war is so terrible—we should grow too fond of it." Almost 13,000 of Burnside's men lay on the field during the cold night; Lee's casualties were 5,300. Burnside was soon replaced by General Joseph Hooker.

Hooker recrossed the Rappahannock at the end of April with a force of 130,000 to challenge Lee in the tangled wilderness country west of Fredericksburg. When the Federals carelessly exposed one flank, Jackson urged an attack, and on May 2 marched through the thickets with an entire corps, while Lee held the line against Hooker with about 14,000 men. Jackson's charge crushed the vulnerable flank, put Federal troops to flight, and caused panic in Hooker's army. As darkness fell, Lee prepared for complete victory the next day—but Jackson, scouting the enemy front by

moonlight, was wounded by his own troops. Lee drove Hooker north of the Rappahannock with ease. Jackson, though he lingered a few days, was soon dead. Lee had lost his most able and aggressive lieutenant.

In June, Lee moved to invade the North once more, leaving a baffled Hooker behind him. Lincoln called a new commander to replace Hooker, this time the veteran George Meade, who promptly followed Lee westward across Pennsylvania. Jeb Stuart, scouting far north to Carlisle, failed to alert Lee to Meade's move, and the Confederate chief learned belatedly, on June 28, that the Federal army was concentrating at Gettysburg. Lee turned from his plan to threaten Philadelphia, Baltimore, and Washington, to confront Meade.

Once more the armies met by happenstance, when a North Carolina brigade, straying into the small town in search of shoes, met Federals there and opened an action that was to change the course of the war.

On July 1, Confederates of A.P. Hill's corps pushed to the center of Gettysburg but were driven back in hard fighting. Lee tried to avoid a general battle until General James B. Longstreet arrived with his corps, but his field officers threw their divisions into battle as they arrived in sequence, and fighting spread.

Meade's troops were pushed from the town and took positions south of Gettysburg along a formidable line —Culp's Hill, Cemetery Hill, and southward along Cemetery Ridge, past a jumble of boulders known as Devil's Den, to the slopes of two rugged hills known as Round Top and Little Round Top. Lee ordered the enemy driven from the heights, but his orders went astray in the confusion and at the end of the first day the Federals still held their position. The Confederates settled to the west, along the heights of Seminary Ridge. Longstreet resisted Lee's plan for an assault the next day and proposed a flank march around the ene-

A small crowd watches Union troops march through the village of Gettysburg on November 19, 1863, before the ceremony dedicating the burial ground for thousands of soldiers who had fallen there.

my toward Washington, but Lee said firmly, "No. If he is there tomorrow, I will attack him."

A frustrated Lee spent the morning of July 2 urging reluctant generals to the attack. The stubbornly defiant Longstreet refused to move until George Pickett's Virginia division had arrived, and as the hours passed fresh Federal troops joined Meade's line. It was mid-afternoon before lines of gray-clad troops attacked from the right under heavy fire from Round Top. General John Hood was shot down but his Texans stormed through a peach orchard under fire and reached Devil's Den. A.P. Hill's men belatedly joined the attack in the center and a few of them fought their way among Federal cannon before being driven back. Only heavy artillery fire halted the charging rebels. Young Lieu-

tenant Frank Haskell watched from Meade's lines:

> We saw the long gray lines come sweeping down upon Sickles' front and mix with the battle smoke. . . . Oh, the din and the roar, and those Rebel wolf cries! What a hell was there down in that valley! . . . The 3rd Corps was . . . swept from the field. . . .
>
> All along the crest everything was ready. Gun after gun, along the batteries, in rapid succession leaped where it stood and bellowed its canister upon the enemy. . . .
>
> Men were dropping, dead or wounded, on all sides, by scores and by hundreds. Poor mutilated creatures, some with an arm dangling, some with a leg broken by a bullet, were limping and crawling to the rear. They made no sound of pain. . . . A sublime heroism seemed to pervade all, and the intuition that to lose that crest was to lose everything.

At sundown the rebel tide ebbed and gray lines retreated into the woods opposite. Lee's piecemeal attacks had failed to dislodge the Federal line. The Virginian ordered Longstreet and Ewell to strike simul-

Renowned orator Edward Everett had consented to be the principal speaker at the Gettysburg dedication, and delivered a two-hour speech. President Lincoln, in the group on the platform, had been asked to follow with "a few appropriate remarks." He did— in 239 words that are among the most memorable ever uttered.

taneously on the right and left in the early morning of July 3. Longstreet still resisted Lee's orders to attack, and not until 3 P.M., after fresh Federal regiments had arrived, did the gray infantry advance. Stuart, arriving belatedly, won a cavalry clash in the Federal rear while the armies exchanged artillery fire across the valley.

The reckless attack to be known as Pickett's Charge moved through dancing heat waves into the open valley and up the slope of Cemetery Ridge under cannon fire from the Federal front. Almost 12,000 rebels crossed the open, most of them from Virginia and North Carolina. About 6,000 Federals awaited them on the crest of the hill, concentrated within the narrow sector of the assault, and about twenty-five cannon raked the Confederates almost every foot of the way. The gunners could hardly miss their targets in the lines moving at a slow march step; it was like practice firing, one of them said, and each bursting shell seemed to knock down at least ten men.

A few hundred graycoat troops clambered among Meade's guns on the heights and one Federal regiment fled, but the Confederates were soon driven out and survivors fell back to their lines. Pickett's command had almost literally disappeared; three generals were lost, only one field officer escaped unwounded, and only 1,000 riflemen reported for duty the next morning.

Lee's army lay in position in the heat of July 4, with the wounded croaking for water and rifling the haversacks of the dead. The rebels began their retreat the next day, slowed by 4,000 Federal prisoners and a wagon train of wounded some seventeen miles long, crossing the Potomac without interference from Meade. Lee had made his last invasion of the North.

The president's critics charged that the Confederacy was a one-man government. Davis, who had become more wan and ill as the war progressed, was dogged by the basic political weakness of the Confederacy—

his states were fierce guardians of their rights and often defied his orders. North Carolina, for example, formed its own "navy," operated a blockade-runner, and stored up plentiful supplies of uniforms and weapons which it was to deny Davis in time of need. Bickering disrupted the Confederate cabinet and Davis, who could not bring himself to delegate authority, presided over an increasingly inefficient government. His wife, for one, complained publicly that inflation had made paupers of her family.

On the day Lee left Gettysburg, U.S. Grant's men marched into Vicksburg, Mississippi, cutting the Confederacy in two, a victory that was the climax of a two-year campaign. The rebel stronghold which anchored the defenses of the mid-Mississippi was not a typical Southern town. Vicksburg's trade was with the northwest and its people had resisted secession to the last, until their state left the Union. The city of 5,000 looked down on the great river from 200-foot bluffs, and about it lay a watery wilderness of swamps and bayous which had defied Grant in six separate expeditions while politicians and the public clamored for his dismissal. But Lincoln had clung to his dogged general. "I can't spare this man," the President told critics. "He fights."

At last, with the aid of the navy, Grant landed an army of 76,000 below Vicksburg and battered his way to the city, defeating two Confederate armies in sharp engagements from Port Gibson to the Black River. Then he hammered Vicksburg's strong defenses for a month and a half. Some 2,800 shells burst in Vicksburg every day. Soldiers and civilians lived near starvation in caves and cellars until General John Pemberton surrendered. Lincoln grasped the meaning of Vicksburg: "The Father of Waters again goes unvexed to sea." The way was now open for Federal armies to drive from the Mississippi to the Atlantic. Confederate military power would ebb steadily after the twin disasters of July, 1863.

ABRAHAM LINCOLN

AND HIS

Emancipation Proclamation

Whereas On the Twenty-second day of September, in the year of our Lord one thousand eight hundred and sixty-two, a Proclamation was issued by the President of the United States, containing among other things the following, to-wit:

"That on the first day of January, in the year of our Lord one thousand eight hundred and sixty-three, all persons held as slaves within any State, or designated part of a State, the people whereof shall then be in rebellion against the United States, shall be then, thenceforward and forever free, and the executive government of the United States, including the military and naval authority thereof, will recognize and maintain the freedom of such persons, and will do no act or acts to repress such persons, or any of them, in any efforts they may make for their actual freedom.

"That the executive will, on the first day of January aforesaid, by proclamation, designate the States and parts of States, if any, in which the people thereof respectively shall then be in rebellion against the United States, and the fact that any State, or the people thereof, shall on that day be in good faith represented in the Congress of the United States by members chosen thereto at elections wherein a majority of the qualified voters of such State shall have participated, shall, in the absence of strong countervailing testimony, be deemed conclusive evidence that such State and the people thereof are not then in rebellion against the United States."

Now, therefore, I, ABRAHAM LINCOLN, President of the United States, by virtue of the power in me vested as Commander-in-Chief of the Army and Navy of the United States in time of actual armed rebellion against the authority and government of the United States, and as a fit and necessary war measure for suppressing said rebellion, do, on this first day of January, in the year of our Lord one thousand eight hundred and sixty-three, and in accordance with my purpose so to do, publicly proclaim for the full period of one hundred days from the day the first above mentioned order, and designate as the States and parts of States wherein the people thereof respectively are this day in rebellion against the United States, the following, to-wit:

ARKANSAS, TEXAS, LOUISIANA (except the parishes of St. Bernard, Plaquemines, Jefferson, St. John, St. Charles, St. James, Ascension, Assumption, Terre Bonne, Lafourche, St. Mary, St. Martin, and Orleans, including the city of New Orleans), MISSISSIPPI, ALABAMA, FLORIDA, GEORGIA, SOUTH CAROLINA, NORTH CAROLINA and VIRGINIA (except the forty-eight counties designated as West Virginia, and also the counties of Berkley, Accomac, Northampton, Elizabeth City, York, Princess Ann and Norfolk, including the cities of Norfolk and Portsmouth), and which excepted parts are, for the present, left precisely as if this Proclamation were not issued.

And by virtue of the power and for the purpose aforesaid, I do order and declare that all persons held as slaves within said designated States and parts of States are and henceforward shall be free; and that the executive government of the United States, including the military and naval authorities thereof, will recognize and maintain the freedom of said persons.

And I hereby enjoin upon the people so declared to be free, to abstain from all violence, unless in necessary self-defence, and I recommend to them that in all cases, when allowed, they labor faithfully for reasonable wages.

And I further declare and make known that such persons of suitable condition, will be received into the armed service of the United States to garrison forts, positions, stations and other places, and to man vessels of all sorts in said service.

And upon this act, sincerely believed to be an act of justice, warranted by the Constitution, upon military necessity, I invoke the considerate judgment of mankind, and the gracious favor of Almighty God.

In testimony whereof, I have hereunto set my name, and caused the seal of the United States to be affixed.

Done at the City of Washington, this first day of January, in the year of our Lord one thousand eight hundred and sixty-three, and of the Independence of the United States the eighty-Seventh.

By the President: ABRAHAM LINCOLN.

WILLIAM H. SEWARD, Secretary of State.

NOTE.---The rest of the slaves were afterwards freed by Legislation and Constitutional Amendments.

the army in disgrace to become a storekeeper and tanner; he still bore a reputation as a heavy drinker. The army was soon chuckling over an updated version of a joke almost as hoary as military history: To a complaint that the new general in chief drank too much, Lincoln was said to have drawled, "Find out what brand he drinks and send a barrel to all my other generals."

Grant was a relentless fighter who felt that the quickest way to end the war would be the cheapest. "Find out where your enemy is, get at him as soon as you can and strike him as hard as you can, and keep moving on." He was also fearless. William Tecumseh Sherman once told a friend, "I'm a damned sight smarter man than Grant; I know more about organization, supply, and administration, and about everything else than he does; but I'll tell you where he beats the world. He don't care a damn for what the enemy does out of his sight, but it scares me like hell."

In the spring of 1864, Grant moved to execute Lincoln's command to destroy the two major Confederate armies, Lee's in Virginia and Joseph E. Johnston's in the west. He ordered Sherman to drive toward Atlanta and set after Lee himself. As clearing weather brought firmer roads to the overgrown country near Fredericksburg, he led the Army of the Potomac toward Richmond. Lee's 65,000 stood in his way.

On May 4, with a column that would have strung out for seventy miles on a single road—120,000 men, 4,000 wagons and 50,000 horses, Grant's army crossed the Rapidan at Germanna Ford and plunged into the country called the Wilderness, where the rebels set upon them in desperate, often hand-to-hand fighting. For two days the armies thrashed about in the forest

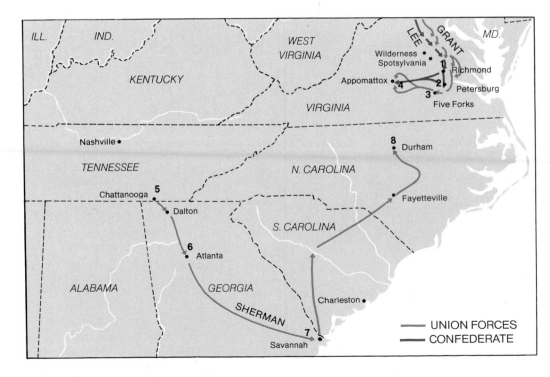

Under Grant's command, the Federal army executed two giant pincer thrusts against the Confederates.

Grant's forces in Virginia drove Lee back to Richmond (**1**) and Petersburg (**2**), and laid siege to the capital. When Lee's defenses broke at Five Forks (**3**), he withdrew and surrendered at Appomattox (**4**) on April 9, 1865.

W.T. Sherman, in the west, advanced from Chattanooga (**5**) to take Atlanta (**6**), then cut a swath through Georgia to Savannah (**7**) and swept north, receiving Johnston's surrender at Durham (**8**) five days after Appomattox.

Sherman's way to Atlanta had been opened by the November, 1863, capture of the heights around Chattanooga: under Grant's orders, Hooker (on white horse in James Walker's painting opposite) took Lookout Mountain; then Thomas's men charged through the rebel line on Missionary Ridge. That defeat destroyed the South's capacity to wage offensive war and win its independence by military victory.

34

in a struggle almost beyond control. Private Warren Goss, in one of Grant's regiments, remembered the scene:

> No one could see the fight fifty feet from him. The roll and crackle of musketry was something terrible. . . . The lines were very near each other, and from the dense underbrush and the tops of the trees came puffs of smoke, the "ping" of the bullets and the yell of the enemy. It was a blind and bloody hunt to the death, in bewildering thickets, rather than a battle. . . .
>
> It was next to impossible to preserve a distinct line, and we were constantly broken into small groups. . . . The uproar of battle continued through the twilight hours. It was eight o'clock before the deadly crackle of musketry died gradually away. . . . The groans and cries for water or for help from the wounded gave place to the sounds of the conflict.

Forest fires swept the field all night, and helpless wounded screamed in agony. Once more General Longstreet moved slowly to obey Lee's orders, but just as the bluecoats had the Confederates on the run, Longstreet and his veterans restored the line. Longstreet was shot through the throat and left the army for some months. The two days cost Grant 17,500 men and Lee 7,500. Grant wrote of the Battle of the Wilderness, "More desperate fighting has not been witnessed on this continent."

Federal veterans expected to retreat across the Rapidan, in the familiar pattern of previous springs. But Lee was convinced that Grant would move swiftly on toward Richmond and, after a day of silence in the torn woodlands, he found the bluecoats marching on his flank, sidling down toward the capital. Confederates, hurrying to block the path once more, won an

all-night race to the crossroads village of Spotsylvania Courthouse, where the adversaries clashed in headlong assaults. As the second great battle of the campaign opened, Grant reported stoically to Lincoln that he had lost almost 20,000 men, but added, "I . . . propose to fight it out on this line if it takes all summer."

The battle of Spotsylvania opened in confusion, as both armies launched night attacks. Union Private Theodore Gerrish never forgot the experience:

> Just at dark there was a heavy crash of musketry and a wild, savage yell as they rushed upon our first line of battle, which soon gave way and fell back upon the second. The confusion was indescribable: it was only with the greatest difficulty that we could tell friend from foe. . . . The Rebels came on with terrible energy. . . .
>
> It was a hand-to-hand conflict, resembling a mob in its character . . . for that hour they were brutes, wild with passion and blood. . . . The air was filled with oaths, the sharp reports of rifles, thuds of clubbed muskets, the swish of swords and sabers, groans and prayers. . . . Federal and Confederate would roll on the ground in a death struggle. Our officers fought like demons. . . . Many of those who were wounded refused to go to the rear but, with blood pouring from their wounds, continued to fight.

At the end of this collision Lee dug a line of works shielded by fallen trees, dominated by a bulge near the center known as The Mule Shoe. Grant struck and pierced this bulge in the midst of a rainstorm at night, a wild scene in which many were killed by bayonets, and men struggled atop piles of corpses, some of them buried alive by the casualties. Lee galloped forward on his gray Traveller to lead a counterattack but his men halted him, shouting, "Lee to the rear!" When their commander had turned back to safety, the rebels drove out the Federals and restored the line.

Colonel Walter Taylor of Lee's staff recorded the ferocity of the fighting:

> Then occurred the most remarkable musketry-fire of the war: from the sides of the salient, in possession of the Federals, and the new lines . . . occupied by the Confederates, poured forth hissing fire, an incessant, terrific hail. No living man nor thing could stand in the doomed space . . . even large trees were felled—their trunks cut in twain by the bullets of small arms.

As the rebels lay in their line at Spotsylvania, Lee had distressing news from the rear. Jeb Stuart was mortally wounded, shot down by a Michigan trooper as 1,100 Confederate riders fended off a raid against Richmond by Phil Sheridan and 10,000 Federal cavalrymen.

On May 18, Grant attacked once more at Spotsylvania and then, turned back by rebel cannon, he moved again to the southeast. The Confederates fol-

Anticonscription rioting erupted in New York and other Northern cities in July, 1863, during which hundreds were killed in clashes with troops (left) and police. The rioters had been inflamed by speakers and writers such as Copperheads—Democrats who advocated peace at any price. Lincoln's problem in dealing with the situation is shown symbolically in D.G. Blythe's painting below, in which the President tries to kill the dragon of rebellion with a gun swab while chained to strict constitutionality by Tammany Hall.

lowed—but in the rear Lee's salvage crews gathered 120,000 pounds of lead in the Wilderness to be melted into new bullets. Now, in the first day of quiet in two weeks, the armies looked back on an incredible series of battles; they had met sixteen times in major clashes, exclusive of the countless waves of attack on The Mule Shoe. Grant had suffered 33,000 casualties and Lee 20,000. Two Federal divisions had simply disappeared, and several brigades had shrunk to the size of regiments. Grant had lost 2,000 men in every twenty-four hours of the campaign.

Lee outmarched Grant to the crossings of the North Anna River, then moved on to a new position of defense, nearer the capital. He wrote his wife, "I begrudge every step he takes toward Richmond."

When Grant moved into the watery thickets of the Chickahominy River east of Richmond, Lee took up an impregnable position at Cold Harbor on one of George McClellan's old battlegrounds. At 4:30 A.M. of June 3 the bluecoats were flung against Lee's guns. More than 7,000 of them fell in the first hour. Robert Stiles, a Confederate gunner, described the slaughter:

> For my own part, I could scarcely say whether it lasted eight or sixty minutes, or eight or sixty hours, all my powers being concentrated on keeping the guns supplied with ammunition. . . .
>
> Here, then, is the secret of the otherwise inexplicable and incredible butchery. A little after daylight . . . infantry discharged their bullets and artillery fired cast-shot and double-shotted canister, at very short range, into a mass of men twenty-eight feet deep, who could neither advance nor retreat, and the most of whom could not even discharge their muskets at us.

After innumerable assaults, Grant ordered a final attack, but the survivors in his lines refused to obey his order, and the slaughter was over. That night Grant said, "I regret this assault more than any one I have ever ordered. I regarded it as a stern necessity." In the end it was useless. The Confederates escaped with

37

fewer than 1,500 casualties. For three or four days Federal wounded croaked for water between the hostile lines, but Grant refused to call a truce to tend them.

On June 13 rebel pickets found Grant's lines empty, and before Lee could give chase it was too late—Grant had eluded him, thrown a 2,100-foot pontoon bridge across the James, and moved against Petersburg. Lee saved the city only by rushing reinforcements at full speed, a vanguard which reached the trenches barely in time to meet determined assaults.

The armies settled down to siege warfare around Petersburg and Richmond, where Lee's defensive lines ran through a bleak landscape for thirty-six miles north and south of the James. In some places the lines were barely 150 yards apart, and sharpshooters made life in the clay pits miserable. The troops burrowed into the soil like animals and raised canvas roofs to escape the broiling sun. The Confederate capital was almost surrounded.

As Grant battered his way down the bloody trail in Virginia, W.T. Sherman drove for the heart of the Confederacy from the west, equally relentless but more artful, an inspired tactician who saved the blood of his 98,000 troops by sweating them on the march. Through the spring and summer he feinted and flanked his way from Chattanooga toward Atlanta, brushing past Joe Johnston's shifting defenses, assaulting only when a collision could not be avoided.

Sherman found the wily Johnston awaiting him before Dalton, Georgia, with cannon frowning from mountaintops, but Sherman avoided the narrow passage of Buzzard's Roost under rebel guns, held the center with General George H. Thomas's Army of the Cumberland, and flanked Johnston with a rapid march to the south by the Army of the Tennessee, which struck for a railroad at Resaca, eighteen miles in the

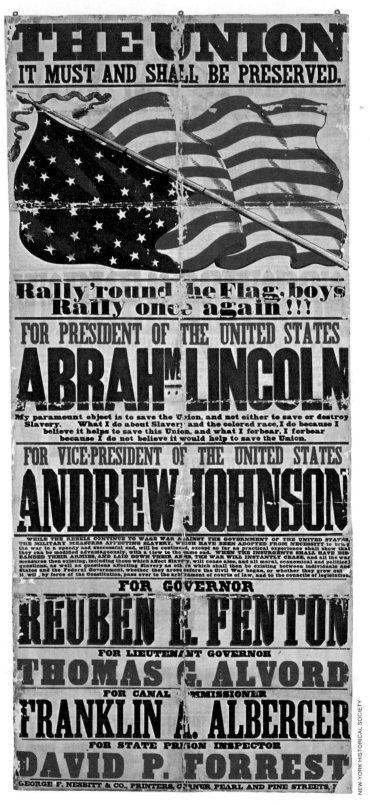

Lincoln ran for reelection in 1864 on the National Union ticket with Democrat Andrew Johnson as his running mate. Although Lincoln doubted he could win the presidency, Union victories on the battlefield renewed the voters' faith in him, and he beat the Democrats' George McClellan by an electoral count of 212 to 21.

Lincoln lantern was carried atop a pole during the 1864 campaign parades in New York. His foes assailed him for such measures as conscription and suspension of habeas corpus.

rear of Dalton. But Johnston was alert and his defenses strong, and in the end Sherman was forced to fight briskly to drive the rebels from Resaca—they fell back ten miles into open country between Kingston and Cassville, where Johnston laid an ambush.

Sherman drove after the enemy on a front so broad that his gunners rolled up Johnston's line and put it into retreat once more. Captured rebels paid tribute to the energetic general: "Sherman'll never go to hell," one of them said. "He will flank the devil and make heaven despite the guards." Another drawled a complaint, "You-uns swings around on your ends like a gate."

When Johnston made another stand at fortress-like Allatoona Pass, eighteen miles below Kingston, Sherman side-stepped once more, flanking to the southwest to New Hope Church, through country he had studied closely as a young officer. "I knew more of Georgia than the rebels did," he said.

As Johnston fell back, combative Southern civilians launched a storm of criticism, protesting his timidity. The belligerent John Hood, one of Johnston's generals who had lost a leg and the use of one arm, clamored for an attack on the enemy. Johnston's hope was that by playing for time he might catch Sherman in an awkward position and destroy him. He also hoped that rising war weariness in the North would lead to Lincoln's defeat in November. Grant's grievous losses in Virginia had caused mourning in virtually every Northern city.

When Johnston pulled back from Allatoona and dug in along a chain of hills—Pine Mountain, Lost Mountain, and Kenesaw Mountain—fighting became more severe. Every day for twenty-seven days troops clashed up and down the ten-mile line. Only twenty miles away was Atlanta, the rail hub of the central South and symbol of Confederate invincibility. Sherman saw the small mountain range as "one vast for-

tress," but edged nearer and nearer the rebel entrenchments until Johnston gave up two mountain positions and withdrew to Kenesaw Mountain, which he had made impregnable.

On June 27, perhaps stung by criticisms of his officers that he was "not a fighting general," Sherman ordered a frontal assault up the slopes of Kenesaw into the face of massed rebel guns and 25,000 entrenched infantry. In less than an hour he lost 2,500 men, including the two generals who led the attack, and Sherman called it off. Less than a week later, having flanked the position, Sherman's men were atop Kenesaw Mountain.

The bluecoats raided widely, burned Rome and Marietta, and plundered civilians in Georgia and Alabama. On July 5 the invaders got their first glimpse of Atlanta, and within a few days Johnston had dug in along Peachtree Creek to fight for the city. The laconic Johnston, accused of "losing 20,000 men without having fought a decisive battle," declined to reveal his plans to Jefferson Davis and was relieved. The erratic Hood, spoiling for a fight, was given command of the army to defend Atlanta.

Hood attacked unexpectedly on July 20 and routed Joe Hooker's corps but was bloodily repulsed by grapeshot from the guns of George Thomas's men which tore great holes in the gray ranks. The stubborn Hood then struck General James B. McPherson's wing at suburban Decatur, a savage assault in which McPherson died and the Army of the Tennessee was almost surrounded and overwhelmed—but in the end Hood was beaten off with ruinous losses. The Federal armies settled down to besiege Atlanta.

In late August, Sherman cut the lone Confederate rail supply line at Jonesboro and drove off the Confederates in heavy fighting, but though he almost captured two entire corps of rebels, he could not force his way into the city. A crisis was at hand in Washington.

Winslow Homer's painting, *A Skirmish in the Wilderness,* (above) shows dense woods surrounding Union soldiers as they fight a hidden enemy. In the drawing at right by Edwin Forbes, Grant is hailed by his troops on the way to Spotsylvania after the carnage in the Wilderness.

Grant leans over the back of
a pew placed in the shade of
trees to talk to his officers
during a council of war at
Bethesda Church on June 2,
1864, after the fighting at
Spotsylvania. The next day
Grant ordered an assault on
Lee's trenches at Cold Harbor
which cost the Union 7,000
soldiers in half an hour.
The Federals had feared the
attack would be suicidal
and had pinned name tags to
the backs of their coats so
that their bodies could be
identified after the battle.

The Wilderness Campaign

*The war's most desperately fought campaign took place in the Wilderness,
a dismal area of underbrush and scrub trees south of the Rapidan River
in Virginia. Grant, hoping for a showdown with Lee, put 120,000 men
into the Wilderness in May, 1864, and was met by Lee's army of 65,000.
Savage fighting in the woods failed to bring about a showdown, and the
armies shifted to Spotsylvania and then to Cold Harbor, fighting
fiercely but inconclusively almost every day for a month. The Union
suffered 55,000 casualties in the campaign; the rebels lost 32,000.*

One of the victories that helped reelect Lincoln was scored by Alabama-born Adm. David Farragut at Mobile Bay. The painting shows him standing in the rigging to see over the smoke as his wooden flagship *Hartford* exchanges fire at close range with the South's most powerful ship, the ironclad ram *Tennessee.*

The presidential election was a month away. A new draft would go into effect on September 5, and in the absence of Union victories, grumbling was widespread.

Lincoln feared defeat by the Democrat, his former general in chief George McClellan. In a somber mood, the President asked his cabinet members to sign a document stating, "... it seems exceedingly probable that this administration will not be reelected. Then it will be my duty to so cooperate with the President-elect, as to save the Union between the election and the inauguration; as he will have secured his election on such ground that he cannot possibly save it afterwards."

After his election in 1860, Lincoln had gathered about him a cabinet of unusually able men—Whigs, converted Democrats, and Republicans, none of whom was a friend or follower of the new President. William H. Seward, an antislavery senator from New York, remained as secretary of state throughout Lincoln's administration, as did Secretary of the Navy Gideon Welles, who had been a journalist in Connecticut.

The Union monitor *Tecumseh* capsizes after hitting a mine as Farragut's fleet enters Mobile Bay on August 5, 1864, in the greatest naval action of the Civil War. Farragut's triumph gave the North complete control of the Gulf of Mexico, further weakening the Confederacy's ability to continue waging war.

Salmon P. Chase, an abolitionist Republican from Ohio, was followed as secretary of the treasury by William P. Fessenden of Maine in July, 1864, and Hugh McCulloch in 1865. Simon Cameron, a Pennsylvania manufacturer, was replaced as secretary of war in January, 1862, by an efficient Democrat, Edwin M. Stanton. Edward Bates of Missouri lasted as attorney general until December, 1864, when James Speed took over, and ultraconservative Montgomery Blair of Maryland was succeeded as postmaster general by William Dennison in October, 1864. Secretary of the Interior Caleb B. Smith from Indiana was replaced by John P. Usher in January, 1863. Four cabinet members—Seward, Chase, Cameron, and Bates—had been Lincoln's rivals for the presidential nomination, and it required all of Lincoln's tact, patience, and intellectual ability to weld his cabinet into a valued group of advisers during years filled with stress and tragedy. Gideon Welles was probably unique among Lincoln's cabinet members— he did not feel superior to the President.

Seward and Chase were antagonistic to each other until Chase's intriguing for the 1864 presidential nomination led to his removal from the cabinet. Stanton connived with the Radical Republicans to wrest con-

trol of policy away from Lincoln. Yet in the many cabinet crises, the President had to retain the support of the radical followers of Chase and Stanton and of Seward's moderate supporters.

The enormous toll of lives on the battlefields in over three years of war, the highly inflated cost of living for civilians, and the inability to see victory in the near future caused a large number of Northerners to lose confidence in Lincoln. Rather than postpone the election on the grounds of war, Lincoln declared, "We cannot have free government without elections; and if the rebellion could force us to forego or postpone a national election, it might fairly claim to have already conquered and ruined us."

In June, 1864, Lincoln was nominated for the presidency on the National Union ticket, representing Republicans and War Democrats. Among those who had backed Chase's bid for the presidency was Horace Greeley, editor of the *New York Tribune*, who groundlessly felt that the Confederate states could be prevailed upon to rejoin the Union through diplomatic approaches. In August, Greeley and Radical Republicans, who differed with Lincoln on plans for reconstructing the Union after the war, called for another

43

Republican convention to nominate someone in place of Lincoln.

As for the Democrats, their convention in August adopted a resolution stating that "justice, humanity, liberty, and the public welfare demand that immediate efforts be made for a cessation of hostilities." Although McClellan accepted their nomination, he repudiated the peace plank in the Democrats' platform, and was able to retain their confidence because many believed he was the Union's greatest general and had been shabbily treated by Lincoln.

The efforts to supplant Lincoln came to nought. Hood evacuated besieged Atlanta, and Sherman sent a telegram: "Atlanta is ours and fairly won." In Virginia, Phil Sheridan swept Jubal Early's rebel army from the Shenandoah Valley. Suddenly, total victory was at hand. McClellan was overwhelmed at the polls.

Sherman ordered Atlanta's remaining civilians evacuated and when its mayor protested replied that safety and humanity demanded that women and children be moved. He added:

> You cannot qualify war in harsher terms than I will. War is cruelty and you cannot refine it. . . . You might as well appeal against the thunder-storm as against these terrible hardships of war. . . .
>
> You deprecate its horrors, but did not feel them when you sent car loads of soldiers and ammunition, and molded shells and shot, to carry war into Kentucky and Tennessee, to desolate the hundreds and thousands of good people who only asked to live in peace at their old homes, and under the Government of their inheritance. . . .
>
> But, my dear sirs, when peace does come, you may call on me for any thing. Then will I share with you the last cracker, and watch with you to shield your homes and families against danger from every quarter. . . .
>
> Now you must go . . . until the mad passions of men cool down, and allow the Union and peace once more to settle over your old homes at Atlanta.

Crippled, gallant Gen. John Hood tried to block Sherman's invasion of the South at Atlanta. The painting shows fierce fighting near the Troup Hurt house after the rebels broke the Union line and met a counterattack. After inconclusive battles outside Atlanta, Sherman laid siege to the city and occupied it on September 2, 1864.

In November, after a brief debate with the distant Grant by telegraph, Sherman burned most of Atlanta and marched toward the sea, cutting communications and ordering his 62,000 troops—218 regiments—to live off the country. He left Thomas behind him with a strong army to follow Hood into Tennessee, convinced that his own foray could end the war.

He wrote Grant:

> Until we can repopulate Georgia, it is useless to occupy it, but the utter destruction of its roads, houses and people will cripple their military resources. . . . I can make the march and make Georgia howl!

Washington was anxious for the safety of Sherman's army, and newspapers in the Confederacy and in England predicted its ruin—but the vast force flowed to

44

the east over many parallel roads, confusing the outnumbered rebel defenders, destroying railroads, plundering plantations, and gathering thousands of freed slaves in its wake. From Mississippi, General Beauregard wired Georgia leaders:

> Arise for the defense of your native soil! . . . Rally around your patriotic Governor and gallant soldiers. Obstruct and destroy all the roads in Sherman's front, flank, and rear, and his army will soon starve in your midst.

And Georgia congressmen urged:

> Let every man fly to arms—Every citizen with his gun and every negro with his spade and ax can do the work of a soldier. Remove your negroes, horses, cattle and provisions and burn what you cannot carry—Assail the invader.

The prophet of total war, Sherman (below) made his prophecy come true in his march through Georgia. After occupying Atlanta for 10 weeks, he began his advance to the sea. In his wake he left an area of destruction 60 miles wide, stripped of anything that could aid the rebels' war effort. Railroads, bridges, factories, machine shops, arsenals, farms—all were destroyed or plundered.

But Sherman was irresistible and rebel troops were few. Confederate cavalry sometimes struck the Federal flanks, and now and then, as at the hamlets of Griswoldville and Sandersville, Confederate infantry gave fight briefly, but was brushed aside. After five weeks of pillaging through the countryside, burning public buildings and factories, but leaving most dwellings intact, Sherman appeared before Savannah and made contact with the U.S. fleet.

General William J. Hardee retreated from the city by night over a pontoon bridge, his only escape route, and the Federals entered Savannah. Sherman offered Lincoln the captured city as a Christmas present, and surveyed the wreckage he had left behind him—200 miles of railroad torn up, an estimated $100 million of food and supplies destroyed. "This may seem a hard species of warfare," he wrote, "but it brings the sad realities of war home to those who have been . . . instrumental in involving us in its attendant calamities."

In January, Sherman invaded South Carolina. In revenge for the state's role as leader of the secession movement, the Federals left behind a sixty-mile-wide trail of ashes, lonely chimneys, and desolation; took Columbia, the capital, and left it in ashes (the blame for its burning a matter of controversy that was to continue for generations).

Sherman entered North Carolina in March, occupied Fayetteville, fought a brief, sharp battle against Joe Johnston and rebel veterans of the western campaigns at the village of Bentonville, and marched to Goldsboro, where he was reinforced to a strength of more than 100,000. As Johnston retreated westward, Sherman took Raleigh, the capital, and rebel resistance in the state was near an end.

Grant made repeated assaults as the weary months passed in the trenches before Richmond and Petersburg, but the stubborn Confederates hung on. A regi-

45

To penetrate rebel defenses around Petersburg (above), Union troops tunneled under a fort (below) and on July 30, 1864, triggered a blast (right). The infantry attack after the explosion faltered, and the Union lost the Battle of the Crater.

Hitting The Rebel Heart

After the bloody fighting at Cold Harbor during the Wilderness Campaign, Grant broke away from Lee on June 12, 1864, and headed for the railroad hub of Petersburg, 23 miles south of Richmond, but lost an opportunity to take the undefended town before Lee slipped in. Both armies dug in for trench warfare—a foretaste of World War I. Grant besieged Petersburg for nine months, lacking enough strength to break the rebel line. He did try to mine under the enemy and blow them up—a costly failure. On April 1, 1865, Philip Sheridan pushed back Lee's right at Five Forks, and the next day Grant pierced the center of the rebel defenses. That night Lee's troops abandoned Petersburg, allowing Grant to take Richmond the following day.

The flames of Richmond light the night as its residents flee the rebel capital on April 3, 1865.

ment of Pennsylvania miners tunneled beneath the rebel works and blew a great hole in the line, but an attack by Negro troops under Ambrose Burnside ended disastrously for the Union as the confused and poorly led blacks crowded into a crater and were slaughtered by the rebels. Grant settled for a long siege, determined to win Richmond at all costs. Lincoln agreed: "I have seen your despatch expressing your unwillingness to break your hold where you are. Neither am I willing. Hold on with a bull-dog grip, and chew & choke, as much as possible."

By winter, men in Lee's trenches were twenty feet apart, and they were limited to eighteen musket rounds daily. Firewood sold for five dollars a stick. In the absence of rations, some soldiers ate rats. A puny network of four surviving railroads barely kept the army and Richmond alive. Prices soared alarmingly—boots sold for $300 a pair, flour for $400 a barrel, and live chickens for $50 each. Wilmington, North Carolina, the last open Southern port, was closed at last by Lincoln's blockade. Official figures showed 35,000 rebels in the defenses, but deserters streamed

More than 700 buildings were destroyed in the Richmond fires, many ordered by rebel leaders to prevent supplies from falling into Union hands. Grant's troops quelled the flames and restored order.

Lincoln rode through the streets of the ruined Confederate capital on April 4. While the white population may not have been quite so welcoming as shown in Denis Malone Carter's painting, the Negroes were truly overjoyed, calling Lincoln "Messiah." He told them, "As long as I live no one shall put a shackle to your limbs."

away by day and night. Facing them were 150,000 well-fed and well-armed Federal troops—and Grant could call in 50,000 more from Tennessee and the Shenandoah Valley.

In February the Confederate congress at last forced Davis to make Lee general in chief, with powers the president had reserved for himself. Lee knew that it was too late, but he went to Richmond to plead for his cold and hungry troops. He told his son Custis, "I have been up to see the Congress and they don't seem to be able to do anything except eat peanuts and chew tobacco while my army is starving." Lee added somberly, "When this war began I was opposed to it, bitterly opposed to it, and I told these people that unless every man should do his whole duty, they would repent it . . . and now they will repent."

On March 2, Lee asked Grant for a conference to discuss an armistice but was refused: "Such authority is vested in the President of the United States alone," was Grant's reply. Lee surprised Grant with an attack on Fort Stedman, a Federal stronghold, and took more than 1,000 prisoners—but victory was fleeting. Heavy

Union fire beat off the attackers with a loss of 5,000 men.

At the end of March, Phil Sheridan's cavalry circled Lee's line to the south, a move urged by Lincoln, who had come down by water to visit the army. Grant told his staff, as he left Lincoln behind and went off to the front, "The President is one of the few visitors I ever had who never tried to squeeze out of me every one of my plans—though he's the only one with a right to know them. . . . I think we can send him some good news in a day or two."

Sheridan and a strong infantry force struck the rebel flank at Five Forks, overwhelmed Lee's cavalry and the shrunken brigade of George Pickett, and the siege line was turned. Federal attacks broke through in several places near Petersburg and Lee began a retreat.

Davis and his cabinet fled southward in a rickety train, and behind them soldiers and civilian looters started fires which destroyed the heart of Richmond. The last graycoats had hardly disappeared when Lincoln entered, to be greeted by thousands of Negroes, some of whom knelt before him. "My poor friends," the President said, "you are free—free as air. You can cast off the name of slave and trample upon it. . . . Liberty is your birthright. . . . Let the world see that you merit it."

The armies pushed westward up the valley of the Appomattox, through a countryside touched with spring, with Federal cavalry hacking at Lee's flanks and rear. President Davis, jostling toward safety, reached Lynchburg, only a few miles in advance. The rebel army disintegrated on the march, burying its cannon and blowing up ammunition.

Federal infantry overwhelmed a wing of Lee's army under Ewell at Sayler's Creek on April 6 and took thousands of prisoners, including half a dozen generals. Grant sent Lee a note the next day, urging his surrender. Lee pushed his troops ahead but asked for more details, and couriers rode continuously between the armies as the commanders negotiated. The one route of escape for the survivors was through Appomattox Courthouse, from where Lee hoped to march to Lynchburg and turn southward to join Joseph Johnston in North Carolina. But in the late afternoon of April 8, Grant barred the way with a cavalry screen and during the night hurried his infantry into position.

Lee's worn regiments went forward at dawn of April 9 but after a brief battle were recalled, and Lee wrote Grant to ask for a conference. The generals met in the simple farmhouse of Wilmer McLean, a civilian who had moved his family from the old field of Bull Run/Manassas to avoid battle. After a brief, rambling talk, Grant offered generous terms under which the rebels would stack their arms and return to their homes, never to fight the U.S. again. At Lee's request,

Confederates were allowed to keep their horses and mules to resume farming.

Lee signed Grant's surrender terms and rode back through tearful troops to his tent headquarters as Federal bands played, cannon roared, and bluecoats frolicked about Appomattox Courthouse. Grant ordered a halt to the celebration: "The Confederates are now our prisoners and we don't want to exult over their downfall." There were still rebel armies to surrender, including Joe Johnston's, near Durham, North Carolina, but when Lee signed the brief surrender agreement in the McLean house the four-year bloodbath was over. The bloodiest war in American history, which had cost more than 500,000 lives, had also ended

Lee, resplendently dressed, signs the surrender agreement at Appomattox on April 9, 1865, as Grant, wearing the dusty uniform of a private, glumly watches. Thus ended a four-year war that had been fought by almost 3 million Federals and about one million Confederates (with more than 620,000 total fatalities). The war cost the Union over $3 billion and the Confederacy about $1.5 billion; it also ravaged large areas of a once beautiful South.

250 years of human slavery in America and reunified the nation.

On April 10, Lee wrote a farewell to his troops:

Headquarters,
Army of Northern Virginia,
April 10th, 1865

After four years of arduous service, marked by unsurpassed courage and fortitude, the Army of Northern Virginia has been compelled to yield to overwhelming numbers and resources. . . .

You will take with you the satisfaction that proceeds from the consciousness of duty faithfully performed; and I earnestly pray that a merciful God will extend you his blessing and protection.

With an increasing admiration of your constancy and devotion to your country, and a grateful remembrance of your kind and generous consideration of myself, I bid you an affectionate farewell.

R. E. Lee, General.

At almost the same moment that Lee returned to his men, Lincoln reached Washington by boat and was surprised to see bonfires blazing and excited crowds milling in the streets. When someone asked the cause

of the celebration, there was a shout: "Why, where have you been? Lee has surrendered!"

A foreign observer, Lord Charnwood, may have summed up Lincoln's achievement best of all:

Many great deeds had been done in the war. The greatest was the keeping of the North together in an enterprise so arduous, and an enterprise for objects so confusedly related as the Union and freedom. Abraham Lincoln did this; nobody else could have done it; to do it he bore on his sole shoulders such a weight of care and pain as few other men have borne. When it was over it seemed to the people that he had all along been thinking their real thoughts for them; but they knew that this was because he had fearlessly thought for himself. . . . This most unrelenting enemy to the project of the Confederacy was the one man who had quite purged his heart and mind from hatred or even anger towards his fellow-countrymen of the South. That fact came to be seen in the South too, and generations in America are likely to remember it when all other features of his statecraft have grown indistinct.

On Good Friday, April 14, Lincoln went with his

51

wife and two friends to Ford's Theater to see a play called *Our American Cousin*. Shortly after 10 P.M. a shot rang out and the President slumped in his seat with a bullet in his head. John Wilkes Booth jumped from the President's box to the stage, breaking a leg, then left by the stage door, and rode off on a horse. Lincoln was carried to a house across the street and died there the next morning.

As might be expected of an ex-newspaperman, Gideon Welles kept a diary. Here is what he wrote in it concerning Lincoln's assassination:

> The giant sufferer lay extended diagonally across the bed, which was not long enough for him. He had been stripped of his clothes. His long arms, which were occasionally exposed, were of a size which one would scarce have expected from his spare appearance. His slow, full respiration lifted the clothes with each breath that he took. His features were calm and striking. I had never seen them appear to better advantage than for the first hour, perhaps, that I was there. . . .
>
> A double guard was stationed at the door and on the sidewalk to repress the crowd, which was of course highly excited and anxious. The room was small and overcrowded. . . . About once an hour Mrs. Lincoln would repair to the bedside of her dying husband and with lamentation and tears remain until overcome by emotion. . . .
>
> I remained in the room . . . there being a vacant chair which someone left at the foot of the bed, I occupied it for nearly two hours, listening to the heavy groans, and witnessing the wasting life of the good and great man who was expiring. . . .
>
> I took a short walk in the open air. . . . Large groups of people were gathered every few rods, all anxious and solicitous. . . . The colored people especially . . . were overwhelmed with grief.

Said Grant on learning of Lincoln's death: "I knew his goodness of heart, and above all his desire to see all the people of the United States enter again upon the full privileges of citizenship with equality among all.

I felt that Reconstruction had been set back, no telling how far." He was right.

Booth, a twenty-six-year-old actor and fanatical sympathizer of the Southern cause, had first planned to kidnap Lincoln and take him to Richmond, but abandoned this scheme after the Confederate capital was captured. He then conspired to kill Lincoln, Vice President Johnson, Secretary of State Seward, and General Grant. Seward narrowly escaped death in his bed from a knife wielded by one of Booth's accomplices, Lewis Paine. Johnson and Grant were not harmed. On April 26, Booth was trapped in a burning barn in Virginia and shot dead. One of the conspirators, John Surratt, escaped, but his mother, Mary, was hanged in July, as were Paine, George Atzerodt, and David Herold. Others in the plot and Dr. Samuel Mudd, who set Booth's leg, were given prison sentences to be served in the Dry Tortugas.

When Lee's army disbanded its men were free to walk homeward to take up farming once more and to begin rebuilding the South. Grant, following Lincoln's orders, avoided mass arrests and executions. Lee and other leaders were paroled and only a few Southern leaders were to be imprisoned, among them Jefferson Davis, who was captured in Georgia on May 10. Only one war criminal was to be executed, Henry Wirz, commander of the infamous prison at Andersonville, Georgia.

Already the world of 1861 seemed long ago. Northern factories which had spewed out weapons and military supplies began mass production of civilian goods; despite the war, the westward tide of settlement had never abated and new territories were filling up, soon to become states. Though the U.S. war debt seemed staggering, it was soon to be dwarfed by the nation's economic growth and its emergence as a continental power. With slavery doomed and secession ended, the U.S. began its rapid development as a modern nation.

At a cabinet meeting on April 14, 1865, Lincoln urged an attitude of forgiveness toward the defeated rebels in implementing Reconstruction of the South. That night he was shot by John Wilkes Booth while watching a play, and died the next morning, leaving Reconstruction in the hands of men who lacked his greatness of spirit or deftness of mind.

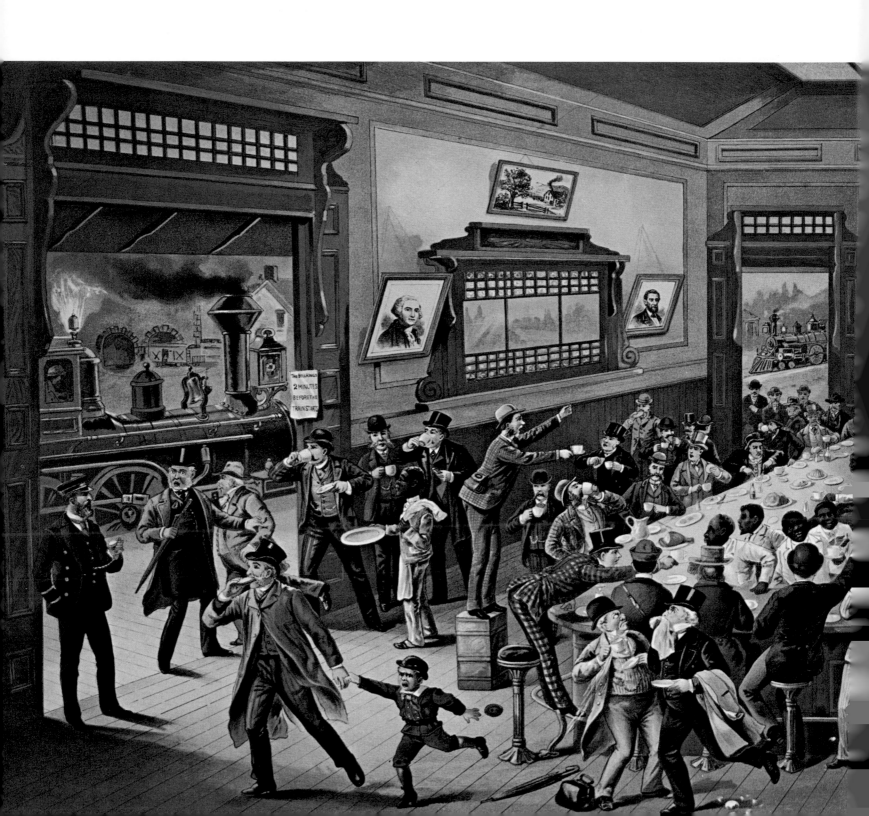

Unifying the Divided Nation

3

"Forty acres and a mule by Christmas." Such was the ardent hope of many freed slaves as the Civil War ended. The hope was encouraged by certain congressmen, who also fostered dreams of education, civil rights, and social reform. Other hopes were stimulated by President Andrew Johnson, the latter-day Andy Jackson who seemed determined to carry out single-handedly a program of instant social and political reform. Perhaps the noblest expression of what must be done for the blacks of the South was uttered by that epitome of abolitionism, Charles Sumner: the South must be reconstructed in accordance with the principles of the Declaration of Independence. Those principles had been denied the Negro ever since the antislavery clause had been eliminated from Jefferson's draft.

The dream of property for freedmen had been given specific expression by twenty black leaders toward the end of the war. Then, in a conference at Atlanta with General W. T. Sherman and Lincoln's secretary of war, they had faced the question of how, slaves no longer, they might successfully establish themselves as free citizens. "The way we can best take care of ourselves is to have land, and . . . till it by our own labor."

With economic freedom a stated objective of both the country's leadership and the South's 4 million blacks (180,000 of whom had fought as soldiers for the Union), it stands as a massive contradiction of American history that so little lasting progress was made towards equality and justice for the Negro in the postwar decade.

The era began auspiciously enough: first, the President's statement (by Lincoln before his assassination) that he would "bind up the nation's wounds"; then the passage of the Thirteenth Amendment that went beyond the Emancipation Proclamation and abolished slavery. But the leadership of the agricultural South was not to be so easily dispossessed of its property.

Lincoln's and then Johnson's program of restoring the defeated and presumably reformed states to the Union soon began to run into roadblocks. The trouble occurred in part because the poorer Southern farmers (whom Johnson favored and sought to elevate) were not separable from the Confederacy's "wealthy" leadership; Southern society remained of a piece. Reported a Union officer who toured the territory in 1865: "Everywhere that I went . . . I found the chivalrous Southron still under the domination of his ancient leaders." In addition, notorious "Black Codes" kept the Negro in chains nearly as strong as slavery.

Johnson's program also failed because he was an inept politician. He had neglected to involve congressional leaders, particularly the triumphant Republicans. They responded by condemning "his Accidency" and by initiating their own vigorous Reconstruction program. Its most notable accomplishments were the Fourteenth and Fifteenth Amendments (which gave the Negroes citizenship and equal protection of the laws) and establishment of the Freedmen's Bureau. The bureau, which was created over Johnson's veto, was responsible for the first legislative effort at social engineering in this country, and until its demise in 1869 rather effectively promoted medical aid and education. In the 4,000 free schools established by the bureau some 250,000 black children began to read and write.

But the most "radical" aspect of congressional Reconstruction—even more radical than the nearly successful attempt to impeach Johnson—was the creation of five military districts to control government in the

Black waiters serve food to transcontinental passengers in the station lunchroom opposite. The Pullman Company, which built its first sleeping car in 1864, established Negro porters and crews as a kind of trademark—thus opening many jobs but maintaining a stereotyped black image long after the Civil War.

A Chance for Equality

"A laborless, landless, homeless class," Abraham Lincoln called the black freedmen (one-third the South's population at war's end). They gained in the Reconstruction decade a Bill of Rights—the 13th, 14th, and 15th Amendments—but fell under Southern states' Black Codes, which perpetuated field labor (opposite) and house service as the black destiny. Even when Negro legislators sought to build equal governments and Freedmen's Bureau teachers opened schools, a working wage—key to American equality—could rarely be found. Nonetheless blacks took what chances occurred. Booker T. Washington, later president of Tuskegee Institute, recalled of his youth (when he worked from 4 A.M. to 9 A.M. in a salt mine before going to school), "Few were too young, and none too old, to make the attempt to learn."

A four-generation family from a plantation near Beaufort, S.C., poses before their one-room cabin shortly after the 1862 Emancipation Proclamation.

Reconstruction, even a century later, remains a controversial issue in the U.S. One historian has written, "The South was [then] plunged into debauchery, corruption, and private plundering." Yet other historians are revising the judgment of the "carpetbagger" period of 1865-1875 when the South was forced to reform its government under Congress-imposed military rule. These revisionists point to legislative and educational gains. In the centrally heated school below at left, a black teacher watches over six grades in one room. The composite of black legislators below includes Pinckney Pinchback, later acting governor of Louisiana.

HARPER'S WEEKLY.
A JOURNAL OF CIVILIZATION

VOL. XI.—No. 568.]　　　NEW YORK, SATURDAY, NOVEMBER 16, 1867.　　　[SINGLE COPIES TEN CENTS.
[$4.00 PER YEAR IN ADVANCE.
Entered according to Act of Congress, in the Year 1867, by Harper & Brothers, in the Clerk's Office of the District Court for the Southern District of New York.

South. By Senator Sumner's Reconstruction theory, the rebellious states had effectively canceled their legality; the Congress would have to lay down rules for the writing of new constitutions and for the election of new state legislatures. In this way—that is, under the gun—Negro suffrage and more broadly based democracy came to the South.

South Carolina was the only state where blacks held a majority (briefly) in one of the legislative houses. Elsewhere the black legislators were—generally— moderate and respected minority members. But the vision of blackness at the state capitals did not please all. Wrote a horrified Northern visitor to South Carolina: "The Speaker is black, the Clerk is black, the doorkeepers are black, the little pages are black, the chairman of Ways and Means is black, and the chaplain is coal black. At some of the desks sit colored men whose types it would be hard to find outside of the Congo."

Southern whites' antipathy and Northern whites' indifference finally did Reconstruction in. Even such ripsnorting radical Republicans as Representative Thaddeus Stevens urged his fellow countrymen to get on with the business of settling the West, encouraging manufacturing, and generally prospering. America was getting ready for that tremendous nineteenth century surge of materialism called the Great Barbecue, in which such men as President Grant's minions and the Tweed Ring would profit hugely from the alliance of industry and government. In the South the revivified leadership accused Northern "carpetbaggers" (many of whom were effective educators and developers) of corruption, sometimes accurately.

The passionate spirit of Reconstruction withered as the 1870s advanced. Had the Northerners not done enough with their amendments and bureaus and new governments? Surely, beyond what had already been accomplished, the best for all would be to forget the

past and unify the entire nation in bonds of steel. For, in Thaddeus Stevens's words, "new railroads, new factories and foundries . . . are linked with the grand march of humanity."

Thus there was no cry of anguish in either North or South when President Rutherford B. Hayes withdrew military forces from the supposedly reconstructed states in 1877. (Indeed, the agreement to withdraw the troops was the tactic by which Hayes won his disputed election.) Nor were there protests across the land in 1883 when the Supreme Court invalidated much of the Civil Rights Act of 1875, which had been in many ways the very flower of the Reconstruction period. The nation was too busy, it appeared—or too prejudiced against the blacks—for the Declaration of Independence to become more than a restricted document.

"Oh, for the pen of a Dickens to describe this wonderful scene," wrote Sarah Herndon in her journal as she witnessed what she estimated to be more than a thousand persons moving westward from the South Platte in 1865. She was alluding to one of countless parties that recommenced to pour into the trans-

Old and young, veteran and laborer, blacks flocked to polls in the South after reforms opened them in November, 1867 (opposite). By then many Northerners, aroused by lethal race riots in Memphis and New Orleans, had turned against President Johnson's lenient policies toward the South (below). Radical Republicans attempted sterner measures. But Southerners struck back: at right, Ku Klux Klansmen prepare to string up a white Republican.

Mississippi frontier almost as soon as the Civil War ended. Black and white, the migrants traveled on foot and horseback, in wagons and stagecoaches, in steamers and trains, seeking new homes on readily available government lands.

The Homestead Act of 1862 represented something of a western triumph over eastern industrialists and Southern landowners who had long fought to keep American manpower in the factory and blacks on the plantation. Indeed, the classless, raceless westward course of the homesteaders and other emigrants of the time represented a theme of national unity nearly as strong as the events and memories of the Civil War. By terms of the Homestead Act, 160 acres of public land were given to every adult who chose to emigrate to the Plains territories and beyond, after payment of a ten-dollar fee. The homesteader would get title to the land after he had "resided upon or cultivated the same for a term of five years." Responding to this invitation—and to Horace Greeley's admonition "Go West, young man"—the nation rumbled across the Mississippi.

Thus in the three decades between 1870 and 1900 Americans occupied more new areas of their continent than they had in the three centuries since 1600. Statistically, most of the westward migrants came from southern Illinois, Missouri, and Kentucky. Many of the homesteaders were war veterans or Southern farmers, unable to make new adjustments in their old homes. Some others were uprooted blacks.

The old Santa Fe and Oregon trails, long utilized to supply military posts and mining communities, also felt the tread of families and farm animals. Most used of all was the Central Overland Road. This took them along feeders of the Missouri River to the vicinity of Fort Kearny, nearly 200 miles to the west of Omaha. There the "overlanders" usually took a cutoff along the southern bank of the Platte, then through South Pass. They continued on one of the trail's two branches, which ran either to the northern end of the Oregon Country or in a southwesterly direction to California. They found the route nearly always in good condition, thanks to the army, which partly maintained it. Indeed, between Fort Kearny and Denver, a distance of about 400 miles, it was, wrote one of them, "as smooth as a table." But elsewhere it snaked over hills and stretched monotonously over seemingly endless sand that often slowed their progress to a snail's pace.

59

Rumbling west like hundreds of thousands of blacks and whites in the first two postwar decades, the pioneers on these pages halt on the trail. The family photographed below has led its stock off to water; the outfit opposite has stopped on a rise so as not to scare the game sought by the hunter in the valley's grasses.

Usually each family traveled in a single Conestoga—a four-wheeled, canvas-covered wagon drawn customarily by four oxen or four plow horses. These sturdy "prairie schooners," admirably suited for long travel, could carry a load of two or three tons. On their whitish tops the owners often inscribed slogans for their outfits: "The Sensible Child," "Hell Roaring Bill From Bitter Creek," or "Mind Your Business."

The overlander, in his lumbering wagon loaded with food, furniture, seed grains, plows, and sometimes shovels, hoes, and rakes dangling from its sides, scarcely averaged twenty miles a day. Toward night-fall the captain looked for grass and water for his horses and a good camping ground for his outfit. At a suitable place, outfits usually joined, set up their tents inside their circle of wagons, and cooked and ate their evening meal while they regaled one another with incidents or experiences or tall tales of the day.

At the age of "seventy-nine going on eighty," Frances Clelland Peabody, whose husband served as governor of Colorado, wrote a short but vivid account of a trip she made across the plains when she was "a little girl of four going on five." She recalled "the creaking and jolting of the wagon, the straining of the oxen over

HARVEY THOMAS DUNN (1884-1952). *SOMETHING FOR SUPPER.* COLLECTION OF SOUTH DAKOTA MEMORIAL ART CENTER

rough places, the odor of the dust and sweat of the oxen, the cracking of the long bullsnake whip as the teamster urged them on, the clanking of the big heavy chains when needed to keep the wheels from running over the oxen on bouncing over a steep place." Her most fearful sights were herds of buffalo and antelope running close to the wagon and then scampering off in clouds of dust at the sound of rifle shots.

She experienced "no startling escapes from the Indians, but lumbered on through sandstorms and rainstorms, the intense heat during the day, the jolting of the wagon hard to endure." The fear of being surprised in the night by Indians kept not only the sentry but even her mother on watch. "My tired father," she recalled, "slept as soundly as if in his own comfortable bed."

The experiences of the westbound stagecoach traveler were perhaps less onerous, though only slightly more comfortable. Several types of stagecoaches were then in use. John Butterfield, winner of the first direct mail service contract to California, preferred the durable but lumbering Troy coach. For fast driving on very muddy or on mountainous roads, many firms favored the so-called "mud coach" because of its light body, narrow wheels, and maneuverability—though it had no springs and sent its passengers skyward with each bump. Much more elegant was the Concord coach made in that New England town by Abbot, Downing and Company. It weighed over a ton and cost over a thousand dollars. Its oval-shaped body was made of seasoned elm, poplar, white ash, or white oak painted in English vermilion and then varnished twice. Suspended on heavy braces and cushioned by

leather straps, it swung and swayed, said Mark Twain, like "an imposing cradle on wheels." Its large wheels derived strength from wide and thick iron tires.

On one or both of the Concord coach's door panels appeared the words U.S. MAIL in gold letters, or pictures of western life. The coach's ornamented oil lamps were kept lit at night. Its front, rear, and central drop seats, upholstered in russet or black leather, accommodated nine passengers. Two more passengers could ride with the driver, who kept his money box well hidden under his seat—for masked "road agents" were a constant threat. Yet no danger was as terrifying to stagecoach drivers and riders as that of an Indian attack. In discomfort and trepidation, the families went west, participating in an epic chapter of the American experience.

Overland transportation brought to the plains wave after wave of miners, expressmen, federal troops, cowmen, and farmers. Each one of the settlers aimed to occupy a certain portion of the Plains Indians' traditional hunting grounds.

There, Indian and buffalo had lived in constant interaction. Indeed, that shaggy animal was virtually the center of the red man's existence—his food, shelter, and clothing; a part of his ethics and religion; the strength against which he tested his strength, courage, and character. The Plains Indians (including the Sioux or Dakotas, Crows, Cheyennes, Arapahos, Comanches, and Kiowas) feared that their fate would be similar to the banishment or extinction suffered earlier by their red brothers living in the mountainous region west and southwest of them. Yet they had good reason to

61

think they might withstand the white settlers. Most of their warriors were skilled horsemen whose favorite tactic was to speed across the landscape, letting their bodies drop behind their horses, quickly rising up again to drive their barbed arrows through their prey. In warfare a Comanche or a Sioux brave could shoot twenty arrows in the length of time a soldier required to reload his Colt six-shooter.

The western tribes had been generally quiet until the last year of the Civil War, when they became correspondingly bold as military defenses weakened. The Cheyenne and Arapaho bands, who had been removed to an inadequate reservation at Sand Creek in southeastern Colorado, were particularly bitter against the constant stream of wagons and stagecoaches rolling westward. They resented the stringing of "talking wires" across their hunting grounds, the railroad builders, and especially the inhuman massacre they had suffered at the hands of Colonel John M. Chivington and his Colorado militiamen. They and neighboring tribes thirsted for revenge, choosing to attack rather than perish, striking first at what they thought they could easily subdue or destroy. Their frequent targets were the poorly guarded stagecoaches and the long, gray immigrant overland wagons that passed near their villages. General Grenville Dodge wrote his commander in the East the estimation that as many as 25,000 redskins were openly hostile in the northern and southern plains. Colonel Robert E. Livingston reported that Indian bands had burned stage stations, ranch houses,

and haystacks, and killed a number of whites between Denver and Julesburg. From the Central Overland Road came word that twelve men and two women had been killed and scalped.

In the summer of 1865, attacks by Arapahos and Cheyennes and other Plains Indians mounted to a peak of destructiveness. The Indians sacked ranches, cut down telegraph wires, plundered towns of merchandise, even struck at army posts. But Appomattox put an end to their season of fury. When cold weather approached, they met peace commissioners accompanied by a large force of cavalrymen. The Indians were persuaded to surrender unconditionally and give up their Sand Creek reservation in return for lands to be assigned to them later. Yet the Senate failed to ratify this treaty, leaving the Arapahos and Cheyennes homeless vagrants.

General Philip H. Sheridan, who had been made commander of the American forces in the West at the war's end, surveyed the situation and understood the Indians' cause. He wrote, "We took away their country

and their means of support, broke up their mode of living, their habits of life, introduced disease and decay among them, and it was for this and against this that they made war. Could anyone expect less?"

No sooner had the government restored some semblance of peace with the Arapahos and Cheyennes than it faced a conflict with the Sioux. This commenced when the tribe learned that miners were planning to build a new wagon road cutoff to the Bozeman mines of western Montana Territory. Red Cloud, chief of the Oglala Sioux, stubbornly opposed such a road, saying that it would cut right through the heart of their hunting grounds. The miners, looking for a better outlet for their supplies, insisted that the road be built. Red Cloud then warned them that, should they attempt to realize their plans, he would take the warpath. In the summer of 1866, Colonel Henry Carrington met this challenge by starting to build a number of forts along the proposed Bozeman Trail. Naturally, Red Cloud broke off talks with N. B. Taylor, whom the government had sent to assure him

63

Col. George A. Custer, often pictured holding out alone with saber in one hand and six-shooter in the other—as in this painting by Cassily Adams—caused the defeat of his 400-man cavalry force by splitting it in three parts before 3,000 Indians.

that it had no intention of fortifying the road. As the Sioux scattered into the hills for action, Carrington continued to work on the forts. In December several bands of Sioux and some Cheyenne allies attacked a wood train near Fort Phil Kearny. Carrington immediately sent Captain William J. Fetterman to its relief. An inexperienced officer, Fetterman pursued the Indians into the wilderness, where he and his entire force of eighty-two men were slaughtered.

The Sioux continued to attack the unfinished forts, while the government, worried by the Fetterman massacre, recalled Carrington, sent reinforcements to the Powder River region, and dispatched a new peace commissioner, John B. Sanborn, to Fort Laramie. But Red Cloud and his aide, Man-Afraid-of-His-Horses, refused to see Sanborn until that official could guarantee that the road and the forts on it would be abandoned. "We are on the mountain looking down on the soldiers and the forts," said Red Cloud. "When we see the soldiers moving away and the forts abandoned, then I will come down and talk." The War Department soon yielded to his demands. In the summer of 1868, the soldiers in the forts hauled down the Stars and Stripes, packed their belongings, and marched away. Red Cloud led a band of yelling and yelping warriors to Fort Kearny and set fire to it. Then, on November 6, he rode proudly into Fort Laramie and made his mark on a treaty signed by less valiant chiefs of his tribe earlier in the year. He and his people and bands of other tribes accepted residence in the southwestern corner of Dakota Territory.

By this time the Arapahos and Cheyennes, tired of homeless wandering, had, by the Treaty of Medicine Lodge Creek, accepted as their reserve a barren and bare piece of ground between the Cimarron and Arkansas rivers. There they faced destitution. Their chief, Black Kettle, still bitter over Chivington's massacre at Sand Creek, allowed some of his young men

to plunder and pillage along the Smoky River road and Saline River valley of Kansas. General Sheridan determined to surround the chief and his warring bands in the Washita Valley, their base of operations, and then send his main force to destroy them.

That force was composed of eleven companies of the Seventh Cavalry under Colonel George Armstrong Custer. Tall and broad-shouldered and usually clad in a buckskin suit, with broad-rimmed hat turned up on one side and enormous yellow gloves, Custer enjoyed a heroic reputation from the Civil War. Unfortunately, glory was the chief aim of this American romantic figure whose blond hair hung down in strands to his shoulders. Learning from his scouts that Black Kettle and several hundred of his warriors were in their village, Custer disregarded Sheridan's orders to wait un-

til the Indians were surrounded and drove toward the village through cold and snow. In a few hours of hand-to-hand combat, Custer killed over a hundred Arapahos, including Black Kettle and his squaw. Then he hurried back to his headquarters before braves from other camps along the Washita Valley could come to the rescue of their comrades.

Custer's next bid for glory was his last. He waited seven years for it, and almost missed it, for by that time (1876) the Indian wars were about over. Rumors of gold in the Black Hills had attracted thousands of prospectors to land guaranteed to the Sioux. The red men feared the transcontinental railroad—which was, in part, a deliberate maneuver against them. (William Tecumseh Sherman had advised, "I think our interest is to favor the undertaking of the Road, as it will help

bring the Indian problem to a final solution.") Recognizing the U.S. government as their enemy, and repudiating Red Cloud, who counseled peace, warriors slipped away from the reservation and joined such young and hostile leaders as Sitting Bull and Crazy Horse.

The Indian agents saw trouble brewing. They ordered all hostile Sioux, regardless of their hunting privileges on the northern plains, to return to the reservation by February 1, 1876, under pain of punishment. Sitting Bull and Crazy Horse and their followers not only refused to return but increased their efforts in gathering ammunition and other supplies on the Little Big Horn. So the military authorities moved against them in three columns. General Alfred Terry warned Sitting Bull that, after the specified date, he

Sitting Bull, a Sioux chief who helped defeat Custer, appears at right in captivity at Standing Rock reservation. A similar reservation, South Dakota's Pine Ridge, extends beyond the waterhole below. In 1889 a religious movement swept the reservations, touching off a massacre by cavalrymen. Sitting Bull was shot resisting arrest; at that Battle of Wounded Knee 300 men, women, and children were killed.

would attack him. "You won't need any guides," the chief is said to have replied. "You will find me easily; I won't run away."

In that year Americans were celebrating their centennial as a nation and were making self-congratulatory speeches about the obstacles they had surmounted in their progress from pioneering to civilization. Alaska had been purchased from Russia in 1867; the continent was coming together. The strongest remaining threat to white advance was the Sioux, and now military authorities were planning to crush them in the Dakotas.

Their plans succeeded despite Custer. That vain and reckless officer, clad in his exotic garb, craved all the glory of victory for himself. Riding along the Rosebud River, he tracked the Sioux to their encampment on the Little Big Horn. Instead of waiting for reinforcements, as General Terry had ordered him to do, he advanced impetuously, while his scouts increased his confidence by telling him that Major Marcus Reno had attacked the Indians and had forced them to flee in considerable numbers. In reality, few Indians fled. Instead of charging their camp, Reno, finding his flank turned, became frightened and retreated into a forest. This was unknown to Custer, who quickened his advance.

On June 25, while some of his army companions were enjoying a reunion at the Centennial Exposition in Philadelphia, George Armstrong Custer stumbled on warriors who outnumbered his soldiers eight to one. What happened next is unknown. Perhaps Custer tried to gain lower ground, cross the river, and join Reno's troops in attacking the encampment, but heavy fire prevented him from doing so and he took his position on a knoll. There the Indians surged around them, says one chief, "like a hurricane," and killed all of them, including Custer, within a few hours.

But theirs was an empty victory. That summer the

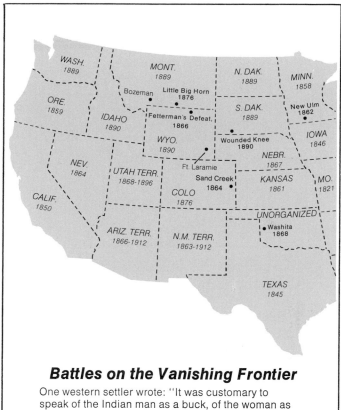

Battles on the Vanishing Frontier

One western settler wrote: "It was customary to speak of the Indian man as a buck, of the woman as a squaw. . . . By a very natural and easy transition from being spoken of as brutes, they came to be thought of as game to be shot, or as vermin to be destroyed." Relentlessly, by occupation of their lands and by battle (see map), the whites eradicated the Indian as a self-sustaining entity. When colonial settlement of U.S. territory began, nearly a million Indians had lived there; by the Battle of Wounded Knee in 1890, hardly 200,000 remained. Even more effective than battle in this process was the slaughter of the Plains buffalo on which the Indians had depended. Buffalo hunting and railroad building went hand in hand; as a hunter for the Kansas Pacific Railroad, "Buffalo Bill" Cody killed 4,000 bison in 18 months. Soon they vanished completely, along with most other vestiges of the wild frontier.

Sioux were driven slowly eastward into the Tongue River valley, where about 3,000 of them became trapped. In the following spring Crazy Horse and his warriors surrendered, but Sitting Bull, stubbornly refusing all terms, fled with his followers to Canada, asking in vain for a reservation. Starving and in rags, his followers gradually deserted him. And in the summer of 1881, even he with 186 tatterdemalions returned to the United States and gave themselves up at Fort Buford. Wearing a ragged calico shirt, a pair of shabby leggings, and a dirty blanket, proud Sitting Bull

agreed to return to his old reservation—a prison, but his prison.

The hunting grounds of the Plains Indians gradually became the pasturelands of the cattlemen. Reaching from central Kansas to the Rockies and from the Rio Grande to Canada, the Great Plains constituted the last frontier of the United States. At first its dry climate, sparse vegetation, and unfamiliar soils discouraged migratory farmers from making any attempt to cultivate and develop it, and it was controlled largely by its tribes until their removal to reservations. Early cattlemen saw little value in its grama or "buffalo grass." But eventually farmers and cattlemen migrating westward in wagon trains were surprised to discover that their oxen throve on bunch grass and that all of their cattle pawed in deep snow to find it and feed on its dried but nourishing blades. And when each spring they found that stray cattle had grown sleek and fat, they began to pay more and more attention to the economic possibilities of the region.

But where could they find the animals to stock this potential cattle empire? Southern Texas was the answer. In that region of warm climate, eternally green grass, and abundant water from the tributaries of the Nueces River, Spaniards for two centuries had raised long-horned Andalusian cattle that multiplied until countless herds of them ran untrammeled over the land. The Americans who settled in Mexico crossed their milch cows and oxen with Mexican cattle to produce a variety of strains. The most common of these was the so-called "Texan-Mexican," a multicolored, tall, gaunt animal with narrow hips, a coarse, thin head, and horns sometimes measuring eight or nine feet from tip to tip.

At the end of the Civil War most Texas ranchers were so impoverished that they turned to their "long-horns" as a desperate means of recouping their fortunes. They learned to their delight that they could sell a five-dollar steer in Minnesota for as much as forty dollars and in New York for possibly seventy dollars. Joe McCoy, an Illinois meat dealer who credited himself with being the originator of the frontier cattle market, discovered a route to riches. He conceived the "Long Drive," walking cattle from Texas nearly a thousand miles north to a shipping point on the Kansas Pacific Railroad (which had by then reached Salina, Kansas). He chose Abilene, "a small dead place, consisting of about a dozen log huts"—future home of President Dwight David Eisenhower.

That fall of 1865 about 35,000 steers passed through Abilene's loading chutes. The following year the number of steers doubled, and the volume continued to grow. In the days of the Long Drive nearly 4 million steers reached Kansas railroads.

The best-known figure of the cattle industry was the cowboy, who adopted the garb of a Mexican *vaquero* and modified it to fit his own needs. His three weapons on the range were his six-shooter, quirt with

C. M. Russell's painting *Jerked Down* shows a cowboy's horse thrown by a steer that has been roped and cinched to the saddle. Black cowboy Bill Pickett (who went west in the '70s just as 100,000 other blacks moved to Texas) was the first to "bulldog" a steer: he bit its upper lip while wrestling it to the ground, thus won the fight.

lashes of twelve inches or more, and lasso eighteen feet long. He usually found entertainment in one of the cattle towns at the end of the Long Drive. The largest of these was Dodge City, a dusty and ugly place of dirty saloons, gambling dens, whorehouses, and dance halls. Despite the presence of such professional gunslingers as Bat Masterson and Wyatt Earp, who pretended to maintain law and order, Dodge City was preposterously lenient with lawbreakers of all kinds. Its authorities sentenced to death only three killers and then spared all of them. The West was proving an open-hearted home to all comers.

No fewer than 5,000 black cowboys trailed cattle from Texas as far north as Montana during the years of the Long Drive. Since they filled necessary duties in the economic and social hierarchy of the cattle kingdom, they were readily accepted. The black cowboy often served as a hand or a top hand, though he rarely became a foreman. "If it weren't for my damned black face," complained Jim Perry, rough rider and cook at the vast XIT Ranch for over twenty years, "I'd have been boss of one of these divisions long ago."

The Long Drive was short-lived (1865-1885). It succumbed to many difficulties. Most of the cattle became so thin in their thousand-mile journey over pastures eaten down by successive herds that they brought poor prices in eastern stockyards. Drovers had to send many of the cattle to Indian reservations in Oklahoma or to Nebraska and Iowa to fatten them on corn. Capitalizing on this situation, Cherokees and other tribes charged drovers ten cents per head for all steers driven through their lands and much larger sums for long-term grazing. More irritating to the drovers was the hostility of farmers who, fearful of fever in Texas cattle, often resorted to firearms (and later to state legislatures, which they controlled) to keep their own cattle from being infected. Later, Kansas and Nebraska farmers used their influence to persuade their legislatures to pass "quarantine laws" forbidding Texas cattle to cross their state boundaries save in winter months, when the fever abated. Under these circumstances, drovers made plans to grow their cattle near newer railroads on the northern plains.

For Indians, cowboys, farmers, and miners alike, the railroads made a vast difference. Developed primarily for commercial reasons, the transcontinental system affected individual American lives in myriad ways. Measured at large, the railroads' effect was the creation of a territorial and industrial empire.

The first two railroads across the Mississippi were Missouri projects connecting St. Louis with Kansas City and Hannibal with St. Joseph. Other pre-Civil War railroads, emanating from Chicago, reached Council Bluffs and Dubuque, Iowa; Fort Kearny, Nebraska; Milwaukee, Wisconsin; and Minneapolis and St. Paul, Minnesota. By 1850 there were nearly 9,000 miles of railroad tracks in the country; ten years later there would be thrice that amount, and double that by 1870.

69

Railroad workmen from west and east stretch across the final gap as Central Pacific (left) and Union Pacific (right) trains meet at Promontory Point, Utah, on May 10, 1869. Advertisements soon invited Americans to ride all the way "through to San Francisco" (opposite).

SOUTHERN PACIFIC RAILROAD

At the century's midpoint Congress gave approval to the idea of a transcontinental railroad; but the idea was delayed because of sectionalism. Southerners and Northerners each demanded the route in their own region. To ascertain which route was feasible, Congress authorized army surveys between the Mississippi and the Pacific; these, by showing that four routes were possible, resulted only in widening the sectional breach. The split became no longer an issue when, early in 1861, the Southern states seceded from the Union. Now controlled by Northerners, Congress agreed to build a railroad on the central route. Still it hesitated; it needed most of its funds to carry on the war.

At this juncture Theodore D. Judah, a brilliant engineer living in California, arrived in Washington with his valise bulging with papers of a grandiose scheme. In California he had joined the Big Four among railroad promoters—Leland Stanford, Collis P. Huntington, Mark Hopkins, and Charles Crocker—in a proposal requesting Congress to charter the Central Pacific Railroad from San Francisco to the eastern border of the state, and promising to finance another railroad to connect their project with the Mississippi Valley. Congress, faced with the recent Union defeat at Bull Run, could give Judah no encouragement. Undaunted, Judah rewrote his proposed bill as a war measure aimed at keeping California and Nevada, with their rich gold and silver mines, on the Northern side. Even so, he had to wait a year before he could lobby the bill through Congress.

On July 1, 1862, Congress passed a law authorizing

Builder of ironclads during the Civil War, James B. Eads constructed the first steel bridge across the Mississippi (below) in 1874. Sited at St. Louis, the railroad-carrying bridge cost $10 million, replaced ferries operating for 110 years at America's gateway.

two railroads, the Central Pacific Railroad and Union Pacific Railroad, to build lines toward each other from, respectively, Sacramento and Omaha. In the Pacific Railroad Act, the U.S. government pledged to give the companies free rights of way; for each mile of completed track, the railroads would get land on either side (in ten-square-mile sections, alternating with sections reserved for the public); they would also receive $16,000 (in the form of loans on bonds) for every mile laid in the plains territories and more for miles laid in the foothills and mountains. "We have drawn the elephant," said Judah, "now let us see if we can harness him up."

He wanted to build his railroad, but his associates wanted to build their fortunes. They organized their own construction company and gave it exorbitant prices (in the manner of the notorious Crédit Mobilier of France). They also falsified their maps, moving

foothills to level country in order to charge the government twice the right amount. When Judah protested, his partners took away his power as their chief engineer. They offered him $100,000 to resign and to turn in his stock. He accepted their offer and, with his wife, boarded a ship for New York, but died in Panama of yellow fever.

Meanwhile, the two railroads began a wild race to lay and complete their tracks. The Central Pacific, favored by a federal loan and by another loan of $1,659,000 from California through the influence of Leland Stanford, now governor of the state, was enabled to break ground for its track long before its rival. As chief of construction contracts, Charles Crocker pushed its varied and weighty work with unceasing zeal. He had boats carry steel and rolling stock from eastern industrial plants to San Francisco and then forwarded them in steamboats to Sacramento, where construction began. He solved his labor problem by hiring Chinese coolies living in and around San Francisco and later even importing them from China.

By the summer of 1867 the Central Pacific reached the crest of the Sierra, descended to less difficult work, and began to anticipate its meeting with the Union Pacific. That railroad broke ground at Omaha with a struggle to obtain workers and material. By the end of the Civil War it had completed only forty miles of track. Then it greatly accelerated its pace, thanks to gangs of Irish veterans who found jobs on construction crews. Still its problems remained difficult, for ties had to be brought in from Minnesota, stone from Wisconsin, and rails from Pennsylvania. In 1866 they laid 266 miles of track; in 1867, 240 miles; and in 1868 they battled through to South Pass, hoping to win the prize of the race and the admiration of the world.

These "Hell on Wheels," as the Union Pacific's crews liked to call themselves, left behind them a number of ramshackle towns, including Julesburg, Cheyenne, Laramie, and, last of all, Corinne, Utah, with many saloons, dance halls, and prostitutes or "soiled doves" as more polite people called them. Murder and outlawry went hand in hand, vigilante committees were formed, and suspects were arrested, given a "jury," and hanged. "Some 3,000 people," wrote Ray Allen Billington, "drifted westward with that peripatetic Gomorrah—workers, bartenders, prostitutes, gamblers, speculators, outlaws, renegades, road agents, outcasts."

Out of this sordid but vigorous scene emerged a unique achievement. On May 10, 1869, some 600 spectators crowded at Promontory Point, Utah, to watch the engines of the two rival railroads creeping nearer to each other. Among the witnesses were Leland Stanford, Thomas C. Durant, and Grenville M. Dodge—politician, robber baron, and engineer.

Western Union Telegraph sent a message by wire to an eagerly awaiting nation: "To everybody. Keep quiet. When the last spike is driven at Promontory Point we will say, 'Done.' Don't break the circuit, but watch for the signals of the blows of the hammer." A little later: "Almost ready. Hats off. Prayer is being offered." And a little later still: "We have done praying. The spike is about to be presented." And, finally, "Already now," as Stanford and Durant, each with a ceremonial spike, one of gold from California and one of silver from New Mexico, swung sledges—and missed. "Done!" announced the telegraph, and bells all over the nation, in large cities and in small, clanged joyously, while multitudes answered them with exultant shouts.

Many expected that the transcontinental railroad would soon bring about national unity and grandeur. One of them was President James A. Garfield (who, while in Congress, had been named as a recipient of the Union Pacific's largess). His optimistic and farsighted verdict: "The railroad is the greatest centralizing force of modern times."

The New Colossus

4

In the year 1886 Wall Street stockbroker Henry Clews offered his view of the American Dream. "The Almighty has made this country for the oppressed of other nations," Clews wrote. "The laboring man in this bounteous and hospitable country has no ground for complaint. . . . Under the government of this nation the effort is to elevate the standard of the human race and not to degrade it."

For others the dream had a different reality. Anzia Yezierska never forgot the day she arrived in New York as a young immigrant from Russia. "Between buildings that loomed like mountains we struggled with our bundles . . . through the swarming streets of the ghetto," she remembered. "I looked about the narrow streets of squeezed-in stores and houses, ragged clothes, dirty bedding oozing out of the windows, ash cans and garbage cans cluttering the sidewalks. A vague sadness pressed down my heart, the first doubt of America. . . . I looked out into the alley below, and saw pale-faced children scrambling in the gutter. 'Where is America?' cried my heart."

It was an era overflowing with such contradictions. In the last quarter of the nineteenth century the United States was transformed—from a society largely rural to one largely urban, from an agrarian economy to one heavily industrialized, from a population essentially nativist to one deeply pluralistic. These were revolutionary changes, achieved at a revolutionary pace. It was exciting and exhilarating, harsh and painful. Above all, it was dynamic.

Which is not to deny that in the dynamic age that began a century ago there were terrible inequalities and injustices. One of the great forces of that era was the tidal wave of immigration washing across the

United States. To landless peasants in Italy or oppressed Jews in Russia or unemployed craftsmen in Germany, America was the font of milk and honey, the Promised Land. Some of the millions who came found it to be so; others struggled and made it so; but in the process many, like the young Russian Anzia Yezierska, cried out in anguish, "Where is America?"

Like so much else in those times, the key fact about immigration was its accelerating pace. In the immediate post-Civil War years, immigrants were arriving from overseas at the rate of 300,000 to 400,000 a year. By 1882 the total was almost 800,000. The pace leveled off for a decade, then shot up again and peaked at over a million and a quarter in 1907. Sources of immigration were also changing. Until about 1885 most of the newcomers were from Britain and northern Europe, more or less reflecting the American ethnic balance and being "absorbed" without great difficulty. Then the immigrant ships began to arrive jammed with the peoples of southern and eastern Europe. For the most part they were the landless, the unskilled, the poverty-stricken, the "huddled masses yearning to breathe free" as Emma Lazarus phrased it in her inscription on the Statue of Liberty. These people, with their alien ways and their babble of tongues, found a bleak welcome inside the "golden door."

Part of their problem was that without money and job skills most of them were trapped in the great eastern seaboard cities, and these cities simply could not handle them. Urban centers were overwhelmed not only with the foreign-born but with native migrants as well. Americans flocked to the cities from farms and small towns in ever-increasing numbers, seeking better jobs and better lives. The growth of cities was nothing less than phenomenal. In the two decades after 1870, Minneapolis grew from 13,000 to 165,000; Denver, from 4,700 to 107,000. By 1890, New York had a population of 1.5 million (with another 800,000 in

Smoke from ships' guns surrounds Frédéric Auguste Bartholdi's statue of *Liberty Enlightening the World* in this painting by Edward Moran of the 1886 unveiling ceremony in New York harbor.

Brooklyn), Philadelphia and Chicago each had over a million, and Boston, Baltimore, and St. Louis nearly half a million each.

The wonder is not that America's cities had their troubles coping with this population explosion, but that they did as well as they did. Housing, water, sanitation, police and fire protection, medical services, public transportation, roads, and bridges—every essential was in short supply, and it seemed as if there would never be enough time or enough money to meet the demand. Land could not be cleared and housing put up and roads laid out and water mains installed fast enough. Tenements sprang up like mushrooms in a dank forest and were immediately filled to overflowing. Garbage was generated many times faster than it could be collected, and fetid privies multiplied at a rate that far outstripped the installation of indoor plumbing. Urban reformer Jane Addams discovered that a supposedly unpaved Chicago street actually was paved; it was simply buried under a foot and a half of debris. A New Yorker complained that "the stink is enough to knock you down," and journalist H. L. Mencken remembered that the Baltimore of his youth, in the 1880s, had a malodorous stench "like a billion polecats."

Finally, toward the end of the century, the cities began to catch up by dint of enormous efforts. Water supplies and sanitation improved. Trolley lines allowed workers to live beyond walking distance of their jobs and spawned "streetcar suburbs." Bridges, most notably the magnificent Brooklyn suspension bridge that opened in 1883, vastly improved the urban transportation network. Streets were paved and electric lighting installed and fire stations built. The steel-skeleton, elevator-equipped skyscraper came into being. Settlement houses aided the underprivileged and new schools "Americanized" immigrant children. Libraries, museums, concert halls, civic centers, and public

parks made urban life more rewarding and more satisfying. Much remained to be done, especially for those —the minorities and the new immigrants—at the bottom of the social ladder, but the cities were showing that they could tackle their problems with imagination and gusto. Walt Whitman, writing in 1889, was impressed with this newly urbanized America:

> As of the building of some varied, vast,
>   perpetual edifice,
> Whence to arise inevitable in time,
>   the towering roofs, the lamps,
> The solid-planted spires tall shooting
>   to the stars.

At the center of this dynamism was the American industrial revolution. That revolution did not spring full-blown upon the nation in the late 1870s, of course; its beginnings went back a half-century and more. But the great impetus came as the country got itself sorted out after the long agony of the Civil War and Reconstruction, when it began to look forward rather than backward. In 1879 the value of American manufactured products was $5.3 billion. By the end of the century it was over $13 billion.

Examples of this industrial growth are legion, but three may be considered both typical and crucial. One was a well-established business that underwent a fantastic expansion; the other two were entirely new industries that produced the steepest of growth charts. The older business was railroads.

Steam locomotives had been chugging across the American landscape since the 1830s, stimulating the growth of fledgling businesses and contributing mightily to the North's victory in the Civil War. The meeting of the rails at Promontory in 1869 dramatically signaled the conquest of the continent, but that was only the beginning. The completion of the first transcontinental railroad raised the mileage to some 52,000; in the next twenty years it more than tripled,

High Tide of Immigration

Between 1783 and 1900 the United States received more than 18 million immigrants, some 13 million of them arriving between 1860 and 1900. They came for many reasons, not the least of which was the hope of a better standard of living than they had endured in their native lands.

For about $30, an immigrant could travel from Europe to America as a minimum cost passenger. They embarked in such scenes as Edgard Farasyn's painting *Les Emigrants* (right), which shows a group preparing to sail from Antwerp. On board, each humble traveler received a lumpy mattress in a crowded, foul-smelling area below the ship's water line ("steerage" meaning the part of the ship near the rudder). To escape these conditions many would sit or sleep on the windy deck (below), arriving in America exhausted from a voyage lasting as long as 15 days.

Most of the immigrants of the mid-1800s had come from northern Europe. At the end of the century the wave began from southern and eastern Europe—Italian peasants tired of fighting fickle weather and malarial mosquitoes; Russian Jews fleeing ghettos and pogroms; rebels in trouble with the Austrian government. The "new" immigrants met hostility from those who had arrived earlier. An 1893 cartoon by Joseph Keppler in *Puck* (below right) shows prosperous Americans, backed by shadows of their former selves, rejecting a newcomer.

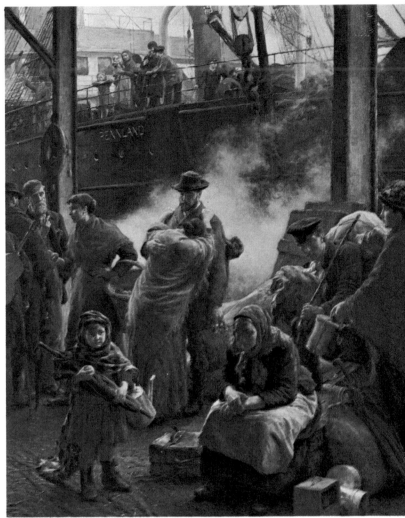

COLLECTION OF AUGUST A. BUSCH, JR., ST. LOUIS

MUSEUM OF THE CITY OF NEW YORK

PRINTS DIVISION, NEW YORK PUBLIC LIBRARY

Immigrants were processed in a huge brick-and-stone
"palace" (above) built on Ellis Island at the turn of the century
in a mixture of architectural styles. The newcomers waited in
alphabetical order according to nationality (below left) for
processing, which included medical exams (below right). Thousands
of them were excluded because of disease and other disabilities.

Ellis Island: Refuge for the Homeless

On January 1, 1892, immigrants began landing at Ellis Island in New York harbor. After their ship docked the steerage passengers were taken to the island by ferry for inspection and baggage examination. Officials could inspect and pass 5,000 immigrants in a day. Those who failed to meet the requirements were detained to await return home at the expense of the steamship company that brought them to America. The few who had to remain on the island overnight were provided with clean beds and wholesome food. Although it was only one of more than 70 processing centers for newcomers, Ellis Island handled nearly three-fourths of all immigrants during its 40 years of full operation.

The New York skyline symbolizes the new life that awaits those immigrants who have passed inspection and will be taken by ferry from Ellis Island to the gateway city.

Street Scene

American city streets filled with immigrants attracted painters and photographers—some to expose the squalid conditions; some to record the vitality. A leading observer of New York slum life was a Danish immigrant, journalist Jacob Riis, who produced a record of the "vile" conditions with pen and film. Warren Dickerson used his camera in New York's Lower East Side to show Hester Street (below), where most of the people were Russian Jews and food was peddled from pushcarts crammed along the sides of the street. One of the artists who found inspiration in the crowded streets was George Bellows, whose work reflected the Ash Can school of artistic realism—as in his painting *Cliff Dwellers* (left). For the adults who had crossed the sea with high hopes, these neighborhoods were misery unrelieved, but for their children it was the way life was: the filthy streets spawned a generation of tough go-getters who made their way upward, some of them even managing to claw their way to fame.

LOS ANGELES COUNTY MUSEUM OF ART

to nearly 167,000 miles. Equally important, the railroad network was consolidated and organized to work smoothly and efficiently.

Steel rails, George Westinghouse's air brake, and better rolling stock, including George Pullman's Palace Sleeping Cars, made rail travel smoother, safer, and more comfortable. The gauge was standardized nationally at four feet, eight and a half inches (on one Sunday in 1886, over 13,000 miles of track were thus modified). And financiers grimly sorted through bad management and flimsy capitalization to get the trains running on time—or at least running. Such rail barons as Jay Gould, Jim Hill, Henry Villard, and E. H. Harriman expanded, financed, and consolidated the network until it crisscrossed the country in every direction. Whatever the industrial revolution needed, the railroads could now deliver it.

Vital to railroad expansion, and to countless other industries, was the spectacular growth of something new under the sun: the steel industry. For years steel had been an expensive luxury. It combines the toughness of wrought iron and the durability of cast iron, but until an Englishman named Henry Bessemer and a Kentuckian named William Kelly came along, getting sufficient carbon out of iron to turn it into steel was too slow and too expensive to be practical. In 1859, independently, Bessemer and Kelly hit upon the stratagem of injecting air into molten iron to purify the mass and "burn off" enough carbon to turn it into steel. When this technique was refined in the open-hearth process, steel suddenly became highly practical to produce. The race began: 77,000 tons were produced in 1870, 1.4 million in 1880, and 11.4 million in 1900.

The dominant figure in steel was Andrew Carnegie, the archetype of a Horatio Alger hero. In 1849 thirteen-year-old Andy Carnegie, newly arrived from Scotland, was earning $4.80 a month as a bobbin boy in a Pitts-

burgh textile mill. In 1901 he retired with a guaranteed income of a million dollars a month for life. In between, he assembled an industrial empire that awed even his most hard-bitten competitors.

Carnegie graduated from bobbin boy to telegrapher for the Pennsylvania Railroad. One day, learning of a wreck on the main line, he took it upon himself to issue telegraphic orders to straighten out matters (signing the name of the company president), a move that was noted approvingly. In the course of time he moved into the iron bridge business and prospered, thanks to a genius for selling and promoting. With one foot firmly in iron, he stepped into steel.

He never professed to know much about making steel, but he gathered around him the best of those who did. (This was a characteristic he shared with the other moguls of the age. His epitaph, he said, ought to read, "Here lies the man who was able to surround himself with men far cleverer than himself.") By 1880 the United States had passed Britain in steel output and technology. Iron ore was beginning to pour into Pittsburgh by lake steamer and rail from the vast deposits around Lake Superior, and join with locally accessible coal and limestone to turn the city into the steel capital of the world.

Carnegie was a tireless promoter of what he called "the gospel of wealth," a philosophy whereby man was ordained to exercise the God-given right to accumulate wealth and the God-given requirement that he not take it with him. By 1900 the Carnegie Steel Company reached a profit level of $40 million, $25 million of which went directly into Carnegie's pocket. The next year, looking toward retirement and good works, he sold out to financier J.P. Morgan, who was putting together the first supercorporation, U.S. Steel. The price was $492 million, $250 million of it Carnegie's personal share. He was the world's richest man, yet when he died in 1919, leaving behind a trail of university endowments, benevolent institutes and found-ations, pension funds, church organs, and 2,800 li-braries, he had given away 90 percent of his fortune.

A second brand-new industry that flourished in this dynamic age was oil. In the early 1860s there was a mini-boom in oil-rich western Pennsylvania. At first the sticky stuff welling up out of the ground seemed of little use beyond greasing farm wagons and enrich-ing nostrums peddled by patent-medicine drummers. Then Professor Benjamin Silliman of Yale subjected it to a careful analysis and reported that, when refined, petroleum would yield such valuable products as ker-osene for lighting, lubricants, naphtha, and paraffin. The boom was on.

Like the California gold rush, it began as a wild free-for-all. Anyone with a few dollars and much rugged individualism could drill himself a well and haul his crude oil off to a backyard refiner. It was a competitive jungle that only a few survived. Watching all this with an unblinking eye was a young, pious, tight-lipped produce merchant from Cleveland named John D. Rockefeller.

Rockefeller had come to Cleveland as a teen-ager in 1853 from upstate New York. He enrolled in a business school and found he had a good head for figures. At the age of twenty Rockefeller took a trip to the oil fields around Titusville, Pennsylvania, and was appalled by what he saw. The production end of the business was to be avoided, he decided, but the refining stage looked as if it might turn a profit if it were properly organized. In the middle of the Civil War he formed a partnership with an inventive Cleveland refiner, Samuel Andrews. By 1870 they were producing 3,000 barrels a day, a tenth of the industry's output, and the Standard Oil Company of Ohio, capitalized at a mil-lion dollars, was in business. Within a decade Standard Oil controlled nine-tenths of the nation's oil-refining capacity. Competitors were invited into the fold, but those who refused were driven out of business. Price-cutting wars, secret rebates from shippers, industrial spying, bribery (it was remarked that the only thing Standard Oil had not done to the Pennsylvania legis-lature was refine it)—all were weapons in the Rocke-feller arsenal. Perhaps his most celebrated managerial device was the trust.

One of Standard Oil's lawyers, Samuel C.T. Dodd, dreamed up the trust. To pull together the far-flung Rockefeller empire, and to shield it from the prying eyes of state legislatures, the stock of all forty com-panies and units was turned over to a nine-man board of trustees, who in turn issued trust certificates to the various company shareholders and provided "general supervision" for the entire operation. The beauty of this was that while the trust ran everything, it had no legal existence. The state-chartered companies were not in charge, the trustees were—headed, to be sure, by John D. Rockefeller.

The trust was quickly and widely imitated by other big businesses. In Standard Oil's case, at least, it was not a device to create a monopoly, for that was already assured by control of refining, pipelines, shipping, warehousing, and marketing. Rather, it made the whole operation efficient—production was stabilized, products were improved, and retail prices went down. Soon after the turn of the century the nation's annual oil output topped a million barrels; perfection of the automobile in the next two decades sent it rocketing right off the charts. And John D. Rockefeller became a very, very rich man. The trusts his organization had originated were not really hit until 1904, when Theo-dore Roosevelt used the Sherman Antitrust Act of 1890 to break up the Northern Securities Company.

Modern America rose directly from the foundations laid by these moguls, yet the methods they used to gain and hold power are generally unattractive to the mod-ern eye. As one observer has noted, under present-day

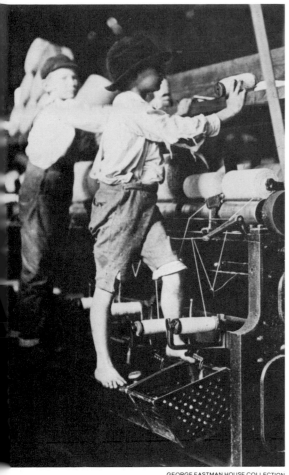

Sweatshops and Child Labor

Many families were able to survive in America only because their children could earn some money.

Georgia textile mills kept wages low by employing children, some of them so small they had to stand on their machines to work (left). The barefoot girl at a thread-spinning frame in a North Carolina mill at right was one of about 40,000 children under 16 who worked in cotton mills in 1908.

Some children began work at home when their immigrant parents set up workshops in their tenement living quarters, sewing clothing (below left) or making cigars or ornaments. They were paid on a piece-work basis, so even very young children helped in the day and night toil.

Those women who went out to work often labored at sewing machines in the intense heat of garment district workshops to earn a profit for their employer or ''sweater'' (below right).

83

DISCRIMINATE AGAINST

INFERIOR
UNCLEAN
SWEAT-SHOP
CLOTHING.

INSIST UPON
THIS LABEL.

ENDORSED BY ALL TRADES UNIONS
AND LEADING REFORM SOCIETIES.

The Roots of Labor Reform

Tenement workshops, child labor, and similar iniquities vanished from the American scene only after organized labor became strong enough to push through reforms. The basis for the modern labor movement was laid in the 1880s by the Noble and Holy Order of the Knights of Labor, led by their Grand Master Workman, Terence V. Powderly (standing above left with his second in command, Charles Lichtman). The Knights clashed with those who favored a labor federation designed on more immediately practical lines, among them Samuel Gompers (above right), an immigrant English Jew who worked as a cigar maker. The discord in the labor movement during its early years is the subject of Frederick Burr Opper's 1886 cartoon in *Puck* below. Powderly fingers the harp at left and Gompers clangs the cymbals in the center. Others seen are the Rev. Heber Newton, Henry George, Father Edward McGlynn, and Robert Ingersoll, all of whom had their own ideas on how to improve the worker's lot. Gompers eventually became the leader of the labor orchestra, heading the American Federation of Labor from its establishment in 1886 almost without a break until his death in 1924. During his leadership the virtues of union-made clothing were extolled in labels and advertisements (above) as part of the reform movement.

rules many of them "would face a good hundred years in prison." Yet in their time they brilliantly stimulated, harnessed, and directed an enormous burst of creative energy, and any judgment of them must be tempered by that fact.

Railroads, steel, and oil are only the most spectacular examples of the period's explosive industrialization. It was going on as well in every field. Hand in hand with all this were breakthroughs in applied science and a flood of inventions. In the decade before the Civil War the U.S. Patent Office issued about 1,000 patents annually; in 1890 it approved over 25,000.

When it came to inventing, there was no one to compare with Thomas Alva Edison. History records few youths with a more highly developed curiosity. He set his father's barn on fire just to see what would happen (what happened was that he got a whipping). He curled up on a batch of eggs to try and discover why fowls nested. He built his own telegraph, and tested, often explosively, all manner of chemical combinations. Three months into his first school year he overheard his teacher remark that he seemed addled, and he stalked out, thereby concluding his formal education. Like Carnegie, Edison had a touch of the Horatio Alger hero about him. One day in 1869 he arrived at a Wall Street communications office for a job interview just as the main stock ticker broke down. Amidst the ensuing panic he looked it over and fixed it on the spot, and got a job on the spot. He was also the original absentminded scientist. On his wedding day, we are told, he stopped by his shop after the ceremony, became involved with some project, and stayed far into the night, oblivious of his bride waiting at home.

While not a theoretician, Edison was unequaled as a master of applied science. In 1876 he established the first modern research laboratory, at Menlo Park, New Jersey, where he and his exceptional assistants (like his illustrious contemporaries in industry, he had an eye

for talent) turned out inventions almost to order. He and his team, he once observed, produced "a minor invention every ten days and a big thing every six months or so." Among his many "big things" were an electric vote recorder, many improvements in telegraphy, the mimeograph, the dictaphone, the phonograph, improved film projectors and storage batteries, an ore separator, the electric dynamo—and the light bulb.

Edison did not invent the light bulb, the principle of which (a filament heated to incandescence within a vacuum) dated back to the 1820s. His genius was to find a practical filament. He simply tried everything he could think of before he hit on carbonized bamboo fibers as the answer (the present-day tungsten filament dates from 1907). His Edison Illuminating Company was financed by such titans as J.P. Morgan, and by 1882 New York City had its first electric power station.

While captains of industry were quite ready to risk great sums of capital and to gamble on new technology and untapped markets, they did not see it incumbent upon them to share their decisions and their profits with the workers. For labor to demand better conditions or a share of the wealth or, worst of all, to band together in unions to obtain these things, smacked to them of radicalism and anarchy.

An important aspect of workers' complaints was the erratic course of the economy. In a business slump the first thing that occurred to employers was to cut wages. They expected the men to see that this was in their own best interests, that their sacrifice would help restore prosperity. But for a coal miner trying to support a family on an annual wage of $200 or a railroad brakeman, with a wife and eight children, earning $360, this was a hard argument to swallow.

These years were a buyer's market in labor. To a destitute and desperate immigrant just off the boat, any job at any pay under any working conditions was welcome, and if an American worker trying to maintain a decent place in life for himself and his family objected to a wage cut, there were plenty of new Americans eager to take his place. And so these became years of extreme labor unrest. Skilled workers were the first to organize. The 1860s and 1870s saw the slow growth of unions among such groups as cigar makers, printers, ironworkers, and railroaders.

In 1877, after two 10 percent pay cuts, workers on the Baltimore and Ohio Railroad struck. The strike spread rapidly across the country until two-thirds of the rail network was idled. Violence spread with the strike. Ten workers died in rioting in Baltimore and another twenty-six were killed in Pittsburgh in a pitched battle between strikers and state militia. Machine shops, depots, and thousands of freight cars were put to the torch. The strike ended only after President Rutherford Hayes called out federal troops.

The great railroad strike failed, many workers believed, because of a lack of central leadership; the arson and pillage that so outraged public opinion was often the work of free-lance hoodlums. The result was the rising strength of a national union, the Knights of Labor. A group of Philadelphia tailors had started the Knights in 1869 as a fraternal order. Terence V. Powderly, a railroad machinist, became head of the union in 1879. Powderly was an idealist, a gentle dreamer who envisioned, over the course of time, a peaceable kingdom of labor and capital. Under his leadership the Knights underwent a spectacular growth, with membership skyrocketing from 10,000 in 1879 to over 700,000 by 1886. Few of these new members, however, cast their eyes upward to Powderly's exalted utopia. They simply wanted better wages, job security, and decent working conditions.

In the early 1880s railroad locals of the Knights struck Jay Gould's Union Pacific over pay cuts, and to their surprise won concessions from Gould. New members flooded into the union but its prosperity was not to last. Powderly's inability to control the rank and file made the national union a hollow shell. Then a tragic incident in Chicago gave the entire union movement a black eye.

In 1886 the McCormick Harvester plant was struck. After violence in which one man was killed, a protest meeting was scheduled in the city's Haymarket Square by a handful of anarchist revolutionaries. The Haymarket meeting produced nothing more violent than some windy, heated oratory, but the authorities overreacted. A column of police arrived as the meeting was breaking up and someone (exactly who was never determined) threw a bomb, killing seven policemen and wounding seventy others. Eight anarchists were arrested and tried for murder, conspiracy, riot, and other charges. Seven received the death sentence and one a prison term. Four were hanged, one committed suicide, and two sentences were commuted. One of those executed had been a member of the Knights of Labor. In the ensuing public outcry the Knights were not specifically blamed, but the incident was seen as bitter fruit of the general labor unrest. "I'm not afraid of anarchy," cried a Chicago businessman, "but I do consider that the labor movement should be crushed!" The Knights of Labor, he went on, should "never dare to create discontent again."

The Knights went into a precipitous decline. In its place rose a new union, Samuel Gompers's American Federation of Labor (AFL). Instead of a general union welcoming workers of any stripe, the AFL was a federation of trade unions. And tough-minded Sam Gompers, a New York cigar maker, had no use for utopian dreams and no expectation that in the foreseeable future labor and management would arrive at any peaceable kingdom. His interests were basic: pay, hours, working conditions. Fifteen years after its founding in 1886 the AFL reached the million-member mark.

The Workers' Revolt

During the depression of the 1870s the number of unemployed peaked at about 5 million. Those still employed suffered pay cuts. In 1877 a strike started by railroad workers over reduced pay spread from West Virginia, and in Baltimore militia fired on strikers and bystanders, killing 10 and wounding scores (above). Outbreaks of strikes continued through the next two decades. A particularly violent one occurred in 1892 at Carnegie's Homestead steel works near Pittsburgh. Fighting began there when 300 guards brought in by the company tried to land from barges (below left). During the battle strikers used a shield (below right) while firing a cannon. Sixteen men were killed and many wounded before the guards gave up. In another violent strike, at the Pullman company near Chicago in 1894, boxcars were set afire (above right). These clashes seemed to bear out tycoon Jay Gould's remark, "I can hire one half of the working class to kill the other half."

Suffragettes Arise

Women had filled the "masculine" roles of clerk and teacher during the Civil War. Many of them were later angered to find that the polling place was to continue as a strictly male preserve. The outraged feminists organized parades (above), gave soapbox speeches (opposite), and took heart from scenes of women voting in the territory of Wyoming in 1888 (right). In the forefront of fighters for women's rights that year were members of the executive committee of the First International Council for Women (below). Among them are Susan B. Anthony (seated second from left) and Elizabeth Cady Stanton (seated fourth from left). The following year, when Wyoming tried to become a state, opponents feared it would open the way for the spread of women's suffrage. The territory's legislature, which had given women the vote in 1869, made its position clear: "We will remain out of the Union 100 years rather than come in without the women." And so Wyoming—with its women voters—became a state in 1890. It took 30 more years for the older parts of the United States to catch up.

Whatever the health of national labor organizations, the grievances of the average workingman did not disappear. In the last fifteen years of the century the number of strikes never fell below a thousand annually, and in some years the total was much higher, but it would be many years before employees achieved the goals for which these workingmen fought. Two of the bitterest strikes of the era took place in the early 1890s. The first occurred at Carnegie's Homestead works near Pittsburgh. Henry Clay Frick, Carnegie's manager at Homestead, was an implacable foe of unions, and he promised to "teach our employees a lesson" when they walked out in 1892 over his refusal to negotiate a new contract with the iron and steelworkers' union. Frick's counter was to recruit 300 private detectives to act as protection for strikebreakers. When a barge load of the detectives arrived at Homestead and the strikers blocked their landing, the Battle of Homestead erupted. The gunfire stopped only after sixteen were dead and sixty wounded. The strike lasted five months and wrecked the union.

Two years later, workers at George Pullman's Palace Car Company near Chicago struck after a series of pay cuts. The American Railway Union refused to move trains containing Pullman cars, tying up some twenty railroads. As in the 1877 railroad strike, federal troops intervened, this time to keep the mails moving. "If it takes every dollar in the Treasury and every soldier in the United States Army to deliver a postal card in Chicago," President Grover Cleveland said, "that postal card shall be delivered." Union leader Eugene Debs was jailed for defying a court injunction and the strike was broken.

CULVER

Millions of Americans had an uneasy sense that all was not well with the system. One thing wrong with the system was that women were far from being full partners in it. In the mid-nineteenth century American women were their spouses' legal chattels. A wife's earnings and property and even her children belonged to her husband. She could not sue or make a contract, she could not write a will unless her husband approved, and she could not vote. Abigail Scott Duniway, an early proponent of consciousness raising, exclaimed, "One-half of American women are dolls, the rest are drudges, and we're all fools!" A bevy of women rose to do battle against these injustices, among them Mrs. Duniway, Lucy Stone, Elizabeth Cady Stanton, and Susan B. Anthony. They wrote, they spoke, they petitioned, they went to court—and they were hounded, derided, vilified, and threatened. Progress came at a glacial pace, but it came. Grudgingly, laws were changed to give women some independence—in part because women workers were pouring into business and industry—and eventually there was even progress on the suffrage front. This was a western movement, where new ideas seemed to take root in new land. Wyoming Territory led the way in 1869, and then women got the vote in Colorado in 1893, in Utah in 1895, and in Idaho in 1896. None of the dedicated female pioneers lived to see national women's suffrage become a fact through the Nineteenth Amendment in 1920.

Discontent was not limited to the factory or the polling place; on the farms there was also a rising tide of complaint. Between 1870 and 1900 the population of the United States almost exactly doubled, to nearly

Coxey's Populist Revolution

Among those who believed they had a cure for the nation's economic woes in the 1890s was a prosperous Ohio businessman named Jacob S. Coxey. In 1894 he organized and led a protest march of the unemployed to present Congress with "a petition with boots on." Coxey was a Greenbacker, advocating the unlimited issue of paper money and a huge public works program to employ the thousands of jobless who were roaming the country. The marchers were in the Commonweal of Christ but became known as Coxey's Army (below). "General" Coxey, a mild-looking 40-year-old who rode in a buggy, started with a hundred marchers in Massillon, Ohio, and gathered several hundred more en route to Washington. On May Day the "army" marched to the Capitol, where there was a confrontation with police and Coxey was arrested for walking on the grass, fined $5, and sentenced to 20 days in jail (right). His "army" was dispersed, but the march helped to make unemployment a national issue, which the Populists—whom Coxey later joined—hoped to use to achieve their goals in the 1896 election.

76 million, and agriculture expanded spectacularly to feed these new millions. Output per acre leaped upward with the use of fertilizers, new machinery, and new techniques, and millions of acres of western land were brought under cultivation. Many farmers profited in this boom but by no means all of them; like industrial workers, most felt they were not getting their fair share. In part this feeling was psychological. It had been an accepted part of the national credo that the man of the soil was the backbone of America. "Those who labor in the earth," Jefferson had said, "are the chosen people of God." With growing industrialization and urbanization, this no longer seemed true, and the farmer was bewildered by his loss of status.

But the farmer also had real grounds for complaint. Farm prices, especially for wheat and cotton, were low; middlemen took an increasingly large share of the proceeds; bankers kept interest rates high; and the cost of the machinery that was now necessary to farm successfully kept going up. His most immediate target, and the one that drew much of his fire, was the railroads. For most southern and western farmers, the railroad was their single lifeline to the marketplace, and they were at the mercy of the rate-setters. Freight rates fluctuated wildly, depending on competitive factors. For example, west of the Missouri River, where it had a local monopoly, the Burlington's rates were four times what they were east of the river.

Like the workingman, the farmer organized to fight for his rights. In 1867, Oliver Hudson Kelley founded the National Grange of the Patrons of Husbandry, soon known simply as the Grange. In the economic slump of the 1870s the Grange grew in size and political clout. The Illinois legislature passed the so-called Granger Laws to regulate railroad and warehousing rates, setting the pace for other state regulatory bodies and laying the foundation for the passage in 1887 of the federal Interstate Commerce Act.

Equitable freight rates might help, but they were not the answer to the periodic economic slumps that drove the farmer to the wall. The depression following the financial panic of 1893 was ruinous. Wheat prices plunged to half what they had been twenty years before; cotton that sold for fifteen cents a pound in the early 1870s was down to less than six cents by the midnineties. Equally serious was the deflationary spiral; farmers who had borrowed heavily to buy land and machinery (as most of them had) were paying off their loans in more valuable dollars. The fact that banks in particular and the hated eastern money men in general were cleaning up on these appreciated dollars did nothing at all for rural tempers. From this discontent there arose a new political force, the Populists.

Throughout most of this new age, the national government had done little more than keep out of the way. Politics was full to overflowing with sound and fury, but it signified close to nothing. The men who entered the White House—Rutherford Hayes in 1877, James Garfield, and, after Garfield's assassination, Chester Arthur in 1881, Grover Cleveland in 1885, Benjamin Harrison in 1889, and Cleveland again in 1893—were honest, competent men who believed that the executive branch should as a rule defer to the legislative. Unfortunately, Congress in these years was inept in picking up the slack reins of government. On such major issues as monetary reform and the tariff, the legislators shamelessly hesitated. On the issue of civil service reform, Congress was goaded to action only by an act of violence, Garfield's assassination. The President's murderer was a deranged man unable to snatch a patronage post, and an outraged public demanded reform of the system. The result was the Pendleton Act of 1883 that initiated a federal civil service.

For the most part, Congress devoted itself to politics, with Republicans waving the bloody shirt—that is, refighting the Civil War issue of loyalty and disloyalty. This might swing an election one way or another, but it begged the main questions. Perhaps one reason government acted slowly, if at all, to solve the current problems was that no one was really sure how to proceed. What was the best way to deal with the new issues of monopoly, trusts, and other immense combinations? How could inflation and deflation be controlled? For government to take action to steer and control the new forces in American life, or even to decide if action was necessary or wise, called for down-to-earth political solutions which the Presidents and the legislators were reluctant to undertake.

The Populists, however, were demanding action, and they would not be put off. Everything came to a head in the election of 1896. The Populists came sweeping out of the South and West, a political amalgam of two farmers' organizations known as the Southern and Northern Alliances. A Nebraska editor put the farmer's plaint succinctly in 1890: "There are three great crops raised in Nebraska. One is a crop of corn, one is a crop of freight rates, and one a crop of interest. One is produced by farmers who by sweat and toil farm the land. The other two are produced by men who sit in their offices and behind their bank counters and farm the farmers."

After scoring heavily in local and congressional elections in 1890, the Populists entered the 1892 national election with a full-blown reform program. Among its planks were comprehensive government aid to farmers, a graduated income tax, nationalization of railroads, and the unlimited coinage of silver. They campaigned hard but the party did not do as well as it had hoped in the election, winning just over a million votes (8.5 percent of the total), but it did raise the issues, and the issues would not go away.

The big issue was silver, and it became bigger as the nation plunged into the deep depression after 1893. Silver meant the money question, and the money question meant the issue of deflation. Since the Civil War the supply of money had not kept up with population growth and economic expansion, and so the value of the dollar had nearly doubled: a dollar borrowed in 1865 had to be repaid in the 1890s with a dollar worth twice as much. If this was discouraging to the borrower, it delighted the creditor. The U.S. had gone on the gold standard in 1873 and discontinued the coinage of silver, but limited silver coinage had later been allowed with the passage of the Bland-Allison Act and the Sherman Silver Purchase Act.

The nation was on a bimetallic standard, with the coinage of gold and silver fixed by ratio. That ratio fluctuated, depending on the availability of the two metals and on the general policy of money supply. There had been a recent vast increase in the supply of silver, and by 1894 one ounce of gold was worth thirty-two ounces of silver (as recently as 1890 the ratio had been one ounce of gold to twenty of silver). Proponents of unlimited coinage of silver were simply seeking an increase in the money supply, an inflationary trend. Gold-standard advocates were intent on preserving "the value of the dollar" and continuing the deflationary trend. What was at issue was the nation's basic economic policy, and it tended to pit East against West, creditor against debtor, conservative against liberal.

The depression led to mass unemployment, creating a climate ripe for change. The Populists made strong gains in the 1894 congressional elections, and as the national nominating conventions prepared to meet in the summer of 1896 the great showdown seemed at hand. Sensing that Cleveland and the Democrats were in trouble, the Republicans confidently nominated William McKinley of Ohio, possessor of sound Civil War and legislative records.

The Democratic convention was a bombshell. Cleveland was renounced and the silverites took control.

When Nebraska's young William Jennings Bryan stood up to speak about silver, he immediately had the delegates in the palm of his hand. "We have petitioned," he cried, "and our petitions have been scorned; we have entreated, and our entreaties have been disregarded; we have begged, and they have mocked when our calamity came. We beg no longer; we entreat no more; we petition no more. *We defy them!* . . . Destroy our farms and the grass will grow in the streets of every city in the country. . . . You shall not press down upon the brow of labor this crown of thorns. You shall not crucify mankind upon a cross of gold!"

It was spectacular and spellbinding, and it won Bryan the nomination. Bryan's reputation comes down to later generations badly tarnished by the last performance of his career—his prosecution in 1925 of a Tennessee schoolteacher, John T. Scopes, for advocating Darwin's theory of evolution. In the "Monkey Trial," Scopes's lawyer, the celebrated Clarence Darrow, mercilessly exposed Bryan's rigid fundamentalist beliefs (he stoutly maintained that the earth was created in 4004 B.C. and that Eve sprang from Adam's rib). Yet in the 1890s, at the top of his form, Bryan was a spokesman for reform, a dedicated fighter for liberal and humanitarian causes. He was proud to be known as the Great Commoner.

Most Populists saw that a third-party ticket would ensure McKinley's election, and endorsed Bryan and the Democrats in 1896. The party platform pledged unlimited coinage of silver. In the campaign the Democrats were definite underdogs, but Bryan was determined to reach the people with his message. Ignoring the tradition that a candidate did not go out to seek votes for himself, he stumped the country from one end to the other. He traveled more than 18,000 miles and made at least 600 speeches, in great halls, in public parks, at crossroads. With superb oratory he spoke to the issues—monopoly, taxes, high interest, attacks on labor unions, and, again and again, the silver question. He was speaking for the farmer and the laborer, for the West against the East, indeed for the nineteenth century against the new century on the horizon. Suddenly the favored Republicans began to run scared.

In charge of McKinley's campaign was a political genius, Cleveland businessman Mark Hanna. Hanna began a GOP blitz. "Assessing" businessmen and corporations ruthlessly, he assembled a campaign chest of $3.5 million and dispatched 1,500 speakers into key areas to spread the gospel. As many as 250 million pieces of Republican literature were plastered across the land. "He has advertised McKinley as if he were a patent medicine," Theodore Roosevelt observed.

McKinley, meanwhile, stayed on his front porch in Canton, Ohio, and held court for thousands of delegations that were paraded across his front lawn with clockwork efficiency. He was dignified and upstanding —and he did just what Hanna told him to do. On election day the South and much of the thinly populated West went for Bryan, but the Republicans captured all of the Northeast and the upper Midwest, including the swing states of Ohio and Illinois. McKinley's electoral college margin was a solid 271 to 176; his popular vote margin was thinner but still substantial, 7,036,000 to 6,468,000.

The Republican victory did not signal an outburst of reactionary policy, as many had feared. The silver issue melted away as new gold strikes in the Klondike and South Africa enlarged the money supply and stopped the deflationary spiral. Prosperity returned. But the voice of reform did not die out; it turned to other issues and became the Progressive movement of the early 1900s.

The election of 1896 symbolized the end of the old America. The new colossus had survived its tempestuous birth and now stood on the threshold of a new century, strong enough to face new challenges.

The Age of Innocence

"Happiness comes to us all with prosperity." Mark Hanna spoke the faith: virtue led to progress, progress to peace, wealth, leisure, all manner of marvelous gadgets. In the buoyant era beginning in 1890 America became the "can-do" nation, innocently blind as the two girls below to inequities or irregularities beneath the veneer of achievement.

FROM THE ROY KING COLLECTION OF CURRIER & IVES

Progress, Invention, Genius

Love of gimmickry matched by inventive genius produced a welter of laborsavers and novelties. By 1900 some one and a quarter million telephones buzzed with business and social talk; 20 million incandescent lamps glowed; elevators and buildings rose to giddy levels.

In 1888 a Rochester, New York, bookkeeper introduced a toy and launched an industry. George Eastman's Kodak "Brownie" (namesake of the little character in the French ad opposite) sold for $1, used roll film, and made everyone a photographer. Other inventions, especially the elevator, encouraged architectural experimentation; skyscrapers, like the Flatiron going up in 1901 (right), began to stud the cityscape. Confident as his era, Thomas Edison promised "inventions to order." Among his 1,093 patents were the incandescent lamp diagramed below, movie camera, and phonograph—which he studies in an early stage opposite.

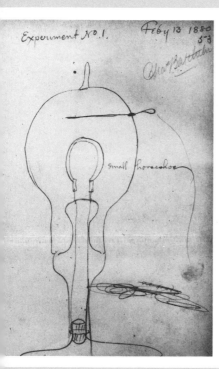

Experiment No. 1.   Feby 13 1880

small horseshoe

COLLECTION OF HENRY FORD MUSEUM

Horsepower for the Farm

The move to cities had begun by 1890, but
8 million farm workers outnumbered those in all
other industries. By 1900 only a fourth of 76 million
Americans lived in towns of 25,000 or more.

BROWN BROTHERS

THE BETTMANN ARCHIVE, INC.

The farmer might have a new laborsaver,
but his wife had a wood stove ($17.48 in
1890). At decade's end she could get a
deluxe, $100 model—still woodburning.

Farms grew, mechanical aids proliferated. Development of combines, like the one above drawn by some 30 horses, was the realization of an old dream, binding and threshing in one operation. Steam-, then gasoline-powered combines followed quickly; by 1912 the horses were gone. Farm output doubled between 1860 and 1880 and doubled again before the end of the century, thanks mainly to the boundless energy of new mechanical marvels.

Smalltown Tempo

The center of population at turn of the century
was at the small town of Columbus, Ohio—
and a typical small town it was. Those
Americans who succumbed to the big city's allure
felt nostalgic about the home town left behind.
Homesick in Chicago in 1905, five "country
boys" founded the Rotary Club to recreate the
warmth and sense of belonging they remembered.

JOHN NOBLE COLLECTION, LIFE © TIME INC.

ANDREWS COLLECTION, UNIVERSITY OF OREGON

LIBRARY OF CONGRESS

Smalltown girls giggled, coveted Valentines, learned reading and
moral precepts from *McGuffey's Readers* for three generations.

Small towns, north (left) or south (below), came with fishing holes and sleepy streets. Most had candy stores. Gerard Jensen recalls one: "Now licorice passays, artificially flavored banana-shaped candies . . . brittle coltsfoot rock rested in the windows, exposed to sun and flies. Two for a cent or three for five."

CHANSONETTA EMMONS, CULVER

Beneath the Big Top

Circus day, preceded by gaudy posters and weeks of suspense, began with an early morning parade of roustabouts and equipment. Then the grand march, led by caparisoned elephants, followed by a gilded and wheezing calliope, drew mesmerized spectators to . . . The Greatest Show on Earth.

To little boys peeping into tents, gazing at the center ring, it
was ever new and wonderful. But circuses had been around since
the Caesars. The golden age of the American circus came between
1870 and 1919. It was a big business, and it owed much to a man
who instinctively combined magic with business: starting with
an old woman he displayed as George Washington's nurse, P. T.
Barnum built a fortune and a legend in the exotic world of the
big top, never forgetting, "There's a sucker born every minute."

103

Shades of Horatio Alger

The dream that riches would reward hard work flowered in the United States with the planting of 8.8 million immigrants who arrived in the first ten years of the twentieth century. For some the dream came true. For others it faded in the despair of slums, filth, and disease.

CULVER

Horatio Alger's poor but clean-cut, fearless young heroes were smart, ready to grasp opportunity. Harvard graduate Alger was pudgy, stoop-shouldered, timid. He hesitated, often sold stories without securing royalties. His heroes succeeded; he was a failure. But the gospel of his hundred-odd books was the faith of the day. If it did not work for all, it did for some, and everyone in the Buffalo holiday crowd opposite and among the newsboys above planned to be lucky. Andrew Carnegie had been a bobbin boy, hadn't he? John Jacob Astor arrived with $5. The sturdy piece-work girl at right might dream of a rich marriage. Why not? It could happen.

High Society

With the era's wealth, much of it held by 4,047 men, came leisure, a new commodity. America must learn to play. None played harder than the rich. Once ruthless business competitors, now they competed socially, each outdoing the others with "cottages" (Vanderbilt's "Breakers," opposite, cost $5 million), parties, and titled sons-in-law.

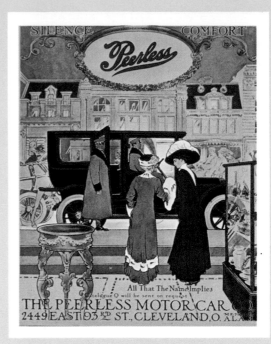

In 1900, America had 8,000 automobiles. They were, as the Peerless ad makes clear, rich men's toys. Few families had as many as the George Goulds, but there were enough speeding (10 miles an hour) status symbols by 1906 to prompt Princeton's Woodrow Wilson to comment, "To the countryman, they are a picture of the arrogance of wealth, with all its . . . carelessness." By then two-time failure Henry Ford was building machines, and in 1913 his workingman's car rolled off the assembly line at $550.

Consuelo Vanderbilt, reluctant duchess, was kept under guard before her wedding.

107

Farewell to an Era

Innocence and industrial might were twins,
nourished during America's isolation from the
rest of the world. In 1914 that separate peace was
threatened by Europe's war. The sailor-suited
lady below ponders the passing of an age.

CHANSONETTA EMMONS. CULVER

PART TWO

The World at War 1898-1945

Chronology:

The Call to Arms

1898 Battleship *Maine* sunk
1898 Spanish-American War
1898 Hawaii annexed
1901 McKinley assassinated
1915 *Lusitania* sunk
1917 War declared on Germany
1918 World War I ends

Boom and Bust

1920 Prohibition goes into effect
1924 Harding administration scandals
1929 Stock market crash
1932 "Bonus March" on Washington
1933 New Deal begins
1940 Roosevelt wins third term

Day of Infamy, Years of Agony

1941 Japanese attack Pearl Harbor
1942 Philippines fall
1942 Doolittle raid on Tokyo
1942 Operation Torch in North Africa
1943 U.S. offensive in the Pacific
1943 Sicily, Italy invaded
1944 D-day invasion of France
1944 France, Belgium, Luxembourg liberated
1944 Germany invaded
1944 Battle of the Bulge
1945 Germany surrenders

CLEAR-THE-WAY-!!

BUY BONDS

FOURTH
LIBERTY LOAN

Over There

5

The American battleship cleared for action, belching black smoke as it churned toward the German squadron. On the bridge, Commodore George Dewey, who despite the torpedoes had steamed into Mobile Bay with Farragut thirty-four years before, recognized he now faced a fight that would make headlines the world over. The German ships were commanded by Vice Admiral Otto von Diederichs, seeking to break up Dewey's blockade off Manila. The kaiser hoped that Germany might grab something in the Philippine Islands as the Spanish empire fell apart under American guns.

Increasing the stakes was a squadron of British ships which sought to aid Commodore Dewey by interposing themselves between the Americans and the Germans. It was 1898, before the dawn of the twentieth century. But already a pattern of international aggression piled on international aggression was visible, a pattern that would become all too familiar as the century grew old by war. The pattern involved immensely powerful weapons, vast commitments of men, globe-girdling alliances that promised to save mankind but actually threatened innocent millions with sudden death.

Commodore Dewey had an answer to the complex situation off Luzon as the three squadrons maneuvered for battle. It was essentially the same answer he had given when his fleet had paraded into Manila Harbor from Hong Kong just a week after the outbreak of the Spanish-American War: "You may fire when ready, Gridley." His words, recorded by correspondents specially brought along for that purpose, immediately blackened front pages across the United States. At his elbow the correspondents were awaiting the reply he would give Kapitän Paul von Hintze, Admiral Diederichs's representative. Hintze, who spoke English, was making last-minute attempts to force an American withdrawal. Dewey turned to the German officer and bellowed, "If your admiral wants a fight, he can have it *now!*"

His bluster scared the Germans off, and made the desired headlines. But the Germans would come on again, at another time and in another place. The fearsome specters that would plague the twentieth century could not be exorcised so easily.

The Spanish-American War, as entertaining and popular as a band concert, was waged by a people with no taste for war on their own soil. Gettysburg was still too strong a memory for Americans to crave the sound of cannon or the smell of powder and seared flesh. Yet a war over the horizon, in an exotic setting, might indeed be a "splendid little war."

Nevertheless, President William McKinley, himself a veteran of 1861, hoped until the last minute that the rising dispute with Spain over rebellious Cuba could be soothed by diplomatic means. If his backbone had been as strong as his face implied, perhaps he could have arranged a settlement, despite the drumbeating of the yellow journals. But such clangorous and influential hawks as Theodore Roosevelt, then assistant secretary of the navy, could not be quieted. They called the President "spineless," and proclaimed that the rebels' cause was freedom's cause.

They were given their war when the U.S.S. *Maine* exploded in Havana harbor on February 15, 1898. With 260 American lives lost, none of Spain's protestations of innocence—not even the Spaniards' urgent assistance to drowning and wounded victims—could satisfy American "honor." Reluctantly, President McKinley put the decision for war in the hands of the Congress, having "exhausted every effort to relieve the intolerable condition of affairs which is at our doors."

Selling war bonds to Americans by posters such as this one by Howard Chandler Christy raised almost $20 billion in 1917-18. Artful propaganda—and the innate desire to save the world for democracy —turned Americans into enthusiastic supporters of the Allied cause.

"Remember The *Maine*!"

Hopes for peace at the 19th century's end were blasted when the battleship Maine *mysteriously exploded in the harbor of Havana, Cuba, killing 260 Americans. Spanish efforts to rescue the Maine's crew were not reported in the U.S., and many Americans blamed Spain for the disaster. Hostility toward Spain had been building for some years as Americans felt increasing sympathy for Cuban revolutionists fighting to free their island from Spanish rule. And so, on April 25, 1898, Congress voted a resolution for what Woodrow Wilson would later call "a war of impulse."*

LOCATION OF THE MAINE—HAVANA HARBOR.

RECOVERING THE DEAD BODIES.

February 25, 1898.

Dewey, Hong Kong

~~Secret and Confidential~~

Order the Squadron except Monocacy to Hong Kong. Keep full of coal. In the event of declaration war Spain, your duty will be to see that the Spanish squadron does not leave the Asiatic coast and then offensive operations in Philipine Islands. Keep Olympia until further orders.

Roosevelt

Commodore George Dewey quickly carried out these orders from Theodore Roosevelt, then assistant secretary of the navy, and in May, 1898, destroyed the Spanish fleet in Manila Bay. The Spaniards suffered nearly 400 casualties in the battle; not one American was killed. As a result of the American victory, the liberated Filipinos were soon under the domination of the U.S. For his victory at Manila, Dewey was promoted to rear admiral

Caricature of William Randolph Hearst as the cartoon "Yellow Kid" in *The Bee* blamed the publisher for raising war fever by administering daily doses of his *New York Journal*. To boost his newspaper's circulation, Hearst sent artist Frederic Remington and writer Richard Harding Davis to Cuba in December, 1896. When Remington told Hearst he wanted to leave Cuba because "there will be no war," Hearst replied, "You furnish the pictures. I'll furnish the war."

NEW YORK JOURNAL, 1897

At the end of April, 1898, with unrestrained enthusiasm both houses of Congress voted for war.

It was a swift and triumphant war of less than four months. To the beat of Sousa's "Stars and Stripes Forever," 150,000 volunteers signed up to "free Cuba" from its Spanish tyrants. Despite wool uniforms, fouled-up transportation, and inaccurate intelligence, some 18,000 American troops landed on the island—right below a Spanish fort. The fort, however, was immediately abandoned, and the Spanish failed to muster more than a fraction of their 200,000-man force. Soon Colonel Roosevelt, who had left his navy post to become a soldier, and his elite but horseless corps of Rough Riders were charging up San Juan Hill, and Admiral Sampson was bagging the hapless Spanish fleet as it steamed out of Santiago Bay on Madrid's orders. Then the only problem was to take over Puerto Rico before the war ended, before the bands struck up "When Johnny Comes Marching Home." Seldom had national spirits soared so high.

Before the October peace conference in Paris, Spain ruefully accepted America's terms: surrender of Cuba to the rebels, cession of Puerto Rico and Guam to the United States. In the wake of Admiral Dewey's Philippine excursions, Spain also let the United States hold Manila but argued during the conference about the final disposition of the islands. McKinley too was undecided about this Pacific prize. Should Americans free the islands? he wondered. Or should they "take . . . and uplift and Christianize" the little brown inhabitants? Finally, as he explained the process to a group of churchmen later, God told him to annex the islands—which was accomplished by means of a $2 million payment to Spain and a roughshod overriding of "anti-imperialists" in the Senate.

Thus America grew out of its historic, isolated position and into a world role. In the words of the astonished and rather perplexed President McKinley:

". . . in a few short months we have become a world power; and I know, sitting here in this chair, with what added respect the nations of the world now view the United States. . . . It is vastly different from the conditions I found when I was inaugurated."

Another result of the peculiarly satisfactory Spanish-American War (which resulted in the deaths of fewer than 300 Americans) was the attractiveness of Theodore Roosevelt as the vice-presidential candidate on the McKinley ticket in the election of 1900. Led by this dynamic campaigner, and bolstered by such slogans as "Prosperity at Home, Prestige Abroad," the Republicans drubbed the Democrats by a count of 292 to 155 in the electoral college. William Jennings Bryan, the still silver-tongued but now unfashionable candidate of the Democrats, lost even his home state

Two key naval victories helped the U.S. to triumph in the Spanish-American War in less than four months. Dewey on the flagship *Olympia* (opposite) gets ready to blow the Spanish fleet out of the water of Manila Bay. At right, U.S. and Spanish warships exchange fire in the harbor of Santiago, Cuba, before the Spanish vessels were destroyed.

of Nebraska. Then, less than a year after the election, McKinley was assassinated at the Pan-American Exposition in Buffalo. Roosevelt, seizing the helm of a surprised but confident nation, devised his own characteristically bold program.

The world watched with little amusement and much respect as Roosevelt brought warring Japan and Russia to the treaty table in Portsmouth, New Hampshire; as he kept the Germans out of Venezuela, and forced them to come to terms with the French in Morocco; as he set up the new nation of Panama by fair means and foul, thereby providing the route for the American "big ditch" that would one day link the Atlantic and the Pacific. Saluting the scope of Roosevelt's efforts, the historian Henry Adams wrote that "for the first time in 1,500 years, a true Roman *Pax* was in sight."

By the time he retired from the presidency in 1908 (having won an election in his own right in 1904), Roosevelt not only had carried through long-needed reforms of America's railways and trusts and initiated a national parks system for which future generations would be increasingly grateful, but had also made the United States look like a "top dog" to the rest of the world. His dispatch of the Great White Fleet—sixteen dazzling warships with white topsides and golden bows sent around the Horn from the Atlantic to envious Japan and home again past proud England's outposts in the Indian Ocean and Mediterranean Sea —struck him as "the most important service that I rendered to peace."

Roosevelt's hand-picked successor, William Howard Taft, tried to maintain an equally strong foreign policy, one that would substitute "dollars for bullets." Valiant but vain was Taft's attempt to uphold the international court at The Hague. He proposed an agreement with France and England whereby the three nations would submit "all questions determinable by the principles of law and equity" to the court. This rule would bind the participants even when the disputes concerned matters of "vital interest and national honor." In a manner that cast a shadow down the next several decades of American history, the U.S. Senate amended the treaty to death after the French and British governments had accepted it. The President, heartsick with disappointment, thereupon refused to sign the treaty.

Nor did Taft triumph on the domestic front. Even though he pursued the trusts under the Sherman Act even more effectively than Roosevelt, and even though his administration fostered two vital amendments to the Constitution (income tax and popular election of U.S. senators), he could neither hold the allegiance of his own party nor command the hearts and minds of the nation. After Roosevelt decided to fling his hat into the ring of the 1912 election, Taft was left with the conservative end of a broken party. Woodrow Wilson, the former president of Princeton and dynamic

A hot and bloody day on San Juan Hill lives on in Frederic Remington's painting depicting the charge of the Rough Riders.

115

CULVER

"Speak softly and carry a big stick" characterized Theodore Roosevelt's leadership of the U.S. Above, he is portrayed as an international arbiter and, in the *Puck* cartoon below, his stick becomes a sword as he takes on the Wall Street giants in his role as trust-buster. One of Roosevelt's biggest coups was the building of the Panama Canal. Jonas Lie's painting (below) depicts the canal's most difficult section, the mountainous Culebra Cut, where the construction men suffered a succession of landslides.

DETROIT INSTITUTE OF ARTS

PUCK, JANUARY, 1904

governor of New Jersey, succeeded in capturing the Democratic nomination and looked like a good wager in a race against the divided Republicans. A wit composed the jape "Vote for Roosevelt, pray for Taft, but bet on Wilson!" And the smart money won handily. Taft, a man out of size and out of style for his leader-seeking era, went on to become chief justice of the United States.

Wilson immediately established himself as a leader for all the nation to see. With courage and legislative skill, he revised the tariff, reformed the banking system, and wrote a new antitrust law. A master of the processes of democratic government, he combined professorial insight with political effectiveness. Yet as he looked overseas at tumultuous Europe, he expressed the hope that his administration would not be judged by its accomplishments in foreign affairs. And after his beloved wife died in 1914, he gazed into the unfamiliar landscape that stretched ahead and said, "This is not the same world in which my dear Ellen lived."

Das Deutsches Reich, the German empire, though small in extent, was a concept hallowed by German-speaking people throughout Europe. Its greatest upholder was Kaiser Wilhelm II, who came to the Prussian throne in 1888. Though Germany had entered the race for colonies after the British and French, the kaiser was determined to find more land rich in raw materials, more markets for its goods, more bases for its fleet. "A place in the sun," Wilhelm called this desired living room. And Wilson, with his aptness for a phrase, remarked that it was a case of "England's having the earth and Germany wanting it."

One of Germany's imperial dreams was to reach south and east through the decaying Ottoman Empire to Persia's oil fields. Such a dream might not have ensnared the United States in an earlier day. But in the early twentieth century, all businessmen read the same stock market reports; women on both sides of the Atlantic watched the same society figures dance and court and marry; children played with dolls from many lands. "God and man have linked the nations together," as President McKinley had pietistically expressed it. And as Germany and her Austro-Hungarian and Ottoman partners planned railways to Baghdad, the other nations of the world shuddered.

Bosnia-Herzegovina, a mountainous little region (now included within Yugoslavia), had long been restive under Austrian domination. Neighboring Serbia, which had won independence in 1878 with Russia's backing, strove to bring about an alliance of all Slavic states, including Bosnia-Herzegovina. So when the crown prince of Austria, Archduke Francis Ferdinand, came to observe military maneuvers in the Bosnian capital with his wife on June 28, 1914, a band of young Serbians awaited him. First the royal couple survived a bomb-thrower's attack as they motored through the streets of Sarajevo. Then they fell beneath the bullets of a successful assassin, nineteen-year-old Gavrilo Princip. As he died, the crown prince whispered, "*Es ist nichts, es ist nichts* (It is nothing, it is nothing)." But it was indeed something—the first death in a ruinous war that would topple his empire and change the face of Europe.

Immediately after the affair at Sarajevo, the interlocking machinery of European alliances went into effect: the Germans backed up Austria's demands against Serbia, home of the assassins; Russia announced that she was mobilizing for war; Austria declared war after Serbia's response to a final ultimatum proved unsatisfactory; Germany declared war against Russia, then against Russia's ally, France; Britain declared war when the Germans invaded Belgium in the first days of August, 1914. It only remained for Italy to decide which side to join. France and Russia and England seemed to offer her more, so she joined the "Allies" rather than the "Central Powers" in the spring of 1915.

By then the war was already becoming a ghastly, stalemated struggle. In but the first year of the war, more than a million Frenchmen had been maimed, killed, or captured. Though the German drive on Paris had been contained, the line of hostilities that stretched from the North Sea to Switzerland continued to bulge ominously westward from the fiercely defended French fortress of Verdun. Wilson's aide, Edward Mandell House, reported after a mission to Europe at this time that America should not expect peace soon. The Allies still yearned for great victories; the Germans still believed they could impose a conqueror's terms.

Wilson pondered how America should comport itself during Europe's death-dance. One possible policy was to follow Jefferson's advice: the New World should "fatten on the follies of the old." This appealed to bankers and progressive isolationists alike. Another policy was to give all aid short of war, as was urged by Theodore Roosevelt and Senator Henry Cabot Lodge. Yet another policy was to ignore the war altogether, though this meant abnegating America's role as a world leader. Wilson showed where he stood when he declined to accept a cutting from a rosebush near the front line at Verdun. Appalled at the President's icy neutrality, Colonel House wrote that Wilson was "singularly lacking in appreciation of this European crisis. He seems more interested in domestic affairs. . . ."

Foreign affairs certainly did not seem Wilson's forte. Since the beginning of his administration he had been jousting with Mexico's dictator president, Victoriano Huerta, who was believed to be responsible for the killing of his predecessor, Francisco Madero. Huerta represented everything Wilson despised; he would

have to be unseated. "I am going to teach the South American republics to elect good men," Wilson explained to one who questioned his interference in Mexico's government.

Such a primly moral view of international politics bespoke Wilson's birth in a Presbyterian parsonage. And when Huerta refused to budge, Wilson's stubborn adherence to an impractical policy reminded some of his former failure at Princeton. There he had stubbornly refused to accept the trustees' decision about where the graduate school should be placed; finally, after entering politics, he had been forced to resign from Princeton. Now that his campus was the world, his pious single-mindedness would have an effect on additional millions.

For Mexico, Wilson felt the best move would be to back Francisco "Pancho" Villa, a bandit whose redeeming feature was his opposition to Huerta. Even as Europe stood poised on the brink of war, Wilson

In the unusual three-way presidential race of 1912, Woodrow Wilson (opposite) waged a whistle-stop campaign and led the Democrats to victory. The intellectual ex-president of Princeton won the voters with his humor and pledges of reforms, but his triumph was assured by the split in Republican party ranks. The faces and figures of two losers in the election were similar though they had little else in common: Theodore Roosevelt (above), trying for a comeback with the Bull Moose symbol of his new Progressive party, called the Republicans' William Howard Taft (below) a "fathead"; President Taft, who had been picked by Roosevelt as his successor four years before, labeled T.R. a "demagogue."

shipped arms to Villa through the port of Veracruz. But at the same time and at the same port arms for Huerta were arriving from Germany. Wilson ordered his forces to block the Germans. A thousand American sailors and marines stormed ashore, followed by 3,000 more, in a scene that recalled 1847 all too vividly. The Mexicans fought back before surrendering their city; 19 Americans were killed and 71 wounded. The German ships, turned away by the blockade, steamed off down the coast—where they landed their munitions without difficulty. Wilson's problems with Mexico were not resolved until 1916, when a much greater crisis pushed the United States to make a peaceful settlement with the Mexicans.

In the meantime, the British liner *Lusitania* had been sunk by a German U-boat with the loss of 128 Americans in May, 1915. Even then Wilson refused to alter his position of strict neutrality in the European war, turning a deaf ear on those who urged a tougher policy toward Germany. "There is such a thing as a man being too proud to fight," he said.

For many other Americans, however, the sinking of the *Lusitania* marked the end of emotional detachment. Henceforth they accorded greater credibility to stories of German atrocities in Belgium, paid more attention to reports of American flying men who had joined the Lafayette Escadrille or of American volunteers in France's Foreign Legion. One of the Legionnaires, poet Alan Seeger, wrote with horror at the end of 1915 that it was "a fight to the finish, just as our Civil War was." Also: "The conflagration, far from diminishing, seems to be spreading."

It spread to the very depths of the sea, where German U-boats now hid between forays on the shipping that kept England alive. General Erich von Ludendorff, who had become Germany's military dictator with Marshal Hindenburg, agreed with the kaiser's admirals that the U-boat campaign must be

119

Mexican bandit "Pancho" Villa led a personal army of 50,000 hard-riding men in 1914. The Villistas were, for a time, looked upon as heroes by Woodrow Wilson, whose missionary zeal almost led the U.S. into war with Mexico and embittered U.S.-Mexican relations for decades.

Wilson shows Mexico his disapproval of its revolution in this *Punch* cartoon.

intensified. All measures for victory must be taken while Germany's diminishing food and industrial resources still lasted.

Throughout 1916 the Germans kept talking peace to Wilson, who had begun to focus his personal concern on the war. But in January, 1917, the High Command made the formal decision to risk all by announcing the total blockade of the British Isles—anything that moved would be sunk.

Woodrow Wilson, who had just won reelection behind the banner "He Kept Us Out of War," was then forced to sever diplomatic relations with Germany. Historians therefore point to the U-boat as one of the chief factors that put American fighting men in European trenches. And what a typical invention of its time the U-boat was: powered with a diesel engine that German technology had developed in 1908; armed with immensely destructive torpedoes and with deck guns; designed to stay out of sight and not engage in conventional gun duels; anonymous, all-powerful, beyond written law.

Another typically twentieth century factor that pushed America into the war was the Zimmermann telegram. It transpired because of a clever British naval action at the very outbreak of the war: seamen hauled Germany's transatlantic cables up from the bottom of the North Sea's floor and hacked them apart. In order to transmit overseas messages thereafter, the Germans had to rely on radio—a device made possible by the invention of the amplifier tube in 1906. Outside Berlin at Nauen they built a powerful wireless station, from which encoded messages began to fill the airwaves as the war burst forth. A British naval intelligence team then succeeded in cracking the German code; from spies and allies, other cryptographic aids

came into British hands. Soon the Germans had no secrets in the air. But, serene in their belief that no one could fathom their technical skill, the Germans persisted in using their established code procedures.

Thus it happened that the British were able to take and decipher a particularly important message from the stream of communiqués that were flowing between Berlin and Washington. This message came from Arthur Zimmermann, the recently appointed German foreign secretary, and was addressed to his ambassador in the United States, Johann-Heinrich von Bernstorff. The message, as amazing for its ignorance as for its impudence, read as follows:

> WE INTEND TO BEGIN UNRESTRICTED SUBMARINE WARFARE. WE SHALL ENDEAVOR TO KEEP THE UNITED STATES NEUTRAL. IN THE EVENT OF THIS NOT SUCCEEDING, WE MAKE MEXICO A PROPOSAL OF ALLIANCE ON THE FOLLOWING BASIS: MAKE WAR TOGETHER, MAKE PEACE TOGETHER, GENEROUS FINANCIAL SUPPORT, AND AN UNDERSTANDING ON OUR PART THAT MEXICO IS TO RECONQUER THE LOST TERRITORY IN TEXAS, NEW MEXICO AND ARIZONA.

At that very moment President Wilson had some 12,000 men in Mexico. After Huerta had gone into exile, "Pancho" Villa had won Wilson's wrath by keeping the border in turmoil. By raising an international rumpus, Villa reasoned, he might succeed in toppling the new president, Venustiano Carranza. On March 9, 1916, he and 400 horsemen galloped through Columbus, New Mexico, killing and burning as they went. Reacting with haste and indiscretion, Wilson sent General John J. Pershing (called "Black Jack" because of his command of a black unit in the Spanish-Ameri-

can War) deep into Mexico. For months the hounds-and-hares pursuit dragged on, Mexicans of all parties finally concluding that the one common enemy was the United States.

Foreign Secretary Zimmermann, aware that the Americans were taking an increasingly partisan view of the European war and that even President Wilson favored the Allies, was delighted to see four-fifths of the U.S. Army committed to Mexico. Perhaps, he concluded, if a genuine war could be stirred up—possibly one that also involved America's Pacific rival Japan (although she was nominally on the side of the Allies) —the Americans could be kept sufficiently busy in their own hemisphere and out of Europe.

"Good Lord! Good Lord!" the President exclaimed on reading the telegram. Shocked to the depth of his being, he could scarcely believe this evidence that America was internationally scorned. He commenced an intense struggle in his mind to construct a rationale for entry, a rallying cry by which he could galvanize a confused and peaceful nation for war. The result of

that struggle: his famous preachment that the war would "make the world safe for democracy."

Diplomatic relations with Germany having been severed, the immediate task before Wilson prior to Congress's convening was to find a commander. And out of the West (where U.S. forces had finally been recalled from Mexico) came the bull-horn voice of "Black Jack" Pershing. "I would like to command the expedition," he unblushingly announced. Wilson assented—having learned that Pershing could speak "a little bit" of French.

Wilson began to feel that he had an armed force and a resolved public behind him. His mind was further eased by news from Russia that revolution had removed the autocratic Romanovs from power. Although the March Revolution weakened the Russian war effort, it allowed the liberal American President to feel that now the Allied cause and democracy were identical.

When President Wilson appeared before the Congress on April 2, many representatives and senators

121

were wearing flags in their lapels. His peroration fell on ears that would listen:

> With a profound sense of the solemn and even tragical character of the step I am taking . . . I advise that the Congress declare the recent course of the Imperial German government to be, in fact, nothing less than war against the government and people of the United States; that it formally accept the status of belligerent that has been thrust upon it. . . . It is a fearful thing to lead this great peaceful people into war, into the most terrible and disastrous of all wars, civilization itself seeming to be in the balance. . . . The day has come when America is privileged to spend her blood and her might for the principles that gave her birth and happiness and the peace which she has treasured. God help her. She can do no other.

The vote to support his declaration of war was 82 to 6 in the Senate; 373 to 50 in the House—not unanimous, but convincing. Americans realized they had a remarkable leader, a leader who would seek to teach the nations the meaning of "democracy and freedom."

To the first American intelligence team arriving in Europe, the English bluntly stated, "It is impossible to go on with the war if [shipping] losses like this continue." England's ships, the critical supply line that kept the Allies in business, were going under the waves at a rate exceeding 500,000 tons per month.

Despite British opposition to the idea, a convoy system was built and the U.S. delivered thirty-six antisubmarine destroyers to a base in Ireland. Within four months the loss rate was halved—a massive contribution to the winning of the war.

As important as the destroyers and submarine-hunting devices was the psychological lift provided by the arrival of fresh fighters. "Never mind the guns, never mind the transport—we'll provide them. Only bring your young soldiers over to fill our thin ranks. The fate of France and of the war is at stake." The same theme was reiterated in the appeals of French and British military and political leaders.

France lay exhausted, her resources bankrupt, her troops in mutiny, her people starving. Two and a half million soldiers had already been killed on the Western Front. But then an American officer, saluting a certain French tomb, proclaimed, "Lafayette, we are here!" And the French, understanding the message, took heart. They heard General Pershing say, "I hope . . . that here on the soil of France and in the school of French heroes, our American soldiers may learn to battle and to vanquish for the liberty of the world."

After a delayed start, the American Expeditionary Force—whose numbers exceeded two million before

"Peace With Honor" provided the theme as Wilson's presidential campaign rolled along in 1916. He narrowly won reelection.

UPI

122

Neutrality Torpedoed

"Fair warning" issued by the German embassy in Washington did not deter Americans from sailing on the Cunard luxury liner *Lusitania* on May 1, 1915. The danger of a wartime crossing provided an extra thrill for the passengers bound from New York to Liverpool. They enjoyed a smooth voyage under sunny skies until May 7. As the ship was nearing Ireland, a German torpedo found its mark. The *Lusitania* sank in 18 minutes. With American women and children among the 1,198 persons who died, U.S. neutrality became a lost cause. Years later it was learned that the *Lusitania* had had munitions aboard.

FROM STEFAN LORANT'S *THE LIFE AND TIMES OF THEODORE ROOSEVELT* (DOUBLEDAY & COMPANY)

the war's end—won respect from allies and foes alike. In the very first American action, at the village of Seicheprey near Saint-Mihiel on April 20, 1918, the "doughboys" of the Twenty-sixth Division outfought the Germans. Though the Germans succeeded in capturing the village and its surrounding woods, "Pershing's babies" staged a counterattack with machine guns and artillery, retaking Seicheprey and clearing the woods of the enemy.

And in the next American action, at Cantigny a few weeks later, it was the same story. U.S. infantrymen counterattacked after the town had fallen, driving the Germans out. Both Seicheprey and Cantigny were tough little battles that got big plays in hometown newspapers. Yet the stories made grim reading: Americans were beginning to die, to be gassed, to be wounded.

To many American readers it appeared that the AEF had arrived just in time to witness the final collapse of the French nation. Diagrams showed the thrusts of the Germans' spring offensives, the *Friedenstuerme* (peace storms), which seemed to have enough fire and fury to sunder the weakened French line near

Reims. Reports indicated that after the Germans had broken through on their left flank, they would then smash the British on the other side of Paris—and all France would fall.

Neither did the Allies have the superior generals nor the harmonious command structure that could turn defeat into victory. At last Marshal Foch was appointed joint commander; the British somewhat reluctantly accepted his combined plan. The Americans consented to Foch's distribution of their forces (though Pershing fought to hold his units together and the AEF was never integrated into the Allied structure). Through wheatfields dotted with poppies, the U.S. Second and Third Divisions hurried to the front. In some cases their truck drivers were Vietnamese, French colonial forces whose grandsons would one day fight for or against the doughboys' grandsons.

The Second Division pressed on toward its assigned objective: the thickly forested *Bois de Belleau*, occupied by some of Kaiser Wilhelm's most seasoned veterans. Led by two regiments of marines, the Americans attacked. Interlocked German machine gun stations ripped the marines apart, shattered the trees, filled the air with "red hot nails." And yet the Americans kept coming. Creeping forward, wiping out the machine gun nests with grenades, hugging the earth, and fighting and dying day after day, the marines and army units finally found themselves in possession of the woods.

The Third Division made its mark less than a month later near Château-Thierry. Crack German forces had succeeded in crossing the Marne River, symbol of French security. Then amidst hilly terrain they locked in combat with the Americans, pulverizing one unit after another. But the American line held. Finally Ludendorff called off his troops and abandoned the offensive on that front.

Impressed, the French passed out medals and changed the name of *Bois de Belleau* to *Bois de la Brigade de Marine*. Ludendorff's officers defended themselves by protesting that the Americans were unprofessional, they didn't fight the way all soldiers on the Western Front had learned to fight in the last four years: "We had Americans opposite us who were terribly reckless fellows." Encouraged, General Pershing began to hope that France might be saved and that, given eighty divisions from home, the war might be won by the end of 1919. And he continued to press his case for a consolidated U.S. Army that would not be fractionalized among Allied divisions.

Through the spring and early summer of 1918 the doughboys fought side by side with the French. They stumbled over the language barriers, learned each other's songs, respected each other's idiosyncracies—the French passion for wine; the American passion for racial segregation. Together they pushed the Germans back: beneath the oaks of Compiègne Forest, along the banks of the Aisne River, eastward from Soissons.

It was the British, however, who gave the kaiser what he called the German Army's "Black Day"—August 8, 1918. Assisted by Canadians and Australians, and meshing their forces with the French, the British fell upon the Germans at Amiens on the Somme. It was not the war's worst battle (some 125,000 men were lost), but it was more than the thinned-out Germans could stand at that stage of the war. Kaiser Wilhelm called a meeting of the High Command; Hindenburg concurred, "The war must be ended."

The end would come swiftly. But not until the Americans had had a chance to launch their own

At last the Yanks were coming, with Gen. John J. Pershing leading the way. Before the war ended, more than 2 million Americans would serve in Europe, tipping the balance in favor of the Allies.

offensive. In August, Pershing finally got his wish, and was given command of the U.S. First Army, a complete and cohesive force. Foch had eventually been won over to Pershing's view, but only with difficulty. During one of their confrontations, Pershing had refused to scatter his units according to Foch's plan. Foch had then sarcastically asked, "Do you wish to take part in the battle?" Adhering to U.S. political policy, Pershing replied, "Most assuredly, but as an American army, and in no other way."

His point won, Pershing now had to make good. His army's assignment in early September: to eliminate the Saint-Mihiel Salient, the sword that Germany had thrust into the vitals of France below Verdun. With primitive air and tank support, Pershing's First and Twenty-sixth Divisions moved in—and accomplished their task in two days. By September 16 the Germans had surrendered some 200 square miles of French territory, plus 15,000 prisoners and 257 guns. Casualties were heavy as ever on both sides (7,000 Americans killed or captured).

Without pause, Pershing then threw his forces into the big Allied drive west of Verdun at the end of September. Known as the Meuse-Argonne Offensive, this sustained action cost more than 20,000 American lives. In a whole month of agonized fighting, little was gained; little but a prolongation of the vast tragedy. There was neither glamor nor glory in worming through a ten-mile-deep German defensive system (denser and more elaborate with its concrete, steel, and wire buttresses than anything American soldiers would encounter in World War II). There was neither exaltation nor honor in blasting German machine gun nests with hand grenades and helping maimed or blinded comrades to aid stations. Terror and exhaustion and shell shock were the souvenirs for those who survived their visit to Europe.

Yet heroism must be recorded. Here in the Meuse-Argonne, Alvin C. York, a former conscientious objector, achieved fame by shooting twenty-five of the enemy platoon that swept down upon him—and the remainder he captured. Here Charles W. Whittlesey, a scholarly-looking major with round, steel-rimmed spectacles, refused to surrender when his "lost battalion" was besieged for five days; when relief came, only 194 of his men were found alive.

It was also in the Meuse-Argonne that Captain Harry S. Truman urged his artillery unit on through the mud, earning from an observant blacksmith this accolade, "I never heard a man cuss so well—or intelligently—and I've shoed a million mules." Truman was in the 129th Field Artillery of the Thirty-fifth Division

The Fourteen Points

Wilson enumerated his formula for a "peace without victory" on January 8, 1918. He asked for:

1. Pacts openly negotiated.
2. Freedom of the seas.
3. Removal of economic barriers.
4. Armament reduction.
5. Colonial claims adjusted in interests of subject people.
6. Russian territory evacuated and Russian national policy freely decided.
7. Belgium evacuated by Germans and restored.
8. French territory evacuated, Alsace and Lorraine returned to France.
9. Italian frontiers adjusted along nationality lines.
10. Autonomous development opportunity for Austria-Hungary people.
11. Rumania, Serbia, Montenegro evacuated and Serbia given sea access.
12. Autonomous development for non-Turks in Ottoman Empire, and Dardanelles opened to all ships.
13. Independence for Poland with sea access.
14. International body to preserve world peace . . . the League of Nations.

France suffered half a million casualties in the 1916 fighting for Verdun under the rallying cry "They shall not pass." At right, U.S. troops overrun a German trench at blood-soaked Verdun in 1918.

in August, 1917. He hoped to become a section sergeant, but in those days enlisted men elected their officers and he was voted into the rank of first lieutenant. He went with his unit to Camp Doniphan, Oklahoma, where he successfully filled the role of regimental canteen officer among other duties. But when he was recommended for promotion to captain, Brigadier General Lucien G. Berry told him, "It will be a disaster to the country to let you command men!"

In the spring of 1918, Truman was sent to France, where he received five weeks of special artillery train-ing on French 75s, the supreme weapon of the war. Now a captain, he rejoined the newly arrived 129th Field Artillery and was made adjutant of its Second Battalion. The battalion's rowdy Battery D had already virtually destroyed the careers of three commanding officers when Truman was asked to take charge of it. He was still trying to attain control of Dizzy D in August when the 129th was ordered to the front. Truman's unit got into position on Mount Her-

Hard training in France transformed recruits into tough fighters such as this doughboy shown in street combat by Harvey Dunn.

renberg in the Vosges Mountains of Alsace. On the night of September 6 the Germans' heavy artillery rained shells on the area and almost all of Dizzy D's "fighting Irish" panicked.

Truman had then been on his horse but it fell into a shell hole and rolled over on him. He regained his feet in time to see his men fleeing. "I got up and called them everything I knew," he recalled. The cowed men returned to their positions and from that point on there was no doubt about who was in command of Dizzy D.

Later, Truman's outfit moved to the Meuse-Argonne sector, where he had many narrow escapes from shells and machine gun fire. Once his men had given him up for dead when he reappeared and led them into no-man's-land. The air was foul, the men were filthy. But not Truman. A fellow officer remarked that "dirt and cooties didn't seem to stick to him the way they did to the rest of us. Harry Truman hadn't had his clothes off his back for two weeks and yet he was immaculate. Moreover, he was clean-shaven. He must have shaved with coffee, because we didn't have plain hot water."

The loathsome life led by the ground fighters—slogging through mud, pinned down in verminous trenches—contrasted sharply with the conditions of warfare high above the scarred earth. Flying fragile aircraft mostly by the seat of their pants after only a few hours of solo time and without parachutes, the fighter pilots earned the war's greatest glory. Their aerial dogfights gave them a lasting romantic image. They were the gallant, daring knights of the war, free of the regimentation that governed the foot soldier's life.

Since April, 1916, 180 American volunteers had been serving as pilots with the Lafayette Escadrille, attached to the French Flying Corps. They had accounted for 199 enemy planes by the time most of them transferred to the American Army Air Service in February, 1918. Back home, the U.S. had had fewer than

The Western Front

American troops arrived in Europe when trench warfare was being replaced by a war of maneuver. The first major engagement for the Americans took place on April 20, 1918, at Seicheprey (**1**), where they outfought the Germans. Then, on May 28, the U.S. 1st Division captured Cantigny (**2**). Next, the Americans helped the French repulse the Germans at Château-Thierry (**3**). On June 6, U.S. marines and soldiers took the offensive at Belleau Wood (**4**), where they suffered heavy losses before winning the battle. The doughboys then participated in a counter-attack at Soissons (**5**) that, according to Pershing, turned the tide of the war against the Germans. The Americans' next big operation was wiping out the Germans' Saint-Mihiel (**6**) salient in September. This was followed by an offensive in the Meuse-Argonne (**7**), the Americans' toughest battle, costing 117,000 casualties. Although logistical problems halted the American advance on October 14, by then the enemy was on the verge of surrendering.

250 planes in April, 1917, and it took the air service a year to get into action. Although no U.S.-built aircraft were flown in combat, Camels, Spads and SE-5s eventually were produced in sufficient quantity to give the Allies superiority over the Germans in the air. T.O.M. Sopwith, who built the Camel and other British fighter planes, said, "We literally thought of and designed and flew the airplanes in a space of about six or eight weeks."

General William Mitchell, who was to be court-martialed in 1925 for untactfully advocating the creation of an independent air force, commanded all U.S. aviation in Europe during the closing months of the war. This included the massing of nearly 1,500 planes at Saint-Mihiel, an unprecedented show of air power.

Some of the heroic knights of the air achieved extra fame by becoming aces. A German flier had to shoot down ten enemy planes to earn recognition as an ace. An American or a French flier could gain the distinction by disposing of five enemy aircraft. The British did not participate in the ace race, choosing not to exalt one fighting man above another. While none of the Americans came close to equaling the records of such aces as Germany's Manfred von Richthofen (80 aircraft downed), France's René Paul Fonck (75 downed), Britain's Edward Mannock (73) and Canada's Billy Bishop (72), several of the U.S. fliers racked up impressive scores during the comparatively short time they were in action.

America's ace of aces was Captain Eddie Rickenbacker, who shot down twenty-six German planes in just seven months. Captain Eddie's jaunty appearance and high spirits typified the prevailing attitude among fighter pilots of all nations. The average life of an airman during the hottest periods of fighting was three weeks. The loss of life was proportionally greater among fliers than for men in the other armed forces. With death so close, they made the most of life. Unlike most of the men in the ground war, the pilots had the opportunity to enjoy comfortable quarters, good food, liquor, and cars, as well as the often reported, but not exaggerated, attractiveness of French women. One-third of the men who had flown were dead by the end of the war. Among this tragic number was America's third-ranking ace, Raoul Lufbery, who had scored seventeen victories.

The zest that Rickenbacker and other fliers found in the war was shared by very few doughboys. Theirs had been an existence alternating between boredom and terror. The optimistic troops of 1917 had lost their innocence. They had lost it while digging battlefield graves for their buddies. They had learned that in war there are no victors, only survivors. Many of them would later echo the views expressed by playwrights Laurence Stallings and Maxwell Anderson in *What Price Glory?*: "There is something rotten about this profession of arms. . . . When they tell you to die, you have to do it, even if you're a better man than they are. . . . What a lot of God damn fools it takes to make a war!"

The end of the war had come not long after the Argonne Forest had been cleared of German defenders and the Germans realized that time to negotiate was running out. Ludendorff had gone into a rage, horrifying his staff by turning livid, foaming at the mouth, and falling to the floor in a convulsive fit. Kaiser Wilhelm, confronted too by revolutionists on the home front, saw that he was cornered. He agreed to modify some of his imperial powers; desperately he cast about for an angel who could help him ease Germany out of the war. It would have to be Wilson. And thus the kaiser, professing agreement with Wilson's Fourteen Points as a basis for settling the nations' complex problems, urged his new foreign secretary, Paul von Hintze (the very same German officer at whom Admiral Dewey had thundered off the Philippines), to

arrange things with the President of the United States.

By this time America had indeed become the "Arsenal of Democracy" by means of a gigantic mobilization effort that few had believed possible. At first it had seemed that nothing warlike could get done: volunteers failed to show up at the enlistment offices, and some 300,000 who were drafted succeeded in evading military service; industry had not concentrated on war objectives until financier Bernard Baruch, appointed to head the War Industries Board in March, 1918, made himself economic dictator of the United States; public opinion, initially confused about whose war this was (particularly in the big cities and in the Midwest's German-American areas), only began to respond en-

thusiastically after George Creel's Committee on Public Information launched an immense campaign of words and graphics.

"Uncle Sam Wants YOU" was Creel's basic message, and it worked effectively on the American conscience. Perhaps too effectively: national tensions, fired by propagandists and censors, reached such an irrational pitch that the music of Wagner was banned from opera houses and labor leader Eugene V. Debs was flung in jail for "subversive" statements of a pacifistic nature. Such hysteria could only be followed by an equally emotional recoil. Wilson himself had earlier warned, "Once lead this people into war, and they'll forget there ever was such a thing as tolerance . . . bru-

AMERICAN RED CROSS

OUR BOYS NEED SOX KNIT YOUR BIT

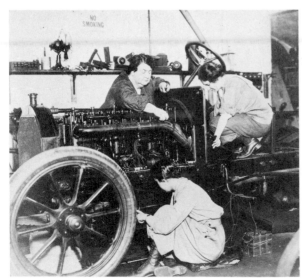

Participation in the war effort took diverse forms for Americans. Above, actor Douglas Fairbanks, famous for his daredevil roles, is armed with a megaphone to sell bonds in Wall Street. Above right, an appeal to wield knitting needles to keep the soldiers warm. At left, in the absence of men, women take on the job of auto repair. And at right, parading Boy Scouts raise their flags and patriotic fervor.

**On the
Home Front**

*Although they were late in entering the war, Americans finally
went all out to insure an Allied victory. They bought amazing
amounts of war bonds, voluntarily rationed their food and fuel,
took jobs to keep factories working around the clock, and blew the
covers of many real and imagined German spies. All their energies
were directed toward the goal of extending democracy to more lands.
This massive effort resulted in their realizing that the U.S.
must act as a major power in world affairs and that the old,
comfortable world they had known was gone forever.*

tality will enter the very fibre of our national life."

Yet for all the national zeal—with civilians contributing vast sums to the war effort via Liberty Bonds, and cooperating without complaint in Food Administrator Herbert Hoover's "meatless and wheatless days"—the American production miracle should not be exaggerated. Most of the American troops sent overseas sailed on British ships; all of the American airmen who dueled against such German aces as Richthofen flew in French or English planes; almost all of the 2,250 artillery pieces with which the Americans defended themselves and prepared their assaults were made in France, including the 75-mm. gun—the deadliest weapon on the battlefield.

And so peace was finally won. Word came from the Middle East that the Ottoman Empire had raised white flags from its minarets. Then came word that red flags had been raised on mutinous ships of Germany's high seas fleet. Word of peace swept through the trenches prematurely, with pathetic celebrations as mud-caked soldiers embraced in joy. And then on November 11, definite word: the kaiser was asking for Allied terms through representatives in Compiègne Forest. The eleventh hour of the eleventh day of the eleventh month—the incredible moment when the Western Front became silent. The moment was too wonderful for telling, particularly for telling that soon twelve o'clock would strike: an even more dreadful war would roll over these same blood-soaked acres in but another generation.

President Wilson issued a statement that indicated the next big task: "The Armistice was signed this morning. Everything for which America fought has been accomplished. It will now be our fortunate duty to assist by example." Foremost in his mind was the final and most important of his Fourteen Points: the establishment of a League of Nations. But soon Colonel House felt compelled to give him the dire report

Schoolgirls draped in American flags strew roses in the path of President Wilson on his arrival at Dover, England, in 1918. By his side is the Duke of Connaught, uncle of King George V.

that "England and France have not the same views with regard to peace that we have by any means."

Sailing to France to contend with the heads of the Allied nations, Wilson prayed that from the ruin of three collapsed empires (the Romanovs' Russia, the Hohenzollerns' Germany, and the Hapsburgs' Austria) could be constructed a Europe of free and independent states. Beyond that, a "universal dominion of right by such a concert of free peoples as shall bring peace and safety to all nations. . . ." With him sailed the First Lady, the former Edith Galt, a sprightly widow who could beat him at golf and whom he had married but a year after the death of his first wife. Also a team of hand-picked advisers, including a token Republican

133

and Colonel House. But House was losing his favored position (possibly because of the new Mrs. Wilson, possibly because his recommendations were presumptuous). Increasingly, Wilson was the lone figure, the leader and teacher, who did everything by himself.

He was indeed the best read, the best informed, and the hardest working of the heads of state who gathered at Versailles. He was also the most applauded by the European peoples, hailed as the "savior," invited to ride under the Arc de Triomphe, cheered as the spokesman for all mankind.

But the premiers and presidents with whom he dealt were not to be lectured at—they had their own views of what peace meant, their own electorates to satisfy. They were fiercely aware that some 6 million Frenchmen and 3 million Englishmen had been killed or maimed in the war, as against less than half a million Americans. And they sensed with seasoned wisdom that Wilson's ideas—his determination to create national boundaries on the basis of linguistic divisions, his disallowance of such old feuds as the French claim to the Rhineland and the Italians' claim to Fiume, and above all his insistence on the League of Nations—were too novel to be acceptable. Concerned about France's future, Premier Georges Clemenceau said, "Mr. Wilson bores me with his Fourteen Points; why, God Almighty has only ten!"

But Wilson pressed on. Tirelessly he debated his way point by point. Even when apparently smitten with a severe thrombosis, he refused to desist. Once when his fellow conferees balked, he ordered his ship made ready and threatened to sail home. Thus, as a devastated Europe waited, as revolution rode the twin steeds of hunger and homelessness, Wilson prevailed. The German delegates were finally summoned to Versailles in May, 1919, to sign a treaty whose terms they had no choice but to accept.

Woodrow Wilson called the League of Nations "the last and best hope for mankind." And when it began operating at Geneva in 1920, it did indeed serve the cause of peace as a firm and just custodian of former imperial territories. But it was a concept too remote and too prejudicial of American sovereignty to appeal to many Americans—Americans who had already begun a frantic search for "normalcy." Having succeeded in convincing Europeans of the League's virtues, Wilson sadly failed at home. His opponents in the Senate, led by Henry Cabot Lodge, successfully blocked passage of the treaty as originally written. They proposed a plethora of amendments that would make our participation in the League nonbinding. And they forced the President to conclude that he would have to take his cause over their heads to the American people.

Off he went on a historic crusade of whistle-stop lectures, a crusade that seemed to be stirring the hearts of the people. But on September 25, 1919, when his special train had reached Pueblo, Colorado, he was seized with indigestion and headaches. The physical breakdown begun in Paris had resumed its course. Ever mindful of the American fighting men who had struggled to go on despite all odds, he too fought to continue. But doctors persuaded him to cancel the tour and go back to Washington.

There he suffered a paralyzing stroke. There from the seclusion of the White House, guarded by the First Lady, he declined to accept compromises that would have ensured the Versailles Treaty's ratification. There he lived out the rest of his term, a wraith occasionally on public view, while his country declined to join the League.

Until Woodrow Wilson's death in 1924, he survived as a ghost of America's fresh hopes in the early years of the century. Then we had dreamed that we could lead the world out of nationalism and imperialism and into a new democratic order of peace and justice. It was a dream hard to surrender.

Collapse and Comeback

6

Out of a sky of vivid blue a brilliant sun shone upon an open car that slowly moved up Pennsylvania Avenue from the White House toward Capitol Hill. The brilliance of the day accorded with the appearance of one of the two men seated on the car's back seat; Warren Gamaliel Harding, who within two hours would be formally installed as the new President of the United States, was a figure of robust geniality. He radiated good cheer and calm confidence as he lifted a tall silk hat above his handsome head and smiled upon the multitude lining his triumphal way.

But though the sun shone, the air was chill in Washington on March 4, 1921, and it was of winter's shivering gloom that sensitive spectators were reminded as they gazed upon the frail figure at Harding's side. Woodrow Wilson—pale, thin, his left side paralyzed by the brain thrombosis he had suffered eighteen months before—huddled, slack-jawed, into his greatcoat. He did not lift his hat or look at the crowds. When the car turned into the Capitol drive, sudden tears rolled down his cheeks and were wiped away before the car came to a halt. He remained seated, a shrunken figure, as a smiling Harding stepped out of the car and briskly mounted the Capitol steps.

The car moved on and stopped at an entrance normally used only for freight. There, screened from public view by mounted cavalrymen, Woodrow Wilson was carried into the building. He remained only long enough to sign a few last-minute bills and go through the brief formality of informing a Senate-House committee that he had no further communication for the Sixty-sixth Congress. Nor did he join

Harding upon the inaugural platform. Instead, he was driven to the house on S Street purchased for him by wealthy friends, where he would live out his few remaining years in retirement from the world.

Thus did the United States as body politic bid symbolic farewell to the highly moralistic idealism of Woodrow Wilson. It was a bitterly disillusioned electorate that had gone to the polls in November, 1920. By and large, Americans had entered World War I in a spirit of self-sacrificial idealism; had been uplifted by their President's assertion that it was a "war to end all wars" and would "make the world safe for democracy."

After the Armistice had come the exposure of truths long hidden behind walls of censorship. A shocked American public learned that the reality of war had been very different from the portrayal of it while war yet raged. They learned that generals glorified as heroes had in fact presided over battlefields from a safe distance. They learned that many of the atrocity stories had been fictions concocted by Allied propagandists. They learned of secret treaties entered into by the governments of Britain, France, Italy, and Czarist Russia whose terms, published by the new Communist government in Russia, flatly contradicted the idealistic war aims proclaimed by Wilson.

The final disillusionment came when virtually all the secret treaty terms, save those relating to Russia, were written into a Versailles Treaty which contained also the Covenant of the League of Nations. Thus a ratification by the U.S. Senate of Wilson's signature to the Versailles document meant that the U.S. became a member of the League while endorsing treaty terms which might breed future wars.

The chief political target of this disillusionment was the crippled and dying Woodrow Wilson. He and "Wilsonianism" had been the real issue of the 1920 campaign. The Democratic presidential nominee,

A revolution in the behavior of urban Americans took place in the 1920s, as prim Victorian standards were replaced by a liberated and sometimes frenzied pursuit of happiness. Foremost recorder of the new emphasis on youthful high spirits was John Held, Jr., whose flapper enlivens this 1926 cover of the humor magazine *Life*.

James M. Cox of Ohio, and his running mate, Franklin D. Roosevelt of New York, had necessarily carried this issue as a burden—and it had proved far too heavy for them. Their Republican opponents won 61 percent of the popular vote while carrying thirty-seven of the forty-eight states, gaining an electoral college triumph of 404 to 127. Harding, the Republican nominee, had struck a responsive popular chord when he asserted that "America's present need is not heroism but healing; not nostrums but normalcy; not revolution but restoration."

Campaigning relaxedly from the front porch of his Ohio small-town home, Harding had seemed the embodiment of the "normalcy" of the farm-and-village America of former years—an America toward whose best features millions of men and women yearned nostalgically. He was the seeming epitome of warmth, kindness, simple goodness, affability, neighborliness. This impression was accented by the very different one made by his running mate, Calvin Coolidge, a shrewd,

Barrels of beer are emptied into Lake Michigan by federal agents during Prohibition. But there were never enough agents to enforce the provisions of the Volstead Act, which outlawed alcoholic beverages during the 14 years of the nation's "noble experiment."

tight-faced Yankee, born and raised in a Vermont village.

The irony is that what Harding-Coolidge really stood for was the precise opposite of a return to the old rural America of farmers and craftsmen, of independent professional men, and of small entrepreneurs. They had been nominated by a Republican convention dominated by big business as none before had been. It was therefore predictable that what they would encourage with government policy was an acceleration of the concentration of economic power in a few huge business organizations, an acceleration of the concentration of population in a few huge cities. Already, for the first time in history, as the 1920 census revealed, more people lived in cities and towns than on farms and in villages of fewer than 2,500 people.

Though corrupt enforcement agents undermined the government's attempt to prevent the sale of liquor, two dedicated agents, Izzy Einstein and Moe Smith, confiscated 5 million bottles of booze and made nearly 5,000 arrests. To get evidence of speakeasy operations, they disguised themselves—as did the pair at right—as gravediggers, musicians, football players, and, not least, judges.

The new President's inner circle of friends and advisers soon became known as the Ohio Gang, though one of its members, Secretary of the Interior Albert Fall, was from New Mexico. The gang's acknowledged leader was the man chiefly responsible for Harding's presidential candidacy, Harry M. Daugherty. A small-town Ohio lawyer, politician, and lobbyist of unsavory reputation, Daugherty was named attorney general and promptly transformed the Department of Justice into a mockery of justice, his office a center of chicanery. Sharing Daugherty's apartment in Washington was his longtime intimate, Jesse Smith, who served as liaison between the Justice Department and the bootleggers, income-tax evaders, lawyers seeking pardons or paroles for convicted clients, and law violators of all kinds who, needing a "fixer," could and would pay highly for one. Also in the gang was a former building contractor named Charles R. Forbes who, though an army deserter in the early 1900s, became head of the Veterans' Bureau; and a director of the 1920 Republican National Campaign Committee, Thomas W. Miller, who became alien property custodian. With the

members of the gang the President of the United States drank and played poker, often in the White House, sometimes in a notorious Little Green House on K Street presided over by Jesse Smith.

The first hint of wrong-doing at the heart of the administration came in early 1923 when Forbes unexpectedly resigned his Veterans' Bureau post. Shortly thereafter gossip about his handling of the bureau provoked a Senate investigation, whereupon Forbes's closest assistant, the bureau's principal legal officer, Charles F. Cramer, committed suicide. This was followed by the suicide of Jesse Smith in Daugherty's apartment while the attorney general was a guest in the White House. On June 20, Harding left Washington for a speaking tour of the West, followed by a ceremonial visit and vacation in Alaska. He was a tired, anxious man when he left—he realized by then how gravely he and his administration had been compromised by "my damned friends, my goddamned friends." He fell seriously ill in Seattle and died in San Francisco, evidently of a cerebral embolism, on August 2, 1923.

The months following Harding's death were crowded with exposures of the corruption of his administration, including Forbes's sale to businessmen of scores of millions of dollars worth of drugs, including war "surpluses" badly needed by wounded veterans, for a fraction of their value, in return for kickbacks. Altogether, as was proved in criminal court, the frauds perpetrated under Forbes cost the taxpayers approximately a quarter of a billion dollars—for which he was sentenced to pay a fine of $10,000 and serve two years in a federal penitentiary.

Then came the exposure of the robbing of the U.S. Navy oil reserves at Elk Hills in California and at Teapot Dome in Wyoming by Edward L. Doheny and Harry Sinclair. Doheny, with a bribe of $100,000 in cash, and Sinclair with a bribe of something over $300,000 in Liberty Bonds and cash, had bought Harding's secretary of the interior, Albert Fall, who was eventually convicted of accepting a bribe, fined $100,000, and sentenced to a year in jail.

Most damaging of all to Harding's personal reputation were repercussions from the exposure of fraud in the alien property custodian's office. The custodian, Miller, having been proved guilty of taking a bribe from a European company, was sent to prison. Some of the bribe money turned up in a bank account kept under the name of Jesse Smith but managed by Daugherty. This led to Daugherty's indictment and trial for bribery. Called upon to take the stand in his own defense, he refused in words that implied Harding had been personally involved in this and/or other dark matters. The result was a hung jury and a stain upon Harding's good name, a stain which was widened when one of Harding's mistresses, Nan Britton, by whom he had a daughter, published a best-selling book recounting her relationship with him.

The "Harding scandals" had no evident depreciating effect upon the Republican party's standing with the electorate. In large part this was due to the character of Calvin Coolidge, Harding's successor in the White House. Another reason why the scandals had so little evident political effect was the prevailing cynical mood of the public. The postwar reaction against "sentimental" idealism grew extreme, so that there developed under the presidency of Coolidge, himself so prim and proper, what has become known as the Roaring Twenties or the Jazz Age. During it, the pursuit of money, of pleasure, and of novel and often morbid sensations appeared the major if not sole preoccupation of most of the public.

Sensationalism and a hysterical faddism became the order of the day, fed by a mass journalism which focused on crimes of passion, on freak accidents, on bizarre divorce cases, on the "private" lives of movie

Women's behavior during the twenties provided the most obvious evidence of the break with old rules of conduct. They wore their hair and skirts short, affected a world-weary air (opposite), literally bootlegged (right), and fought arrest for wearing "indecent" swimsuits (below).

OVERLEAF: While moral laxity became common in the cities, rural folk clung to the old-fashioned virtues and participated in such rituals as shown in John Steuart Curry's painting *Baptism in Kansas*. President Harding preached the old virtues while practicing the opposite; he surrounded himself with corrupt cronies who eventually brought shame upon his administration.

personalities, and on stunts of all kinds. The public was swept by successive crazes for a Chinese game called Mah-Jongg, for bridge, for crossword puzzles, and for dance marathons, six-day bicycle races, and flagpole sitting. A revolution of sexual mores occurred, encouraged by the publication in America of the psychological theories of Sigmund Freud. The nicest girls began to use rouge and eye makeup as only harlots had done before the war. They bobbed their hair. Their hems climbed above their knees. They danced cheek-to-cheek and loin-to-loin with their boyfriends, and "necked" and "petted" with them in parked cars.

The most blatant antisocial behavior stemmed from Prohibition. The temperance movement of the nineteenth century had grown to the point where by the outbreak of the World War it had gained immense political strength. State after state had outlawed the manufacture, transport, and sale of alcoholic beverages, and there were organizations which insisted that the whole country "go dry" by means of a constitutional amendment. After America entered the war this insistence had its way. The Eighteenth (Prohibition) Amendment, passed by Congress in December, 1917, and ratified on January 29, 1919, was imple-

STOCK PRICES SLUMP $14,000,000,000 IN NATION-WIDE STAMPEDE TO UNLOAD; BANKERS TO SUPPORT MARKET TODAY

| Sixteen Leading Issues Down $2,893,520,108; Tel. & Tel. and Steel Among Heaviest Losers | PREMIER ISSUES HARD HIT |

In October, 1929, America's good time came to an end. The *New York Times* headline was another way of saying that the bottom had fallen out of the market. In Wall Street (right) crowds milled about the Stock Exchange as fear of the future struck their hearts. Before long, virtually everyone was affected by the crash. Some committed suicide rather than live in poverty. But most Americans chose to face the bad times ahead—the years of the Great Depression.

mented by a National Prohibition Enforcement Act (the Volstead Act), which went into effect January 16, 1920.

Prohibition's only really solid support came from rural areas; in a very real sense it was an attempt to overcome city wickedness with country virtue. Yet it became the law of the land in the very year when the census showed urban population larger than rural for the first time, and it soon proved to be unenforceable in urban areas and in many ways disastrous. No one can say how great was the reduction in the consumption of alcohol nationwide in consequence of the Volstead Act, but the good of such reduction was outweighed by speakeasies, bootleggers, police corruption, gang war in the streets, and an increasingly potent fusion of crime with politics. The city government of Chicago by the late 1920s was under the strong influence if not the actual control of an exceptionally ruthless hoodlum named Al ("Scarface") Capone, and similar situations prevailed in other metropolitan areas.

Amid the prevailing mood of political apathy, only slightly more than half those eligible to vote bothered to cast presidential ballots in 1924. They had in any case little to choose between the two major candidates as regards fundamental issues that year. The Democratic nominee, John W. Davis, a wealthy lawyer, was as conservative basically as his Republican opponent, Calvin Coolidge, and vainly strove to make viable issues out of the League of Nations (he favored America's entrance) and "Republican corruption." Coolidge won a landslide victory.

Four years later, in 1928, the people were presented with a somewhat clearer choice between progressiveism and conservatism when the Democrats nominated Governor Alfred E. Smith of New York and the Republicans, Herbert C. Hoover. Smith shared Hoover's conviction that businessmen were the creators of American prosperity, and he abandoned his party's

traditional hostility to the protective tariff in order to embrace a tariff policy indistinguishable from Hoover's. But as New York's governor he had effected progressive measures as regards hydroelectric power and social welfare, and he stressed these in his campaign. Hoover opposed public power developments and any governmental activity directly beneficial to individual people. This was a significant difference between the two candidates. It might have narrowed the margin of Hoover's victory if popular attention had not been diverted from it by religious bigotry (Smith was a Roman Catholic) joined to temperance fanaticism (Smith opposed Prohibition). Hoover won by 21.4 million to 15 million of the popular vote, by 444 to 87 of the electoral vote.

All through these years the industrial economy was booming as never before. The average individual income and the general standard of living steadily rose. Hoover's election triumph sparked another spectacular surge in prices on the New York Stock Exchange that had been steeply rising since the preceding March, a rise that continued through the spring and summer of the following year in what has become known as the Great Bull Market of '28 and '29.

144

As millions lost their jobs and the unemployment rate neared 25 percent, the ''self-employed'' apple seller became a familiar sight on the streets of U.S. cities.

Only in embittered hindsight would it become clear to all that the Exchange price index in those months was as a thermometer in the mouth of a sick man who does not yet feel ill: it recorded a high fever which told of a fundamental malfunctioning in the economic system. The policies of the business community and the government it dominated resulted in too high a percentage of the national income going into the pockets of too low a percentage of the population. Industrial wages failed to rise in anything like a fair proportion to the increase in per-worker production that resulted from new technology. Corporate profits, on the other hand, increased rapidly. Farmers, having greatly expanded their production to supply war needs, lost their foreign market with the war's end, and were now overexpanded in terms of effective market demand. In general, too much of the total national income, instead of going into the consumer market, was going into savings; and as the totality of savings outstripped the totality of valid offsets for them, investments in stocks and bonds, whose prices had been steadily inflated, became increasingly speculative.

New residential construction, which had been a major prop of basic prosperity, came very near a total halt soon after Hoover's inauguration. The rate of increase in automobile sales, which every year had been markedly greater than the year before, was slowing down. By late summer of 1929 the most reliable indices showed declines in industrial production and consumer spending, while business inventories increased at an alarming rate; they more than trebled between the fall of 1928 and the fall of 1929. Yet stock prices soared to astronomical heights.

Then the crash!

The stock market, which had become wildly erratic in September of '29, remained so into October; and on Wednesday, October 23, it broke sharply, generating a wave of selling orders which on the following day (Black Thursday) hit the market with demoralizing force. Total collapse was averted only through huge if largely nominal purchases made by a floor representative of a bankers' pool formed in an emergency meeting at the offices of J.P. Morgan and Company; and the price level thus bolstered was held relatively steady by a somewhat renewed confidence among smaller traders for a few days thereafter. The ultimate debacle came on Tuesday, October 29. A record 16 million shares changed hands during the day and the price of every one of them was drastically lower at the market's

145

The Depression hit farmers hard; the drought just about destroyed them. During the thirties the misused land of the Great Plains became the Dust Bowl as the dry topsoil was blown away. A man and his sons (opposite) head for shelter in Oklahoma during one of the dust storms that turned farms into wastelands. Then began an exodus as farm families packed up and headed west in old cars (right) to seek work. California received 300,000 of the refugees in four years.

close than it had been at the opening. Nor was there any recovery in the days that followed.

By November 13, when the market hit its low for the year, industrials were 228 points lower than they had been on September 3 and the value of all stocks listed on the Exchange had been reduced by 40 percent—a paper loss of nearly $30 billion!

This was only the beginning of disaster. Unemployment mounted steadily all through 1930 as the Depression fed upon itself in endless downward spiral. Because there was industrial and agricultural "overproduction," measured in terms of effective market demand, production was cut back; which meant that payrolls declined and unemployment increased; which meant that a contracted consumer market was still further contracted; which meant more cutbacks in production; which meant, finally, before the year was out, the closing of many factories, the failure of 1,325 banks, the abandonment of thousands of acres of farmland, and the creation of a mass of unemployed so largely concentrated in industrial centers that its existence could no longer be denied even by the White House. Total national income, which had been $81 billion in 1929, fell below $68 billion in 1930, and there were over 4 million unemployed by year's end.

The next year was worse, and 1932 far worse. By 1932 industrial production was approximately half what it had been in '29, with the automobile industry operating at a fifth of its '29 capacity and steel plants, that summer, at a mere 12 percent of capacity. Factory payrolls were down from $12 billion to $7 billion. Gross farm income fell from nearly $12 billion to $5 billion.

As every index of production and distribution went down, unemployment, having doubled in '30, at least doubled again in '31, and doubled yet again in '32, when between 15 million and 17 million workers—a fourth of the national labor force—were out of work.

Behind these grim statistics lay vast human tragedy. For millions of self-respecting, hard-working men the first personal shock of the Depression came with cuts in their hours of work. Then came wage cuts. Finally came the dreaded slip in the pay envelope saying, however euphemistically, "You're fired!", followed by months of futile search for new employment. The savings of a lifetime, if not already lost through bank failure, were used up. Clothing wore out, was patched, and could not be replaced. Moves were made to cheaper dwellings. The quality of food upon the table, and then the quantity, too, were reduced, often below the level needed for strength. As this happened—an initial determined effort at optimistic courage gave way, through a period of angry bitterness, to apathetic despair shot through with anxiety and times of naked terror. The Depression thus became a psychological as well as an economic phenomenon. There came at last what subscribers to the Protestant work ethic deemed the ultimate humiliation and confession of failure, that of "going on relief," of "living off handouts," and as millions were forced to do so, the burden imposed upon local relief agencies was greater than they could bear.

Countless thousands took to the road. Often jailed as vagrants, always forced to move on by local authorities, they "bummed" their way around the country aimlessly, sleeping in flophouses, in hobo "jungles," in parks and vacant lots when the weather was mild and wherever they could find some sort of shelter when the weather was cold. Soup kitchens and breadlines became a thrice-daily sight in every large city, but there were not enough of them. Hundreds of thousands were driven by hunger to become scavengers, picking over the refuse of restaurants and city dumps in search of food. In every city there sprang up beside the dumps and on other wasteland collections of shacks made of old boards, flattened tin cans, and

Dream Land

The worse real life became, the more Americans sought escape in dreams. The supreme purveyor of dreams was Hollywood, whose products achieved their greatest popularity in the thirties. During the Depression most people could sometimes spend the few cents necessary to gain admittance to a marble and gilt dream palace where beautiful women, handsome men, and adorable children lived in luxury or achieved rags-to-riches success, where comedians could make them smile and forget the grim world waiting outside. Some of the era's most popular performers appear in John Steuart Curry's dreamscape Comedy *(opposite).*

Hollywood scored a big success in 1939 with a colorful musical version of *The Wizard of Oz* starring Judy Garland. The film became an often revived classic.

The most renowned stars were Rudolph Valentino (below) and Greta Garbo (right). Valentino, who caused women to swoon in theaters, died in 1926, but Garbo continued to fascinate movie-goers until retirement in 1941.

sheets of corrugated iron, where jobless men, some with their wives and children, lived in misery. A derisive name was bestowed upon these pitiful villages by those condemned to live in them: they were called Hoovervilles.

For by 1932 Herbert Hoover was hated by masses of Americans as perhaps no other President had ever been. He was a man of rigid principles, highly moralistic in his approach to public affairs. The core of his basic belief was a commitment to what he called "rugged individualism" with an inflexible opposition to "socialism," a term he defined so broadly as to include almost every kind of direct economic activity by government. He was not, however, opposed to government measures directly and exclusively beneficial to business. In 1930, despite vehement protests from more than a thousand American economists and some thirty-four foreign governments, he signed a tariff measure (the Smoot-Hawley Tariff) which raised the highest tariff walls in American history. It amounted to a declaration of economic war upon the rest of the world, and it became a major incitement of the world economic collapse which followed the onset of the American Depression.

Cigarette holder at a jaunty angle, Franklin D. Roosevelt began his four-term presidency with a New Deal to combat America's economic ills.

Hoover was inclined to blame a "loss of confidence" by American businessmen for the lack of recovery following the crash. When he took positive action to "restore confidence," it was designed primarily to benefit big businessmen, and thereby encourage them to lead America back to prosperity.

In the summer of 1932, after his party had nominated him for a second term, Hoover was engaged in an election campaign while mass miseries gave clear signs of coalescence into revolutionary movements. In early July, Congress passed a bill which provided for direct relief to the unemployed and a massive public works program whose principal aim was to provide employment. Hoover promptly vetoed it as subversive of "our whole conception of governmental relations." He had by then already blocked passage through the Senate of a House-passed bill authorizing immediate payment to war veterans of a $2.4 billion bonus due them under existing law in 1945.

Present in Washington that summer was an "army" of some 12,000 to 20,000 jobless veterans, many with their wives and children, who called themselves the Bonus Expeditionary Force. Some of them had taken over unoccupied buildings; others were scattered through twenty makeshift camps in and around the city. They had come from all over the country to demonstrate for passage of the bonus bill and a few thousand of them remained, having no better place to go, after the measure's defeat. Hoover refused to acknowledge publicly that the bonus marchers existed until some of them became involved in a riot in which two were killed by police gunfire. He then ordered the army to remove the marchers from the capital, whereupon six tanks and a thousand troops under the command of the chief of staff, General Douglas MacArthur, marched against a crowd of unarmed men, women, and children, injuring scores while evicting all from the shacks they had erected.

150

The Democrats had nominated for President the successor to Al Smith as governor of New York, Franklin D. Roosevelt. In 1932 he won a landslide national victory—23 million to 15 million of the popular vote, 472 to 59 in the electoral college—after an energetic campaign conducted on vaguely liberal principles.

An interregnum of four months then separated the election from the inauguration. In mid-February, 1933, when two giant Detroit banks proved hopelessly insolvent, Michigan's governor declared a "bank holiday," closing all his state's banks and presaging a wave of such holidays all across the country. By March 1 thirty-eight states had ordered or were about to order their banks closed. On the eve of inauguration day, Saturday, March 4, 1933, the lifeblood of the economy, its money and credit, had virtually ceased to circulate as the financial heart of the American community slowed to nearly a complete stop. The total stop came in the early morning hours of March 4 when the governors of New York and Illinois, whose banks were dominant over the nation's private financial operations, ordered the closing of all banks in their states. A few hours later, the New York Stock Exchange failed to open as usual for Saturday morning trading. Around what seemed the dead body of the American economy was wrapped in thickening layers a shroud of gloom and terror as at noon the inaugural ceremony began.

Then came a miracle. Or so it seemed at the time. So it continued to seem in retrospect to millions of Americans. The shivering hundred thousand gathered before the Capitol, the millions huddled beside their radio sets across the land, heard a calm, resolute, wonderfully vibrant voice saying, "This great nation will endure as it has endured, will revive, and will prosper. So, first of all, let me assert my firm belief that the only thing we have to fear is fear itself." He blamed "the rulers of the exchange of mankind's goods" for the current disaster. He said he would not hesitate to ask for

In a mighty endeavor during the New Deal, the Tennessee Valley Authority built dams such as this one, provided electric power, and helped rehabilitate farms in the Tennessee River region.

"broad executive power to wage a war against the emergency, as great as the power that would be given me if we were in fact invaded by a foreign foe." Over and over again he promised "action . . . direct, vigorous action."

And action followed in flood. During the famous First Hundred Days of what Roosevelt called the New Deal, major attention was given the financial crisis. Having declared a national bank holiday and invoked federal controls over gold exports, Roosevelt called to Washington several of the "money-changers," whom he had excoriated as a group in his inaugural address, to help patch up the collapsed credit structure. They proved barren of ideas, according to Raymond Moley, who headed FDR's advisers, popularly known as the Brain Trust. But the New Dealers nevertheless fashioned with amazing swiftness the Emergency Banking Act, which was adopted without debate by fear-stricken Congress and signed on March 9. This, the first important piece of New Deal legislation, did at last "restore" a measure of "confidence," enabling all banks not palpably insolvent to reopen in a few days with a vast renewal of deposits instead of ruinous runs upon them.

There followed in swift succession legislation and executive proclamations establishing a Civilian Conservation Corps (CCC), to take unemployed youth into camps for healthful living and useful work on conservation projects; abandoning the gold standard, substituting a managed currency; establishing a federal relief system; establishing an Agricultural Adjustment Administration (AAA), whereby farmers received federal payments for *not* producing "surplus" crops and livestock; providing for refinancing of farm mortgages; establishing a Tennessee Valley Authority (TVA) for public power and economic development; requiring a full disclosure of relevant information regarding securities issues; enabling refinancing of home mortgages; establishing a National Recovery Administration (NRA), intended to replace chaotic competitiveness with a planned partnership of business and government; divorcing commercial from investment banking and guaranteeing bank deposits; providing for a drastic overhaul of agricultural credit services; and providing for coordination of the nation's railroads. There was also enacted a bill legalizing the sale of beer and wine with an alcoholic content of no more than 3.2 percent, anticipating adoption of the Twenty-first Amendment to the Constitution, repealing Prohibition.

CULVER

Recipes for Recovery

While their critics complained about the "alphabet soup" the New Dealers were cooking up, Roosevelt and his Brain Trust created the WPA, TVA, AAA, NRA, CCC, SEC, REA, and many other projects designed to revive America after three years of Depression.

The NRA (National Recovery Administration) was launched in mid-1933 with enormous fanfare. There were parades, and posters, and the emblem of the blue eagle was even displayed on the sunburned backs of Hollywood starlets (above). The NRA provided jobs, established minimum wages and maximum hours for workers, and outlawed child labor in the two years of its existence before it was abolished by a decision of the Supreme Court.

Also created in 1933, the CCC (Civilian Conservation Corps) became the most popular of the alphabet agencies. It provided socially useful and healthy outdoor work for 2.5 million young men such as those below. In the nine years the CCC camps operated, the men fought forest fires, fed wildlife, cleared brush, surveyed game, but most of all planted trees to restore the ravaged land.

In the first year of the New Deal more laws of social and economic significance were passed than in all of the nation's previous history. By 1934 the worst of the Depression was behind Americans.

WIDE WORLD

Simultaneously, the character of the Reconstruction Finance Corporation was greatly changed. Instead of lending money to financial institutions on the basis of "adequate security," thereby adding to the debt burden under which they already staggered, RFC began to purchase preferred stock in these institutions, thereby strengthening their capital resources.

The immediate effect of the Hundred Days was to dissipate the fog of fear—"nameless, unreasoning, unjustified terror"—against which Roosevelt had inveighed in his inaugural address. The worst miseries of the unemployed were alleviated by direct federal relief and expanded state aid, and the number of unemployed was reduced as factory production took a sharp upturn and industrial stocks rose in proportion on the Exchange. Other indices of economic activity also showed marked upturns. Farm prices advanced—in part because of New Deal measures, in part because midwestern drought cut farm production—and individual farmer incomes were boosted by AAA checks.

The country seemed on its way to total recovery in the early summer of 1934. In that fall's elections the Democrats increased their already substantial majorities in both houses of Congress, something that seldom happens for the party in power. But there followed five months of frustration and increasingly dangerous drift. What had seemed in June of 1934 a rising slope of prosperity turned out to be a plateau of partial recovery. National income was only slightly more than half that of 1929. An increase of 2 million in the number of employed still left jobless some 10 million of those unemployed in March of '33.

During these months of apparent indecision and drift, Roosevelt pushed through Congress the Emergency Relief Appropriation Act of 1935, authorizing the President to spend, largely at his own discretion, nearly $5 billion on emergency public employment projects in place of direct federal relief. So there was

established a Works Progress Administration (WPA), which soon had thousands of projects under way, many of them of the make-work variety but many others of genuine value. Under WPA were a Federal Arts Project, a Federal Theater Project, a Federal Writers Project, each of which made valuable contributions to American cultural life in the 1930s.

Roosevelt then launched the Second New Deal. It included the establishment of a National Labor Relations Board, operating under the Wagner Act, guaranteeing collective bargaining rights of employees and limiting or preventing antiunionism by employers; a social security program setting up a federal payroll tax to help finance unemployment insurance, old-age pensions, and grants of relief; and a greatly strengthened Federal Power Commission, Federal Trade Com-

By the mid-1930s businessmen were often the target of dissatisfied workers, and pickets like those in Joe Jones's *We Demand* (opposite) were much in evidence. Many artists were supported by government projects. They celebrated the might and majesty of blue-collar workers in such works as Philip Guston's *Maintaining America's Skills* (right) at the 1939 New York World's Fair, and William Gropper's *Construction of the Dam* mural (below) in the Department of the Interior building in Washington.

mission, and Securities and Exchange Commission (SEC). A Revenue Act was passed to effect a more equitable distribution of wealth and income through a high surtax and corporate income tax, along with inheritance and gift taxes. On the agricultural front were launched a Soil Conservation Service to help farmers fight erosion, a Resettlement Administration to help rural families relocate to better land, and a Rural Electrification Administration (REA) to build power lines and provide electricity through government-sponsored cooperatives in areas not served by utility companies.

The Neutrality Act, forbidding the transport of munitions to any belligerent, rolled through Congress on a tide of isolationist sentiment. The act seriously inhibited the President's conduct of foreign affairs, denying him authority to discriminate between aggressor and victim in a world increasingly at the mercy of Nazi Germany, Fascist Italy, and militaristic Japan.

From the Roosevelt administration's first days there had hung over its head the decisions to be rendered by the Supreme Court upon New Deal legislation. It was a unanimous decision of the court that invalidated the National Industrial Recovery Act, thereby abolishing the NRA. The NRA was designed to impose "codes" of "fair practice" upon industry and commerce, inclusive of a pledge by industry to maintain a minimum wage and bargain collectively with labor. Regarded by Roosevelt as one of the two main New Deal thrusts toward renewed prosperity (AAA was the other), NRA had been launched with immense fanfare under the sign and symbol of a blue eagle. Roosevelt was

155

shocked by the court decision, not only because of its destruction of NRA but because of its threat as precedent against nearly every other key piece of New Deal legislation.

Adverse Supreme Court decisions increased in direct proportion to the increase in liberal New Deal legislation. The precedents thus established spelled doom for virtually every New Deal reform. It was in the shadow of this crisis that the presidential campaign of 1936 was waged. The Republican nominee, Governor Alfred M. Landon of Kansas, was a reasonable, moderate man but was cast by his big business supporters in the role of a reactionary. Roosevelt received nearly 28 million votes, to less than 17 million for Landon, carrying every state except Maine and Vermont.

After the election, organized labor, taking full advantage of the Wagner Act's guarantee of the right to organize, launched unprecedentedly huge membership drives among steel and automobile workers. A new tactic was used, the sit-down strike, in which workers occupied plants and made it clear they could not be ousted without a battle that would destroy property as well as lives. Within a few months, as federal and state governments pursued a hands-off policy, General Motors, U.S. Steel, much of little steel, the giants of the tire and rubber industry, and the largest textile companies were organized and committed to collective bargaining.

Buoyed by his enormous election triumph, Roosevelt attempted to remove the threat to his administration posed by a Supreme Court whose docket was now crowded with pending New Deal test cases. On February 5, 1937, he sent a special message to Congress asking for authority to "vitalize the courts" through new judicial appointments. He proposed that, when a federal judge who had served for ten years did not resign within six months after his seventieth birthday,

the President be empowered to add a new judge to the bench. He might in this way add six new justices to the Supreme Court. His "court-packing scheme," as it was dubbed, foundered on opposition from liberals as well as conservatives. This defeat was, in one sense, a victory: it occurred in large part because the Supreme Court, under the pressure of this attack upon it, began to reverse itself. During thirty months, deaths and retirements enabled Roosevelt to make five appointments to the court.

All the same, the President had suffered a grave loss of prestige and a graver loss of power over Congress. For one effect of the court battle was to split the Democratic congressional delegation, driving the party conservatives into coalition with Republicans. The seriousness of Roosevelt's loss of power and prestige was first made clear to him when, in Chicago on October 5, 1937, he made a speech calling for an international "quarantine" of "aggressors," indicating his desire to repeal or revise the Neutrality Act. There had begun in Spain in 1936 what most knowledgeable people recognized as a probable dress rehearsal for World War II. A democratically elected left-wing government in Madrid was forcibly challenged by a right-wing minority that included the bulk of the Spanish army, under the command of General Francisco Franco. To the frankly Fascist Franco's aid came planes, troops, and munitions from Fascist Italy and Nazi Germany. To the Spanish Loyalists came aid, on a far smaller scale, from Soviet Russia, but none from the democracies. The public response to the "quarantine" speech appeared to be overwhelmingly negative. In the face of vehement isolationist attacks, Roosevelt drew back. His subsequent efforts to repeal the Neutrality Act were all in vain.

In 1939, Roosevelt presided over a deeply divided America facing, or refusing to face, the most serious threat to its survival as a free society.

Struggle for the Pacific

7

It was 6:30 on the morning of Sunday, December 7, 1941, when the U.S.S. *Ward,* a destroyer patrolling outside the entrance to Pearl Harbor, the big naval base on the Hawaiian island of Oahu, spotted the conning tower of a small submarine. Captain William Outerbridge's orders were unequivocal: no American submarines were operating in this "defensive sea area," so any sightings should be considered hostile. The *Ward's* gunners put a three-inch shell into the sub and depth charges finished the job. Outerbridge reported the sinking to naval headquarters at Pearl Harbor. Unbelieving officers insisted on confirmation. At 7:40 A.M. they called Admiral Husband E. Kimmel, commander of the U.S. Pacific Fleet, at his home. He set out for headquarters and the checking continued. But no alert was sounded.

There was a similar flurry at army headquarters on Oahu. Just after 7:00 A.M. two young privates at a radar post on the northern shore of the island reported a bright "blip" on their screen, the largest they had ever seen. They calculated that a very big formation of planes was about 130 miles north of Oahu and heading their way at 180 miles an hour. The army duty officer was new on the job and concluded that the blip must be the dozen army B-17 bombers due in from the States that morning. He told the radarmen not to worry, to close up shop and come in for breakfast.

It had also been an unusual Sunday morning for officers in the War and Navy departments in Washington, where the clock was five and a half hours ahead of Pearl Harbor. For more than a year, ever since Colonel William F. Friedman broke the Japanese diplomatic Purple Code, American intelligence had figuratively been reading over the shoulders of Japanese diplomats

as they received their instructions from Tokyo. This morning there was a fresh radio intercept to study. The Japanese diplomatic corps in Washington was being instructed to break off diplomatic negotiations with the United States. This in itself was not particularly startling in view of the increasingly tense situation in the Pacific and the Far East; what was unusual was that the diplomats were to tell their American counterparts this news at exactly 1 P.M. Washington time.

A quick calculation showed that 1 P.M. Washington time was 7:30 A.M. at Pearl Harbor. General George C. Marshall, army chief of staff, drafted a dispatch to Hawaiian headquarters, noting the deadline and adding, "Just what significance the hour set may have we do not know, but be on the alert accordingly." Since Pearl Harbor had been on "war alert" status for the past ten days, Marshall felt that this fresh warning was justified. It was 6:30 A.M. Hawaiian time when he filed the dispatch at the army's Washington message center, and he later checked to see that it was sent. It had been sent, but the message center had neglected to tell him how. Army radio was having problems that morning, so Marshall's warning was sent through commercial channels—via Western Union. Not until mid-afternoon did a telegraph messenger pedal his bicycle up to Pearl Harbor headquarters with the dispatch.

Three chances, three foul-ups, and so December 7 was not just a day of infamy, in President Roosevelt's celebrated phrase, but a day of military humiliation as well. When the cream of the Imperial Japanese Navy's carrier pilots winged in over Pearl Harbor at 7:55 that morning, not a single interceptor or antiaircraft gun was manned. Of the eight Pacific Fleet battleships in port, just one had any steam up. Recalling the scene, Japanese Commander Itaya, who led the first formation of attacking aircraft, remarked that "Pearl Harbor was asleep in the morning mist. Calm and serene inside the harbor . . . important ships of the Pacific Fleet,

Shocked sailors watch the battleship Arizona explode at Ford Island Naval Air Station during the December 7, 1941, attack on Pearl Harbor. "Battleship Row" was the main Japanese target.

strung out and anchored two ships side by side."

There were any number of acts of bravery to soothe American pride—gunners manning their weapons under intense enemy fire, two army pilots somehow getting their P-40s airborne and shooting down seven of the attackers, the battleship *Nevada*'s gallant sortie— but these could not conceal the fact that Pearl Harbor was a stunning, lopsided defeat. Of the eight U.S. battleships, one had her back broken, a second capsized, three sank to the shallow harbor floor or ran aground, and two were grievously crippled. Ten other ships were sunk or badly hit, and 347 planes were destroyed or damaged. A total of 2,335 American servicemen were killed. The Japanese lost only twenty-nine planes and fifty-five airmen. Their six-carrier task force steamed away unscathed. Thus was America sucked into the maelstrom of World War II.

When at dusk on December 8 the carrier *Enterprise* and its escort of cruisers and destroyers entered Pearl Harbor the naval men were aghast at the devastation. "Morale went to nothing just about then," noted a cruiser officer. "We weren't frightened—or maybe we were. But we certainly were sick and shocked. We couldn't believe this had happened to us."

If the Pearl Harbor attack was a surprise, the attacker was not. When Plan Orange, the American military's first between-wars contingency plan, was drafted in 1924, Japan was assumed to be the one potential enemy in the Pacific. Beginning early in the century, the Japanese had industrialized rapidly and pursued an expansionist foreign policy. Korea they forcibly annexed in 1910; three strategically important Pacific island groups, the Marshalls, the Carolines, and most of the Marianas, were their reward for helping the Allies in World War I; in 1931, on the basis of a contrived "incident" by army extremists, they wrested Manchuria from China; in 1937 another such incident precipitated a full-scale war against the Chinese.

Japanese policy was aimed at solving two critical domestic problems: a rapidly growing population crowded into a limited insular homeland, and a severe shortage of the natural resources needed by an industrialized society. In theory Emperor Hirohito presided over a parliamentary government, but in fact the nation rapidly fell into the iron grasp of an Imperial Army clique known to their opponents as the Manchuria Gang. Aggressive, expansionist, silencing opposition by the brutally direct method of assassination, the Manchuria Gang aligned Japan with the saber-rattling German and Italian dictatorships in 1940 by means of the Tripartite Pact, which bound them to aid each other if the U.S. entered the war. The Far Eastern colonial holdings of Britain, France, and the Netherlands were left dangling like so many ripe plums when war broke out in Europe. The Japanese militarists envisioned an enormous Asian and Pacific empire, the Greater East Asia Co-Prosperity Sphere, rich in resources and controlling half the world's population.

Former U.S. Ambassador to Japan Edwin O. Reischauer, writing of "700 years of unbroken rule by warrior aristocrats," expressed this view: "Small wonder that the impress of feudalism lies so heavily upon the nation and that the attitudes and ideals of the feudal warriors have sunk so deeply into the consciousness of the Japanese people. Accustomed for so long to rule by wearers of the sword, even in recent times the Japanese have looked instinctively to their military men for leadership and have been prone to assume

Shouting "Banzai!" the crew of a Japanese carrier (opposite) waves to pilots about to leave on a 275-mile flight to attack Pearl Harbor. At right: the target area, with the U.S. ships lined up, as seen from an attacking plane.

that military men *per se* were honest and sincere."

Since ancient times the Japanese state had been based on war. In the medieval civil wars, great warriors became the heroes of the Japanese people and remained so for future generations. Powerful chiefs had their *samurai* (feudal retainers) whose contempt for death and loyalty to their chiefs became models for Japanese into modern times. In 1876 the *samurai* were forced to lay aside their swords. Social classes were abolished and compulsory military training instituted, but most of the leaders of the new Japan came from the ranks of the ex-*samurai*.

This long history of military influence made Japan quick to learn the techniques of modern warfare. She became feared by the West and felt the need to defend the Far East against the Western nations. During this period Japanese leaders were somewhat surprised by the new respect with which the West eyed their country and reportedly remarked, "When we sent you the beautiful products of our ancient arts and culture, you despised and laughed at us; but since we have got a first-class army and navy with good weapons, we are regarded as a highly civilized nation."

Japanese army officers rarely went abroad and were more arrogant and nationalistic than their navy counterparts who often visited foreign ports. The army knew it could hold its own against other military forces in the Far East; the navy knew its strength was inferior. For these reasons, the Japanese navy was more cautious and moderate than the army. Most Japanese civilians supported the army because of its traditional prestige.

The Japanese sank or damaged 19 U.S. warships at Pearl Harbor, including the *Arizona* (right) and the destroyer *Shaw* (below), but were disappointed that no aircraft carriers were in port at the time.

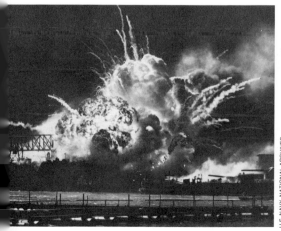

The Other End of the Axis

By the time Pearl Harbor was attacked, large areas of the world had fallen under the Axis yoke. Germany had taken over the Rhineland, Czechoslovakia, Austria, Denmark, Norway, the Netherlands, Belgium, and France, and had divided Poland with Russia. Italy had seized Ethiopia and Albania. Britain stood alone against the aggressors. While millions died in concentration camps and bombed cities, Americans were split into those who favored isolation from "foreign" wars and those who could hear the bell tolling for America in Europe's ruins.

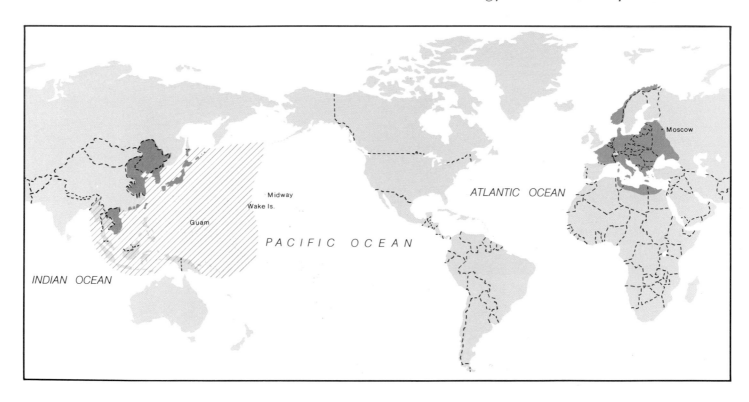

In the above map the dark areas are territory controlled by the Axis in December, 1941. Diagonally shaded areas show the maximum Japanese expansion, in May, 1942, after the fastest, most valuable conquests in modern history. At right, Field Marshal Erwin Rommel, the "Desert Fox," gives orders during a battle in Africa. He was a master in making armored strikes, also in regrouping after a strike to administer a swift coup de grace. His domination of supply problems and his scorn of opposition also won him the grudging respect of his Allied opponents. "A great general" was Churchill's tribute to Rommel.

Parading under the Arc de Triomphe, German occupation troops (above) filled most Parisians with shame. The City of Light became a center for underground resistance to the conquerors. Before taking over France, the Germans had tested their blitzkrieg in Poland and achieved air supremacy in just one day. At right, German soldiers destroy a border barricade at the beginning of their invasion of Poland.

Winston Churchill found that "the hierarchy of the Japanese army formed a series of concentric circles united by the *samurai* tradition, which inspired all its chiefs and their subordinates to die for the military honor of Japan and to face each man's court of ancestors with confidence." And Reischauer, noting the continuation of *samurai* influence, writes that the medieval warrior of Japan "made a cult of his sword, a cult still kept alive as late as World War II by Japanese officers who proudly lugged long, cumbersome curved swords into the jungles of Southeast Asia."

By 1941, Japan was on a collision course with the United States. American strategy in case of war with Japan called for General Douglas MacArthur's undermanned army in the Philippines to fight a delaying action for up to nine months while the navy's First World War-vintage battleships battered their way across the Pacific to his relief. In 1941 there was not an American official, from the President on down, who had any faith in this will-o'-the-wisp. The best hope was that the Japanese might stay their hand while America went about the painfully slow process of rearming.

Lacking force yet unwilling to resort to appeasement, the American government tried bluff. A series of economic embargoes, supported by the British and Dutch, reached a climax in July, 1941, when the Japanese army moved into French Indochina. These embargoes cut off 75 percent of Japan's foreign trade and 90 percent of its oil. President Roosevelt announced that only when Indochina was evacuated and the fighting halted in China would the embargoes be lifted. This was a hard line, far too hard for the Japanese militarists to swallow. The moderate prime minister, Prince Konoye, was forced out, to be succeeded by General Hideki Tojo, leader of the Manchuria Gang. Finishing touches were put on plans for war with the United States.

Admiral Isoroku Yamamoto, commander in chief of the Imperial Japanese Navy, was under no illusions that his nation could defeat the Americans with their tremendous industrial potential in a toe-to-toe slugging match. "I can raise havoc with them for one year," he said, "but after that I can give no guarantee." He contemplated a sharp wounding blow to buy Japan time to seize its objectives—the oil, rubber, tin, rice, and other resources of Southeast Asia and the Dutch East Indies—and to build a defense-in-depth across the Pacific so strong that the Americans would settle for a negotiated peace. His wounding blow was Pearl Harbor. For all its tactical brilliance Pearl Harbor was a major strategic blunder, for this sneak attack was the one act absolutely certain to arouse and unite the American people in unbending determination to destroy, rather than negotiate with, Japan.

Ironically, Yamamoto's Pearl Harbor attack achieved the success it did primarily because of a similar misreading of Japanese capabilities by the Americans. The nearly universal reaction to December 7 was utter disbelief; it was simply inconceivable to American minds, military and civilian, that those diminutive people from the other side of the world, perhaps clever but certainly inferior, would dare to attack the United States Navy in its own backyard. In the next six months both sides would have a great deal of reevaluating to do.

Having secured their Pacific flank, the Japanese skillfully went about assembling the Co-Prosperity Sphere. The American island bases of Guam and Wake were taken. The Philippines were invaded and MacArthur's army driven into last-ditch positions on the Bataan Peninsula near Manila. Britain's outpost of Hong Kong surrendered, as did supposedly impregnable Singapore, the "Gibraltar of the Far East," with its 70,000 defenders. Allied defenses in the Dutch East Indies collapsed like a house of cards. It was the same

The Allied cause suffered grave losses soon after the attack on Pearl Harbor. The disasters included the fall of the British colony of Hong Kong (shown at left with fires blazing before its surrender) and the sinking of the British dreadnoughts *Prince of Wales* and *Repulse* by Japanese aircraft in the Gulf of Siam (depicted below by Japanese artist Kenichi Nakamura). Other early blows at the Western colonial powers deprived them of the Netherlands East Indies, Burma, Singapore, Guam, the Philippines, and the Solomons.

Victorious Japanese soldiers wave their swords, guns, and flags in Bataan. In contrast to the jubilant Japanese, the faces of the defeated defenders of Bataan (below) show the misery they suffered during the "death march" —the 85-mile trip to prison camp during which about 10,000 of the 75,000 prisoners perished from disease, starvation, or torture.

story in Burma. All this was achieved in three months; two months later American resistance in the Philippines ended with the surrender of the island fortress of Corregidor.

The one bright moment for Americans was the Doolittle Raid on Tokyo and other Japanese cities on April 18. The damage done by Doolittle's bombers was mostly to Japanese pride, but the sheer audacity of the raid was a tonic to American morale. Army Air Force Colonel Jimmy Doolittle had led his sixteen B-25s off the deck of the aircraft carrier *Hornet,* proof enough to Admiral Yamamoto that his flank was not secure after all. As long as American carriers were loose in the Pacific, he could not rest easy.

It was pure good fortune that the three carriers assigned to the Pacific Fleet had been absent from Pearl Harbor on December 7. With the battle force crippled,

they became the navy's first and only line of defense and offense. Ernest J. King, the new commander in chief of the United States fleet, and white-haired Chester W. Nimitz, Kimmel's replacement as head of the Pacific Fleet, were determined to act as aggressively as possible with their limited resources. "Hold what you've got and hit them when you can" was how King put it.

Japanese strategists were debating their next step when Doolittle's B-25s made up their minds for them. They decided on twin objectives: first to sever Australia's lifeline to the United States by establishing air bases in eastern New Guinea and the Solomon Islands, and then to lay a trap for Nimitz's carriers.

Early in May, 1942, a Japanese invasion force moved toward Port Moresby in New Guinea, supported by a carrier task force in case the Americans should try to interfere. Admiral Frank Jack Fletcher's Task Force Seventeen, the carriers *Yorktown* and *Lexington* and their screen of escorts, steamed into the Coral Sea intending to do just that.

The Battle of the Coral Sea opened on May 7 when American planes found the light carrier *Shoho* escorting the invasion convoy and sent her under in just ten minutes; "scratch one flattop" was the terse report to the *Lexington.* The next day the main contestants traded blows, with the Japanese landing the harder punches. The venerable old *Lexington* was mortally wounded by torpedo planes and the *Yorktown* took a bomb hit that caused serious internal damage. The best the American pilots could do was to put three bombs through the flight deck of the fleet carrier *Shokaku,* which limped away. "Lady Lex" was not so fortunate; torn apart by internal explosions, she had to be abandoned by her crew, who reportedly first finished the ship's supply of ice cream and also made sure the captain's dog was brought to safety.

Admiral Fletcher ordered a destroyer to torpedo the

Before the fall of the Philippines, defense headquarters went underground on the island of Corregidor (left). After Bataan's surrender, the Rock's 10,000 defenders, some of whom are shown below, held out nearly a month.

blazing *Lexington* so she wouldn't guide the Japanese to the task force. Three torpedoes struck her and she slid under. "There she goes," said one of her officers. "She didn't turn over. She's going down with her head up . . . a lady to the last!"

If the fighting edge had gone to the Japanese, the Americans had won their primary objective when the Port Moresby invasion convoy retreated. For the moment the Australian lifeline was safe. The Coral Sea fight was notable in one other respect: for the first time in history a naval battle was fought entirely by "aerial artillery"; not once did the opposing fighting ships sight each other.

But Coral Sea was only the preliminary to the main event—Yamamoto's effort to finish the job begun at Pearl Harbor and put the U.S. Pacific Fleet out of action. The Japanese admiral conceived a complex plan to draw the Americans out into the open by threatening their vital Pearl Harbor base. At the heart of his scheme was the seizure of Midway, the westernmost island in the Hawaiian chain. Supporting the invasion transports would be Admiral Chuichi Nagumo's four-carrier striking force. Lurking in the background to mop up anything the carriers missed was a powerful force of battleships. Finally there was a decoy force to strike at the Aleutians to the north to draw out Nimitz should he not take the Midway lure. Even though it would be scattered over a large area of the Pacific, Yamamoto's force was enormous—four fleet carriers, four light carriers, eleven battleships, more than a hundred other fighting ships—and he had every reason to expect surprise to be on his side. If all went according to schedule, the decisive battle would take place early in June.

At Pearl Harbor, meanwhile, Nimitz and his admirals were beneficiaries of one of the major intelligence coups of the war. Navy cryptanalysts led by Commander Joseph Rochefort had broken some of the Im-

perial Navy's codes, and they figured out the strength, timing, and objectives of Yamamoto's mighty force. This knowledge could not win the coming battle for Nimitz, of course, but it at least gave him a fighting chance. He also benefited from the prodigious efforts of the Pearl Harbor shipfitters, who patched up the battered *Yorktown* in two days, a job first estimated to take many weeks. This gave him three fleet carriers— the *Hornet* and the *Enterprise* in Task Force Sixteen under logical, cautious Raymond Spruance, and the *Yorktown* in Task Force Seventeen under the more impetuous Fletcher—to Yamamoto's four. However, the available U.S. escorts totaled just eight cruisers and fourteen destroyers. The Americans had to avoid a sur-

167

face engagement at all costs and fight with carrier planes alone. The best way to do that seemed to be to lay an ambush.

By June 2 the two American task forces were cruising well to the north of Midway, waiting. Fletcher and Spruance were depending on Midway's search planes to be their eyes. June 3 passed in mounting tension. When a report came in of Japanese raids on the Aleutians, Nimitz ignored it. When a scout plane radioed a sighting of the enemy's invasion transports, he ignored that too. He knew that somewhere off to the northwest was bigger game—Admiral Nagumo's Carrier Striking Force.

At first light on June 4, Nagumo sent off a strike force to knock out opposition on Midway. Marine defenders flying obsolete fighters were shot out of the sky and the island took a severe pounding. Meanwhile, a Midway Catalina scouting plane spotted the Japanese carriers and radioed their position. As the three U.S. carriers raced forward to get within launching range, Midway threw everything that could fly at the enemy fleet: dive bombers and torpedo bombers and big army bombers. But none scored a hit and most of them were shot down by Zeros and antiaircraft fire.

By studying the Catalina's sighting data and the time of the attack on Midway, Spruance's chief of staff, Captain Miles Browning, calculated when the Japanese planes would land to be refueled and rearmed— an aircraft carrier's most vulnerable period. For the American planes to strike then meant immediate launching at the very limit of their range; many might not make it back to the carriers. Yet springing the ambush looked like the only hope for victory. Spruance emptied the *Enterprise* and the *Hornet* of attack planes. After waiting an hour in case of a later sighting, Fletcher sent off the *Yorktown*'s planes.

First to spot the Japanese carriers were the torpedo bombers. These old Devastators were slow and obso-

lete, and although their pilots pressed their attacks gallantly, not one of their torpedoes hit anything and thirty-five of the forty-one were shot down by the Zeros of Nagumo's combat air patrol.

Now the Japanese began to taste victory. They had easily beaten off every attack, one of their scout planes had spotted an American carrier *(Yorktown)*, and Nagumo had a fresh attack force spotted on his decks ready for takeoff. At 10:20 A.M. he gave the order to launch.

The first good news for Americans in the Pacific war was delivered by Lt. Col. James Doolittle (left) when he led 16 B-25s to bomb Tokyo and other Japanese cities in April, 1942. Above, Doolittle lifts his heavy bomber from the short flight deck of the carrier *Hornet* to fly 650 miles to Japan. Most of the planes, including Doolittle's (opposite), made crash landings in Japanese-occupied China after carrying out the bomb strike, but Chinese guerrillas guided the Americans to safety.

Six minutes later his world fell apart. From high above plummeted waves of American Dauntless dive bombers, fifty-four in all. The Zeros, fresh from their slaughter of the low-flying torpedo bombers, were unable to climb fast enough to interfere. Two bombs crashed into the flagship *Akagi*, triggering explosions among the armed planes that tore the ship apart. The *Soryu* took three 1,000-pounders that killed her engines and started terrible fires. Four hits were scored on the *Kaga*, setting off stored bombs and aviation

gasoline. Only the fourth carrier, the *Hiryu*, escaped.

Said *Enterprise* pilot Lieutenant Clarence Dickinson, "The target was utterly satisfying. The squadron's dive was perfect. This was the absolute. After this, I felt, anything would be just anticlimax. . . . I had determined during that dive that since I was dropping on a Japanese carrier I was going to see my bomb hit. After dropping I kicked my rudder to get my tail out of the way and put my plane in a stall. So I was simply standing there to watch it. I saw the 500-pound bomb hit."

Nagumo desperately counterattacked with the *Hiryu's* planes, and they wounded the *Yorktown*. She took on a critical list and was abandoned. But revenge came swiftly. Spruance sent off another strike force of Dauntlesses that caught up with the *Hiryu* and blasted her into a flaming hulk. By dawn the next day the last of the Japanese carriers had gone to the bottom, and Nagumo's Carrier Striking Force ceased to exist. The following day the *Yorktown* was torpedoed by a Japanese submarine while being towed toward safety. She lingered on through the night. "At dawn it was evident she was doomed," wrote naval historian Samuel Eliot Morison. "The escorting destroyers half-masted their colors, all hands came to attention, uncovered; and at 0600, with her loose gear making a horrible death rattle, *Yorktown* rolled over and sank in a 2,000-fathom deep."

Yamamoto tried to retrieve success by forcing a shoot-out with his battleships, but the prudent Spruance, who took command when Fletcher's *Yorktown* was crippled, carefully stayed out of their range and made the last score when his pilots sank a heavy cruiser. With control of the air lost beyond recall, Yamamoto had no choice but to retreat.

Since only six of the forty-one American torpedo planes returned to their carriers, that night in the *Hornet's* ward room it was felt that "the empty chairs

Dauntless dive bombers head for the enemy during the Battle of Midway (opposite). They destroyed four Japanese aircraft carriers, turning the tide in the Pacific and giving Japan her worst naval defeat in history. The news of the American victory made happy headlines back home.

stood there in silent question and even on a night of victory voices were hushed."

The first major Japanese defeat in battle in three and a half centuries had a strong effect upon Admiral Yamamoto. Described as having "strangely glittering eyes" in an "ashen face," he reportedly suffered stomach trouble and nervous depression for a week, eating only rice gruel.

Of the Battle of Midway, Masanori Ito wrote:

> Japan thus lost four fleet carriers in less than 24 hours! The magnitude of this defeat was beyond imagination. . . . News of the loss of the four fleet carriers was dribbled out to the homeland public over a period of a year following the battle. In addition to Japan's loss of ships and planes there was the serious loss of men, especially of skilled pilots, who were thereafter in short supply for the remainder of the war. Survivors of sunken ships were held incommunicado until reassigned, and they were under strict injunction to keep silent about the terrible defeat Japan had suffered. . . . The facts of the Midway battle were not divulged to the people of Japan until after the end of World War II. . . . So great was Japan's defeat in this one battle that the resourceful and skillful enemy must have been supported by the wrath of an avenging god.
>
> There were many reasons for the defeat suffered at Midway. The ultimate blame, however, may be laid to Japan's unbelievable successes during the first six months of the war. These early successes gave rise to an arrogance—aptly characterized as 'victory disease'—which engendered negligence and a lack of vigilance.

Midway was one of the decisive naval battles of all history. Just six months after war began, the Japanese tide in the Pacific was checked. Yet ahead lay Japan's stout outer ring of Pacific defenses. It was anchored in the north by the lodgment in the Aleutians won during the Midway campaign. In the Central Pacific were the well-fortified Marshall and Gilbert island groups, and farther south the Bismarcks and northern New Guinea. The twin centers of this spiderweb of interconnected posts were the Imperial Navy's fleet anchorage at Truk in the Carolines and the air and army base at Rabaul in the Bismarcks. It looked tough and it was, and then came word that the enemy was again moving to sever the Australian lifeline. A month after Midway a Japanese airfield was reported under construction on Guadalcanal in the Solomons, from which raids could be launched against Allied shipping routes and bases to the south.

Admiral King had been eyeing the Solomons for several months. Allied global strategy specified "Europe first," on the indisputable ground that the Nazis were the greater threat to Western civilization and had to be stopped from swallowing up all Europe. Yet to back off further in the Pacific could mean forfeiting the key springboards to future victory; if Australia and New Zealand were lost or isolated, the road back would be brutally hard. So Ernie King fought and clawed in the councils of the Joint Chiefs of Staff for a limited offensive in the Solomons. The Joint Chiefs opposed King's "defensive-offensive" strategy on the ground that it would be a diversion. King countered that if the Americans did not take Guadalcanal, the Japanese would advance from Rabaul into Papua, New Guinea, Australia, New Caledonia, and Samoa. President Roosevelt was under pressure from many Americans to shift the emphasis of hostilities from Germany to Japan on the grounds that the "Yellow Peril" was worse than Hitler. Roosevelt's order of priorities did not change, but on July 2 the Joint Chiefs issued a directive for offensive operations in the area of New Ireland, New Britain, and New Guinea. These operations would include taking the Santa Cruz Islands, Tulagi, and adjacent positions in the lower Solomons, including Guadalcanal. King was a thorny enough character as

The perilous path to Tokyo began at one of the Solomon Islands— Guadalcanal. Although 10,000 marines went ashore almost unopposed (opposite), it took six months of fierce fighting to gain control of the island. The Americans had to fight the steaming jungle (right) as much as they did the Japanese.

it was and his stance had won him no new friends, but news of the Guadalcanal airfield had got him the go-ahead he sought. He bluntly ordered his commanders to invade Guadalcanal within a month.

It was labeled Operation Watchtower, but Operation Shoestring became its real name. Everything was in short supply and everything was frantically rushed. The key was the First Marine Division, the one trained Allied fighting force in all the Pacific. By hook and by crook, the assault force, the shipping, the supplies, and the support were cobbled together, and on August 7, 1942, the First Marines splashed ashore and grabbed the newly completed airfield—just hours before the first flight of Japanese planes was due to arrive. It was that close.

There is nothing quite like Guadalcanal in the chronicle of the Pacific war. For three months the decision was in the balance; several times the Allies were perilously close to defeat. Before the fight for control of the seas around the Solomons ended three months later, twenty-four American warships were sunk, including the fleet carriers *Wasp* and *Hornet*. The climax was the Battle of Guadalcanal on November 12-15. In a desperate sprawling struggle, the battleships *Washington* and *South Dakota* finally turned the tide; the enemy lost two battleships and saw a troopship convoy slaughtered.

Ashore it was the same story—a series of desperate Japanese assaults that severely bloodied the marines but never quite broke them. The leathernecks endured air attacks and naval bombardments and suicide charges, and they also endured Guadalcanal itself. Here was no travel agent's glittering South Seas isle, but a rank, rotting jungle that stank of death and disease. When victory was assured at last and the First Marines were withdrawn on December 9, each one of them could claim without qualification, "I've served my time in hell." Perhaps the highest tribute was paid

them by a surviving Japanese soldier who said, "It was no disgrace to be beaten by such men."

Assessing the Guadalcanal action, Morison wrote, "The recommendations of Guadalcanal commanders became doctrine for Allied fighting men the world over.... For us who were there, or whose friends were there, Guadalcanal is not a name but an emotion."

The commissioning of the U.S.S. *Essex* on the last day of 1942 signaled the beginning of rejuvenated American power in the Pacific. Within a year six more of these modern 27,000-ton, 100-plane carriers joined the Pacific Fleet to furnish the tools for a strategic offensive. The high command hammered out a plan for breaching Japan's outer defense ring. In the South Pacific the brilliant, ambitious General MacArthur was to dislodge the Japanese from eastern New Guinea and then leapfrog into the Bismarcks. Admiral William F. Halsey, meantime, would "island-hop" up the Solo-

173

mons. The objective of this pincers was, first, Rabaul on New Britain, Japan's defensive linchpin in the South Pacific, then the Philippines. Simultaneously, Admiral Nimitz honed his carrier striking forces to support a flanking advance in the Central Pacific aimed at Truk in the Carolines. Also due for attack were the Japanese-held islands of Attu and Kiska in the Aleutians. All the while, American submarines would continue to prey on the shipping arteries that carried lifeblood to Japan's war machine.

In January, 1943, MacArthur's Australian and American infantrymen, after a hard fight to secure a foothold, began a long and bloody effort to conquer the huge island of New Guinea. In one of the war's more unappreciated campaigns, they won out against a determined enemy and a hostile land. By the end of the year they had invaded New Britain to threaten Ra-

Americans invade Makin atoll in the Gilbert Islands on November 20, 1943, after it was pounded by U.S. carrier-based aircraft.

baul. Meantime, beetle-browed, barrel-chested "Bull" Halsey was "climbing the ladder" in the Solomons to approach Rabaul from another direction. Both drives were supported by land-based planes, with the carriers helping out on occasion. Admiral Yamamoto dispatched some of his best naval pilots to fly out of Rabaul, but to no avail; they were destroyed by the score. Yamamoto himself was killed when his aircraft was shot down in Bougainville by P-38s in an aerial ambush made possible by a code-breaking coup which revealed his flight schedule. In early 1944 the Japanese withdrew their surviving planes and pilots from Rabaul. Leaving the fortress and its 100,000-man garrison to wither, the Allies turned to other targets.

"This was the type of strategy we hated most," said General Matsuichi Ino. "The Americans attacked and seized, with minimum losses, a relatively weak area, constructed airfields and then proceeded to cut the supply lines. . . . Our strongholds were gradually starved out. The Japanese army preferred direct assault after the German fashion, but the Americans flowed into our weaker points and submerged us just as water seeks the weakest entry to sink a ship."

Nimitz's carrier striking force had to come back a long way: at the Battle of Guadalcanal in November, 1942, the gallant *Enterprise* was the single U.S. carrier left in the Pacific, and she fought limping, patched together in desperate haste. Yet a year later the new carriers, the new planes, the new fliers, and the new amphibious forces were ready to go to war. Their first target was Tarawa atoll in the Gilberts, with D-day set for November 20, 1943. The Japanese commander, Admiral Keiji Shibasaki, confidently predicted, "The Americans could not take Tarawa with a million men in a hundred years."

The main objective was Betio, 300 acres of coral sand crowned by a stand of palm trees, that had the only airstrip in the atoll. This was the first American

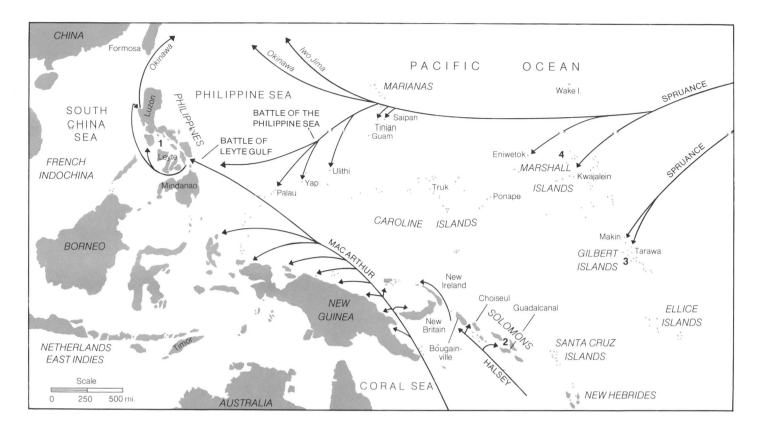

The Pacific war was enormous in scope, complex in strategy. The American plan was to reach the Philippines (**1**) by two routes, one beginning at Guadalcanal (**2**) and the other at the Gilbert (**3**) and Marshall Islands (**4**). En route, islands would be either conquered or bypassed if possible. Nowhere was this itinerary so agonizing as for the marines at Tarawa atoll (below) in the Gilberts. The bitter fighting earned Tarawa a dreadful distinction: ''the very essence of the horrors of war.'' The Gilbert Islands were taken within four days, and soon after American forces captured the Marshalls—adding stepping stones on the watery route to Japan.

amphibious assault on a solidly dug-in enemy, and mistakes were made. Japanese strength and tenacity were underestimated and the effects of naval and air bombardment overestimated. There were also unpredictable misfortunes; an exceptionally low tide prevented landing craft from getting over a coral reef, and many marines had to wade a quarter-mile to shore under savage fire. When they reached the beach many of them were under direct machine gun fire. "It was like being in the middle of a pool table with no pockets," said Sergeant Welles Grey.

On the beach Lieutenant William D. Hawkins became a marine legend. Leading a scout-sniper platoon, he was hit by many bits of shrapnel on the first day. On the second day he got a bullet in his shoulder but continued to fight despite the loss of blood. He then received a bullet wound in his other shoulder. Refusing to be evacuated, he said, "I came here to kill Japs; I didn't come here to be evacuated." One man who observed Hawk in action said, "He's a madman. He cleaned out six machine gun nests with two to six Japs in each nest. I'll never forget the picture of him standing on that amtrac, riding around with a million bullets a minute whistling by his ears, just shooting Japs. I never saw such a man in my life." Hawk died from loss of blood during his second night on the beach.

Paying tribute to men like Hawk, Colonel Merritt Edson said after the battle, "The reason we won this show was the ability of junior officers and noncoms to take command of small groups of six to eight or ten men, regardless of where those men came from, and to organize and lead them as a fighting team." The fierce dedication of the marines on Tarawa was made evident on the second day of the fighting when Colonel David M. Shoup, commanding the landing force, radioed, "Casualties: many. Percentage dead: not known. Combat efficiency: we are winning."

The cost of taking the tiny coral isle: Americans,

Combat artist William Draper shows the Palau Islands being bombed by Dauntlesses from Task Force 58. The action was designed to support General MacArthur by preventing Japanese reinforcements from reaching New Guinea. In the photo below, paratroops land on the Japanese-built airstrip at Noemfoor Island, near New Guinea, in July, 1944, in the leapfrog campaign to reach the Philippines.

it was demonstrated that a full-fledged offensive could be mounted under the wing of the carrier task forces alone. The overall goal would remain the Philippines and then a stepping-stone for the final assault on Japan, but there was going to be a detour—into the Marianas.

The Mariana island chain lay in the Central Pacific just 1,500 miles from Tokyo, and it was this statistic that made it so inviting. When the Boeing B-29 Superfortress started coming off the production lines in the fall of 1943, Allied planners had a weapon capable of

1,026 killed and 2,296 wounded; Japanese, 4,690 killed and 17 taken prisoner. No Japanese escaped. Summing up Tarawa, Andrew A. Rooney commented, "There were other battles longer, others in which more men died, others of greater importance; but Tarawa was the bitterest, the fiercest, the most concentrated battle of World War II."

The next step was Kwajalein atoll in the central Marshalls. This complex operation began at the end of January, 1944, and went without a hitch, although the fighting was hard and costly. When the westernmost atoll in the Marshalls, Eniwetok, was captured in February, the United States had the bases it needed for the next seven-league stride forward.

That stride would go in a different direction than originally planned. Grand strategy as conceived back in 1942 called for an advance via the southern route (New Guinea to the Philippines to a lodgment on the China coast from which to hit Japan itself) under General MacArthur, with powerful flank support from the Pacific Fleet. In the Gilberts and Marshalls, however,

Fulfilling his promise to return, MacArthur waded ashore at Leyte 948 days after he had left the Philippines. Then he broadcast: "This is the voice of freedom. General MacArthur speaking."

With the carrier's Hellcats behind him, Admiral Mitscher eyes the action from the *Lexington*'s bridge during "The Great Marianas Turkey Shoot."

revolutionizing the Pacific war. From bases in the Marianas, the long-range B-29s could strike any city in Japan with ten tons of explosives per plane.

First it was necessary to eliminate the threat of a flank attack being launched from Truk against the Marianas-bound force. That job went to Admiral Spruance's powerful Fifth Fleet, with its five fleet carriers and four light carriers of Task Force Fifty-eight under the command of Marc Mitscher. The wiry Mitscher had been with the naval air arm since 1915, had made the first takeoff and landing on the old *Saratoga* back in 1928, and knew just about all there was to know about carrier operations. In February, 1944, Mitscher sent in his new Hellcat fighters to work over Truk's defenses, then followed up with his bombers. By the time Task Force Fifty-eight was through, 275 Japanese planes were demolished, 200,000 tons of merchant shipping and two destroyers were at the bottom of Truk's harbor, and the Japanese "Gibraltar of the Pacific" had lost its power.

Planning for the Marianas operation moved ahead rapidly. In the meantime, MacArthur was brilliantly sweeping along New Guinea's long northern coast, using the amphibious capabilities of the Seventh Fleet assigned to him to make end sweeps around enemy strongholds. Before long he had seized the bases and airfields needed for his spring into the Philippines.

In the Gilberts and Marshalls, the Japanese high command had left garrison troops to do the fighting, preserving their lean resources of naval and air striking power for more critical situations. When American carrier planes began hitting the Marianas, the situation was critical; here was the central link in the home islands' inner defense ring. Admiral Soemu Toyoda, commander in chief of the Imperial Navy, alerted his carrier forces for action.

Since Guadalcanal, the Japanese, like the Americans, had been rebuilding their carrier arm. By May,

1944, the First Mobile Fleet under Jisaburo Ozawa—five fleet carriers and four light carriers, plus a powerful force of escorts—was assembled in a southern Philippines anchorage. (The murderous campaign against tankers by the U.S. submarine fleet had forced the Imperial Navy southward, a thousand miles from the Marianas, to be nearer the East Indies oil supplies.) Although Ozawa's fleet was strong, he was weak in well-trained pilots and his planes were something less than a match for the new American types.

Admiral Richmond Kelly Turner's amphibious assault on Saipan, which opened the Marianas campaign on June 15, was expertly carried out: 8,000 marines

The Japanese carrier *Zuiho,* camouflaged to resemble a battleship, suffered extensive damage in an attack by Mitscher's raiders in the Philippine Sea. A flier from the *Enterprise* took the photo, showing the carrier's deck buckled by explosions, before she sank October 25, 1944, off Cape Engaño during the Battle of Leyte Gulf.

U.S. Pacific Fleet carriers, led by the *Essex*, plow through the ocean. The 27,000-ton *Essex*-class carriers were introduced into the Pacific war in mid-1943. Eventually 18 of them were in service, insuring U.S. air superiority before invasions and destroying Japanese war and merchant ships.

scrambled ashore in twenty minutes. But after that the Japanese reacted savagely, and the American advance became slow and costly.

Before D-day was over Admiral Spruance received reports from his scouting submarines that the Japanese fleet had sortied northward at high speed into the Philippine Sea, west of the Marianas. Spruance postponed a second landing, on Guam, and had Mitscher's Task Force Fifty-eight clear for action.

Ozawa's battle plan was shrewd. Lacking self-sealing gas tanks and with little armor plate, Japanese carrier planes were lighter than the American planes and outranged them by a good 200 miles. His scheme was to keep well out of reach of Task Force Fifty-eight while he attacked with everything he had. He further planned to use the Guam airfields for refueling and rearming planes and so keep up the offensive pressure. Ozawa anticipated (correctly) that Spruance would not dare to leave the Saipan beachhead uncovered to come out and pursue him.

Early on the morning of June 19, Ozawa sent off his first strike wave, sixty-nine planes, to keep the American combat air patrol busy while a second and stronger strike wave hit the carriers. American search radar picked up the first wave 150 miles out and Mitscher scrambled his fighters. He launched his dive bombers and torpedo planes with orders to orbit out of the way so that the flight decks would be clear to service the fighters, and he called in the Hellcats that had been sweeping the Guam airfields. Interception was made well to the west of the U.S. fleet. One-third of the first wave went down in this clash, and the survivors were mauled when they reached the U.S. fleet.

When the second wave of Ozawa's bombers and fighters came in, they found great swarms of Hellcats waiting for them. The slaughter was incredible. Japanese planes by the dozens, by the score, went careening into the sea. Lieutenant Alex Vraciu got six of them in a dazzling display of marksmanship. The half-dozen that eluded the gauntlet to reach the carriers were all shot down. This time the score added up to 98 lost out of the second wave's 130 planes. A third wave of attackers never found the American fleet at all and took a beating, and a fourth wave flew far astray before making contact; it was very nearly wiped out, only nine of eighty-two surviving.

179

Guam was no haven at all for the battered attackers. Relays of Mitscher's Hellcats prowled the airfields and riddled dozens of Japanese planes trying to land or take off. The *Hornet*'s Wilbur Webb had a field day there, scoring six to match Vraciu. Darkness finally ended the massacre. The Japanese had lost 346 planes, the Americans just 30. It is little wonder that June 19, 1944, has gone down in the history of World War II as "The Great Marianas Turkey Shoot."

Yet this was only part of Ozawa's disaster. Early that morning, just after completing launching, the brand-new carrier *Taiho* took a torpedo hit from the U.S.S. *Albacore*, one of the submarines assigned the job of shadowing the Japanese fleet. The damage was inconsequential, but some hours later a blunder by a damage-control officer ignited aviation gasoline fumes, tearing Ozawa's flagship to pieces and sending her to the bottom with 1,600 crewmen. Shortly after noon a second submarine, the *Cavalla,* scored three torpedo hits on the veteran carrier *Shokaku;* three hours later she too broke up and sank.

One dramatic final act remained in the Battle of the Philippine Sea. It began at 4 P.M. the next day, June 20, when an American scout plane at last spotted the First Mobile Fleet. Mitscher faced a nasty decision. The sighting was at the maximum range of his planes, and they would not return until after dark—and few pilots had training in night landings. But in war no chance to enlarge a victory dare be overlooked. Mitscher sent a 216-plane strike force winging off westward and ordered Task Force Fifty-eight after it at full speed to shorten the return flight.

It was sunset when Ozawa's fleet was sighted. The attackers endured a sharp fight from the combat air patrol, for only the best Japanese pilots had survived the Turkey Shoot. Twenty U.S. planes were shot down against sixty-five Zeros. Mitscher's dive bombers and torpedo planes sank the fleet carrier *Hiyo* and only

brilliant damage-control efforts saved the severely injured fleet carrier *Zuikaku*. A light carrier also was badly damaged.

It was fully dark as the strike force headed home. One after another, planes ran out of gas and had to ditch. When the rest reached Task Force Fifty-eight they found it blacked out and under radio silence as protection against submarines and aerial snoopers from Guam. But if Marc Mitscher had to make the decision to send his airmen out, he could now make the decision to get them home. He ordered the fleet to light up—running lights, floodlights, searchlights, even flares—and he radioed his pilots to land on the first carrier they could find. One grateful flier recalled, "The effect on the pilots . . . was magnetic. They were open-mouthed at the sheer audacity of asking the Japs to come and get us . . . to hell with the Japs around us! Our pilots were not to be expendable." It was a wild hectic scene and there were many landing accidents and many close calls but most of the airmen got aboard safely.

The Battle of the Philippine Sea was the war's greatest carrier fight, and one of the war's most one-sided victories. Just two years earlier the Imperial Japanese Navy's carrier force was the best in the world; now it was all but wiped out. After the Philippine Sea, Japan had only a handful of trained carrier pilots left and few prospects for increasing that number. With its new carriers, its new planes, and its well-trained airmen, the U.S. Navy had set Japan on the road to defeat.

The major islands in the Marianas—Saipan, Guam, and Tinian—were soon secured by the marines, and engineers swarmed over the airfields to lengthen them for the B-29s. The Pacific war still had more than a year to run and there would be scores of pitched battles and thousands of lives lost, but after June, 1944, there could be no doubt of the outcome—Japan was doomed.

D-Day to V-E Day

8

For anyone with a sense of history, it was a portentous moment: Sunday evening, June 4, 1944; Southwick House, Allied naval headquarters on England's Channel coast; a gathering of the high command to decide whether to give the go-ahead for the Anglo-American invasion of France. (June 4, in fact, was already momentous. Earlier in the day the U.S. Fifth Army had captured Rome. In the war against Japan on the other side of the globe, a mighty 535-ship expeditionary force was moving out for the decisive attack on the Marianas.) Never before in history had so many fighting men and so much striking power been gathered together for that most difficult of all military operations, an amphibious assault on a defended coast. Now it all hung on the vagaries of the weather.

Rain and high winds were rattling the windows of Southwick House as Supreme Commander Dwight Eisenhower opened the meeting. Already the invasion had been postponed twenty-four hours because of bad weather. A second postponement would mean at the least a two-week delay and more likely a month's delay; it depended on moonlight conditions and the Channel tides—and the weather. The huge secret invasion spring was coiled tight, and whether it could be recoiled without the Germans learning of it was highly dubious.

In this tense atmosphere Royal Air Force weather expert J.N. Stagg presented his forecast. His meteorologists had detected a clearing front moving up the Channel, Stagg said, that seemed to promise barely tolerable conditions for the twenty-four hours beginning around midday the next day, June 5. That was their best estimate, but like any weather forecast, it was not a sure thing. Eisenhower polled his lieuten-

The Supreme Commander for Operation Overlord, Gen. Dwight D. Eisenhower, talks to paratroopers before they take off on D-day, June 6, 1944, to drop behind German lines in invasion of Europe.

ants. His deputy, Arthur Tedder, and his air force commander, Trafford Leigh-Mallory, hesitated; air support and the scheduled parachute drop would be "chancy." His chief of staff, Walter Bedell Smith, urged that the invasion proceed. So did his ground commander, Bernard Montgomery: "I would say—go!"

The final decision was of course Eisenhower's. The complications and the potentially grave risks of a postponement had to be balanced against the possibility of a disastrous landing attempt. Eisenhower pondered silently for several minutes and then looked around the table. "I'm quite positive we must give the order," he said. "I don't like it, but there it is. I don't see how we can possibly do anything else." D-day for Operation Overlord, the assault on Hitler's Europe, would be Tuesday, June 6, 1944.

There was going to be a cross-Channel invasion because, as the more hard-headed military thinkers had predicted, it was the only way to defeat Nazi Germany. The strategy of pecking around the edges of Hitler's Europe had failed to leave the enemy in disarray after all; the current Italian campaign was terribly slow and costly and promised little in strategic advantage. Nor had the air power enthusiasts delivered; Germany showed no signs of going to her knees under the relentless bombing campaign. As so often seemed to happen in war, it was going to be up to the foot soldier.

The American high command had promoted a cross-Channel attack as early as 1942. The British, experienced in fighting the tough German war machine, counseled caution until the Nazis were considerably thinned and stretched, especially by their struggle with Russia. As it happened, a frustrating shortage of one essential, landing craft, meant postponement until 1944. "The destinies of two great empires," British Prime Minister Winston Churchill grumbled, "seem to

be tied up in some God-damned things called LSTs."

So England became, from 1942 on, a great armed camp; only the antiaircraft barrage balloons, said the wits, kept the island from sinking under the load. Airfields and truck parks and infantry barracks sprouted like mushrooms. Quiet tree-lined country lanes concealed mile upon mile of stacked artillery shells and ranks of cannon parked hub to hub and endless rows of silent, menacing tanks. Slowly, steadily, under the direction of Supreme Commander Eisenhower, the spring was coiled.

This mighty buildup was the measure of a major Allied victory already won—the Battle of the Atlantic. As recently as a year earlier that battle was being lost. In March, 1943, U-boat wolfpacks sank 108 ships totaling over 625,000 tons. But that was the peak. Slowly, month by month, the toll of merchant ships fell off—and the toll of German submarines went up. Better convoy methods, more destroyers and destroyer-escorts, electronic search gear, escort carriers for air cover—all contributed to one of the decisive Allied victories of World War II. Even a standoff in the Atlantic battle could have compromised Operation Overlord; a defeat would have left Britain starving and helpless.

So by the spring of 1944 the men and the weapons were massed in sufficient numbers. But there was one further essential before the invasion could proceed— control of the air over France. This too was finally won, but it was a close-run thing and the cost was high. Continuous raids on aircraft plants put a dent in German fighter plane production, but more important, the massive air battles left the Luftwaffe critically short of trained pilots. The invasion force need have little fear of hostile aircraft.

The Germans knew an invasion was coming, of course, but exactly where and exactly when they could only guess. Terrain and logistical requirements limited the Allies to the French coastline between the Belgian border and the Cotentin Peninsula in Normandy. The Germans fortified it all, but saved their strongest defenses for the Pas de Calais across from Dover, where the Channel is at its narrowest. The

The Allies landed on the Italian mainland in September, 1943, but it was not until June, 1944, that U.S. forces entered Rome and rolled past the Colosseum. They had been delayed on the road to Rome by hard fighting at Salerno, Anzio, and Cassino.

184

Officers of an American reconnaissance patrol (opposite) study a map in Tunisia as their crew takes a break.

Allies went to great effort to encourage the belief that they would strike at this point, since they were actually going to land in Normandy.

The German commander in the west, Gerd von Rundstedt, was a wily old veteran who had masterminded the conquests of Poland and France back in the Nazis' glory days. In tactical command of the Atlantic Wall was Erwin Rommel, the "Desert Fox," whose genius in a war of maneuver had stretched the fight for North Africa into three costly, grueling years. Rommel was convinced that the invading Allies must

be defeated on the beaches if they were to be defeated at all; their command of the air, he said, would make them unbeatable if they ever got ashore. "The first twenty-four hours of the invasion will be decisive," he told an aide in April. "For the Allies, as well as for Germany, it will be the longest day." With furious energy he set about sowing the French beaches with land mines and landing-craft obstacles and concrete bunkers and pillboxes. By June he had the task well begun, but nowhere did he consider the defenses as strong as they needed to be. The war of attrition on

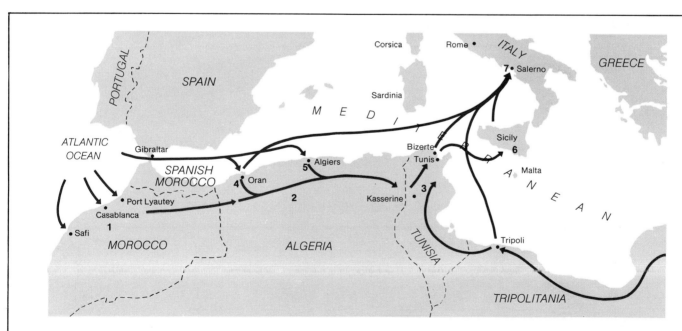

North African Campaign

Not yet strong enough to attack the Nazis across the English Channel, the Allies decided to hit the Axis forces in North Africa and then in Italy. The plan was to land in French Morocco (**1**) and Algeria (**2**), and advance into Tunisia (**3**) to trap Gen. Erwin Rommel. Operation Torch consisted of three forces: 35,000 Americans landed in Morocco directly from the U.S.; 39,000 Americans sailed from Britain to seize Oran (**4**) in Algeria; and 10,000 GIs

and 23,000 British troops left Britain to capture Algiers (**5**). More than 800 ships carried and protected the invaders, commanded by Gen. Eisenhower. As these troops thrust eastward, British forces under Gen. Montgomery swept westward from Egypt to catch the Germans in a vise. The Axis desert fighters held the Allies to a stalemate during the winter of 1942-43, but by mid-May, 1943, the Allied forces had conquered North Africa and were on schedule for the summer invasion of Sicily (**6**) and Italy (**7**).

Meanwhile, Back Home . . .

In preparation for an all-out assault on Hitler's Europe, American industry poured forth an astonishing quantity of planes, tanks, ships, guns, and ammunition—more than double the Axis powers' production in 1944. Companies that in peacetime had produced Kodaks and Quaker Oats operated plants turning out bombs and shells. More than half the workers in war plants were women, many of whom had never held jobs before. Civilians grumbled about shortages of butter, meat, gasoline, and textiles, but their dedicated labor shortened the war.

Even children played a part in the war effort, collecting metal (left). Many families responded to the poster below, and prepared for air raids that happily never occurred.

186

Working night and day and using prefabricated sections (above), a shipyard turned out cargo ships in 17 days. On the assembly lines, women (below left) waged war against Hitler and Tojo with acetylene torches. Boeing's Seattle plant rolled out its last B-17 (below right) in April, 1945. Its successor, the B-29, stands in the background. Wartime America produced nearly 300,000 aircraft, 87,000 tanks, 320,000 artillery pieces, 12,000 war and cargo ships, 65,000 landing craft, plus 42 billion bullets.

the Eastern Front had stretched German resources too thin to build a proper Atlantic Wall.

The bad weather early in June caused the Germans to relax their vigil. Defense exercises were canceled and many officers took leave. Rommel left the coast to be with his wife at their home near Ulm, Germany, on her birthday, June 6.

The harbingers of invasion came from the air—18,300 American and British paratroopers who tumbled out of the dark sky into the area behind the Normandy beaches in the early hours of June 6. Their mission was to seize bridges and causeways for use by the invaders coming across the beaches a few hours later. The air drops were badly scattered and many paratroopers were killed, captured, or drowned in flooded marshlands, but they won most of their objectives and spread confusion far and wide.

The gray, hazy dawn revealed calm seas in the Channel; the meteorologists had been right. In their coastal emplacements German troops stared in stunned silence at the sight revealed to them—a panorama of ships spreading solidly, without a break, across the horizon. The armada totaled nearly 5,000 vessels, 900 of them warships, carrying 174,000 troops and over 20,000 vehicles. As the landing craft broke out of their impatient circling and began to head for the beaches, the Germans opened fire.

Allied bombers and fighter-bombers swept in to

Ammunition stored along an English country road (left) is concealed by trees from Nazi reconnaissance planes. By May, 1944, supplies filled 64 million square feet of indoor and outdoor storage space. The invasion fleet included many landing ships and boats. These powerful, shallow-draft vessels, such as the LSTs (Landing Ship, Tank) at right, were unknown until shortly before the war. The Allies had a difficult time building enough of them to carry simultaneously more than 20,000 vehicles and 174,000 troops to France.

ROBERT LANDRY

U.S. ARMY

rake the beach defenses and reinforcement routes behind the coast. Battleships, cruisers, and destroyers added their powerful voices to the pounding. On the beach code-named Utah at the base of the Cotentin Peninsula, forming the right flank of the Overlord assault, American troops poured ashore against almost no return fire. By day's end the Americans manned a solid beachhead and had linked up with the paratroopers, at a cost of fewer than 200 casualties.

On the left flank, the three British and Canadian beaches, opposition was stiffer but there was never any doubt that a firm hold would be won on D-day. Soon a link-up was made with the paratroopers and substantial armor was ashore. The one disappoint-

ment, which would loom large in the coming weeks, was the failure to win the city of Caen, with its network of roads leading inland.

It was in the center landing area, designated Omaha, that Rommel had come closest to his goal of building adequate beach defenses, and it was at Omaha that the Anglo-American invasion came closest to foundering. The narrow beach was a devilish tangle of concrete and steel obstacles laced with barbed wire and mines. The bluffs behind were honeycombed with concrete pillboxes and bunkers from which artillery and machine guns commanded every inch of the landing area. For the American invaders, it was like entering the mouth of hell; two-thirds of the first wave was shot down in the surf.

Landing craft of succeeding waves were soon milling around, one man said, like "a herd of stampeded cattle" as they sought clear unloading places. For a time the high command debated evacuating the troops huddling behind any shelter they could find on the deadly beach. But then a handful of men here, a squad there, began creeping forward to get at their tormentors. "They're murdering us here!" yelled one officer. "Let's move inland and get murdered!" A sergeant was blunter. "Get your ass up that hill!" he bellowed at every soldier he saw. In the crisis, destroyers maneuvered through the fire of shore batteries until they nearly ran aground to provide gunfire support for the beleaguered infantrymen.

And slowly, as what Rommel had prophetically called "the longest day" wore on, they scratched out first a toehold, then a beachhead. Some 2,500 fell in the effort, but they were now solidly ashore and could not be pushed off. As darkness fell and reinforcements and guns came in over the bloody sands of Omaha, Adolf Hitler's Atlantic Wall was breached.

"One of the forty-seven immortals of Omaha," according to historian S.L.A. Marshall, is Lieutenant

189

Awaiting H-hour to land, invaders crouch in an assault craft (left) in the early morning light. Photographer Robert Capa went in with the first wave and took the photo opposite of GIs trying to take cover among the anti-invasion obstacles at the "Easy Red" section of Omaha. On that June day, Capa thought it "the ugliest beach in the whole world."

Walter Taylor, who led his section crawling across the beach and over the seawall, losing four men killed and two wounded, then led them straight up the bluff and into Vierville, where in a two-hour fight they whipped a German platoon without losing a man. From there, he led the men to a château, capturing twenty-four Germans en route and two more in the château. They then fought three truckloads of German infantry throughout the day. Fifteen Rangers joined them at sundown and Taylor told the group they must go to their original objective for the end of D-day. He led the thirty-three men nearly to the village of Louviers—"almost one-half mile in front of anything else in the United States Army." There they learned that the remnants of their battalion were assembling 700 yards closer to the sea, so Taylor's group joined them there.

Staff Sergeant Frank M. Price later said of Taylor, "We saw no sign of fear in him. Watching him made men of us. Marching or fighting, he was leading. We

followed him because there was nothing else to do." Says historian Marshall, "Thousands of Americans were spilled onto Omaha Beach. The high ground was won by a handful of men like Taylor who on that day burned with a flame bright beyond common understanding."

D-day—and the GIs drop into the water from an LCT (Landing Craft, Tank) and wade to the shore in the face of enemy fire at Omaha Beach. The in-depth German defenses included underwater mines, mined obstacles on the beach, then casemented and mobile guns, backed by land mines. Some 2,500 men fell at bloody Omaha.

Having won the battle of the beaches, the Allies now set about winning the battle of logistics. With total air and naval superiority, Eisenhower was able to deliver more reinforcements and supplies across the English Channel to the beachhead than Rundstedt could dispatch to Normandy over a transportation network crippled by air attacks and sabotaged by the French Resistance. Three weeks after D-day, utilizing such ingenious inventions as artificial harbors assembled off the beaches and gasoline pipelines laid on the Channel floor, the Allies had a million men, half a million tons of supplies, and over 175,000 vehicles ashore in France.

Efforts by Rommel and Rundstedt to counterattack with reserve panzer (armored) divisions were blocked by Hitler, who was convinced that the Normandy invasion was only a feint to distract him from the main blow soon to hit the Pas de Calais, and they were further hampered by watchful Allied fighter-bombers that pounced on anything German that dared to move in daylight. (One of their victims was Rommel himself, gravely injured in a strafing run on his staff car.)

If the Germans could not break into the beachhead, the Allies were having a hard time breaking out of it. Part of the trouble was the terrain. The Americans on the right flank faced the *bocage* country, a checkerboard landscape of sunken roads and small fields divided by hedgerows—thick earth ridges crowned with trees and bramble bushes. It was an area perfectly suited to defense and almost impervious to armored thrusts. The advance was agonizingly slow, field by field rather than mile by mile. There was open country in front of Montgomery on the left flank, but it was kept out of reach by the stubborn German defenders of Caen. The cautious Montgomery was content to tie down the strongest of the enemy forces on his front and let his American colleagues on the right do the breaking out.

193

This they finally did, in late July, at Saint-Lô. Eisenhower's right wing was under Omar Bradley, a mild-looking man whose homespun manner concealed a sharp intelligence. Eager to be free of the slugging match in the hedgerows, Bradley suddenly sprang armored spearheads through Saint-Lô in the wake of a "carpet bombing" by the strategic air forces that left the area looking, said a German general, "like the face of the moon."

Once through the crust of defenses, the American tanks found little opposition. Swinging right into Brittany and left toward central France, they made twenty-five miles a day and more, their flanks often protected solely by the deadly fighter-bombers. Spurring the breakthrough was the flamboyant George Patton, a controversial, sometimes unstable soldier but the best general in the Allied camp at directing pursuit warfare.

With the stalemate broken, there began a reverse blitzkrieg (lightning war), a turnabout of the Nazi drive across France in 1940. Montgomery finally got past Caen and advanced on Falaise. Patton hooked his Third Army in from the southwest, threatening to encircle the main Nazi force in Normandy. The Allies failed to slam the door completely shut on the "Falaise pocket" and some 35,000 of the enemy escaped. Yet the carnage was great: 10,000 killed, 50,000 captured, 500 tanks and uncounted numbers of other vehicles wrecked. In nearly complete disorganization, the Germans fled pell-mell for the Seine. The great pursuit was on.

Patton's spearheads smashed ahead, one of his armored divisions taking Orleans on August 16 after a drive of 250 miles in a day and a half. American columns reached the Seine on both sides of Paris. Taking shorter jumps, the British and Canadians closed up to the river downstream from the capital. Once more the Germans avoided entrapment, but those who escaped

across the Seine did so with only about 100 of the 2,300 tanks and assault guns that once faced the Normandy beachhead. On August 25, a Free French column entered the City of Light, and the liberated Parisians went wild.

For the German forces in northern France there was no haven short of the defenses of the West Wall on the frontier of the Third Reich itself. They slogged along, much of their transport horsedrawn, constantly harried by what they called the *Jabos*—Thunderbolts, Hurricanes, and Typhoons of the Allied tactical air forces. Armored columns snapped at their heels, probing eastward on a broad front. By this time the Allies had even opened a second front, landing on the French Riviera on August 15 and driving swiftly northward for a linkup with the main force.

So it was in late August. But by early September the

Soon after D-day, a group of high German officers tried to kill Hitler because he would not seek peace. Their bomb killed four men but only slightly injured Hitler, shown discussing the event.

Allied blitzkrieg was faltering, a victim of the tyranny of logistics. The unexpected German collapse played havoc with the supply echelons. Already the Allies were more than three months ahead of their pre-invasion timetable, to which logistical schedules were geared, and in the front lines there were growing shortages of almost every tool of war—most especially gasoline. Improvisation was the standing order of the day: hastily organized airlifts, a truck convoy system called the Red Ball Express that operated on one-way roads, even thefts from other units (the U.S. First and Third Armies were particularly adept at this), but one by one the armored spearheads ran out of gas and watched the enemy slip away. "My men can eat their belts, but my tanks have gotta have gas!" Patton raged.

There was a moment of fresh hope on September 4, when the British Second Army captured Antwerp in Belgium, the greatest port in northwest Europe, in one of the coups of the campaign—and captured it so quickly that its docks and cranes and warehouses were taken intact. Then Montgomery and his generals threw away their sparkling victory by neglecting to sweep down the sixty-mile Schelde estuary that connects Antwerp with the North Sea. The Germans dug in along the Schelde, and for almost three months they denied the Allies this vitally needed entry for supplies.

Meanwhile, Montgomery was embroiled in a bitter argument with Eisenhower over grand strategy. The Briton pleaded for "one really powerful and full-blooded thrust" under his command in the northern sector that would plunge ahead with full supply priority to blast through the West Wall and jump the Rhine, then threaten the Ruhr, Germany's industrial vitals. In Montgomery's view, nothing could stop him; in Eisenhower's, it was altogether too risky, inviting flank counterattacks and failing to take advantage of the classic military stratagem of parallel advances to divide and confuse the enemy. The argument has since fueled many a battle among armchair generals, but after Montgomery's failure to open Antwerp promptly, no forces, full-blooded or broad-front, were going to get very far in the face of a supply crisis.

October brought with it the vanguard of bad winter weather and a breathing space for Hitler. The Anglo-American forces might have reclaimed most of France and Belgium, but so far they held only the barest of footholds in the Third Reich itself. In the east, the massive Russian summer offensive was also finally slowing down due to supply problems—but only after it had chased the last Nazi from Russian soil and driven deep into the Balkans, Poland, and the Baltic states.

The weather put a damper on still another Allied offensive, the strategic bombing campaign. Once the Luftwaffe was smashed and the troops were rolling ahead in France, Carl Spaatz, head of the U.S. bomber force, won approval for his pet scheme: the destruction of Germany's oil supply. By late summer Spaatz's Flying Fortresses and Liberators were succeeding brilliantly. Their strikes on refineries and synthetic-oil plants slashed Luftwaffe and Wehrmacht gasoline stocks by 75 percent. Under the protective cloud cover of fall, the gasoline began to flow again, but then only in limited quantities.

While the Allies and the Axis were locked in deadly battle on the land and sea and in the air, another war was being fought "underground." For the Americans, this war was led by Major General William Joseph ("Wild Bill") Donovan as head of the Office of Strategic Services. The OSS (also known as "Oh, So Secret") was a remarkable espionage organization, the forerunner of today's Central Intelligence Agency.

In its global operations, the OSS employed more than 30,000 persons, not counting the many thousands of partisans in the occupied countries who were paid and equipped by the OSS and performed OSS missions. More than 800 OSS members were decorated for gallantry, some posthumously. Paying tribute to Donovan, his deputy director Ned Buxton said, "He was given a fantastic assignment—to create and operate a

CIVIC CENTER COMMISSION, DETROIT

An Allied tank column and infantrymen move through the ruins of St.-Lô in the painting at left by Ogden Pleissner. A 2,500-plane attack preceded the St.-Lô breakthrough, which opened the way to Paris. One day after the liberation of Paris, Free French leader Gen. Charles de Gaulle heads a parade (right) from the Arc de Triomphe down the Champs Elysées on August 26, 1944.

secret intelligence agency after the enemy had erected his barbed wire and contrived every conceivable scheme to make himself impregnable. The general founded the organization; he formulated the program; he devised the tactics; he penetrated the barriers. He personally attended the invasions. . . . He extemporized; he devised; he asked for the improbable and confidently achieved it."

Super-spy Donovan recruited an extraordinary group of agents, researchers, and administrators. They included playwright Robert E. Sherwood, authors Thornton Wilder and Stephen Vincent Benét, film director John Ford, future CIA chiefs Allen Dulles and Richard Helms, historian Arthur Schlesinger, Jr., polo player Raymond Guest, New York socialite Prince Serge Obolensky, Hollywood stunt man Rene Dussaq ("The Human Fly"), professional wrestler Jumping Joe Savoldi, circus owner John Ringling North, film star Sterling Hayden, explorer Ilya Tolstoy—the novelist's grandson, Quentin Roosevelt—Teddy's grandson, and many talented if lesser known men and women from all walks of life. Author Corey Ford, noting the extent of OSS operations in Europe, wrote:

> Prior to the invasion of Africa, covert installations began to function in Casablanca and Tangier and Algiers, later in Marrakesh, Rabat, Alexandria, Cairo. The Italian campaign was served by forward units in the islands of Sicily and Corsica . . . Capri, Caserta, Bari, Naples, Rome, Milan. By 1944 the clandestine web stretched from Norway and Denmark to Albania and Poland and Greece, to inconspicuous . . . villas in Madrid and Lisbon and Barcelona, to Abadan and Istanbul and Baghdad. From the neutral capitals of Bern and Stockholm, from Copenhagen and Brussels and Antwerp, it spun its way stealthily into Austria and the German homeland. . . . When D-day dawned, Anglo-American teams were already operating inside France at St.-Lô, Grandville, Ste.-Mère-Eglise. An OSS cell hidden in a modest apartment in Nazi-held Paris directed a string of substations in Toulouse, Dijon, Nice, Marseilles.

Sicily and Corsica fell to the Allies almost without a fight, due in part to the OSS having previously infiltrated the islands and organized the local resistance. During the Italian campaign, OSS teams slipped into Naples by boat, carrying arms for the guerrillas whom they organized to fight the Nazis; agents infiltrated frequently through the German lines to obtain tactical information; the OSS secret radio in Rome supplied detailed information on the German units deploying against the Allied landing forces, and recommended bombing targets.

197

Supreme Commander Eisenhower argued about strategy with the British ground forces leader, Gen. Sir Bernard Law Montgomery (at left), who wanted to make a single thrust to the Ruhr. Eisenhower favored continuing the advance to the Rhine on a broad front.

U.S. ARMY

By October, 1944, the underground war had achieved such success in German-occupied Italy that Field Marshal Albert Kesselring proclaimed October 8-14 "Anti-Partisan Week" to exterminate guerrilla resistance. Sabotage had been tormenting the Germans as they moved north through Italy after evacuating Rome. Their water supplies were poisoned; their vehicles disabled; their sentries garroted; their troop trains wrecked; their communication lines cut. Kesselring ordered his men to shoot on sight any Allied agent caught working with the partisans. Still the OSS agents infiltrated Italy by parachute and from boats. They equipped and trained the partisans so that they were able to rout the Germans from parts of northern Italy and could help the Allied forces hold various sectors of the fighting front.

OSS officers parachuted to help the Maquis—the French underground—create chaos behind the German lines, block escape routes, and prevent demolition of key installations by the retreating enemy after D-day. By the end of August, after Patton's breakthrough, many of these little armies of Maquis were being led in forays based on the guerrilla strategy: surprise, kill, vanish.

Hitler's one-time dream of world conquest was shattered, but he still hoped for a stalemate and a negotiated peace on his own terms. For one thing, he now gripped both the state and the military high command in an iron fist, with the slightest deviation from orders punishable by death. This was the result of the bomb plot. On July 20, 1944, a group of Wehrmacht officers, believing the war lost and Germany doomed, had smuggled a bomb into the fuehrer's East Prussian headquarters. But the explosion only slightly wounded the target. A swift and savage bloodbath left the military cowed. Hitler detected in his escape from assassination the intervention of fate, "the guiding hand of Providence directing that I must and will carry out my task." His task he defined as leading the Third Reich to either triumph or destruction.

His fevered hopes were boosted by the German *Vergeltungswaffen* (vengeance weapons) program. In June, the first V-1 "buzz bomb," a jet-propelled projectile, had swept down on London, and since then several thousand more had caused widespread if random damage and many casualties. Then, early in September, the first V-2 hit the British capital. This was a true terror weapon, a ballistic rocket that plunged out of the stratosphere at supersonic speed without the slightest warning. The Luftwaffe also had a jet fighter in limited action that completely outclassed any Allied aircraft. On the drawing boards or under testing was a variety of other exotic advanced weapons. The Germans had pioneered atomic research, but had not yet succeeded in producing a chain reaction and in 1944 were far behind the Americans and British in the production of an A-bomb. To realists on the German side of the lines, all this added up to the slenderest of hopes in the face of overwhelming Allied power. (When asked what was to be done after the Allies secured their Normandy beachhead, Rundstedt had replied, "Make peace, you fools!") But to Hitler's warped mind there were omens everywhere, glimmerings of another glorious phase in the life of the "Thousand-Year" Reich. He began plotting a counterstroke to confound his enemies.

By mid-October, 1944, the Anglo-American forces had a solid 500-mile front stretching from the Swiss border to the North Sea, and their supply crisis was easing. Eisenhower now determined to launch a major offensive to crack through the West Wall and close up to the Rhine before winter. Rundstedt was still outnumbered and outgunned, but his forces had recovered their poise. They had the benefits of the West Wall's defenses and of solid, experienced leadership. Every Allied thrust was fiercely opposed.

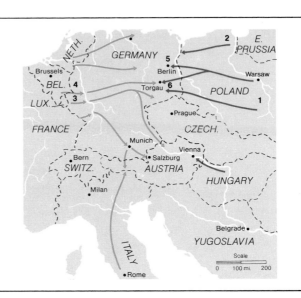

Into the Heart of Hitler's Germany

After the Battle of the Bulge ended in January, 1945, the Allied forces entered Germany. The Russians opened an offensive from Poland (**1**) and East Prussia (**2**) on January 12 and were inside Germany within two weeks. The Americans, British, French, and Canadians began their offensive in the west on February 23 in conjunction with bombing of oil depots, large cities, and transportation centers. They captured the Saar (**3**) by March 23. After taking the industrial Ruhr (**4**) in April, they met no further major resistance. The Russians fought their last big battle in Berlin (**5**), and on April 25, American and Russian soldiers met at Torgau (**6**) on the Elbe. Germany surrendered May 7.

The Allied air offensive intensified after D-day. While providing tactical support for the ground forces, the airmen also had the job of knocking out the German war economy. Here, a Flying Fortress passes over a burning target on the Baltic island of Peenemuende, where the Germans carried out research on the powerful V-weapons.

Courtney Hodges's U.S. First Army tried to exploit a breach in the West Wall resulting from the capture of Aachen. It was soon embroiled in one of the most hellish fights of the war, the Battle of the Huertgen Forest. No war of maneuver was possible in this thick forest of firs; the victor would be the side that could jam the most men into the cauldron. The struggle recalled the horrors of the Battle of the Wilderness in the Civil War or of the Argonne Forest in World War I. "Once magnificent trees were now twisted, gashed, broken, their limbs and foliage forming a thick carpet on the floor of the forest," writes historian Charles MacDonald. "Some trees stood like gaunt, outsized toothpicks. Great jagged chunks of concrete and twisted reinforcing rods that together had been a pillbox . . . here and there bodies of the dead in grotesque positions. . . . It was misery unrelieved."

It was well into December before Hodges's troops finally secured the Huertgen Forest. Eight divisions had been ravaged; there were more than 24,000 combat casualties and another 5,000 men lost to trenchfoot and disease. Worst of all, the carnage was largely pointless. The high command had failed to give top priority to seizing the key to the whole sector, a pair of dams on the Roer River. By their control of the dams' sluice gates, the Germans could flood the Roer Valley and block any major Allied advance.

Still, substantial gains were made in this fall offensive, especially by "Jake" Devers's Sixth Army Group in the south. Nearly everywhere the Allies had closed up to the West Wall and at several points had won jumping-off places for a continuing push to the Rhine. With the docking of the first supply ship at Antwerp on November 28, the logistical crisis would in time become a thing of the past. Eisenhower and his gen-

erals had every reason to be optimistic as they prepared for the final drive into Germany. What they were not prepared for, however, was the paranoid determination of Adolf Hitler.

At a conference in mid-September, with the situation grim and unsettled everywhere, Hitler had astounded his generals with a sudden outburst: "I have made a momentous decision. I am taking the offensive!" Pointing to a map, he exclaimed, "Here—out of the Ardennes! Across the Meuse and on to Antwerp!"

At the time it was utterly impossible. But when supply problems and bad weather and stiffening resistance combined to slow his enemies on both the Eastern and Western fronts, the idea of a counterstroke was suddenly not so impossible after all. A thrust to Antwerp, Hitler reasoned, would not only deprive his enemies of their key supply port but would isolate Montgomery's entire army group. He was confident that in the face of such a calamity the Western powers would agree to a negotiated peace, leaving him free to continue his fight against bolshevism.

The Allies' advance had flowed on either side of the Ardennes, a large patch of militarily uninviting terrain in the southeastern corner of Belgium at about midpoint on the Western Front. This was a hilly, heavily forested area with a poor road network, and Eisenhower had quite properly shunned it in favor of more inviting targets north and south. In mid-December this front was lightly held by a single corps of Hodges's First Army. The men of Troy Middleton's VIII Corps were a combination of combat-weary veterans, many of whom had fought in the Huertgen Forest, and rookie regiments fresh from training centers. Bradley frankly called it "a nursery and old folks' home," but this caused no particular worry, since it was known that the Germans used the Ardennes for precisely the same purpose.

They did, that is, until December; then, quietly and stealthily, the forests east of the Ardennes began to fill up with a staggering array of fighting men and equipment. There were almost 1,000 tanks and assault guns and almost 2,000 artillery pieces; there were 15,000 tons of artillery shells and 4.5 million gallons of precious gasoline; and there were some 200,000 men in thirteen infantry divisions and seven armored divisions. Hermann Goering promised that 1,000 planes, including many of the new jets, would support the operation, but the German generals had heard Goering's promises before and largely discounted any help from the Luftwaffe. All they wanted was weather bad enough to ground Allied *Jabos*.

This buildup was a major feat of logistics and planning, doubly so since it was carried out under the nose of an enemy who had complete domination of aerial reconnaissance. The Allied high command never suspected a thing. There were many reasons for this intelligence failure, but the main one was simply overconfidence. It was an article of faith that the terribly battered German army was incapable of a major counterattack. On December 12, four days before Hitler's assault began, a Twelfth Army Group intelligence summary stated that "attrition is steadily sapping the strength of German forces . . . the crust of defenses is thinner, more brittle and more vulnerable than it appears on our G-2 maps or to the troops in the line." If anyone remembered that in 1940 the Germans had launched a surprise attack through the Ardennes that

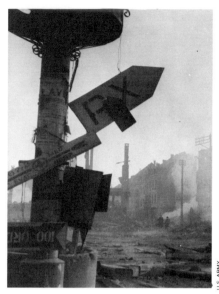

GEORGE SILK, LIFE © TIME, INC.

U.S. ARMY

In the Battle of the Bulge, the Germans' surprise counteroffensive of December, 1944, the GIs had to fight the weather as well as the enemy in Belgium's Ardennes Forest. At left above, a big gun moves up in heavy snow past one in a ditch. Above right and below: devastated Bastogne, where surrounded Americans refused to surrender and were finally rescued. At the end of the battle the Ardennes front stood nearly where it had been a month before.

ruined the French army, they did not bother to mention it.

At dawn on December 16, behind a massive artillery barrage, the Germans smashed into the VIII Corps's thin line. Outposts were overrun and armored probes quickly slid through weak spots and gaps. Middleton's men fought desperately, but the sheer weight of the assault drove them back. With foul weather preventing counterstrikes from the air, sixty-ton German Tiger tanks rumbled unhindered through sleepy Ardennes villages.

Late in the day, studying fragmentary reports from the front, Eisenhower concluded that this was no local

U.S. ARMY

spoiling attack as some of his officers believed. He ordered in reinforcements from both flanks of the breakthrough. It was now a question of time: whether the battered American line in the Ardennes could hang on until help arrived.

For some it was already too late. On the second day of the offensive most of an infantry division of newly arrived draftees was cut off, and 9,000 men were forced to surrender. Squads of English-speaking Germans, dressed in American uniforms and driving jeeps, spread confusion behind the lines. A battle group of SS (*Schutzstaffel,* "defense echelon") troops scored a breakthrough and ranged deep into the American rear. Capturing a convoy of artillerymen near the village of Malmedy, they disarmed their prisoners, marched them into an open field, and machine-gunned them. Eighty-six Americans died in this Malmedy massacre. If the beleaguered GIs needed any encouragement to stand and fight, news of the atrocity provided it.

The Germans had to seize the roads and bridges to the Ardennes quickly if they were to have any hope of reaching the Meuse River and the open country beyond. GI clerks and cooks and engineers, often armed just with bazookas, waged bitter fights for isolated crossroads and rustic bridges. Sometimes they were overrun quickly; sometimes they hung on long enough for a bridge to be blown or a crossroads village to be held a few hours longer. All they were winning was time, but time was what counted as the Allies brought up reinforcements.

The twin keys to the Ardennes road network were Saint Vith and Bastogne. Saint Vith, in the northern sector of the German bulge—almost by common consent the Americans began calling the struggle the Battle of the Bulge—was manned by a pick-up force of survivors from Middleton's VIII Corps and an armored division sent in from the northern flank. For five days Saint Vith held out against savage attacks, denying the enemy the roads they desperately needed. Finally the defenders were routed out, but they had so impeded the main thrust of the German drive that it no longer had any hope for a decisive breakthrough to Liege on the Meuse, the shortest route to Antwerp.

Bastogne commanded most of the roads in the central Ardennes, where the primary weight of the Nazi thrust now shifted, and both sides raced for it. The U.S. 101st Airborne Division, ordered up from a rest area where it was refitting after a battle at Arnhem in Holland, got to Bastogne first, thanks to delaying roadblocks thrown up by Middleton's men. But it was soon surrounded there.

To defend Bastogne, Brigadier General Tony McAuliffe had his paratroopers plus a mixed bag of stragglers blown loose from their commands and part of an armored division rushed in from the south. The Germans smashed at his perimeter from every point on the compass, but each time they were beaten back.

On December 22, under a flag of truce, a German officer arrived with a demand for surrender. The note was delivered to McAuliffe, who glanced at it, said, "Aw, nuts," and tossed it away. Reminded that he should make some formal response, he was stumped for an appropriate answer. "That first remark of yours would be hard to beat, General," one of his aides said. So the celebrated one-word message—"Nuts!"—was handed to the German officer. Perplexed, he asked if the reply was negative or affirmative. "If you don't understand what 'Nuts' means," he was told, "in plain English it's the same as 'Go to hell!' "

Only a statue appears intact in this view of once-lovely Dresden, which suffered the worst destruction ever visited upon a city. Allied bombing raids in February, 1945, created a great fire storm that killed 135,000 persons in scenes of apocalyptic horror.

203

An American and a Russian embrace after their units met at the Elbe River, accomplishing the final act in the conquest of Nazi Germany.

On Christmas Day the enemy launched its biggest assault yet on besieged Bastogne. It was a desperate struggle of bazookas and grenades, of tank charges and countercharges, of American paratrooper against German grenadier. When the firing at last dwindled away at dusk, the perimeter was still intact. The next afternoon a tank column from Patton's Third Army reached Bastogne. The siege was lifted.

That day, December 26, the German tide began to recede. The Saint Vith and Bastogne bottlenecks had crippled German attempts to supply and reinforce their spearheads, and in clearing weather Allied fighter-bombers came out in force to bomb and strafe.

The road back was brutally hard. Some of the most savage fighting of the entire battle took place in late December and early January, 1945, often in blizzards and waist-deep snow. Losses were extremely heavy on both sides, but relentlessly Hodges's First Army and Patton's Third Army constricted the Bulge from north and south. On January 16, they made contact, forming a solid front and flattening the Bulge.

The Battle of the Bulge was the U.S. Army's biggest single action of World War II: 600,000 men engaged; 800 tanks lost; 81,000 casualties, including 19,000 dead. German losses were at least 100,000. It was, Winston Churchill proclaimed, "undoubtedly the greatest American battle of the war and will, I believe, be regarded as an ever-famous American victory."

Hitler's gamble had failed utterly. He succeeded only in delaying a renewal of Eisenhower's offensive by perhaps six weeks—at a cost the Third Reich could not afford. When the Russians opened a winter offensive on January 12, and smashed through German lines thinned by the demands of the Ardennes counteroffensive, there were no reserves left to plug the holes. In two weeks, the Red Army advanced 220 miles.

In 1936, Hitler had trod the first step on his road to war by snatching up the Rhineland in violation of the Versailles Treaty; now, in February, 1945, the Western Allies were finally set to snatch it back. Eisenhower assigned the main weight of the offensive to Montgomery in the north. As soon as Bradley drew up to the Rhine farther south to keep the enemy divided and off balance, Montgomery's Twenty-first Army Group would launch a massive assault crossing of the great river, Germany's historic barrier to foreign enemies.

The Wehrmacht had few resources left to counter the new offensive, and the Allies' worst enemy was the weather. Under gray, dripping skies, American GIs and British Tommies slogged through mud and

Victorious Russians stand in the ruins of Berlin after their 10-day battle to capture the capital of Hitler's Reich.

204

Churchill, Roosevelt, and Stalin—architects of the Allied victory over the Nazis—planned the final attacks on Germany and Japan in February, 1945, during their meeting at Yalta in the Crimea. Stalin wanted to impose harsh peace terms on Germany in revenge for the brutality of the Germans who had invaded Russia, but Churchill and Roosevelt did not fully agree with this view. It was decided that East Prussia be divided between Russia and Poland, and that $20 billion might be exacted from Germany in reparations. Free elections were pledged for eastern Europe. Russia was promised the return of territory lost in her 1904-5 war with Japan, and agreed to enter the Pacific war within a few months after Germany surrendered.

flooded streams. With Hitler's rigid orders to stand and fight denying his troops maneuvering room, thousands were cut off. Patton and Hodges dispatched armored columns with orders to probe for cracks, wriggle through, and range deep into the enemy's rear areas. On March 7 a rampaging unit from Hodges's First Army pounced on the defenders of the Ludendorff Bridge spanning the Rhine at Remagen, and the GIs sprinted across to the east bank.

Although the terrain beyond Remagen was ill-suited for a major Allied drive, the establishment of a bridgehead there panicked the Germans. Frantic, fruitless counterattacks on Remagen further sapped their strength. Then came fresh disasters. On the night of March 22, Patton easily moved troops by assault boats across the Rhine at Oppenheim, and two days later Montgomery was also on the east bank. (Patton's glee at beating his arch-rival was undisguised; his surprise crossing cost but twenty casualties, while the careful Montgomery had mounted an operation that rivaled the Normandy invasion in complexity.) Having already lost 300,000 men in the Rhineland, the German command in the west was all but helpless.

The once-mighty Third Reich armies were now at bay between the Rhine and the Oder. Over 4 million Americans, Britons, Canadians, and Frenchmen on the Western Front, and a like number of Russians on the Eastern Front were poised for the final campaign.

The Wehrmacht was bloody and bowed, the Luftwaffe powerless to halt the rain of bombs from the Allied air forces. Factories and refineries were in ruins; railroads and bridges shattered. Devastated cities lay silent and smouldering, their citizens cowering in cellars and air raid shelters.

The newest such urban horror was Dresden. There was nothing of military significance in this lovely and historic city, and by early 1945 it was crammed to overflowing with refugees fleeing the advancing Russians. However, Churchill had just met with Roosevelt and Stalin at Yalta, and the idea prevailed among British leaders that destroying cities in eastern Germany would somehow aid the Red Army—which at this point needed no aid from anyone. The British strategic bombing planners added Dresden to their target list, and on February 13-14 it was gutted by two huge RAF night raids and an American daylight raid. An immense fire storm was set off, an explosive mountain of flame that created a typhoon-like wind to feed itself. Some victims were burned to cinders; others were found unmarked, suffocated when oxygen was sucked up by the fire storm. An estimated 135,000 persons died. In all history, no city—not even Hiroshima or Nagasaki—suffered so great a calamity.

The bizarre horror of Dresden is described by author John Toland: "The bombers watched in awe. . . . It was fantastic, unearthly; a shocking sight, with entire streets etched in fire. . . ." In the city "the fire roared like cannon, the wind shrieked, and the dust and smoke swirled furiously. . . . The roar of engines was shattering as the bombers passed overhead. Then there was abrupt silence except for the crackle of flames and the crash of falling walls. . . . People were staggering . . . faces black, hair burned off, clothes smoldering. They were clutching babies, suitcases, even incongruous things like pots and pans. A few moaned but the majority were unnaturally silent, star-

ing blankly with wide eyes. . . . Some who had tried to escape in between raids were caught in the open by bombs; others tried to find shelter inside the round metal advertising kiosks but were literally roasted to death."

At the Central Station, which had been only lightly damaged in the first raid, trains were loaded for evacuation, children having priority. Before the trains could leave the station, the second raid began. Incendiaries smashed through the glass roof and the station burst into flames. "Rescue workers fought their way into the fiery building," Toland writes. "Hundreds of people were slumped along the station walls as if asleep, but they had been suffocated by carbon monoxide. The children in the trains were found huddled in heaps; they too were dead. In the cellars where thousands had rushed for shelter, the floors were covered with lifeless bodies."

A million smaller horrors were taking place on the Eastern Front. As the Red Army crossed the German frontier, it embarked on an orgy of rape, murder, and pillage. German troops had visited a similar barbaric scourge on Russia early in the war, and writer-propagandists like Ilya Ehrenburg did not forget. "A pool of blood for a drop of blood!" he cried. "All the trenches, graves, and ravines filled with corpses of the innocents are advancing on Berlin. . . . Germany, you can whirl around in circles, and burn, and howl in your deathly agony; the hour of revenge has struck!"

The Russians advanced in the east like an implacable glacier, slowly grinding down the desperate German troops buying time for their civilian countrymen to flee. The push in the west was spectacularly rapid against often half-hearted opposition. On April 1 the great industrial area of the Ruhr was surrounded, trapping more than 300,000 German troops. American columns ranged deep into central Germany toward the Elbe, into southern Germany toward Austria and

Czechoslovakia. In Italy—the "forgotten front"—the long-suffering Allied army broke out of the mountains into the open Po Valley and drove rapidly northward.

These headlong advances uncovered the worst of all Nazi atrocities—the concentration camps. Some inmates greeted their liberators with hysterical joy. Others, the shriveled living dead, could only stare uncomprehendingly. In some camps the conquerors found only silent gas chambers and crematory ovens and great mounds of ashes and bones and neat bureaucratic balance sheets that calculated the profit exacted from a slave laborer right down to gold fillings and the "rational utilization of corpse."

And all the while, in his bunker under the *Reichskanzlei* (National Chancellery) in Berlin, Adolph Hitler continued to dispatch orders directing phantom armies to fight to the last breath. In his maddened dream world he plotted to hold out in Berlin for weeks and months until the Western powers quarreled with their Russian ally and joined him in his fight against bolshevism. At other times the mood in the bunker was apocalyptic. "When we step down," raged Propaganda Minister Joseph Goebbels, "let the whole earth tremble."

At the end of March, the most advanced Anglo-American army was 275 air miles from Berlin, while the Russians were but 30, and Eisenhower struck the German capital from his list of objectives. But in mid-April his hard-driving forces were only a twenty-four-hour march from Berlin. Pressure on him mounted to capture the city, but he refused on the grounds that the recent Yalta conference had established that Berlin would be in the postwar Russian occupation zone under joint Allied control. He saw no reason to risk lives to take a city that would only have to be evacuated at the war's end.

On April 11 leading elements of the U.S. Ninth Army reached the Elbe and halted as ordered. Three days later, Patton's spearheads were at the Czech frontier and Devers's Sixth Army Group was closing in on Nuremberg, the showplace of Nazism. More than 2 million Russian troops were about to weld an iron ring around Berlin.

The end was in sight, but Franklin Roosevelt was not to see it. Early on the afternoon of April 12, at his retreat in Warm Springs, Georgia, the President was struck down by a massive cerebral hemorrhage, and a little more than two hours later he was dead. Sixteen days later, a second major figure on the world stage, Benito Mussolini, met a more violent end. Captured by Italian partisans, the Sawdust Caesar was summarily executed and strung up by the heels with his mistress at a gas station in Milan, his corpse reviled and spat upon by the people to whom he had pledged a new Roman Empire. Then, on April 30, as his capital burned around him, Adolph Hitler sat down at a table in his quarters in the *Fuehrerbunker* and shot himself through the roof of the mouth. Henchmen carried the corpse into the *Reichskanzlei* garden and, as Russian shells exploded nearby, doused it with gasoline and burned it. Eva Braun, the mistress Hitler had married the previous day, took poison and died.

Five days earlier, American and Russian troops had met along the Elbe, and the German plan was to surrender as many troops as possible to the Americans to avoid becoming prisoners of the Russians. The news of Hitler's death accelerated wholesale surrenders to the Western Allies. At last Admiral Karl Doenitz, Hitler's successor as head of state, agreed to surrender unconditionally. On May 7, at Eisenhower's headquarters in a school building in Reims, the instrument of surrender was signed. The Supreme Commander signaled V-E (Victory in Europe) Day to the Combined Chiefs of Staff: "The mission of this Allied force was fulfilled at 0241, local time, May 7, 1945. Eisenhower."

Europe's agony was stilled at last.

Picture Portfolio
Artists to the World

Americans, it's been said, will tinker with anything but an abstract idea. It might better be said that Americans tinker their way into science and art. There was Jefferson, tinkering with plows and philosophy; Samuel Morse, at home with telegraphy and palette. Charles W. Peale was archeologist, revolutionary soldier, and artist. From our creative tradition has come a welding of technique and genius, producing such obviously American works as Jasper Johns's flags. Now American art is giving back to the world treasures as diverse as the people who have come flocking to our shores.

Tradition and Action

No longer meekly following, American art of the twentieth century has blazed its own, often controversial, trail for the world to follow. With realism, abstract expressionism, action painting, U.S. artists—since their international debut at the Brussels exposition in 1910—have influenced the work of artists everywhere.

DENNIS STOCK, MAGNUM

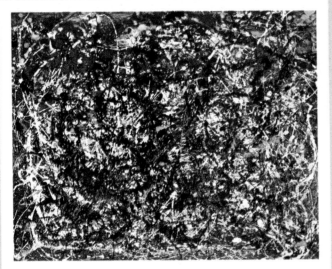

FRANK LERNER, LIFE © TIME, INC.

Gimmickry or art? Blacksmith or artist? Jackson Pollock, whose *Mural* (above) seems to vibrate, was action painting's prime practitioner. Alexander Calder, at home in Roxbury, Connecticut (right above), or Saché, France, gave the world kinetic sculpture with his whimsical mobiles.

DENNIS STOCK, MAGNUM

Andrew Wyeth, perhaps America's best known and best loved living artist, has been called a realist. But he says he is "pure abstractionist in my thought." Such categories matter little to those who see stern Yankee pride, touched with sentiment for the past, in his *The Patriot*.

Light and Shadow

Photography's practical magic entranced
Americans. Inventors supplied do-everything
cameras; the group "snap" became part of
every gathering. By 1920 men like Edward
Steichen were creating a new art. Steichen
made all photography, commercial or purely
creative, a step in pursuit of perfection.

Steichen died in 1973, nearing his hundredth birthday as America neared
the Bicentennial. Among his achievements was the enduring meaning of
the show he created for the Museum of Modern Art, "The Family of Man."

WAYNE MILLER, MAGNUM

EDWARD STEICHEN, MUSEUM OF MODERN ART

EDWARD STEICHEN, MUSEUM OF MODERN ART

Art student turned photographer,
Steichen explored the farthest reaches
of image-making on film. Each
picture—Garbo, a glowing tree,
spirals representing the universe—
makes a technical statement as well
as a comment on the passage of time.

LLOYD ARNOLD

The Rugged Hero

Every era has its heroes—and its troubadours who tell the heroes' stories. In this era the two fused in Ernest Hemingway. War correspondent and hunter, novelist and international personage, he sang his heroism. Loving life, he chose to meet death on his own terms, by his own hand.

PUBLIFOTO, BLACK STAR

Fascinated by the danger and tragedy of the *corrida* (above), he joined the amateurs at Pamplona and wrote of the bond between man and bull in *Death in the Afternoon*. "It is a strange feeling to have an animal come toward you consciously seeking to kill you, and see the oncoming of the lowered horn that he intends to kill you with."

GEORGE LEAVENS, LIFE © TIME INC.

Hemingway, who hated all pretense, scraped his writing to bare, clean truth. Achieving this style was "tough . . . but I love it more than anything." Challenged by brute strength, he went for the big fish off Cuba and for the big animals on African safari.

214

Jazz and the Blues

"I invented jazz in a barroom in New Orleans in 1910," Jelly Roll Morton liked to say. In fact, no one invented jazz. It grew, rooted in slavery, nurtured in New Orleans's red-light district. It went "upriver" to Chicago, to the world. Chicago added the piano and solos; New York brought in "big bands." And so it grew, and spread.

PETER SAMERJAN

The blues is a woman thing—Bessie Smith sang it in the '20s; today Ella Fitzgerald (right) tells life's sad story.

LEE BATTAGLIA

Jazz: good-time music from the tragedy of life. Bands played for dances and marched in funerals, taking a lost friend to the cemetery with dirges, leading the parade away, honoring him, wishing him well with a celebration of life. Bands march today (left), but they are few. The great Louis Armstrong (opposite) started with Kid Ory's New Orleans band. In 1922 "Satch," like many others, followed his music north, took it overseas. From Moscow to Australia, tumultuous, sometimes riotous, crowds greeted "their" Louis; for them he was jazz.

FRED FEHL

The Singing, Leaping Stage

Its folksy openness marks the musical as American, partly derived from those old river-boat "drammers" with mustached villains in black capes. Also American is its creative use of dance. Agnes de Mille's choreography moved easily from ballet stage to Rodgers and Hammerstein set.

Oklahoma! (below), Rodgers and Hammerstein's all-time great, was a loser, critics said. It lacked froth; had a killing. But its success opened a new avenue, one further explored by Leonard Bernstein in his American Romeo and Juliet, *West Side Story* (left).

As all living art, the musical continues to evolve. Leaving the simple stories of its early days, it tackled reality. Rodgers and Hammerstein followed *Oklahoma!* with an attack on prejudice in *South Pacific*. Serious social comment combined with beautiful songs in a modern genre made the off-Broadway rock musical *Hair* (above) an international success.

219

JOHN ENGSTEAD

PEDRO GUERRERO

Form and Function

Organic architecture never "outrages" the landscape, but, growing out of its surroundings, enhances them—a radical theory when Frank Lloyd Wright offered it. Turn-of-the-century designers of gargoyle and gingerbread sneered. Tenaciously, he stuck to his dictum that form and function are one. Today, no architecture remains untouched by his ideas.

Impatient with college courses, Wright went to Chicago and learned from skyscraper-builder Louis Sullivan. Still designing at 85 (top), his ideas remained young.

In building office towers or homes, Wright's inspiration came from nature. From trees he took the theory of cantilevering. In the Price tower in Bartlesville, Oklahoma (opposite) floors branch out from a central, cross-shaped pylon. For New York's Solomon Guggenheim Museum (left), Wright went to the spiral. Not floors, but a winding ramp divides the gallery's space. At his death in 1959, Wright's career had spanned nearly 70 years. He left to those who would study his principles the Frank Lloyd Wright School of Architecture (above), located in Arizona's desert.

LOUIS REENS

221

Hall of Nations

The American arts, at their best, glint with
the ingenuity, perseverance, and idealism of
pioneers who found a new shore and made it theirs.
More and more they are, like the Kennedy
Center, of America but for all the world.

LEE BATTAGLIA

PART THREE

A New Universe 1945-1976

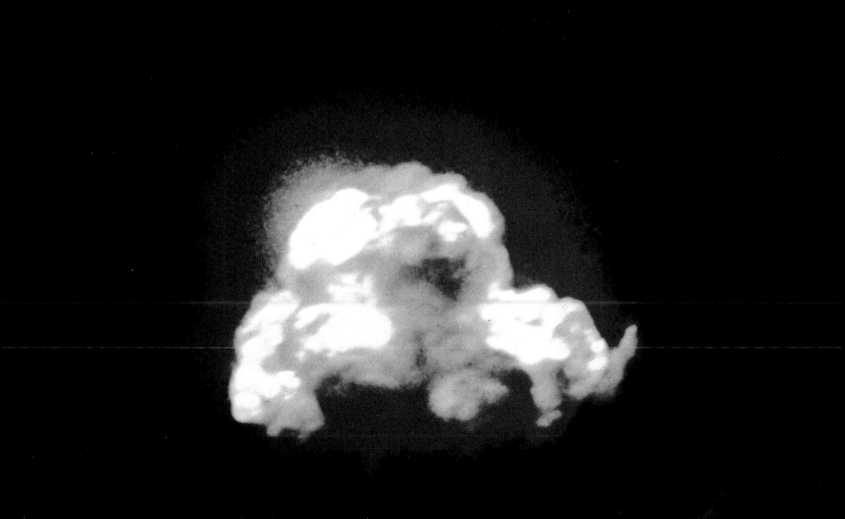

On July 16, 1945, the dawn came up like thunder at Alamogordo, New Mexico. "It was a sunrise such as the world had never seen," wrote William L. Laurence of the *New York Times,* "a great, green supersun . . . lighting up earth and sky with a dazzling luminosity." From a 100-foot tower the first atomic bomb exploded with the power of 20,000 tons of TNT. As Dr. J. Robert Oppenheimer, director of the Los Alamos atomic laboratory, watched the awesome blast, he recalled a line of Hindu scripture from the Bhagavad-Gita: "Now I am become death, destroyer of worlds."

Another observer, General Thomas F. Farrell, saw the dawn of a new era—the Age of Atomic Energy. "Atomic fission would no longer be hidden in the cloisters of the theoretical physicists' dreams," he stated. "It was almost full grown at birth. It was a great new force to be used for good or evil."

Word of the successful test was sent to President Harry S. Truman, meeting with Winston Churchill and Joseph Stalin in Potsdam, Germany, to decide Europe's future and Japan's fate. Upon Truman, who had not known about the development of the new weapon until after Roosevelt's death, fell the responsibility for using it in warfare. Actually the decision to drop the bomb on Japan had already been made by consensus of leading military, scientific, and political participants privy to the Manhattan (A-bomb) project. To its commanding general, Leslie R. Groves, Truman was "like a little boy on a toboggan." The President's role, Groves reasoned, "was one of non-interference—basically a decision not to upset the existing plans." Truman didn't.

Although Admiral William Leahy, chief of staff and Truman's principal military adviser, opposed nuclear

After Japan's Premier Suzuki scorned a surrender ultimatum as "unworthy," President Truman decided to drop the atomic bomb. Japanese aggression had already caused 300,000 U.S. casualties.

war, the prevailing opinion was that hitting Japan with the atomic bomb—Groves had predicted two would be required—should greatly shorten the war and thereby save lives. On Okinawa alone the United States had suffered 42,000 casualties, the Japanese twice that many. In the projected campaign to invade Japan, scheduled to begin in November, 1945, estimates of American casualties ranged to 750,000 or more. Japanese losses were expected to be in the millions. "To avoid a vast, indefinite butchery . . . at the cost of a few explosions," reflected Churchill, "seemed, after all our toils and perils, a miracle of deliverance."

This had been the pragmatists' view all along; but, to a group of atomic scientists in Chicago, it was dangerously narrow thinking. A month before the Alamogordo test, they drafted a report stating that "the military advantages and the saving of American lives achieved by the sudden use of atomic bombs against Japan may be outweighed by the ensuing loss of confidence and by a wave of horror and repulsion sweeping over the rest of the world. . . . A demonstration of the new weapon might best be made, before the eyes of all the United Nations, on the desert or a barren island." The report was intended for Secretary of War Henry Stimson; if he received it, he never read it. Even if he had, it would not have changed the course of events for, as he said a year later: "Nothing would have been more damaging to our effort to obtain surrender than a warning or a demonstration followed by a dud. . . . Furthermore, we had no bombs to waste." There were, in fact, only two completed bombs after the Alamogordo test.

The programmed decision to use them on Japanese cities was apparently inexorable and inviolate. Nothing short of presidential intervention or unconditional surrender by the Japanese could halt the momentum. Ironically, a few days before the Potsdam conference, Japan, oblivious to Russia's imminent invasion of Man-

A Kamikaze pilot in a flaming Zero (above) just misses the *Hornet* as crewmen scatter in combat artist Dwight Shepler's painting of fierce action at war's end. The first carrier *Hornet* had been scrubbed in the 1942 Battle of Santa Cruz. Nagasaki, blasted by nuclear fury (below), raises but a few chimneys above its scarred landscape. When viewing the 40,000-ft. mushroom shaped cloud that rose above Hiroshima after the preceding nuclear explosion, the co-pilot of the *Enola Gay* asked, ''My God, what have we done?''

Japan's Fiery End

Peace came to the Pacific only after both sides had resorted to desperate measures. The Japanese—so exhausted of matériel that bamboo spears were issued to some army units—intensified training of Kamikaze or suicide pilots. Against the U.S. attack force at Okinawa (only 325 miles from Japan) the Kamikazes took a toll of some 5,000 American sailors and 130 ships. Yet Okinawa fell, and the belligerents girded for a mutually disastrous invasion of Japan's home islands—an invasion which never came. Instead, two atom bombs, dropped in August, 1945 (annihilating more than 140,000 in Hiroshima and Nagasaki), swiftly brought the Japanese military leaders to the Missouri's deck (below). There they signed surrender documents before General MacArthur on September 2, 1945.

Marines flush a wounded civilian out of his hiding place on Okinawa—the last and largest U.S. amphibious operation of World War II.

churia, sought to enlist the Soviet Union as mediator to end the war. Having broken the Japanese code, the United States quickly learned of the overtures for negotiations but, rigidly committed to the policy of demanding unconditional surrender, did nothing to exploit them.

On July 26, an ultimatum from the United States, Great Britain, and China demanded that Japan surrender unconditionally or face "prompt and utter destruction." That the ultimatum would be flatly rejected was anticipated, for on the previous day the air force had been ordered to "deliver its first special bomb as soon as weather will permit visual bombing after about 3 August, 1945." With that order, Truman recalled, "The wheels were set in motion for the first use of an atomic weapon. I had made the decision."

As Japan had given no warning on December 7, 1941, when Pearl Harbor was attacked, it would receive none on August 6, 1945. That sun-drenched morning the B-29 *Enola Gay*, named after pilot Paul Tibbets's mother, dropped the bomb on the industrial city of Hiroshima. It exploded 1,800 feet above the ground in a blinding flash that pierced the airmen's dark goggles. Shock waves rocked the plane. A huge "bubbling mass of purple-gray smoke" with a fiery red core mushroomed high into the sky. One crew member looking down on the city said it resembled "a cauldron of boiling black oil." The pilot reported later: "As far as I was concerned it was a perfect operation."

More than 70,000 people died in the blast and about the same number were injured, many of them dying years later from the effects of radiation. Investigators from Tokyo flew over Hiroshima two days after the explosion and found "but one black dead tree, as if a crow was perched on it. . . . The city itself was completely wiped out."

U.S. policy, as Secretary of the Navy James Forrestal understood it, was "to get the Japanese affair

over with before the Russians got in." But Stalin, eager to be in on the kill—and the spoils—struck first. Just after midnight of August 8, he sent the Red Army into Manchuria. Only hours later the B-29 *Bock's Car*, piloted by Major Charles Sweeney, took off from Tinian in the Marianas. Aboard was a plutonium bomb earmarked for Kokura. Smoke and clouds obscured the city, forcing Sweeney to head for Nagasaki, the secondary target. It was overcast there too, but at 11 A.M. he "found a hole in the cloud and let go." Nearly 40,000 people were killed by the bomb.

At the moment the bomb exploded, Japanese leaders in Tokyo were debating terms on which to surrender. The Nagasaki bomb and the threat of more to come convinced a majority of them to accept the Potsdam declaration, with the proviso that the emperor would be retained as the sovereign. This was granted, and after an abortive coup by die-hard militarists, Emperor Hirohito announced to his people that Japan had surrendered.

On September 2 the formal documents were signed aboard the battleship *Missouri* in Tokyo Bay. After the ceremony General Douglas MacArthur pro-

Guarded by MPs and flanked by Allied judges, remnants of the Nazi command listen to the Nuremberg proceedings. War criminals Hitler, Goebbels, and Himmler had already committed suicide. Goering (writing at far left opposite) poisoned himself an hour before his Nuremberg sentence— death by hanging—could be executed.

claimed: "A new era is upon us. . . . The destructiveness of the war potential, through progressive advances in scientific discovery, has in fact now reached a point which revises the traditional concept of war. . . . If we do not now devise some greater and more equitable system, Armageddon will be at our door."

The best—if not the only—hope for world peace seemed to lie in the newly chartered United Nations, the "town meeting of the world," as Senator Arthur Vandenberg characterized it. At the first meeting of the UN General Assembly in 1946, a committee to control atomic energy was created. Before that international forum Bernard Baruch, representing the United States, said its business was "to make a choice between the quick and the dead. . . . Behind the black portent of the new atomic age lies a hope which, seized upon with faith, can work our salvation. If we

fail, then we have damned every man to be the slave of fear. Let us not deceive ourselves: We must elect world peace or world destruction."

His plan for peace would prohibit the manufacture of atomic bombs, destroy existing bombs, and place all atomic energy data under UN authority. This authority would exercise control over development and usage, safeguard against violations by inspections and penalties, and be exempted from the great power veto. Having a monopoly on atomic power—at least temporarily—and theoretically capable of holding the entire world hostage, the United States had made what seemed to nearly all Americans a magnanimous proposal.

A few days later Soviet delegate Andrei Gromyko offered a counterproposal. He outlined a plan to outlaw production and application of atomic bombs and

At least 5,700,000 European Jews died at the hands of Germany's Nazi lords—a fact of Western culture that haunted the peace-makers. How could they make it be remembered? At right, Germans, nudged by U.S. medics, observe corpses of Jewish women who starved during 300-mile forced march.

On entering Germany in 1945 U.S. soldiers discovered the horrors of Buchenwald, Dachau, Bergen-Belsen; Russians found starvation and death at Auschwitz (left) and Lublin-Maidanek. Against such outrages the victors sought to create a new international system that would be stronger than the 1920s' League of Nations.

While President Truman beams, Secretary of State Edward Stettinius signs the UN charter for the U.S. in June, 1945 (left). Truman went on to lead the nation during the "cold war" which the UN failed to thaw.

UPI

to provide "the setting up of a system of supervision and control to see that the conventions and agreements are observed." But the proposal was toothless; it contained no machinery for international inspection; nor did it waive the veto power, crucial to enforcement of atomic controls.

Unable to reach a compromise, the UN atomic commission left the bomb dangling over a fearful world. The U.S. resumed tests, in a few years developing the even more deadly hydrogen bomb. Russia accelerated her atomic timetable through espionage, notably by Klaus Fuchs, a British scientist who worked at Los Alamos. In 1949 the Soviets exploded their first atomic bomb. Within a decade both countries would possess the power to destroy all mankind. The arms race triggered a war of nerves or, as Baruch dubbed it, "a cold war."

Churchill, in a speech at Fulton, Missouri, in March of 1946, early defined the demarcation of power in Europe: "From Stettin in the Baltic to Trieste in the Adriatic, an iron curtain has descended across the continent. Behind that line lie all the capitals of the ancient states of central and eastern Europe . . . subject, in one form or another, not only to Soviet influence but to a very high and increasing measure of control from Moscow. Athens alone . . . is free to decide its future."

A year later not even Athens seemed safe. Britain, strapped economically, announced she would have to discontinue aid to Greece and Turkey. Stepping into the breach, Truman, in what he termed "the turning point in American foreign policy," asked a joint session of Congress to approve his request for assistance to the beleaguered countries. "I believe," he declared, "that it must be the policy of the United States to support free peoples who are resisting attempted subjugation by armed minorities or by outside pressure." That support, he said, though primarily economic, would include "American civilian and military personnel

230

"Don't mind me—just go right on talking," says the A-bomb to the UN diplomats in the cartoon at right. The veto, held by the "big five" on the Security Council, ruled out action on many crucial issues.

FROM *THE HERBLOCK BOOK* (BEACON PRESS, 1952)

... to assist in the tasks of reconstruction" in the ruins.

From new ground broken by this Truman Doctrine, as it came to be known, sprang two developments in foreign affairs of far-reaching significance. The first was the vast European reconstruction program enunciated by Secretary of State George C. Marshall: "Our policy is directed not against any country or doctrine but against hunger, poverty, desperation, and chaos. Its purpose should be the revival of a working economy in the world so as to permit the emergence of political and social conditions in which free institutions can exist." The United States ultimately pumped into the Marshall Plan some $12 billion in aid. By 1951 a Europe once on the brink of famine and bankruptcy had surpassed wartime levels of production.

The second development in foreign policy was the formation of a military alliance between the United States, Canada, and the countries of Western Europe to resist Russian aggression. Backed by American money and arms, this North Atlantic Treaty Organization (NATO) stipulated that an attack against any member country would be considered an attack against all. An "offensive-defensive alliance to maintain the peace," the treaty, Truman hoped, "would serve to prevent World War III."

Despite NATO, tensions continued to mount, the Communist coup in Czechoslovakia and Russia's blockade of Berlin shrouding 1948 with forebodings of doom. General Lucius Clay declared that the Western powers would not be driven out of Berlin "by any action short of war." The British foreign minister said Britain was prepared to fight. But rather than risk war

by sending in supplies by armed convoy, the United States and Britain resorted to a massive airlift that, after almost a year, broke the Russian will to continue the blockade.

While transports were flying around the clock into Berlin, President Truman was crisscrossing the United States by train in a whistle-stop election campaign that spanned more than 30,000 miles. Inflation, low farm prices, crippling strikes—which he blamed on the Republican-dominated Eightieth Congress—plagued his bid for election. Delegates at the Democratic convention, unable to persuade General Eisenhower to seek the presidential nomination, sported campaign badges that read, "We're just mild about Harry."

The entire country seemed to be mild about Harry, even after he won the nomination. Thomas E. Dewey of New York, the Republican nominee, led public opinion polls by up to 15 percent. That didn't bother Truman. Sensing grass-roots support responding to his

On Manhattan's East Side (opposite) the UN opened the doors of its permanent home in 1950 after five years of temporary lodging on Long Island. Eleanor Roosevelt, a member of the first U.S. delegation, is seen at right conferring with two who would play major roles as U.S. foreign policy sought to contain communism: Adlai Stevenson, later ambassador to the UN, and John Foster Dulles, adviser to Truman and eventually Eisenhower's secretary of state.

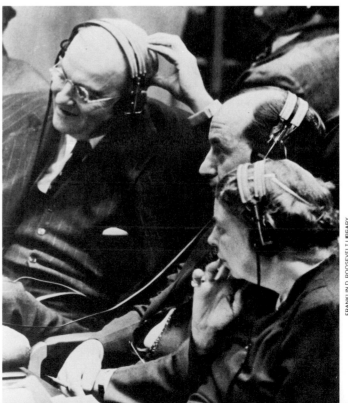

off-the-cuff oratory, he lashed into the "do-nothing" Congress. The crowds loved it. While Truman gave them hell—in as many as sixteen speeches a day—Dewey mouthed such platitudes as, "Our future lies before us."

"DEWEY DEFEATS TRUMAN" bannered an early edition of the *Chicago Daily Tribune* on election night. *Life* carried a picture of the "next President"—Dewey. Syndicated columnists, anticipating what seemed inevitable, filed election-day stories on the Republican victory. When all the returns were counted Truman had 2 million more popular votes and 114 more electoral votes than Dewey. The President had pulled off the biggest political upset of American history.

Truman's 1949 State of the Union message proclaimed that "every segment of our economy and every individual have a right to expect from our government a fair deal." An extension of Franklin Roosevelt's New Deal and anticipatory of Lyndon Johnson's Great Society, the Fair Deal called for an increased minimum wage, farm price supports, federal aid to schools, low-cost housing, slum clearance, compulsory health insurance, increased social security benefits for the aged, civil rights for Negroes, and repeal of the Taft-Hartley Act—the "slave-labor act" to union leaders.

Though the Eighty-first Congress boasted a Democratic majority, it was, through coalitions of Republicans and southern Democrats, almost as "do-nothing" as the Eightieth. Civil rights bills died in committee. Health insurance, stigmatized as socialized medicine by American Medical Association lobbyists, was stifled. Taft-Hartley survived unscathed.

Truman fared better in securing foreign-aid legislation. Congress approved funding the so-called Point Four program, the fourth point of foreign policy recommendations outlined in Truman's inaugural address. Forerunner of the Peace Corps, it called for "making the benefits of our scientific advances and industrial progress" available to underdeveloped areas in Africa, South America, and Asia.

One area, however, in which Truman and Secretary of State Dean Acheson thought United States aid should be suspended was Nationalist China. Driven from the mainland in late 1949 by Mao Tse-tung's Chinese Communists, the Nationalists were confined to the island of Formosa. There the Chiang Kai-shek regime, past beneficiary of some $2 billion in American assistance, learned—as Truman stated in January, 1950—that the United States "will not pursue a course which will lead to involvement in the civil conflict in China." A week later Acheson indicated that Formosa—and also Korea—lay outside the "defense perimeter"

Milk flies into Berlin by means of the airlift. During "Operation Vittles," the Americans delivered up to 7,000 tons of supplies a day.

Amid ruins of World War II, Berliners watch an American C-47 arrive at Tempelhof Airport in 1948. They and the rest of the anxious world wondered if this confrontation with the Russians—who had determined to shut off western access routes and bring all Berlin under Communist control—would cause another war of even greater destruction. Two giants faced each other head-on.

the United States felt it was necessary to defend.

The administration's position brought howls of protest from the press and some members of Congress. Senator Joseph McCarthy projected himself into national prominence by seizing upon the China issue. He also tackled Alger Hiss, a former State Department official accused of passing government documents in the 1930s to Whittaker Chambers, a former Communist. The State Department, McCarthy claimed, was "thoroughly infested with Communists." He denounced Acheson as a traitor for expressing moral support of Hiss. McCarthy branded Acheson and his predecessor, Marshall, "executioners" of the Chinese Nationalists. Although a Senate subcommittee in 1950 found the charges "a fraud and a hoax," McCarthyism continued to flourish.

That year was the most trying of Truman's presidency. Korea exploded on June 25, 1950, when North Korean Communist troops supported by Russian-built tanks invaded South Korea. They captured Seoul, the capital, and threatened to overrun everything below the thirty-eighth parallel, the demarcation line drawn near the end of World War II. "If this was allowed to go unchallenged it would mean a third world war," Truman feared. He acted quickly, requesting a special session of the UN Security Council and ordering General Douglas MacArthur to speed air and naval support to South Korea.

The Security Council, with Russia absent because of its opposition to membership for Nationalist China, voted unanimously to condemn the North Korean aggression and called upon all member nations "to render every assistance" to the UN resolution.

Coming less than five years after the atomic bomb put an end to World War II, the fighting in Korea was to be our first limited modern war, the first in which the combatants would have to accept a "no-win" policy for fear of starting World War III and a nuclear holocaust. Those who had lived through World War II were so fed up with war, both hot and cold, that the Korean clash was not called a war: it was officially designated a "police action" or a "conflict." Whatever

it was called by the politicians and other civilians, the men who fought in it called it hell.

The blood of 2 million dead and wounded men from eighteen countries soaked the rugged mountains and valleys of the primitive land during three years of fierce fighting that finally ended where it had begun—a "no-win" for sure. The U.S. supplied 33 percent of the UN forces; South Korea, 61 percent.

The Korean War was fought for the most part with the weapons of World War II. American infantry used the M-1 rifle, the .30-caliber carbine, the .45 pistol, the Browning automatic rifle, and the bazooka. The Sherman tank, workhorse of World War II, was the main battle tank in Korea after being fitted with a new 76-mm. gun. The United States provided 90 percent of the munitions used by the UN forces, and the Russians delivered most of the Communist weapons. The Russian equipment was of simple design and easy to maintain, making it more suitable for use by peasant armies than the more complicated American arms.

The first UN troops put into the grinder were Americans who had been living easy as occupation forces in Japan. They were soft, in no shape for the hard conditions they would find in Korea. Another minus was that they had been trained to fight in an unbroken battle line. When the enemy separated them by thrusts into the American lines during the first weeks, the GIs frequently panicked and fled through the steaming rice paddies. But by August the Americans had toughened enough to set up a defense perimeter around the port of Pusan at the southern end of the peninsula, and General Walton Walker gave them the hard words: "There will be no more retreating, withdrawal, or . . . anything else you want to call it." It was the unbroken battle line the Americans had been trained to hold, and they held it.

In those six weeks of the "conflict" the Americans had suffered 6,000 casualties, the South Koreans 70,000. After fresh troops arrived from the United States, the North Korean advance was halted and it was the UN forces' turn to take the offensive. MacArthur decided to launch a bold amphibious assault far behind the North Korean lines. "We shall land at Inchon and I shall crush them," he announced. And he did. The landings at Inchon enabled Seoul to be retaken. A few days later American and South Korean soldiers reached the thirty-eighth parallel.

Although the South Koreans and the Americans shouldered the heaviest burden in the war, the other UN forces were highly thought of, each country having sent its best battalion or regiment to Korea. The Turks and the Ethiopians, particularly, won respect from both friend and foe for their fighting ability, and the British occasioned some awe by wearing berets instead of the helmets the other troops would not part with.

In early October, Chou En-lai, premier of Communist China, stated his country's policy to the Indian ambassador in Peking: "The South Koreans did not matter, but American intrusion into North Korea would encounter Chinese resistance." The warning was ignored. On October 7, the UN General Assembly, with the Soviet bloc opposed, passed a resolution sanctioning the invasion of North Korea for the purpose of establishing a "unified, independent, and democratic government." The action was not unexpected. A week earlier MacArthur had been authorized by the U.S. Joint Chiefs of Staff "to conduct military operations north of the thirty-eighth parallel," though "under no circumstances" were non-Korean forces to be used "in the areas along the Manchurian border." On October 1, MacArthur demanded that North Korea "cease hostilities." Receiving no reply, he sent the U.S. Eighth Army toward Pyongyang, the capital of North Korea (which fell October 19), while South Korean troops stormed up the east coast to seize the port of Wonsan.

On October 15, MacArthur was summoned to Wake

Demagogue Senator Joseph McCarthy accused the Democrats of ''twenty years of treason'' in which they ''conspired to deliver America to the Reds.'' At left he points to map of Communist organization; at right he hushes mikes while conferring with brash aide Roy Cohn.

Island for a meeting with Truman. "What are the chances for Chinese or Soviet interference?" Truman asked. "Very little," replied MacArthur, ". . . if the Chinese tried to get down to Pyongyang, there would be the greatest slaughter."

South Korean troops dashed northward vowing, "We will not stop until we bathe our sabers in the Yalu River," the North Korean-Manchurian border. In Tokyo, MacArthur confidently told a press conference: "The war is definitely coming to an end shortly." On October 24 he commanded his officers to "drive forward with all speed and full utilization of their forces." When the Joint Chiefs questioned this apparent violation of orders forbidding use of non-Korean troops in border areas, MacArthur cabled it was "a matter of military necessity."

Thus began the general's feud with the administration on how to run the war. When the presence of Chinese Communist troops became increasingly evident in North Korea and fighter planes darted across the border, MacArthur advocated retaliatory strikes and "hot pursuit" into Manchuria. Washington relented only to the extent that he could bomb the Korean side of Yalu bridges—"the most indefensible and ill-conceived decision ever forced on a field commander in our nation's history," in MacArthur's view, and in the view of many Americans who feared the rest of Asia would fall to the Communists as China had done.

Truman's position was, "If we had gone ahead and bombed the Manchurian bases, we would have been openly at war with Red China and, not improbably,

Even with Republicans in office, McCarthy would not let up; he implied that President Eisenhower himself was ''soft on communism.'' In the notorious Army-McCarthy hearings of 1954—best TV show of the decade—the administration fought back by means of witty counsel Joseph Welch (at microphone at left). Finally, after the Senate censured him by an emphatic vote, McCarthy collapsed (right).

With the USSR seat empty (left), the UN Security Council votes on June 27, 1950, to send troops to stop the Communist invasion of South Korea. Thus for the first time in history, a world body agreed to "repel armed attack and to restore international peace and security."

UPI

with Russia, World War III might very well have been on."

A man under fire from all sides—in a very real sense on November 1, when two fanatic Puerto Rican nationalists tried to shoot their way into Blair House, where the President was napping—Truman had to contend with Soviet threats in Europe, French demands for U.S. involvement in Indochina, and Republican criticism for plunging the country into war without a congressional declaration. Republican Senator Robert Taft charged that Truman's decision to commit American troops to combat in Korea "usurped the power of Congress."

The day after Thanksgiving, MacArthur issued a communiqué announcing that the "United Nations massive compression envelopment in North Korea against the new Red armies operating there is now approaching its decisive effort." Behind the heaviest artillery barrage of the war, the Eighth Army struck out for the Yalu. Two days later Chinese Communists, bugles blowing, cymbals clanging, swarmed down from high ridges and cut the scattered Eighth Army to ribbons. In sub-zero cold, ill-clad marines fought and fell back. South Korean units were annihilated. Writing of the decimation of the U.S. Second Division at this time, S.L.A. Marshall says:

> At Valley Forge, in the birth struggle of a nation, but 3,000 of 7,000 Continentals died or faded from the force in one terrible winter. In round figures, the wasting away of the 2nd Division and its attachments is roughly comparable. But it all happened in one day. . . .
> That was on December 1. By Christmas Day, 2nd Division was again a going concern, en route to a new battlefield.

Our aerial reconnaissance failed to detect the Chinese movement into Korea because they hid by day

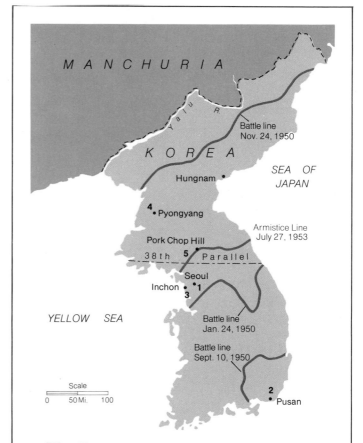

The Korean War 1950–1953

With the backing of most Americans, President Truman committed limited U.S. forces to help the UN halt the Moscow-ordered invasion of South Korea in June, 1950. Sweeping down from the 38th parallel, the North Koreans captured the southern capital, Seoul (1), and soon hemmed in UN contingents at Pusan (2). But, after executing a brilliant amphibious counter-thrust on Inchon (3), UN units recaptured Seoul and went on to take the northern capital, Pyongyang (4) in October, 1950. Yet as the UN armies pressed north toward the Yalu, enjoying complete air superiority, they fell into a trap: strengthened by Chinese might, the Communists surged south and recaptured Seoul in March, 1951. It took the UN team two more weary years to reclaim Seoul, to win such costly battles as Pork Chop Hill (5), and to dig in north of the 38th parallel.

Chinese forces beyond the Yalu (left) were feared as Asia's best. Tough and battle-hardened, they marshalled a variety of captured Japanese and Russian-supplied arms.

American marines helped hold the critical Pusan perimeter (map opposite) and thus save Korea from the first swift Communist attack. Marines in the David Douglas Duncan photograph above cross a rice paddy under fire, a fallen North Korean in their path.

and marched by night. And how they did march! Three of their divisions walked 286 miles from Antung in Manchuria to their assembly area in the North Korean combat zone in a period of sixteen to nineteen days. General Walton Walker, Eighth Army commander, estimated that the Chinese had thrown 200,000 men into the attack. It was, as MacArthur stated, "an entirely new war."

The Chinese "volunteers" wore clothing of padded, quilted cotton. They wore no underwear and no socks; they wrapped rags around their feet before putting on their sneakers. According to the Americans who fought them, the Chinese soldiers were "strong as oxen," carrying all their provisions on A-frames on their backs, even while scaling and descending Korea's ridges. Each of them had in his pockets three days' rations— cooked rice wrapped in seaweed or boiled leaves. Their only medical supplies were vials of morphine.

Sometimes the Chinese would attack in waves. The first wave consisted of human pack animals, carrying ammunition and grenades. The second was armed with rifles. A green flare was the signal to attack. According to an American captain, "As we shoot the first attack waves down, a third wave from behind—at the outset armed only with grenades—now picks up their rifles and automatic weapons and moves on in." An American officer noted they "fight in a way which seems fanatical to us. We crawl on our bellies to take a machine-gun post" but they "go head on into a machine-gun position" because their "value of life is low. Our boys would mow down twenty or thirty of them before one Chinese finally reached it, killed off our men with a grenade, and took the weapon."

An officer who flew over the front found that the Chinese "camouflage is perfect. . . . From the air you can spot an American outfit ten miles away but, even when I knew I was right over the Chinese, you couldn't see them." Because of their excellent camouflage, the

237

Hunched against the spray, marines move in toward the Inchon beachhead at dusk on September 15, 1950 (opposite). The war's most desperate phase was the U.S. Army's winter retreat south from the Yalu (right) after 300,000 Chinese "volunteers" attacked in irresistible strength. Both sides practiced psychological warfare; one of Gen. MacArthur's appeals to the enemy appears below.

DAVID DOUGLAS DUNCAN

Chinese were able to stage surprise attacks, pouring out of apparently empty hills in trotting columns.

Weapons used by the Chinese included new rifles abandoned by our forces during their retreats as well as Mausers dating from the twenties and thirties when Germans had been hired to train the Chinese army. But "the worst thing they have," according to many who fought them, was the Soviet burp gun, which held seventy-five rounds: "They can clip a couple of ammunition drums on its bottom—br-r-r-r-rp! —and in a minute the damned thing is empty!" What it lacked in accuracy of aim, it more than made up in fire power: "At any range short of 20 yards it is unexcelled. If one of its quick shower of slugs doesn't get you, another will."

A huge new Chinese offensive began New Year's Day. The U.S. Eighth Army fell back to positions some seventy miles below the thirty-eighth parallel, again abandoning Seoul to the Communists. Criticized for miscalculating Chinese strength and intent, MacArthur lashed back at the administration for making him fight a limited war. If he could have his way, he wrote the Joint Chiefs, he would blockade the coast of China, destroy the Communists' industrial capacity to wage war, reinforce his army with troops from Formosa, and have Chiang Kaishek's Nationalists make a diversionary landing on the mainland. "If I were still not permitted to attack the massed enemy reinforcements across the Yalu," he threatened, ". . . I would sever Korea from Manchuria by laying a field of radioactive wastes . . . across the major lines of enemy supply."

The Joint Chiefs, according to General Omar Bradley, felt that MacArthur proposed to wage "the wrong war, at the wrong place, at the wrong time, and with

U.S. ARMY

the wrong enemy." Denied all of his proposed options, MacArthur sent the Eighth Army back up the peninsula against weakened resistance. Seoul was recaptured March 15. Five days later the Joint Chiefs dampened any new desires he might have had for the Yalu by informing him of UN preparations "to discuss conditions of settlement in Korea." Venturing north of the thirty-eighth parallel was not advised. MacArthur responded, at least indirectly, in answering House minority leader Joe Martin's request for his views on foreign policy. Taking a jab at the administration, the general wrote, "It seems strangely difficult for some to realize that here in Asia is where the Communist conspirators have elected to make their play for global conquest. . . . There is no substitute for victory."

The letter, released by Martin to the press, and a public statement by MacArthur that a lifting of restrictions by the UN "would doom Red China" ended Truman's patience. "In effect, what MacArthur was doing was to threaten the enemy with an ultimatum," Truman concluded. "I could no longer tolerate his insubordination." On April 11 he relieved MacArthur of command.

This caused a furor in the United States. MacArthur's admirers—and there were many—lowered Old Glory to half-mast. There was talk in the Senate of impeaching Truman. Senator Richard M. Nixon demanded that MacArthur be immediately reinstated. Senator Joseph McCarthy called the President "an s.o.b. who decided to remove MacArthur when drunk." The results of a Gallup poll showed that the public favored MacArthur against Truman 69 to 29. MacArthur returned to the United States and was wildly greeted.

239

He addressed Congress and drew tears when he quoted an old army song saying, "Old soldiers never die, they just fade away."

Negotiations for an armistice began on July 10, 1951, and dragged on until it was finally signed on July 27, 1953, while men continued to kill each other for the ravaged earth of Korea. What prolonged the peace talks was the issue of repatriation of prisoners. The UN forces were holding more than 70,000 prisoners, and the Communists demanded that all return, but most of them did not want to return. They finally were allowed to choose their fate, and three-fourths of them chose to remain in South Korea.

GIs served in Korea under a points system. A man could go home—rotate—when he got thirty-six points. Those fighting on the line got four points a month; those anywhere in the combat zone as far back as regimental headquarters got three; and those anywhere else in Korea got two. Under this system the average infantryman knew he had a year to sweat out, and this kept his spirits up, since it was not an open-ended deal as in World War II. The points system also

Recognizing Gen. MacArthur's leadership of UN forces in Korea, President Truman gave him the Distinguished Service Medal at Wake Island in October, 1950 (above). But as the war progressed, MacArthur urged more aggressive policies toward the Red Chinese. In this "Great Debate," Truman replied, "We are trying to prevent a third world war." In April, 1951, he removed MacArthur from command, to the displeasure of John Q. Public (right).

Candidate Dwight Eisenhower proposed in his 1952 campaign that he would go to Korea and seek settlement to the drawn-out war. True to his word, President-elect Eisenhower— back in uniform—shares chow with GIs in Korea before Christmas, 1952.

MICHAEL ROUGIER, LIFE © TIME, INC.

had the effect of filling the war zone with reservists, national guardsmen, and draftees. Many of the officers were "retreads" who had served in World War II. Settled married men with children, they had been recalled to service from their civilian jobs and were trying to get through their second war alive. The worst result of the Big R—rotation—was that it replaced men who had learned the answers in Korea with men who were green. S.L.A. Marshall recalls that when he arrived in Korea in 1953 a few months before the war ended:

> I began to hear pessimistic reports about how gravely our musical-chairs rotation policy had downgraded the fighting spirit of the average young American in the combat line. Worried senior officers expressed the view that if the war's pace changed and the pressure rose suddenly, troops might be found lacking in the old drive and guts. Line captains told me that morale had so far deteriorated that when units came under full attack more men died from taking refuge in the bunkers than from fighting.

And then he found after the battle for Pork Chop Hill:

> The in-fighting which took place in the entrenched works of the outposts was as hard-pressed and bloody as Cold Harbor, Attu, or the Argonne. The Americans won, not simply by the superior weight of their artillery, but because the infantry, man for man in the hand-to-hand battle, outgamed the Red Chinese.
>
> In two vital particulars these Americans outshone any of our troops with whom I have ever dealt: there was a superior command presence in their young officers, and a higher ratio of enlisted men exercised strong initiative in the most dangerous moments.
>
> The one manifest weakness in our youngsters was in their leg muscles and not in their fighting spirit.

The battle for Pork Chop—"a contemptible hill, ill-formed for all-around defense and too loosely tied in to the supporting neighborhood"—was primarily an artillery duel won by the American guns. Marshall says the artillery fire reached a rate greater than at Verdun or Kwajalein—World War's II "most intense shoot." Pork Chop set "the all-time mark for artillery effort" with over 115,000 rounds expended in two days.

The Korean War was generally unpopular with the American people. Many felt it was "better to fight the Commies in Korea now than in our own backyards later," but others could raise no enthusiasm for a crusade against Communist aggressors in a far-off land. One of the aspects of the war that helped to make it unpopular was the use by the Communists of a technique that came to be known as "brainwashing." While some American prisoners were able to withstand the physical and mental torment, others broke and collaborated with their captors.

Seventy-eight captured American airmen were subjected to psychological and physical torture in 1952 to make them confess to having waged germ warfare against North Korea, and thirty-eight of them did so. After the germ warfare charges were unsuccessfully brought to the United Nations, the U.S. delegate, Dr. Charles Mayo, described the brainwashing technique:

> The total picture presented is one of human beings reduced to a status lower than that of animals, filthy, full of lice, festered wounds full of maggots, their sickness regulated to a point just short of death, unshaven, without haircuts or baths for as much as a year, men in rags, exposed to the elements, fed with carefully measured minimum quantities and the lowest quality of food and unsanitary water served often in rusty cans, isolated, faced with squads of trained interrogators, bulldozed, deprived of sleep, and browbeaten with mental anguish.

In April, 1953, the two sides exchanged sick and

wounded prisoners in Operation Little Switch. The UN forces handed over 6,670 and the Communists returned 684, among them 149 Americans. The freed Americans brought with them the shocking story that some American prisoners had been cooperating with their captors. When Operation Big Switch—the exchange of prisoners after the armistice—took place three months later, details of these allegations became known. The 3,597 Americans who were released provided evidence that prisoners collaborated with the Communists without being subjected to the torture experienced by the airmen during the "germ warfare" hoax. The Communists had gained the collaboration of these men by merely exploiting their racial or economic discontent, or playing upon other psychological weaknesses. Because of this, there had been hostility among the American prisoners toward each other, sometimes ending in murder. Their collaboration with their captors most often took the forms of informing on fellow prisoners, denouncing America in Communist publications, and praising the Communists in broadcasts.

The U.S. Army found that 15 percent of its men taken prisoner actively collaborated with the enemy, 5 percent resisted, and 80 percent were in the gray area of signing peace petitions and such. Perhaps even more shocking was that not one American had tried to escape. Then came a bigger shock: seventy-five American soldiers had agreed to become Communist spies after returning to the U.S. and twenty-one others refused to return home at all.

Added to this was the revelation that 38 percent of the American prisoners—2,730 out of 7,190—died in captivity, a considerably higher rate than in previous wars. Most of them died during the first year of the war. Many of the prisoners starved themselves to death, refusing to eat the unfamiliar food, such as soybeans, given them.

A captured American doctor, Major Clarence L. Anderson, found that a common ailment among the prisoners was "give-up-itis":

> The sufferer first became despondent; then he lay down or covered his head with a blanket; then he wanted ice water to drink with his food; next no food, only water; and eventually, if he was not got to and helped, death would come. . . . If you didn't get to him within three weeks, he would be gone. . . . One of the best ways to get a man on his feet initially was to make him so mad by goading, prodding, or blows that he tried to get up and beat you. If you could manage this, the man invariably got well.

Anderson also found that the high death rate was largely due to a lack of discipline among the prisoners, many having no sense of loyalty to their country or to their fellow prisoners:

> They refused to obey orders, and they cursed and sometimes struck officers trying to enforce orders. The result was a general collapse of that unity that is so essential to survival in enemy hands. . . . The strong regularly took food from the weak. . . . Instead of being helped and nursed by the well, the sick men were ignored, or, worse, even helped to their deaths.

UNITED NATIONS

MICHAEL ROUGIER, LIFE © TIME, INC

In a flimsy hut at Panmunjom negotiators sign a Korean cease-fire agreement on July 27, 1953 (left). As peace came to the war-torn land and bewildered prisoners were exchanged (right), Americans assessed the "police action" in which they suffered 140,000 casualties.

It was the worst showing by prisoners in the history of America. A result was that President Eisenhower issued a new Code of Conduct for Members of the Armed Forces of the United States in 1955. The code, to be memorized by every American serviceman, confined them to providing only their name, rank, serial number, and date of birth if questioned while a prisoner. But some still questioned whether Americans had become so liberal-minded, so soft, so scornful of authority that they were misfits in the military, where any man is a misfit if he cannot obey orders unquestioningly, withstand intense physical and psychological pressure, and be willing to fight well in a war for purely ideological reasons.

U.S. MARINE CORPS

A Helping Hand for Korea

Homeward-bound from Korea, GIs took some comfort from having made a contribution beyond blood and guts to the embattled land. Battalions had founded and supported orphanages; millions for missions and charities had come from soldiers pay. For the marine-sponsored orphanage at left a Santa Claus sergeant unpacks clothing collected in California. Yet in the eyes of other American warriors, Korea remained "Gookland," which they would help most by leaving immediately.

Assessing the performance of our troops in Korea, T. R. Fehrenbach wrote:

> The enemy is no superman, as was proved on Pork Chop Hill. Anything he can do, we can do better—if we have the will. . . . It was time for free, decent societies to continue to control their military forces, but to quit demanding from them impossible acquiescence in the liberal view toward life. A "modern" infantry may ride sky vehicles into combat, fire and sense its weapons through instrumentation, employ devices of frightening lethality in the future—but it must also be old-fashioned enough to be iron-hard, poised for instant obedience, and prepared to die in the mud.

The Korea "police action" claimed 33,529 American lives. No formal peace treaty was signed; an armed truce still exists there along the thirty-eighth parallel. It was truly "the war we can't win, we can't lose, we can't quit."

The Truman administration's inability to bring the war to an early end was a liability for the Democrats in the 1952 presidential election. The previous year the Twenty-second Amendment had gone into effect, limiting a President to two terms. Although Truman had been exempted from the restriction, it was felt the amendment would greatly hamper his reelection to a third term. Truman tapped Adlai E. Stevenson, governor of Illinois, to succeed him. Stevenson attracted the support of labor and liberal intellectuals—dubbed "eggheads" by the Republicans. If elected, Stevenson confided to aides, he would try to restore morale in a visit to Korea, the scene of a bloody stalemate and on-again, off-again peace negotiations. But to disclose his plan publicly "would, in his view, amount to an attempt to buy votes in the coin of others' sacrifices."

"I like Ike" was the Republican party's battle cry and the broad Eisenhower smile its image in 1952.

Eisenhower also had in mind such a visit—and he said so a week before the election: "To bring the Korean war to an early and honorable end. That is my pledge to the American people. . . . I shall go to Korea. That is my second pledge to the American people."

When the votes were counted, Eisenhower had swamped Stevenson by 34 million to 27 million. He received 442 electoral votes to Stevenson's 89. It was a personal triumph for Ike; his party won control of Congress by only a slim margin.

In his inaugural address Eisenhower promised there would be no startling policy changes, and he kept his word: his administration was devoted to balancing the budget, halting inflation, and achieving efficiency in operations. To achieve these goals he put businessmen into key government positions.

Despite pressure from the Republican right wing to follow MacArthur's plan for a total military victory in Korea, Eisenhower continued Truman's efforts to negotiate an armistice. Before his inauguration he fulfilled his promise to go to Korea, but found "no panaceas" for ending the bloody war. A few months later, the Communists having eased their demands, a cease-fire agreement was signed.

By the end of Eisenhower's first term inflation had been checked and social security extended. The piercing cries of McCarthyism had been quieted. The Supreme Court, under the leadership of Chief Justice Earl Warren, had advanced the cause of civil rights by striking down segregation in schools. The only big cloud on the horizon was shaped like a mushroom, the Russians having detonated a hydrogen bomb in August, 1953, and the United States having exploded a bomb in the spring of 1954 that was 100 times more destructive than any previous man-made blast. As Nobel Prize winner Harold Urey had said earlier: "There is only one thing worse than one nation having the atomic bomb—that's two nations having it."

Toward a New Frontier

Two generations clashed on the proper goals for America during the late 1950s and early 1960s. The older, more conservative generation found its symbol in the steady, quiet, benign public image of Dwight D. Eisenhower. For the younger, less patient generation, John F. Kennedy's vigor and drive "to get this country moving again" was supremely attractive. Each generation eventually won converts from the other in their debates on domestic issues, civil rights, and foreign policy that rang through the halls of Congress, the corridors of the Pentagon, and the streets of Little Rock. Yet these clashes of generations at the end of the postwar era—sometimes violent, sometimes cerebral—left many of the basic issues unresolved.

For many people the period offered the best in America, usually expressed in material terms: television sets, hi-fis, two automobiles, a secure job with a large corporation, a house in the suburbs. Yet for others it seemed a troubled time. Television constituted a vast cultural wasteland; hi-fis blared the gyrating rock 'n' roll; cars sported more horsepower, more chrome, and more lethal tail fins. The organization men in gray flannel suits preached rugged individualism, but practiced a rigid conformity, living in a suburbia of prefabricated boxes, each sprouting a TV antenna on the roof.

The cult of conspicuous consumption was the result of much of the nation achieving middle-class status following World War II. A booming economy, wartime savings, credit plans, and the urgings of Madison Avenue created a heady atmosphere for the generation of Americans that had suffered the economic frustrations of depression and the material sacrifices of war. Tired

Triumphant John F. Kennedy at inaugural ball radiates the vigor that would characterize his brief leadership of the U.S. His enthusiasm, wit, and style as a political campaigner had captured the hearts, minds, and votes of a new generation of Americans.

of crises, the growing middle class sought only to return to the tasks of raising a family, making money, and living comfortably. Over millions of television sets the fatherly face of President Eisenhower smiled approvingly.

Critics, however, were greatly disturbed by the predominant materialism. The society was indeed affluent, yet there were embarrassing pockets of poverty in urban ghettos and rural areas. The society preached equality, yet winked at racial prejudice. Public transportation sputtered, urban areas crumbled, the quality of public education declined, and the government refused to deal substantively with any of these issues. It would take a new generation of politically concerned Americans, the critics agreed, to move the nation.

"We want Ike. We want Ike. We want Ike," campaign workers and well-wishers chanted, sniffing victory on election night, 1956. The early returns were significant. Key precincts in urban areas were voting Republican for the first time since 1928, signaling that labor and blacks had abandoned their allegiance to the Democratic party. Several southern states were also swinging to the Republican column. Eisenhower's popularity and the campaign slogan "Peace and Prosperity" had kept the Democratic candidate, former Illinois governor Adlai E. Stevenson, on the defensive.

Eisenhower wanted to win big; to retain any political clout the margin had to be substantial. Hopefully, a Republican Congress might be returned on his coattails. As the votes were being counted, it became evident that while Ike was winning a smashing victory, his coattails were of little help to other Republican candidates. Ike swamped Stevenson by nearly 10 million votes; his percentage of the popular vote had been surpassed only by Roosevelt's in 1936 and Harding's in 1920. He carried the electoral college 457 to 73. A victorious President faced a Congress controlled by the opposition party. Democrats captured the Senate 50 to 46 and held a margin of twenty-one seats in the House. Ike had won a popularity contest, but the Democrats had won an election.

While Ike could attract Democrats and independents, he could not convince them to support his party, which, below the presidency, still carried the twin scars of the Depression and do-nothing conservatism. An urbanized America was reordering its priorities, and these changes were reflected at the presidential rather than the congressional level. The situation arose, in great part, because the men on Capitol Hill had remained predominantly rural in outlook while the nation had become increasingly urban.

The question during Eisenhower's second administration was: Would the President and Congress continue to recognize and respond to the shifting nature of American society? For those interested in continuing domestic social legislation, the answer was a disappointing no. Eisenhower Republicanism combined a moderate amount of social welfarism with a sound fiscal policy. After projecting expenses to be $73.3 billion for fiscal 1958, Eisenhower came under attack as a profligate spender. Agonized by the charge, Ike insisted on cutting costs. So domestic programs would have to wait, and the Democratic Congress, led by Senate Majority Leader Lyndon B. Johnson, agreed. After all, Johnson felt, the do-nothing Republicans had been receiving too much credit for the successes of the first administration.

For decades American Negroes had protested against second-class citizenship, but had found the road to equal rights twisting and arduous. The National Association for the Advancement of Colored People (NAACP), founded in 1909 by white liberals and militant blacks, had achieved a number of small but not insignificant steps toward equality by the end of World War II. A more direct protest took form during the war when millions of southern blacks migrated to northern cities to escape the most vicious aspects of a caste society and find work in defense industries. The migration did not destroy southern traditions, however, and Jim Crow continued to loom tall in the South, effectively blocking the road to freedom.

The legal fortress that protected Jim Crow was the "separate but equal" doctrine enunciated in an 1896 Supreme Court ruling, which upheld a Louisiana law requiring segregated railroad facilities. Segregation in itself did not constitute discrimination, the court said, as long as the accommodations were equal. By mid-century, however, this decision was being eroded. In May, 1954, Chief Justice Earl Warren spoke for a unanimous court in *Brown* v. *Board of Education of Topeka.* "In the field of public education the doctrine of 'separate but equal' has no place," Warren said. "Separate educational facilities are inherently unequal." Within two years the Warren court had enlarged this principle, banning segregation in parks, swimming pools, public transportation, and public housing. Schools, the court maintained, should be integrated "with all deliberate speed." When white southerners balked at the rulings, blacks sought a more direct method to overcome Jim Crow. They found it in Montgomery, Alabama, the old capital of the Confederacy, on the front seats of a bus.

Early in the evening of December 1, 1955, this particular Montgomery City Lines bus was quickly filling with Christmas shoppers and store clerks returning home. At a stop in front of the Empire Theater six whites stepped on board. As usual, the driver walked back and asked the foremost Negroes to stand so the whites might sit. Several did so, but Mrs. Rosa Parks, a forty-two-year-old seamstress, refused to budge. She was arrested and fined ten dollars for violating a state law requiring bus passengers to obey the driver's seat-

Adlai Stevenson: Ambassador for Peace

"The hardest thing about any political campaign is how to win without proving that you are unworthy of winning," commented the wise and witty Stevenson in 1956, when he once again vainly represented the Democrats' hopes of beating Eisenhower. For liberals, the "hard-boiled egghead" symbolized internationalism and concern for the common man. He was governor of Illinois when President Truman first presented him as the Democratic candidate in 1952 (above). After Kennedy appointed him ambassador to the United Nations (right), he dutifully defended Kennedy's and later Lyndon Johnson's actions with regard to Cuba, the Dominican Republic, and Vietnam, in opposition to the views of Soviet leader Nikita Khrushchev (below right). The day before he died in 1965 aged 65, Stevenson remarked, "Oh, what I would really like is to just sit in the shade . . . and watch the dancers."

249

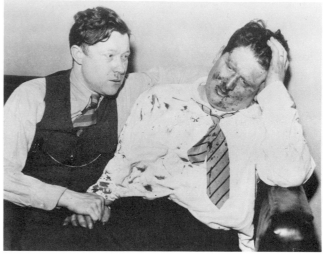

Walter Reuther: Responsible Union Chief

Walter Philip Reuther worked as an organizer for the infant United Auto Workers union in 1937 when it had a victorious showdown with General Motors. The union then signed up Chrysler and tried to organize the Ford Motor Company. At Ford's River Rouge plant, guards confronted Reuther and other unionists (above left) and beat them up in the Battle of the Overpass (above right, Reuther at left with Richard Frankensteen after the battle).

Ford was finally organized in 1941. Reuther became the UAW's president in 1946, and in 1952 president of the CIO. He and AFL leader George Meany both wielded the gavel in 1955 at the first convention of the newly merged AFL-CIO (below). The merger, representing 15 million workers, made organized labor a new power in the American political process. Also in 1955, Reuther won what amounted to a guaranteed annual wage for auto workers (below left).

ing assignments. She had not planned her now historic decision. She was, she later explained, simply tired from standing all day and her feet hurt.

The arrest of Mrs. Parks catalyzed a black community already angered by the bus company's rudeness and inadequate service. On the following Monday the buses rolled almost empty. Blacks, who had constituted 75 percent of the line's regular patrons, walked, drove in private cars, or rode mules. The boycott, black leaders claimed, was 95 percent effective. For the first time the black community had demonstrated the power of solidarity. As one old woman said, "My soul has been tired for a long time. Now my feet are tired and my soul is resting."

Initially, whites ignored the blacks' demands: courteous treatment, black bus drivers, and seating on a first come, first served basis. But as the boycott continued, guided by the gentle hand of Martin Luther King, Jr., a young Baptist minister steeped in the precepts of Mahatma Gandhi's nonviolent resistance, the whites' complacency turned to fury. Yet obscene phone calls and letters, police harassments, and the bombings of King's home and several Negro churches failed to shake the protesters' determination. As violence increased, white opinion, fearful of random terrorism by a small minority, demanded a peaceful solution. On a day more than a year after it began, the boycott ended. Rosa Parks boarded a bus and gazed out a window from a seat near the front. No one asked her to move. Jim Crow would never be the same.

President Eisenhower had not committed his administration to any civil rights legislation during his first term, primarily because he felt that the federal government should not aggressively enter the battle. Attorney General Herbert Brownell's four-point program—to create a civil rights commission, authorize the attorney general to bring injunctions where civil rights were violated, aid in voting procedures in the states, and strengthen the civil rights section of the Justice Department—was largely ignored by Ike. While balking at new federal legislation, Eisenhower silently moved into areas where federal authority had been clearly established. By executive decree he ended segregation in the District of Columbia and the armed forces, and appointed several blacks to important government positions. The tactics worked, and many blacks voted Republican in 1956.

After the election the Brownell program for civil rights—now backed by the President—passed the House and went to the Senate, where Majority Leader Johnson tried to hammer out a measure less offensive to southerners and thus avoid a filibuster. Brownell's suggestion to permit the attorney general to act when civil rights had been violated was dropped, and the new bill focused on voting rights and the creation of a civil rights commission. In this form Johnson steered it through the Senate 72 to 18.

To get the Civil Rights Act of 1957 through Congress, however, Johnson had scrapped a section which would have given the federal government more power to deal with the school desegregation issue. And it was in southern schools that the battle for equal rights was most crucial. To evade the Supreme Court's ruling to integrate "with all deliberate speed," many southern school districts simply shut down. White "private academies" sprang up. When the Eisenhower administration hesitated to move against these deceptions, some southerners took heart in hoping that the ruling could be defied. The governor of Arkansas arrived at this position, and national attention was focused on a high school in Little Rock just a few days after Eisenhower had signed the bill.

Little Rock was quiet; there was no hint of trouble on the eve of school integration. Then, around 9 P.M. the peaceful night was shattered by the rumblings of trucks, half-tracks, and jeeps. A National Guard unit unloaded tear gas, guns, and billy clubs, then fixed their bayonets, and set up a defense perimeter around Central High School. Within the hour Governor Orval E. Faubus explained to a television audience that he had ordered the Guard to the school to "maintain or restore the peace and good order" of the community. He did not mention that the troops would also prevent nine Negro students from integrating the school. Southern extremists flocked to Little Rock to keep the schools from integrating. When black students tried to enter Central High School, they were driven back by white toughs screaming threats.

To enforce the integration rulings of the federal courts and to demonstrate the authority of the federal government, Eisenhower ordered regular army troops into Little Rock, and Central High was desegregated. Slowly, over the next decade, further court rulings and a growing realization on the part of southern moderates that a more normal educational system was imperative overcame massive resistance to integrated schools.

The announcement came quietly. Tass, the Soviet news agency, routinely mentioned that on October 4, 1957, Russian scientists had orbited a small earth satellite. The reverberations from Sputnik's beeps were profound in the United States. Americans saw their technological superiority dangerously threatened and with it their security. The space race was under way and the United States had not even left the starting blocks. The reason, many argued, was the state of American education. Ivan was a highly selected and rigorously trained scientist or technician; in our overcrowded schools we were having difficulty teaching Johnny to read. A massive influx of students, products of the postwar baby boom, had created a classroom shortage. In addition, thousands of underpaid teachers had found more lucrative positions outside their pro-

fession, creating another U.S. education deficiency.

Since the 1952 presidential campaign, Eisenhower had advocated federal aid to education, but legislation had met strong opposition. Sputnik's beeps drowned out the partisan bickering and in a new atmosphere of crisis Congress enacted the National Defense Education Act (NDEA) of 1958. The act set up a loan fund for students and provided money for language, mathematics, and science instruction, laboratories, and vocational training in scientific and technical subjects.

The consensus formed for the education bill soon broke apart over the issue of additional federal spending, and the political deadlock in Congress resumed. Between October, 1957, and February, 1958, unemployment more than doubled. Many suspected that businessmen and the administration had planned the recession to moderate inflation. This hurt the Republicans in the 1958 off-year elections. Democrats, mostly liberals, swept the Congress, gaining thirteen seats in the Senate and forty-seven in the House. Sensing a mandate for change, the freshmen congressmen traveled to Washington with visions of a new era of social legislation in the fields of civil rights, school aid, and medicare.

Their hopes were dashed on the rocky conservatism of more experienced legislators. Because of the opposition of Howard W. Smith, chairman of the powerful Rules Committee, most of their liberal proposals never reached the floor of the House. Other committees, controlled by conservative southerners, acted similarly.

In his second inaugural Eisenhower had stressed the need to work for world peace. Yet to wage peace he had to escape from the cold war rhetoric associated with his secretary of state, John Foster Dulles, who had coined such terms as "liberation for captive peoples" and "massive retaliation." Dulles's illness facilitated things, and Eisenhower assumed a more active

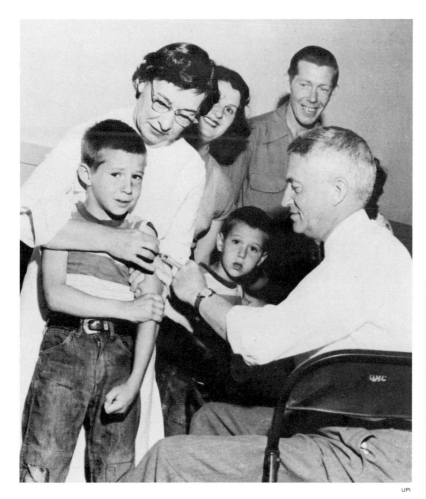

Jonas Salk: Scientist for Society

Dr. Salk (right) appeared like a white knight armed with a needle instead of a lance in 1954 when almost 2 million American children participated in tests of his polio vaccine. The acute infectious virus disease had repeatedly struck terror to the hearts of parents as epidemics killed or crippled thousands of children in many lands. While youngsters were its chief victims, adults were not immune— Franklin D. Roosevelt had been crippled by polio when nearly 40 years old. By 1955, Salk's vaccine was being administered to millions of children (above) and proved effective for about 90 percent of them if they received at least two injections. In 1956 vast amounts of the vaccine were produced (below), and health officials felt it might be the last year of polio's reign of terror.

JFK: *Camelot Under Fire*

Admirers of President and Mrs. John F. Kennedy's charismatic style likened their White House tenancy to Camelot. But the idealistic programs outlined by Kennedy (above) in his inaugural address were soon overshadowed by plans to outmaneuver his foreign opponents, notably Cuban Premier Fidel Castro (below left) and Soviet Premier Khrushchev. The President's admirers surprisingly increased after he approved an invasion of Cuba that met disaster at the Bay of Pigs. He gratefully remarked, "The worse I do, the more popular I get." Kennedy (left) was later burdened by the arrival of Soviet missiles in Cuba. In the UN (below) Adlai Stevenson showed photos of the launching sites, and the U.S. again prepared to invade Cuba. After tense days, a peaceful solution was reached—and Kennedy was hailed for avoiding nuclear war.

role in the conduct of the nation's foreign affairs. His search for peace was aided by a softening of Russian attitudes following the launching of Sputnik.

In part it was this softening of the Soviet line which led to a toughening of the American position in the Middle East. In the summer of 1958, Washington believed that the growing power of the United Arab Republic (Egypt, Syria, and Yemen) gravely endangered stability in other Arab nations. In Lebanon, pro-Nasser Moslems initiated a civil war against the pro-Western Christian government of President Camille Chamoun, who requested American military assistance. Eisenhower, assured that the Russians would not attack, ordered American troops into Lebanon. The same morning that Chamoun asked for help, Lebanese at the beach watched three battalions of marines wade ashore. The crisis was ended.

Eisenhower had used the marines reluctantly and afterward began to turn toward personal diplomacy on a scale that would capture the attention of the world. In his last two years in office Ike would meet with Khrushchev and make four goodwill tours abroad, visting Europe, Asia, the Middle East, Africa, Latin America, and the Far East. The journeys were rousing successes.

Eisenhower's first trip was to Europe for talks with West German, British, and French leaders before Soviet Premier Nikita Khrushchev visited the United States. When Khrushchev arrived at Andrews Air Force Base near Washington, he proudly announced that a Soviet rocket, Lunik I, had hit the moon. While in the United States he continually spoke of an easing of cold war tensions and proposed a four-year plan for disarmament. With much enthusiasm he toured the country and ended his trip with a long weekend with Eisenhower at Camp David in Maryland. There Eisenhower insisted that the Berlin issue be solved before a summit meeting take place. Khrushchev agreed to this,

and invited Eisenhower to visit the Soviet Union the following summer.

After the Camp David meeting, the sixty-nine-year-old Eisenhower set out on his travels once more. His itinerary included Italy, Turkey, Pakistan, Afghanistan, India, Iran, Greece, Tunisia, France, Spain, and Morocco. The framework for peace, built upon Eisenhower's personal diplomacy, continued to be strengthened during his visit to Latin America in early 1960. Out of Ike's visit would come the Act of Bogota, which established American aid for education, land use, public health, and economic development in Latin America.

On May Day, 1960, Eisenhower's framework of world peace collapsed. For Francis Gary Powers, flying over Sverdlovsk in the Soviet Union, it was a dull thud and a lingering orange glow; then his U-2 high-altitude photo reconnaissance plane began to fall apart. With the crumbling plane went Eisenhower's dream for a breakthrough at the summit meeting in Paris. Initially, the United States denied that it had been sending planes over Russia, but did admit that a weather research plane might have crashed in Soviet territory. Then Khrushchev, speaking before the Supreme Soviet in Moscow, displayed Powers, part of his U-2, and the plane's equipment. The United States had been caught spying and lying. Eisenhower absorbed the blame for the whole episode, explaining that Soviet missile developments demanded such American surveillance.

Two weeks after the U-2 was shot down, Eisenhower, French President Charles de Gaulle, British Prime Minister Harold Macmillan, and Khrushchev attended a summit conference in Paris. Khrushchev insisted that Eisenhower apologize for the U-2 incident, punish those responsible, and promise not to renew the flights. Then he told the President that his trip to Russia was canceled. Eisenhower did apologize, but would not punish those involved. He proposed that the United Nations control such aerial surveillance in the future. One observer recalled the dramatic confrontations of the Paris summit talks. The big four, he said, "looked like heavy-stakes poker players late at night. It was the coldest gathering of human beings I believe I've ever seen. Not once in three hours was there a smile . . . to relieve the tension."

The international situation continued to deteriorate after the Paris fiasco. Eisenhower journeyed to the Far East as scheduled in June, although anti-American feeling in Japan forced him to cancel his visit to that country. Relations with Cuban Premier Fidel Castro became more strained and Eisenhower ordered the training of Cuban exiles in Guatemala. Terrorism by the Viet Cong, Hanoi's recognition of the National Liberation Front, and spreading dissatisfaction with the Diem government in South Vietnam, as well as an increase in Pathet Lao strength in Laos had brought the situation in Indochina to a critical point.

Thus, in the summer of 1960, with the domestic economy stalled and the cold war heating up, the Republicans and Democrats moved toward another presidential campaign. The Republican heir to the presidency and Eisenhower's policies was Vice President Richard Nixon. A Quaker from California, Nixon had considered himself a liberal, but a brief stint in the Office of Price Administration during World War II soured his taste for big government. After the war he returned to California, and ran successfully for Congress in 1946, hitting hard against communism in his campaign. His handling of the Alger Hiss case attracted the attention of California Republican leaders, who urged him to run for the Senate in 1950 against Helen Gahagan Douglas, a liberal. Nixon again won handily with a tough attitude toward communism. When the eastern wing of the Republican party secured Eisenhower's nomination in 1952, Nixon was selected to balance the ticket and appease the more conservative forces.

Eisenhower and his supporters never quite trusted Nixon's rough-and-tumble style of politics. Attempts to dump him as the vice-presidential candidate in 1952 and again in 1956 had failed, but Eisenhower never took Nixon into his confidence. In 1960, as Nixon was beginning his campaign for the presidency, a newsman asked Ike what important decisions his subordinate had made after eight years in office. "If you give me a week, I might think of one," Eisenhower replied.

Nixon, however, had worked hard for this chance at the top spot. He had campaigned tirelessly for Republican candidates in 1954 and 1958, establishing a grateful following among party regulars. After New York Governor Nelson Rockefeller withdrew from the race, Nixon had a clear path to the nomination. To add balance to the ticket, he selected Henry Cabot Lodge, the ambassador to the United Nations.

For the Democrats the path to the presidential nomination was more difficult; there were more candidates jostling for the lead position, but the early leader was John F. Kennedy.

A Roman Catholic from Boston, Kennedy had been groomed for politics by his father, a multimillionaire businessman who had served Franklin D. Roosevelt as ambassador to Great Britain prior to World War II. A Navy man like Nixon, Kennedy returned to Boston after the war and won a House seat, joining Nixon in Washington as a freshman congressman. Six years later he moved to the Senate. His record-breaking reelection in 1958 thrust him to the forefront of the presidential race in 1960. Kennedy had almost unlimited funds, a superb organization, and a reputation for winning. He had only to prove to the party bosses that his Catholicism would be no handicap and this he could do with a strong showing in the state primaries.

Kennedy's chief opponent in the race for convention

John Glenn: Man in Space

The mysteries of space inspired both fear and hope in 1961 when a baby chimpanzee named Ham (right) lived through a 15-minute flight aboard a Mercury spacecraft. Ham pioneered a path in the space race with the Soviet Union that enabled marine Lt. Col. John H. Glenn, Jr., to become the first U.S. astronaut to orbit the earth. On February 20, 1962, an Atlas rocket launched (below) at Cape Canaveral, Florida, thrust Glenn into space, where he was weightless for almost five hours in his capsule, Friendship 7 (bottom left). The attention of the world and particularly of America focused on him as he circled the earth three times. A crowd in New York's Grand Central Station (bottom right) reacted to his flight with cheers and prayers. Glenn's flight was followed by three Mercury missions and by the Gemini program, preparing for the Apollo adventure.

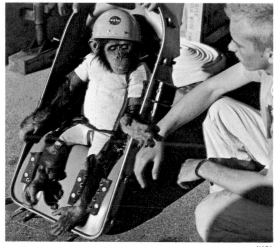

NASA

ALBERT FENN, LIFE © TIME, INC.

NASA

WIDE WORLD

Martin Luther King:
I Have a Dream

One of the greatest orators of modern times, the Reverend Martin Luther King, Jr., used his verbal power as a crusader in the civil rights movement. The Baptist preacher from Atlanta, who headed the Southern Christian Leadership Conference, provided an example of nonviolence for his followers during the 1957 Montgomery bus boycott, the 1960 sit-ins, the 1961 "freedom rides," and the 1963 confrontation with Birmingham police. King was arrested and jailed in the U.S. on such charges as "loitering" in Montgomery (left), but he was regarded as a hero in other lands and in 1964 he received the Nobel Peace Prize. Despite threats on his life and the bombing of his home, he was still advocating nonviolence in 1968 when he was shot dead at age 39. On his tomb are words from a slave song: "Free at last, free at last, thank God Almighty I'm free at last."

delegates was Senator Hubert Humphrey of Minnesota, a long-time liberal who had crusaded for the rights of blacks and labor unions. Humphrey hoped to sidetrack the Kennedy express in Wisconsin and then in heavily Protestant West Virginia, but the voters found Kennedy more attractive than Humphrey, particularly since the Kennedy organization spent freely, overwhelming Humphrey's meager efforts.

At the Democratic convention in Los Angeles that summer John Kennedy's personal attributes plus the energetic efforts of aides directed by his brother, Robert, won him the nomination. He then offered the vice-presidential spot to Lyndon B. Johnson, hoping to restore relations with the most powerful man in the Senate and to strengthen the ticket for the South. Johnson seized the opportunity, no doubt viewing the vice presidency as a way to shed his southern regional image.

Before 80,000 cheering admirers, Kennedy formally accepted the nomination. His speech noted the new priorities of Americans. It was time for a new generation to cope with new problems and employ new solutions, "young men who can cast off the old slogans and delusions and suspicions." Americans stood "on the edge of a new frontier—the frontier of the 1960s."

In the 1960 campaign Nixon tried to manage everything himself, to prove that he could do it without Eisenhower. Midway through the campaign he suffered a knee infection and was hospitalized. Haggard after his illness, and badly made-up, he plunged into a series of television debates with Kennedy, whose good looks and debating ability decided the outcome for millions of Americans. Of those influenced by the debates, according to a Roper poll, three-fourths voted for Kennedy.

Nevertheless, the Republicans, with Ike on the stump, finished the campaign strongly. Although Kennedy's margin in the electoral college was wide, 303

to 219, the popular vote in 1960 was the closest since 1888. Of 68 million votes, only 119,000 separated the two candidates. Moreover, a shift of 35,000 votes in Texas and Illinois, where there had been numerous instances of voting irregularities, would have elected Nixon. Most encouraging for Democrats was the fact that Kennedy had restored some of the old Roosevelt coalition into which Eisenhower had cut deeply. Catholic, blue-collar, and black voters in industrial areas came back to the Democratic party. In Congress the Democrats had retained substantial majorities. On the surface it appeared that the legislative program of the New Frontier would experience few difficulties.

The youngest man to be elected to the presidency, Kennedy was succeeding the oldest person to occupy the White House. And he emphasized youth in his inaugural address: "The torch has been passed to a new generation of Americans" who would offer bold new approaches to challenges at home and from abroad.

"And so, my fellow Americans: ask not what your country can do for you—ask what you can do for your country. My fellow citizens of the world: ask not what America will do for you, but what together we can do for the freedom of man."

Kennedy and his liberal following realized that the success of their domestic program depended upon reform of the House Rules Committee. They hoped to enlarge the committee with more tractable men, and break the legislative logjam. The administration's efforts produced a narrow five-vote victory. While it failed to stop the packing of the Rules Committee, the conservative coalition could, and would, block any of the President's proposals not to its liking.

Kennedy's struggles with Congress were largely overshadowed by foreign crises, and his handling of those crises had not been of a caliber which commanded much admiration. The initial concern was Cuba, where Americans had controlled 40 percent of the island's sugar, 80 percent of its utilities, 90 percent of its mines and cattle ranches, and nearly all of its oil until the Castro regime seized most of the properties. In the summer of 1960, Congress cut American imports of Cuban sugar. Immediately, the Soviet Union offered to buy the excess sugar and increase trade with Castro. In return, Cuba would support Soviet foreign policy in Latin America. Eisenhower, furious that Castro could agree to this, severed diplomatic relations with Cuba just two weeks before he left office.

Kennedy inherited this situation along with a Central Intelligence Agency plan to invade Cuba. The CIA had been training thousands of anti-Castro Cuban exiles in the Guatemalan mountains for such a move. Most of Latin America, including Castro, suspected that an American-backed invasion was in the works. Lacking the element of surprise, the mission should have been scrapped, but for Kennedy to halt the operation might be interpreted as a sign of weakness. In addition, the CIA gave the President inaccurate information and bad advice. So on April 15, 1961, three American-made B-26s bombed Cuba. The attacks, Castro declared, were "a prelude to invasion."

He was right. Two days later 1,500 men landed at the Bahia de Cochinos (Bay of Pigs). The invaders, lacking adequate air cover (Kennedy decided against using more planes) and facing a heavily reinforced Cuban militia, were pinned down on the beach. Within three days all the attackers had been killed or captured. The disaster, critics claimed, was due to Kennedy's vacillation. If the government was going to back such an operation, they said, it should go all the way.

Kennedy was shortly to be tested again. Six weeks after the abortive invasion, he journeyed to Vienna for two days of summit talks with Khrushchev. Tension hung like a dark cloud over the meeting. They agreed on little of substance during the two days, and Khrushchev became militant about eliminating the Allied presence in West Berlin.

Khrushchev's saber-rattling over Berlin filled the President with a grim foreboding. Fortunately, a military response was ruled out by both sides. But no diplomatic solution was found either. On August 13 the East Germans began erecting a wall between the eastern and western sectors of Berlin, and within two months the Berlin Wall was effectively blocking further escapes by East Germans to the West. Neither side could claim a victory in Berlin. The hot spot in the cold war remained; the mutual testing continued.

In September, 1962, intelligence sources heard rumors that the Soviet Union was sending surface-to-surface missiles to Cuba. Khrushchev denied it. Then, in mid-October, a U-2 overflight revealed that Soviet ballistic missiles capable of carrying nuclear warheads were being installed less than 100 miles from the United States. Once the missiles were set, the Soviet Union would have, at minimum cost, an unsinkable launching site for the medium-range missiles already developed. Thus, the continental United States could be brought within range of Soviet weapons and the expense of developing Russian-based intercontinental ballistic missiles could be avoided.

Events moved swiftly. On Monday, October 22, Kennedy announced that the United States was imposing a "strict quarantine on all offensive military equipment" being shipped to Cuba. The next day American vessels started forming the blockade. The world shuddered on the brink of nuclear holocaust. On October 24 reconnaissance planes over the Atlantic reported that Soviet ships carrying offensive weapons had altered course and would not test the American blockade. Khrushchev seemed to be backing down. In a long, emotional letter to Kennedy, the Soviet premier offered to remove the missiles in return for an

Peace Corpsmen: Heroes of the New Frontier

Responding to President Kennedy's urging that they "ask not what America will do for you, but what together we can do for the freedom of man," thousands of Americans volunteered to serve in the Peace Corps when it was formed in 1961. By 1968 more than 25,000 men and women had served by invitation in over 50 countries; the work now continues with a smaller Corps. The volunteers, ranging in age from the teens to the seventies, have performed such jobs as helping villagers in Colombia build a road (right) and treating sick babies (below right) in a primitive Niger village (below). Summing up their achievements, Peace Corps director Jack Vaughn said, "We have learned in Ghana, in the Dominican Republic, and a dozen Vietnams that progress for mankind can never really be measured in causes and coups, but in precious inches of human understanding and enlightenment."

RAY WILTIN, BLACK STAR

CARL PURCELL, PEACE CORPS

CARL PURCELL, PEACE CORPS

The Looming Struggle in Vietnam

Under a policy of containing communism, during Kennedy's presidency 16,000 American ''advisers'' were sent to South Vietnam to help achieve a military victory over northern invaders. In 1963, while the Joint Chiefs of Staff formulated strategy in the Pentagon (below), Buddhist opposition to South Vietnam President Ngo Dinh Diem took the form of Thich Quang Duc's flaming suicide in Saigon (above right). After Diem's death in a coup, the Pentagon's boss, Defense Secretary Robert McNamara, visited Saigon (above left) and dissuaded Gen. Nguyen Khanh, who had seized power, from invading North Vietnam. When Kennedy died the Vietnam problem was inherited by Lyndon Johnson (above with Kennedy) and then by President Nixon.

American guarantee not to invade Cuba. On Sunday morning, October 28, thirteen days after the crisis had begun and just as the Air Force prepared to strike the missile installations, the diplomatic settlement was reached: no missiles, no invasion.

At no time had the world been so close to atomic destruction. But instead of radioactive fallout, the crisis brought a clearing of the air. World leaders had been badly frightened. Kennedy pushed through a test-ban treaty ending nuclear explosions in the atmosphere, and made arrangements to sell American wheat to the Soviet Union. A hot line was installed between the White House and the Kremlin. The Russians began to stress peaceful coexistence. With the test ban, the first step had been taken away from war and toward peace. For the young President, too, the era of testing had passed.

A new generation on the national level injected added momentum into the civil rights movement after 1960. President Kennedy, who had attracted black support during the campaign by telephoning Mrs. Martin Luther King as her husband sat in a Georgia jail, and his brother, Robert, the attorney general, had made a firm commitment to civil rights. A massive protest against discrimination in interstate travel gave the administration its first opportunity to act decisively.

Southern blacks, armed with Martin Luther King's teachings, were continuing their crusade for equal rights. Again, the initial action had been unplanned. One February afternoon in 1960 four Negro college students had walked into a Woolworth store in Greensboro, North Carolina, and had sat at the lunch counter. Custom ruled that Negroes be served standing; seats were for whites only. Refused service, they had sat until closing time. The next morning they had returned, joined at their vigil by twenty-five more students, including some whites. Within a week the sit-in movement had spread into other southern states and the North. White collegians had rallied to the cause, picketing Woolworth stores. Shortly thereafter, the lunch counters of most chain stores had been quietly desegregated. The Student Nonviolent Coordinating Committee (SNCC) was a product of this white-black cooperation.

Older civil rights organizations had joined with King's Southern Christian Leadership Conference (SCLC) to aid the students. The Congress of Racial Equality (CORE), organized and led by whites until 1961, offered years of experience and advice on nonviolent protest techniques. The NAACP provided much of the legal assistance that the tactics of passive resistance required.

As the sit-in demonstrations continued, Negroes and white liberals, sponsored by CORE, planned to test a Supreme Court ruling that buses and trains, as well as terminals and their restaurants, be desegregated. In May, 1961, the first contingent of "freedom riders" boarded a bus in Washington and headed for New Orleans. At Anniston, Alabama, white segregationists burned the bus; elsewhere, riders were beaten or arrested. Immediately, Kennedy ordered federal marshals to Alabama to protect the riders. The road south was terrifying and sometimes violent, but gradually the terminals and restaurants opened their facilities to all.

In spite of black advances, one southern city had not surrendered to desegregation. Its schools, restaurants, pools, drinking fountains, parks, and toilet facilities remained totally segregated. Birmingham, Alabama, Martin Luther King said, was the "symbol of segregation." It was here that King brought his passive resistance techniques in the spring of 1963; it was here that nonviolence tragically ended.

Demonstrations for desegregated public accommodations and for equal job opportunities were met with

The horror began on November 22, 1963, as President and Mrs. Kennedy were riding in Dallas with Texas Gov. John Connally and his wife. Three shots rang out, killing the President and wounding the governor. A spectator took the above picture just after the bullets struck. Two days later the President's assassin, Lee Harvey Oswald, was fatally shot (left) by Jack Ruby. The next day the dead President was carried past his family (right), receiving a salute from his three-year-old son.

Time of the Assassins

It seemed to many Americans watching it all on TV that the whole thing was unreal, another example of unnecessary violence in television programming. They could hardly believe that such things were actually happening—that a young, popular President was shot dead and a governor wounded by a man who was shortly afterward shot dead by another man, and that the dead President's brother was later shot dead and so was a civil rights leader who advocated nonviolence. And who had done all the shooting? Nobodies who wanted to be somebodies. "Violence is as American as cherry pie," said black militant H. Rap Brown, and it seemed in the sixties that he might be right—that our nation had been born violently, lived violently, and would die violently.

At the side of Jacqueline Kennedy during the burial ceremony at Arlington National Cemetery was the slain President's brother, Robert, who five years later would also fall victim to an assassin's bullet. Observing the reaction to John Kennedy's death, Alistair Cooke found that "along with the sorrow, there is a desperate and howling note over the land." It was the people grieving not only for their lost leader but for their lost dreams.

water hoses and snarling dogs. Then, shortly after a Ku Klux Klan meeting, two bombs shattered the home of King's brother, the Reverend A.D. King. Two more exploded at the motel which served as the demonstrators' headquarters. Enraged, the black community poured out of the ghetto and surged through the streets throwing bricks and beating policemen. Tongues of fire flickered from white-owned stores. The city was at war; blacks had fought back. The era of urban rioting had begun.

The civil rights coalition between blacks and liberal whites began to change. Black leadership became more militant as the protest tactic of direct action, so successful in the South, failed in northern urban areas. Blacks and whites—200,000 of them—participated in the March on Washington for Jobs and Freedom in August, 1963. As the demonstrators reached the Lincoln Memorial they joined hands to sing "We Shall Overcome," the battle hymn of the crusade. Leaders appealed to President Kennedy and Congress to pass a strong civil rights program. They would continue the march for integration. Others echoed the militant Malcolm X, a Black Muslim leader, who preached total separation of the races. All received polite attention. Then Martin Luther King stepped to the rostrum. The throng roared its approval.

"The Negro lives on a lonely island of poverty in the midst of a vast ocean of material prosperity and finds himself an exile in his own land," King said. "It would be fatal for the nation to overlook the urgency of the moment and to underestimate the determination of the Negro."

As the crowd thundered its agreement, King cried, "I have a dream that my four little children will one day live in a nation where they will not be judged by the color of their skin, but by the content of their character."

Many nightmares would interrupt that dream.

Concerned with the problems of reelection, Kennedy traveled to Texas in November, 1963, in pursuit of that state's twenty-five electoral votes. Texas was enemy territory, Kennedy was warned. In October, Adlai Stevenson, the ambassador to the United Nations, had been roughed up by a Texas crowd. Contrary to expectations, however, the crowds in San Antonio, Houston, and Fort Worth had been large and friendly. Thousands of people waited at the Dallas airport to cheer the President. Crowds, ten to twelve deep, lined the route of the motorcade as it wound its way toward the city. Mrs. Kennedy sat in the back seat of the President's car with her husband. In front of them sat Texas Governor John Connally and his wife Nellie. Waves of applause rolled through the spectators. As the car passed the Texas Book Depository building Mrs. Connally turned to Kennedy and said, "You can't say that Dallas isn't friendly to you today." The President did not answer; he was dying of an assassin's bullet.

About an hour later police arrested the suspected killer in a Dallas movie theater. His name was Lee Harvey Oswald, a former marine sharpshooter who moved to Russia in 1959 and declared his intention to become a Soviet citizen. Three years later he returned to the United States, and allied himself with the Fair Play for Cuba Committee in his native New Orleans. Soon afterward he moved to Dallas, taking a job in the Texas Book Depository warehouse. Although Oswald maintained his innocence, Dallas police believed the evidence was overwhelming. In the basement garage of the City Hall, as millions watched on television, Oswald was shot and killed by Jack Ruby, a Dallas nightclub owner.

The assassination gave birth to a cult which made Kennedy larger in death than he had been in life. The errors of judgment, the inability to move Congress were lost amid the dreams of what might have been.

"*Let Us Reason Together*" 11

An incident in the Gulf of Tonkin ignited the longest war in U.S. history. On August 2, 1964, the American destroyer *Maddox,* patrolling off the North Vietnam coast, was attacked by three torpedo boats. They inflicted no damage and were driven off. A second attack was alleged to have taken place on the night of August 4 against the *Maddox* and her sister ship, the *Turner Joy,* although evidence of this attack consisted of only a few mysterious radar blips. Shots in the dark from the destroyers apparently hit nothing but salt water.

Although ambiguous reports from the scene cast doubt on the entire episode, President Lyndon Johnson ordered retaliatory air strikes "against gunboats and certain supporting facilities" in North Vietnam. He then asked congressional approval of a resolution "to promote the maintenance of international peace and security in Southeast Asia."

The House voted for the resolution unanimously, 416 to 0. The Senate passed it 88 to 2, the dissenters being Oregon's Wayne Morse and Ernest Gruening of Alaska. Morse predicted that the senators who voted for the resolution "will live to regret it." One who did was J. William Fulbright, chairman of the Senate Foreign Relations Committee. In his book *The Arrogance of Power,* he confessed that the resolution "was a blank check . . . signed by the Congress in an atmosphere of urgency that seemed at the time to preclude debate."

Johnson, as Vice President in 1961, had told President Kennedy that "the participation of American ground troops in the war in Vietnam is neither desirable nor necessary." He said it again, a few weeks after the Tonkin incident, while campaigning for a full term as President: "We are not about to send American boys nine or ten thousand miles away from home to do what Asian boys ought to be doing for themselves." He ran as the peace candidate, promising "no wider war." His Republican opponent, Senator Barry Goldwater of Arizona, fulminated against communism.

After the election—Johnson's 61 percent of the vote surpassing Franklin D. Roosevelt's landslide in 1936 and Warren Harding's victory in 1920—the nation awakened to the reality of war in Vietnam. From 23,000 military advisers stationed there in 1964, U.S. troop strength grew to 184,000 in 1965. Johnson had come "to the painful conclusion that an independent South Vietnam could survive only if the United States and other nations went to its aid with their own fighting forces."

In the spring of 1965, following Communist attacks on the American stronghold at Pleiku in South Vietnam, Johnson invoked "a policy of *sustained reprisal* against North Vietnam." Air strikes by U.S. planes escalated to levels exceeding the heaviest bombings of Germany during World War II. Johnson sent an additional 200,000 troops to Vietnam in 1966. Two years later American forces in Southeast Asia numbered more than half a million. American battle deaths climbed past 30,000.

The political consequences of what became known as the President's war were immense. Public opinion polls showed that Johnson's popularity with voters plummeted from around 80 percent during the 1964 campaign to about 35 percent in 1967, when, according to pollsters, any one of several Republicans could have defeated the President. Left for dead after Goldwater's crushing defeat, the Republicans suddenly found there was still life in the Grand Old Party, with Governor Nelson Rockefeller of New York, Governor George Romney of Michigan, Governor Ronald Reagan of California, and former Vice President Richard Nixon all showing surprising strength. But most sur-

American youth of the turbulent 1960s were insistent in their demands for an end to the Vietnam war and for reform of the U.S. political process. These demonstrators in Chicago's Grant Park typified the generation's efforts to make its views heard.

prising would be the backlash appeal of ex-Governor George Wallace of Alabama, who geared up for a third-party campaign, which he hoped might thrust him into the position of being the broker of the 1968 election in the event it was forced into the House.

The decline of the President's popularity paralleled the nation's deepening involvement in the Vietnam war. "Were there no outside world," wrote Theodore White, ". . . Lyndon Johnson might conceivably have gone down as the greatest of twentieth-century Presidents." The boldest innovator in domestic affairs since Franklin D. Roosevelt in his first term, Johnson fashioned a program of legislation designed to produce, as he dubbed it, The Great Society. Pleading "let us reason together" and persuading old colleagues, Johnson freed John F. Kennedy's New Frontier legislation logjammed in Congress. He signed into law the Civil Rights Act of 1964, the Economic Act establishing the antipoverty program, and a tax reduction bill designed to stimulate the economy. Other significant legislation was passed in 1965, including a voting rights bill, Medicare, and three bills to fund the war on poverty.

With Congress in his pocket—although less so after the off-year elections in 1966—Johnson proceeded to reshape the cabinet, creating a Department of Transportation and a Department of Housing and Urban Development. HUD administered the Model Cities Act, "one of the major breakthroughs of the 1960s" in Johnson's opinion. The first President to name a black to a cabinet post—Robert C. Weaver, head of HUD—and to appoint a black Supreme Court justice—Thurgood Marshall—Johnson confronted the issue of racism being exploited by George Wallace, militant blacks, and right-wing extremists. At Gettysburg, on the 100th anniversary of the battle fought there, the President warned that "patience" would no longer serve as the answer to the Negro's demand for justice:

With the law's backing, a long-deferred equality seems possible for American Negroes. After the Civil War the Freedmen's Bureau set up schools for them (left), but whites burned schools and persecuted teachers to prevent education from "spoiling" Negroes. Now, in affluent Montgomery County, Maryland, black children attend integrated schools (opposite).

PENN COMMUNITY SERVICES, FROGMORE, SOUTH CAROLINA

New Frontier Legislation

President Kennedy's program—much of it carried out by President Johnson after the assassination—resulted in these benefits:

LABOR:
Minimum wage raised from $1.00 to $1.25 an hour and protection extended to some 4 million workers in retail trade, construction, and service industries.

HOUSING:
Grants of $5.6 billion, increased aid for elderly, moderate-income groups, urban renewal.

REDEVELOPMENT:
Loans for new businesses and grants for retraining unemployed in distressed areas.

EDUCATION:
Over $1 billion in federal grants and loans for construction of classrooms and libraries; vocational training broadened.

HEALTH:
Greater government control over drug industry; $175 million to help medical schools expand and make loans to students; federal financial aid to states to care for mentally ill and retarded.

CIVIL RIGHTS:
Poll tax not required to vote in federal elections; racial bias banned in public accommodations, jobs, and schools.

FOREIGN AFFAIRS:
Agency for International Development and Peace Corps established; nuclear test-ban treaty; broad tariff-cutting powers to expand trade.

SPACE:
Appropriations increased to race Russians to moon.

JOE DIDIO, NEA

"Until justice is blind to color, until education is unaware of race, until opportunity is unconcerned with the color of men's skins, emancipation will be a proclamation but not a fact."

The right to vote, historically denied Negroes in the South, was put to the test in Selma, Alabama. There, freedom marchers singing "We Shall Overcome" were brutally treated by police wielding bullwhips and billy clubs. In the bloody aftermath Ku Klux Klansmen clubbed to death a white Unitarian minister from Boston, the first—but not the last—murder in what Martin Luther King feared would be "a season of suffering."

"At times history and fate meet at a single time in a single place to shape a turning point in man's unending search for freedom. So it was at Lexington and Concord. So it was a century ago at Appomattox. So it was last week in Selma, Alabama." Speaking before a joint session of Congress in the glare of television lights, Johnson, with bursts of applause interrupting him, continued in a style almost Lincolnesque: "There

is no Negro problem. There is no southern problem. There is no northern problem. There is only an American problem. . . . There is no constitutional issue here. The command of the Constitution is plain. There is no moral issue. It is wrong—deadly wrong—to deny any of your fellow Americans the right to vote in this country. There is no issue of states' rights or national rights. There is only the struggle for human rights."

Looking squarely at his southern colleagues, the President from Texas defined the challenge in unmistakable terms, pausing at one point between words to emphasize their meaning: "It is the effort of American Negroes to secure for themselves the full blessings of American life. Their cause must be our cause too. Because it is not just Negroes, but really it is all of us who must overcome the crippling legacy of bigotry and injustice. And . . . we . . . shall . . . overcome."

After a moment's stunned silence, the chamber erupted. Congressmen stood and cheered. People in the galleries wept unashamedly. It was, Johnson recalled, "a shouting ovation that I shall never forget as

271

long as I live." It climaxed perhaps the finest hour of the first President to come from the South in decades.

On August 6 he signed into law the historic Voting Rights Act of 1965, one of its provisions outlawing poll taxes. Five days later a race riot, triggered by a drunk-driving incident, exploded in the Watts section of Los Angeles. Crowds chanting "Burn, baby, burn!" fire-bombed buildings and overturned cars; thirty-five persons were killed.

"We were beset by contradictions—movement and progress alongside stalemate and retrogression," reflected Johnson. "Nowhere were these contradictions experienced more deeply than in the black community, where hopes aroused by the early victories were bright, but hostilities caused by the persistent gap between promise and fulfillment were deep. It was a volatile mixture." In the long, hot summer of 1967, the volatile mixture blew up in black ghettos across the nation. Newark counted twenty-five dead and millions of dollars in property damage. Detroit, where forty-three were killed, "looked like Berlin in 1945." President Johnson appointed a commission to study civil disorders. Its report concluded, "Our nation is moving toward two societies, one black, one white—separate and unequal."

In April, 1968, a month after the report was published, a sniper shot and killed Martin Luther King as he stood on the balcony of a Memphis motel. Within hours of King's assassination, rioters were roaming the streets in the nation's capital. Breaking windows, flinging Molotov cocktails, they embarked on a three-day orgy of looting and burning. More than 11,000 federal troops were called in. Six months earlier, soldiers had sealed off the Pentagon from antiwar protesters. Now an army of occupation manned every intersection, ringed the White House, mounted a machine gun on the steps of the Capitol. Not since 1814, when the British sacked the city, had Washington seen

The fiery heart of racial rioting blazed in Detroit during the summer of 1967 (above). As city blocks were consumed in flames and bullets whined through the smoking ruins, guardsmen and police were reinforced by paratroopers to gain control of the situation. Innocent persons as well as looters and snipers were among the 43 killed and 1,000 injured. Rising urban expectations and demands had also led to clashes with enforcers of law and order in earlier times. New York police wielded clubs (below) to break up a strike by streetcar workers in 1886. This use of force caused another 15,000 trainmen to join the strike, which ended when all had their pay raised to $2 for a 12-hour day.

272

But the war in Vietnam heated up. During Tet, the Vietnamese lunar new year holiday, Viet Cong and North Vietnamese forces, attacking at night, launched a widespread offensive against cities and military installations in South Vietnam. Hue fell, and thousands of its citizens were massacred. American air bases at Bien Hoa and Tan Son Nhut were shelled. In besieged Saigon, a Viet Cong suicide squad blasted its way into the American embassy compound. Despite Johnson's claims that the Tet offensive had failed militarily—the Communists lost an estimated 45,000 men—he conceded it had produced a psychological victory for the enemy. Reduced to ashes were hopes in America that the war was nearing an end.

Johnson could not ignore the political implications of Senator Eugene McCarthy's showing in the New Hampshire presidential primary. An avowed peace candidate, McCarthy polled almost as many votes as the President. Then, four days after the primary Senator Robert F. Kennedy—no admirer of Johnson or the war—declared his candidacy for the Democratic nomination on March 16. That day public opinion polls revealed that Johnson's popularity had dropped to a new low.

On March 31, in a television address to the nation, the President announced that he was de-escalating the war. He had ordered a cessation of bombing over most of North Vietnam. He hoped that even limited bombing could soon be halted, so that peace negotiations might begin. Toward the end of the speech Johnson dropped a bomb of his own: "There is a division in the American house. . . . I have concluded that I should not permit the presidency to become involved in the partisan divisions that are developing in this political year. . . . Accordingly, I shall not seek and I will not accept the nomination of my party for another term as your President." The following month peace talks began in Paris.

anything comparable. Like a virulent fever, violence spread to Baltimore, Boston, Chicago, Pittsburgh, Memphis, San Francisco, and a hundred other cities.

During 1968, one of the most agonizing years in U.S. history, nowhere was the burden felt more than in the White House. Lyndon Johnson in his book *The Vantage Point* recalled the gloomy January 23 meeting there with foreign affairs advisers. Opening the meeting, retiring Secretary of Defense Robert McNamara turned to his successor, Clark Clifford, and wryly remarked, "This is what it is like on a typical day. We had an inadvertent intrusion into Cambodia. We lost a B-52 with four H-bombs aboard. We had an intelligence ship [*Pueblo*] captured by the North Koreans."

Unlike his handling of the Tonkin Gulf affair, Johnson used diplomacy rather than retaliation in the *Pueblo* incident. "I do not want to win the argument and lose the sale," he explained. Restraint paid off. The *Pueblo*'s crew was released at the end of the year. War on another front had been avoided.

273

The "only effective way" to peace was to "prosecute the war more effectively," said Richard Nixon shortly after announcing that he would seek the Republican nomination. He swept aside all opposition and, at the Republican convention in Miami Beach, won the nomination on the first ballot. It was a remarkable political comeback. But violence stalked the convention. Three blacks died in a gun battle with police in Miami. Accepting his party's nomination Nixon called for law and order: "The wave of crime is not going to be the wave of the future in the United States." In foreign affairs, he pledged "to bring an honorable end to the Vietnam war." For a running mate, he selected Spiro Agnew, governor of Maryland.

When Vice President Hubert Humphrey announced his candidacy after Johnson withdrew, the Democrats had a choice of three liberals. Robert Kennedy decisively defeated McCarthy in the California primary on June 4 and established himself as the front runner for the nomination, but as he savored his victory in a Los Angeles hotel a young Jordanian named Sirhan Sirhan shot him to death. For the second time in this cursed year the nation mourned a leader cut down by an assassin's bullets.

Chicago, scene of the Democratic convention, was an armed camp. Its streets became a battlefield. National guardsmen and Mayor Richard Daley's police, clubs flailing, tear-gas canisters hissing, waded into mobs of young antiwar protesters, supporters of McCarthy and of Senator George McGovern of South Dakota, a late entry in the Democratic race.

On the convention floor bitter arguments raged over rules, platform, delegate seating. Humphrey, shackled to Johnson's record and his failure to denounce Daley's police, won a Pyrrhic victory—the Democratic party was in a shambles; Humphrey felt as if he "had been in a shipwreck." In November, with 40 percent of the voters staying home, Nixon outpolled Humphrey by less than one percent of the popular vote but garnered a 31-vote electoral majority.

Before the year ended, 1968 crowded in one more headline. On Christmas Eve three American astronauts circled the moon in Apollo 8. Space flights reached a climax July 20, 1969, when Neil Armstrong climbed out of his Apollo 11 lunar module and stepped onto the moon's surface. "That's one small step for man," he said, "one giant leap for mankind." While the world watched via television, he and Edwin ("Buzz") Aldrin planted an American flag and read the inscription from a plaque they left there: "Here men from the planet Earth first set foot upon the moon July, 1969, A.D. We came in peace for all mankind." Before this "year of the moon" ended, U.S. astronauts made another lunar landing.

In his inaugural address, President Nixon had said, "No man can be fully free while his neighbor is not. To go forward at all is to go forward together." He pointed out, "We find ourselves rich in goods, but ragged in spirit; searching with magnificent precision for the moon, but falling into raucous discord on earth. We are caught in war, wanting peace." The attainment of peace proved more elusive than the moon. In

Paris peace negotiators bickered even over the shape of the conference table. Communist rockets again fell on Saigon; U.S. B-52s bombed near the Cambodian border; and the American death toll rose to nearly 40,000—more than were killed in the Korean War.

At home students burned draft cards in nationwide Vietnam Moratorium Day demonstrations. In November a second moratorium effort was focused on Washington, attracting a quarter of a million marchers—the largest mass demonstration in the capital's history. Barricades surrounded the White House. Nixon vowed he would not be swayed by antiwar protests, but he began to withdraw American troops from Vietnam.

As the 1960s drew to an end, the nation was stunned by reports of American atrocities in Vietnam. Borrowing Viet Cong tactics, U.S. soldiers had massacred villagers in My Lai and Song My.

"It has been an awful decade," author Richard Rovere wrote in the *New York Times,* "a slum of a decade."

The new decade began on a note of urgency. After signing the National Environmental Quality Improvement Act on New Year's Day, President Nixon warned, "The 1970s absolutely must be the years when America pays its debt to the past by reclaiming the purity of its air, its waters, and our living environment. It is literally now or never." During Earth Week—inspired by Interior Secretary Walter J. Hickel—many Americans joined the fight against pollution. Students fanned out along roads to collect litter. Recycling stations were set up. Said one biologist, "The affluent society has become the effluent society. The 6 percent of the world's population in the United States produces 70 percent or more of the world's solid wastes." Said comic-strip character Pogo, "We have met the enemy and he is us."

In Vietnam pollution was used as a weapon of war. Tons of herbicides sprayed from planes defoliated for-

Although they were both held In Chicago during times of popular unrest, the Democratic convention of 1968 was a far cry from that of 1896. At the earlier convention William Jennings Bryan (below) won the presidential nomination with his oratory. At the 1968 gathering the talk was secondary to the clash in the streets between young antiwar demonstrators and the police force of Mayor Richard Daley (right). As a result of the confrontation and of protests at the convention regarding rules and delegates, the Democratic party instituted reforms. The Republicans planned to do the same.

STANLEY MELTZOFF, LIFE © TIME, INC.

BURT GLINN, MAGNUM

ests, poisoned water supplies, destroyed rice crops. Intensive bombing, stepped up as American troops were withdrawn, produced what has been described as the most massive excavation project in history. When Nixon extended this scorched-earth policy into Cambodia, sending American forces across the border to destroy enemy sanctuaries and supply routes, accusations that he was widening the war resounded in Congress, foreign capitals, and hundreds of American campuses. At Kent State University in Ohio, national guardsmen fired into demonstrators, killing four students. Police killed two students at Jackson State College in Mississippi.

The repeal of the Tonkin Gulf resolution—tacked on as a rider to an appropriations bill—went almost unnoticed when President Nixon signed it January 14, 1971. Nixon felt he did not need the additional authority given the President by the resolution, believing his authority as commander in chief was sufficient to deal with developments in Indochina. The repeal of the resolution had no teeth, for the proposed McGovern-Hatfield amendment requiring complete withdrawal of American forces by the end of the year had been killed. Four days later, McGovern, by then the leading dove on Capitol Hill, announced his candidacy for the presidency, although the election was almost two years away. Motivating him to start campaigning early was his intense opposition to the Vietnam War, "the cruelest, most barbaric, and most stupid war in our national history."

McGovern's campaign, aided by the revelation of the secret "History of U.S. Decision-Making Process on Vietnam Policy"—otherwise known as the Pentagon Papers—received its first setback on July 15, 1971. On that date President Nixon announced he would undertake "a journey for peace, peace not just for our generation but for future generations." He would visit the People's Republic of China. In October, Nixon announced he would also visit the Soviet Union.

His two trips in 1972—to China in February, to Russia in May—combined with troop withdrawals from Vietnam, established Nixon, his supporters claimed, as the real peace candidate.

As the campaigns heated up, George Wallace, running this time as a Democrat, found broad support on a close-to-home issue—the practice of busing children to achieve integration in public schools. His opposition to busing and emphasis on law-and-order issues won him the Florida primary by a lopsided margin, brought him in a close second in Wisconsin, and made him a winner in Maryland and Michigan. These last two victories came the day after a would-be assassin shot him

as he campaigned in Maryland. Paralyzed from the waist down, Wallace was unable to continue in the race. Most of his support shifted to Nixon.

At Miami Beach—site of both conventions—McGovern fought off a late challenge by Humphrey to win the Democratic nomination on the first ballot. He selected Senator Thomas Eagleton of Missouri as his running mate but, after learning of Eagleton's history of psychiatric problems, replaced him with former Peace Corps director Sargent Shriver. Facing an uphill struggle even before the switch, McGovern now lost ground he could not recover. Not even tainting the White House with scandal—the arrest of Nixon campaign workers for wiretapping Democratic party headquarters in a Watergate office building—could make up the difference.

The President's prospects for victory received a final boost two weeks before the election when his national security affairs adviser, Henry Kissinger, returned from Paris to pronounce "peace is at hand." Bombing of North Vietnam was halted above the twentieth parallel. With the signing of a peace agreement apparently imminent, there was no denying Richard Nixon a second term. He crushed McGovern at the polls in one of the biggest landslides in American history, losing only Massachusetts and the District of Columbia as he racked up a popular vote of well over 46 million against McGovern's nearly 29 million and an electoral vote of 520 to 17.

After the election, peace negotiations broke down.

COME IN AND LEARN
WHY WOMEN
OUGHT to Vote.

THE BETTMAN ARCHIVE, INC

The week before Christmas, Nixon ordered a resumption of the bombing "until such time as a settlement is arrived at." In round-the-clock raids B-52s battered the Hanoi-Haiphong area in the heaviest bombing of the war—or any war. On January 15, 1973, five days before his inauguration, the President directed that "the bombing, shelling, and any further mining of North Vietnam be suspended." Kissinger returned to Paris "for the purpose of completing the text of an agreement" to end the war. After a few days of bargaining, an accord was reached, and on January 27—at last—the cease-fire went into effect.

The coming of peace found Americans strangely silent, as if troubled by the thought that they had paid an enormous price in blood and money for an uncertain outcome. For a victory? None felt the sense of victory, as after previous wars. For a defeat—or at best a failure? Some thought so—at least that it had been too high a price for a doubtful success in checking Communist advances. Unlike the riotous celebrations that took place in New York's Times Square at the end of World Wars I and II, people went about their business quietly in the square as the electric letters of the moving sign on the Allied Chemical Tower spelled out the cease-fire.

The terms of the Vietnam peace settlement provided for the withdrawal of American forces from Vietnam within sixty days and the return of all American prisoners of war. In the twelve years of the war, the United States military had suffered 45,033 men killed, 303,616 wounded, 587 captured, and 1,335 missing. For Americans it had been the most divisive conflict since the Civil War. Some believed that the opposition of the younger generation to the war had led to a decline in their respect for the moral authority of the government and, by extension, of the schools, the church, the press, and the family. Others saw the youngsters' disrespect for the Establishment as a natural extension of their lack of respect for their parents who had reared them in a permissive mode. Whatever the cause, the effect—a change in attitude toward authority—would make itself felt in American life for years to come, some believing that it would eventually produce a wiser, though less confident nation.

In his second inaugural address, President Nixon spoke of seeking a world peace which would be "not merely an interlude between wars, but a peace which can endure for generations to come." Our role would not be that of global policeman to enforce that peace, but rather we would "do our share" and "expect others to do their share." We would continue to work for the limitation of nuclear arms and to reduce the danger of confrontation between the great powers, but "the time has passed when America will make every other nation's conflict our own, or make every other nation's future our responsibility, or presume to tell the people of other nations how to manage their

own affairs," the President told war-weary America.

Despite the isolationist tone of Nixon's program, the fact remained that the U.S. was a world power and could not escape international commitments as long as it hoped to retain a dominant position. Among the international affairs that required action from the administration was the assumption of responsibility to help North and South Vietnam rebuild after the war's terrible devastation, caused primarily by our bombers. In that same part of the world a peaceful solution to the problems of Laos and Cambodia also ranked high on the American foreign policy agenda. Strengthening the new ties with China without jeopardizing better relations with the Soviet Union was another intricate problem for the second term of Nixon's presidency.

Below these concerns, but still requiring the intervention of the United States if it wished to maintain its position as a major power, were attempts to help the Israelis and Arabs arrive at a detente.

The public's quiet acceptance of the Vietnam cease-fire was followed by emotional scenes when the prisoners of war began coming home. Some of them had been away for eight years; it was a new world they entered. Nearly all of them, especially those held captive longest, had been sustained by old ideas of God, flag, and country during the months and years in prison. President Nixon's "peace with honor" found favor with the returning men, one saying that

280

"all the prisoners think Nixon is the greatest thing that ever came down the pike." The newly freed men were much interested in learning who won the war. American officials assured them that South Vietnam did not lose and North Vietnam did not win. The ex-prisoners seemed virtually unanimous in opposing amnesty for draft evaders and deserters, saying such men should not be allowed to enjoy the privileges of an America for which they were not willing to fight.

This was one of the hardest decisions facing the administration. President Nixon told the nation, "Amnesty means forgiveness. We cannot provide forgiveness for them. Those who served paid their price. Those who deserted must pay their price. . . . The price is a criminal penalty for disobeying the laws of the United States. If they want to return to the United States, they must pay the penalty."

Many thousands of Americans were directly involved in the amnesty question. During the Vietnam War the rate of desertion from the military reached the highest point in our history, with upwards of 32,000 men listed by the Pentagon in 1972 as deserters "at large." About 10,000 other men had evaded the draft, some of them having fled to foreign lands.

Many men who had served in Vietnam found civilian life hard on their return home. Unemployment,

281

low GI benefits, and hostility on the part of those who did not go to war combined to fill many veterans with bitterness and frustration. Black veterans particularly found the adjustment to civilian life difficult, suffering an unemployment rate of nearly 15 percent. The veterans' problems were due at least partially to the publicity given the use of drugs by soldiers in Vietnam. As one of their spokesmen said, "There's a cruelly false image of the veteran. The man who served in Vietnam has been stereotyped as a hop-

U.S. NAVAL ACADEMY MUSEUM

headed killer." Because of the war's unpopularity, the servicemen received a cool reception when they came home. Most of them did not mind the lack of victory parades; it was the lack of jobs that hurt.

The problem of unemployment was not confined to veterans in the early 1970s. Inflation worsened the situation of those seemingly doomed to chronic poverty, and the President's budget for fiscal 1974 imperiled many welfare programs to achieve his goal of not raising taxes.

At a time when prices and unemployment were both high, President Nixon, in his second inaugural address, spoke of attaining "a new era of progress at home" by "turning away from old policies that failed." These old policies included "attempting to gather all power and responsibility in Washington"—the opposite of laissez faire. Reversing decades of increasing governmental control, he urged, "Let us measure what we will do for others by what they will do for themselves. . . . Let each of us remember that America was built not by government, but by people—not by welfare but by work."

The Vietnam peace accord removed the major foreign affairs issue of the time. Extensive surveys showed that Americans had turned inward and had become less interested in the cold war than they had been during the years following World War II. In 1964, for example, researchers had found that the five primary concerns of Americans involved international affairs or national defense. By 1972 the top concern was inflation, and other major problems were violence, drugs, crime, and pollution. By 1973 many people had added distrust of the government to this list of concerns, due to further revelations concerning the wiretapping of the Democrats at the Watergate. The scandal involved some of the President's closest aides and developed into demands for Nixon's impeachment. Agnew, meanwhile, was forced to resign as Vice President following charges that he evaded income taxes while governor of Maryland.

In his second term the Republican President faced a series of confrontations with the Democrat-controlled Congress over his policies and powers, with Congress claiming that Nixon's unusually strong presidency was usurping the legislature's constitutional powers. Many congressmen felt that the President believed he could run the government without Congress and intended to do so. Republican Senator Edward W. Brooke of Massachusetts said, "If you continue to invest more and more power into the executive, if one man can start a war, conduct a war . . . or end a war without congressional approval, then you're getting perilously close to a dictatorship." The Senate's leading constitutional authority, Democrat Sam J.

Ervin of North Carolina, expressed the view that the executive branch had usurped the legislative branch's power, but he also claimed that Congress was guilty of giving its power away.

Nixon's fight with Congress over power was typical of strong American Presidents. Even George Washington had confrontations with the legislature because of the tension created between the branches of government by the Constitution.

While cutting back on many projects, Nixon's budget for 1974 nearly doubled appropriations for the endowments of the National Foundation on the Arts and the Humanities established by Congress in 1965 to encourage the nation's cultural growth. The increased appropriations were largely intended for use in connection with the American Revolution Bicentennial celebration of 1976.

"The Spirit of '76" had been the theme of President Nixon's second inaugural. America—from its beginning at Jamestown to the moon landing—was depicted in the parade's floats so that our nation's major achievements could be assessed. What was less easy to assess was whether the optimism, ingenuity, and tenacity that had accomplished the goals of the past were equal to the struggles ahead.

After two centuries as an independent nation, one might indeed ask: Where are we headed? What will America be like in 2076, or even in 1986?

We are obviously in the midst of vast, disturbing changes, of conflicting trends, rival hopes and anxieties. But to say this is to say nothing new. The first great anniversary of the United States occurred in 1826 in celebration of the fiftieth "birthday" of the Declaration of Independence. The nation was prosperous and growing, but there were also bitter divisions within the society. North and South were already at odds over slavery. The last presidential election had been contested by no less than four major candidates; no one obtained a majority and the new President, John Quincy Adams, had to be chosen by the House of Representatives after what Adams's enemies called a "corrupt bargain" with Henry Clay. Nevertheless, the dominant mood was one of confidence and pride, catalyzed by an extraordinary coincidence: both John Adams and Thomas Jefferson, last of the Founding Fathers, died on July 4, exactly fifty years after they had signed the Declaration, and Americans took this as a sign that the nation and its historical mission were divinely inspired.

At the time of the first centennial, in 1876, the national situation also seemed unclear. While dignitaries extolled the virtues of the American people and their fantastic achievements since the signing of the Declaration, they knew (and some were candid enough to say) that the country faced staggering problems.

284

UNITED STATES CENTENNIAL COMMISSION.
INTERNATIONAL EXHIBITION.
1876.
OFFICIAL
CATALOGUE.
MAIN BUILDING AND ANNEXES.
DEPARTMENT I. MINING AND METALLURGY.
DEPARTMENT II. MANUFACTURES.
DEPARTMENT IV. EDUCATION AND SCIENCE.
FIFTH AND REVISED EDITION.
PHILADELPHIA.
PUBLISHED FOR THE CENTENNIAL CATALOGUE COMPANY BY
JOHN R. NAGLE & CO.
PRINTED AT THE RIVERSIDE PRESS, CAMBRIDGE, MASS.

THE BETTMAN ARCHIVE, INC.

It was wallowing in the worst industrial depression it had yet experienced. The government in Washington was being rocked by a succession of scandals involving corruption and influence peddling. Indian warfare was searing the frontier.

All in all, however, the mood of the centennial year was optimistic. The symbol of the celebration was the giant Corliss steam engine at the Philadelphia Centennial Exposition. When President Grant and his guest, Dom Pedro, the emperor of Brazil, pulled the two levers that set it in motion, some 8,000 machines connected to the engine were activated. This marvel of industrial technology was for most observers decisive; problems there were, but on balance the future of a country that could produce such a device was bright.

As the second centennial approached, some Americans wondered if it would also be the occasion of some extraordinary event, or if some new technological marvel would serve the function of George H. Corliss's steam engine. At times of national stock-taking, such as the Bicentennial, even a chance happening can have a lasting effect on public attitudes, and thus can shape the course of events for a long period of time.

The difficulty is that ours does not seem to be an age of heroes and we have become jaded by a surfeit of technological marvels. We said in our introduction to this volume that progress appears to have become self-defeating and that, as the United States has matured, its people have ceased to believe the future is boundless.

The naive optimism of youth is being replaced by a sober awareness of limitations that is characteristic of middle age.

Let us examine briefly some of the sources of this view of our present condition. Who can deny, in the abstract, that material progress is a good thing? And if life is good, should we not all have families as large as we can afford, and thus extend life's bounty? It is today immediately obvious that these are only half-truths. Material goods are desirable because they make possible "the good life," and the more goods produced the more people can live the good life. But . . .

Goods can only be turned out in the mass by expending large amounts of energy; producing this energy causes pollution; producing the goods uses up limited natural resources and degrades the environment. Producing people causes overcrowding, which makes the good life harder to achieve; it strains the food supply, leading to hunger for uncounted millions; increasing the food supply by the intense use of chemical fertilizers leads to pollution; increasing it by killing off crop-destroying insects with poisons leads to the destruction of birds, fish, and other creatures, eventually even human beings.

These paradoxes are now understood by nearly everyone. What is not so widely recognized is that they appear to illustrate a more fundamental paradox: progress toward a desirable goal drives us farther away from one or more other desirable goals.

Putting aside the simple examples mentioned above,

286

consider the following. Freedom of the individual is one of our most cherished ideals, and democracy is the best form of government for protecting freedom that we have yet devised. But freedom can lead to fragmentation; if every individual can do as he pleases, the infinite variety of human nature may make each of us a majority of one. This is perhaps only theoretically true, but it is a fact that in our complex world, where every jack-of-all-trades has been replaced by a dozen specialists, it becomes ever more difficult to put together a real majority—a state of affairs where more than half the people prefer one individual leader or one course of action. Real conflicts of interest proliferate—between producers and consumers, between workers and their bosses, between city dwellers and suburbanites, blacks and whites, the old and the young, developers and conservationists.

In a society that reveres tradition and defers to entrenched status, such conflicts can usually be resolved in an authoritarian manner. In a society (such as existed in the United States in the nineteenth century) that sees itself unique and divinely inspired, most conflicts can be compromised, all the contending factions accepting half a loaf in order to pursue larger common goals. But when individuals and pressure groups put their own interests first, as seems increasingly to be the case in our own time, conflicts of interest generate demonstrations, non-negotiable demands, passive resistance, open violence, and other socially disruptive tactics. All are defended in the name of right and justice and equality, but even if the right and justice and equality are conceded, the effects upon the larger society are frequently unfortunate. What compounds the seriousness of this state of affairs is the aforementioned tendency toward specialization, which, by vastly increasing the interdependence of individuals, multiplies both conflicts of interest and the power of the aggrieved to inconvenience their fellows.

None of this means that the United States is coming apart at the seams. The unexpected and unwanted results of recent "progress" that we have been examining are at least potentially stimulants to true progress, the necessities that mother inventions, the irritants that can goad our creative imaginations and compel us to adjust intelligently to change.

The greatest danger that looms ahead is the temptation to grasp at oversimplified solutions to our problems. All history teaches that social panaceas are illusory. Dissatisfactions with the results of change must neither cause us to turn our backs on past experience nor send us rummaging in the attic of our history in search of worn-out, rightly discarded social tools. All our ingenuity and strength are needed to confront today's tasks. Ingenuity and strength we have, as a nation, in abundance.

Other peculiarly American qualities also emerge and assert themselves as we study our 200 years of nation building. Perhaps the most valuable of these strengths is our system of government—not only the democratic process of voting for the better man, but also the republican process of restraining headstrong executives and reviewing unconstitutional legislation. Armed with such a mighty inheritance, the turmoils of the future begin to seem slightly less formidable.

It may be worthwhile to consider how Walt Whitman reacted to the first centennial. Whitman saw more clearly than most of his contemporaries the paradoxical character of American civilization. He gloried in the nation's accomplishments, but he also wrote about the "pathology" of the country, "the morbid facts of American politics and society." Like nearly everyone in 1876, he reached positive conclusions when he tried to strike a balance: "I count with . . . absolute certainty on the Great Future of the United States." We might well repeat these words on the occasion of our second centennial.

In Their Own Words

The voices of the American past speak to us across the years. From letters in our grandparents' attics, from newspapers tucked in old books, from songs still sung and stories still told we hear them speaking—the four generations of Americans between us and the Civil War.

Theirs is a different "Song of Myself" than that of the Founding Fathers or the antebellum framers of our national heritage. No longer the great classical sentences of Washington or the pithy backwoods observations of Lewis and Clark (see Reading Portfolio, Volume One). Now, instead, records tell of the process of city building: an immigrant to San Francisco exclaims rapturously, "It's like Norway!" Other documents tell of the first mass enthusiasms of urbanized Americans, such as the euphoria in New York when they welcomed "Lucky Lindy" home from Paris.

Also, instead of frontiersmen with long rifles opposing the serried British ranks, Americans of these recent generations fought for (or against) the industrialized Union—then their grandsons marched forth to save the world for democracy. Curiously, the diary of a Union volunteer at Vicksburg is marked by lusty pride much like that of Eddie Rickenbacker's World War I reminiscences. But such soldierly accounts differ radically from the horror-stricken narratives of World War II.

In peace, strife still sounds. We hear the eloquence of Frederick Douglass as he advocates desegregated education,

Proclaiming the value of newspapers, a boy hawks his wares on a street in Alaska.

his words foreshadowing Martin Luther King's "I Have a Dream." We feel the conflicting emotions of a crowd witnessing vigilante action in the rude West. ("An attempt was made by the police on the plaza to get Jenkins away from the committee, but the effort was hopeless. . . .") And we admire the dignity of black legislator Henry Macneal Turner as he resists being expelled from his seat in Georgia's House of Representatives in 1868: "I shall neither fawn or cringe before any party, nor stoop to beg them for my rights. . . . Never [before] has a man been arraigned before a body clothed with legislative, judicial, or executive functions, charged with the offense of being of darker hue than his fellowmen."

Because of our internal divisions and occasional manifestations of violence, many suffer the unspeakable humiliation of having to plead for their American freedoms, including life itself. Victims of the Ku Klux Klan, as well as Indians, Chicanos, and the urban poor raise their voices in protest from the accounts that follow.

But sometimes the struggle for rights has its humorous aspect. During Prohibition Americans opted for moral freedom of a sort by gathering in speakeasies. The *New York Times* wrote up a raid on one such outpost: "The revelers refused to be routed by the dry agents, but continued to make merry for several hours after the sleuths had gone in search of more victims."

Labor too has had to find its own way of speaking up to demand freedoms, freedoms for the working man. John L. Lewis stands forth as one of the mightiest of these spokesmen. He pointed out that bare-knuckled, creative struggles within our democracy are essentially good: "Labor, insistent upon its rights, should not be annoying to the ears of justice nor offensive to the consciences of the American people."

Indeed, the translation of oppressed citizens' cries into legislative and judicial reform is the business of American statesmen. The best of them learn to keep their ears tuned to the winds of controversy, distinguishing truly vital causes from mere howls that might disrupt our workable, but fragile, majority government.

The War Between Brothers

*Victors and vanquished viewed the same battles
differently. From letters, diaries, and orders we are
allowed to observe four critical struggles through
both Union and Confederate eyes.*

FIRST BULL RUN

**This first battle of the Civil War
quickly turned into a Northern rout.
William Howard Russell, a war
correspondent, wrote of the terror-
stricken Union retreat; J. C. Nott, a
doctor in the Confederate army,
described the thrill of the Southern
victory:**

Russell:
I perceived several wagons coming from
the direction of the battlefield, the drivers of which were endeavoring to force
their horses past the ammunition carts
going in the contrary direction near the
bridge; a thick cloud of dust rose behind
them, and running by the side of the
waggons were a number of men in uniform whom I supposed to be the guard.
My first impression was that the waggons
were returning for fresh supplies of ammunition. But every moment the crowd
increased; drivers and men cried out
with the most vehement gestures: "Turn
back! Turn back! We are whipped."
They seized the heads of the horses and
swore at the opposing drivers. Emerging
from the crowd, a breathless man in the
uniform of an officer, with an empty
scabbard dangling by his side, was cut
off by getting between my horse and a
cart for a moment. "What is the matter,
sir? What is all this about?" "Why, it
means we are pretty badly whipped,
that's the truth."

Nott:
The enemy had concentrated all his
forces on this one point [top of a hill]
while ours were scattered around a half
circle of ten miles, and the few regiments
who received the first onset were most
terribly cut up. It was far greater odds
than human nature could stand, the regiments were torn to pieces, driven back,

and so overwhelmed by numbers that I
feared the day was lost. . . .

At this juncture I saw our reinforcements pouring in with the rapidity and
eagerness of a fox chase, and was satisfied that they would drive every thing
before them. No one can imagine such a
grand, glorious picture as these patriots
presented, rushing to the field through
the masses of wounded bodies which
strewed the roadside as they passed
along. For half a mile behind me the
road passed down a gradual slope, and
through an old field, as I looked back, I
could see a regiment of infantry coming
in a trot, with their bright muskets glittering in the sun; then would come a
battery of artillery, each gun carriage
crowded with men and drawn by four
horses in full gallop. Next came troops
of cavalry, dashing with the speed of
Murat; after these followed, with almost
equal speed, wagons loaded with ammunition, &c., screaming all the while,
"push ahead boys," "pitch into the d—d
Yankees," "drive them into the Potomac."

∽

NEW ORLEANS

**In the fall of 1862, New Orleans fell to
Northern forces. Julia LeGrand, an
unconquerable resident, described
the surrender and the determination
to continue resistance. General
Benjamin F. Butler, the Union
commander, issued his now famous
proclamation and Order No. 28 in an
attempt to tame the hostile populace:**

Miss LeGrand:
Flag officer Farragut demanded the unconditional surrender of the town. He
was told that as brute force, and brute
force only, gave him the power that he
might come and take it. He then de-

manded that we, with our own hands,
pull down the flag of Louisiana. This I
am happy to say, was refused. Four days
we waited, expecting to be shelled, but
he concluded to waive the point; so he
marched in his marines with two can-
nons and our flag was taken down and
the old stars and stripes lifted in a dead
silence. . . .

I never wished anything so much in
my life as for resistance here. I felt no
fear—only excitement. The ladies of the
town signed a paper, praying that it
should never be given up.

Butler's Proclamation:
No publication . . . giving accounts of
the movements of soldiers of the United
States within this Department, reflecting in any way upon the United States
or its officers, or tending in any way to
influence the public mind against the
Government of the United States, will
be permitted; and all articles of war
news, or editorial comments, or corre-
spondence, making comments upon the
movements of the armies of the United
States, or the rebels, must be submitted
to the examination of an officer who will
be detailed for that purpose from these
Headquarters. . . .

The municipal authority, so far as the
police of the city and crimes are concerned, to the extent before indicated, is
hereby suspended.

All assemblages of persons in the
streets, either by day or by night, tend
to disorder, and are forbidden.

Butler's Order No. 28:
As officers and soldiers of the United
States have been subject to repeated in-
sults from women calling themselves
ladies, of New-Orleans, in return for the
most scrupulous non-interference and

courtesy on our part, it is ordered hereafter, when any female shall by mere gesture or movement insult, or show contempt for any officers or soldiers of the United States, she shall be regarded and held liable to be treated as a woman about town plying her avocation.

∽

VICKSBURG

The siege of Vicksburg, crucial citadel of the Mississippi, is vividly recalled by two participants: an unknown woman caught in the city; and George W. Driggs, a soldier in the Eighth Wisconsin Volunteers:

The besieged woman:
We are utterly cut off from the world, surrounded by a circle of fire. Would it be wise like the scorpion to sting ourselves to death? The fiery shower of shells goes on day and night. H.'s occupation, of course, is gone; his office closed. Every man has to carry a pass in his pocket. People do nothing but eat what they can get, sleep when they can, and dodge the shells. There are three intervals when the shelling stops, either for the guns to cool or for the gunners' meals, I suppose,—about eight in the morning, the same in the evening, and at noon. In that time we have both to prepare and eat ours. Clothing cannot be washed or anything else done. On the 19th and 22d, when the assaults were made on the lines, I watched the soldiers cooking on the green opposite. The half-spent balls coming all the way from those lines were flying so thick that they were obliged to dodge at every turn. At all the caves I could see from my high perch, people were sitting, eating their poor suppers at the cave doors, ready to plunge in again. As the first shell again flew they dived, and not a human being was visible.

The Union soldier:
The tumultuous chaos of two great contending armies have ceased their struggles, and the Federal arms have gained another victory over the wily foe. Vicksburg, as you have long ere this been informed, has surrendered, after being besieged for forty-seven days. It was a gala day for our troops, I assure you, and the 4th of July was never before celebrated in Vicksburg with such a right

hearty good feeling as on yesterday. The mortars on the point opposite the city, with the accompanying chorus from the distant gunboats had kept our ears in a perfect hum for many long weeks, until they became like household words, familiar to the ear, and no longer a terror, as its introduction. But the sound of battle strife has ceased for a while, and our army now breathes the pure air of freedom once again. Victory is perched upon our blood-stained and tattered banners, and the heart of the great North, which has evinced so much restlessness and anxiety for the result of our success, may now leap for joy, and smile at the happy and successful achievements of the Federal arms.

From a family album: the face of a Georgia private who was doomed to die in the Civil War.

SHERMAN'S MARCH TO THE SEA

Sherman's devastating march left an undying hatred of Yankees. A lieutenant in the Grand Army, Charles Booth, apologetically describes the "Bummers" who ravaged the land; Eliza Andrews, a Georgia girl, describes the highway of destruction Sherman left behind:

Lieutenant Booth:
These "Bummers" were detailed for foragers, and upon them the army depended for subsistence; . . . consequently the "Bummers" were the life of the army. About 5,000 strong, not a field or house or barn, but was searched by them; nor

a town or hamlet but the "infernal bummers" managed to plunder before his cavalry came up. . . . To enter a house and find the feather bed ripped open, the wardrobes ransacked, chests stripped of contents, looking glasses taken from the walls, cooking utensils gone, and all the corn meal and bacon missing, bed quilts striped from the beds, the last jar of pickles gone, was no uncommon sight, and one to make a soldier blush with indignation. Every effort that could be made was made to check the demoralization of the foragers; but . . . "the army must be fed, and the Bummers must feed us."

Miss Andrews:
About three miles from Sparta we struck the "burnt country," as it is well named by the natives, and then I could better understand the wrath and desperation of these poor people. I almost felt as if I should like to hang a Yankee myself. There was hardly a fence left standing all the way from Sparta to Gordon. The fields were trampled down and the road was lined with carcasses of horses, hogs, and cattle that the invaders, unable either to consume or to carry away with them, had wantonly shot down, to starve out the people and prevent them from making their crops. The stench in some places was unbearable; every few hundred yards we had to hold our noses or stop them with the cologne Mrs. Elzey had given us, and it proved a great boon. The dwellings that were standing all showed signs of pillage, and on every plantation we saw the charred remains of the ginhouse and packing screw, while . . . lone chimney stacks, "Sherman's sentinals," told of homes laid in ashes.

BIBLIOGRAPHIC CREDITS: William Howard Russell, *My Diary North and South* II (1863); Frank Moore (ed.), *The Rebellion Record* (1862); Kate Mason Rowland and Mrs. Morris L. Croxall (eds.), *The Journals of Julia LeGrand*, Everett Waddey Company, 1911; Headquarters, Department of the Gulf, New Orleans, May 1, 1862; George W. Driggs, *Opening of the Mississippi* (no date); George W. Cable (ed.), "A Woman's Diary of the Siege of Vicksburg Under Fire from the Gunboats" *Century Illustrated Magazine* VIII (1885); G. S. Bradley, *The Star Corps; or Notes of an Army Chaplain during Sherman's Famous March to the Sea* (1865); Eliza Frances Andrews, *The War-Time Journal of a Georgia Girl*, Appleton-Century-Crofts, 1908, reprinted by permission of Hawthorne Books, Inc.

Blacks' Role in Reconstruction

*Black leaders of the former slaves worked toward
one goal—equality. With eloquence and courage these spokesmen
fought a losing battle to secure their newly granted rights.*

WE CLAIM THE SAME RIGHTS

Following the passage of the first Reconstruction act in 1867, Alabama blacks met in Mobile and drafted the following definition of their status:

As there seems to be considerable difference of opinion concerning the "legal rights of the colored man," it will not be amiss to say that we claim exactly *the same rights, privileges and immunities as are enjoyed by white men*—we ask nothing more and will be content with nothing less. All legal distinctions between the races are now abolished. The word white is stricken from our laws, and every privilege which white men were formerly permitted to enjoy, merely because they were white men, now that word is stricken out, we are entitled to on the ground that we are men. *Color can no longer be pleaded for the purpose of curtailing privileges, and every public right, privilege and immunity is enjoyable by every individual member of the public.* The law no longer knows white nor black, but simply men, and consequently we are entitled to ride in public conveyances, hold office, sit on juries and do everything else which we have in the past been prevented from doing solely on the ground of our color.

∽

THE CRY FOR LAND REFORM

Black leaders felt land ownership was the key to success in freedom. Delegate Francis L. Cardoza argued this before the South Carolina Constitutional Convention of 1868:

What is the main cause of the prosperity of the North? It is because every man has his own farm and is free and independent. Let the lands of the South be similarly divided. . . . We will never have true freedom until we abolish the system of agriculture which existed in the Southern States. It is useless to have any schools while we maintain this stronghold of slavery as the agricultural system of the country. . . . If they [the lands] are sold, though a few mercenary speculators may purchase some, the chances are that the colored man and the poor [white] man would be the purchasers. I will prove this . . . by facts. About one hundred poor colored men of Charleston met together and formed themselves into a Charleston Land Company. They subscribed for a number of shares at $10 per share, one dollar payable monthly. They have been meeting for a year. Yesterday they purchased some 600 acres of land for $6,600 that would have sold for $25,000 or $50,000 in better times. . . . This is only one instance of thousands of others that have occurred in this city and State.

∽

THE RIGHT TO HOLD ELECTIVE OFFICE

In the fall of 1868 the white majority of the reconstructed Georgia legislature expelled all black members. Henry Macneal Turner defended his right to hold his seat in the House:

Before proceeding to argue this question upon its intrinsic merits, I wish the members of this House to understand the position that I take. I hold that I am a member of this body. Therefore, sir, I shall neither fawn or cringe before any party, nor stoop to beg them for my rights. . . .

The scene presented in this House, to-day, is one unparalleled in the history of the world. . . . Never has a man been arraigned before a body clothed with legislative, judicial or executive functions, charged with the offense of being of a darker hue than his fellowmen . . . charged with an offense committed by the God of Heaven Himself. Cases may be found where men have been deprived of their rights for crimes and misdemeanors; but it has remained for the State of Georgia, in the very heart of the nineteenth century, to call a man before the bar, and there charge him with an act for which he is no more responsible than for the head which he carries upon his shoulders. . . .

. . . Did half the white men of Georgia vote for this Legislature? Did not the great bulk of them fight, with all their strength, the Constitution under which we are acting? And did they not fight against the organization of this Legislature? And further, sir, did they not vote against it? Yes, sir! And there are persons in this Legislature to-day, who are ready to spit their poison in my face, while they themselves opposed, with all their power, the ratification of this Constitution. They question my right to a seat in this body, to represent the people whose legal votes elected me.

∽

A PLEA FOR INTEGRATED SCHOOLS

Segregated schools were set up from the outset of Reconstruction. In his newspaper in 1871, Frederick Douglass argued that separate schools would mean unequal education:

We hope for the speedy passage of the bill of Mr. Sumner's [to integrate the schools of Washington, D.C.], in order that the mad current of prejudice against the Negro may be checked; and also that the baleful influence upon the children of the colored race of being taught by separation from the whites that the whites are superior to them may be destroyed.

Throughout the South all the schools should be mixed. From our observations during a trip to the South we are convinced that the interests of the poor whites and the colored people are identical. Both are ignorant, and both are the tools of designing educated white men; and the poor whites are more particularly used to further schemes opposed to their own best interests. In that section everything that will bring the poor white man and the colored man closer together should be done; they should be taught to make common cause against the rich land-holders of the South who never regarded a poor white man of as much importance as they did slaves. Educate the poor white children and the colored children together; let them grow up to know that color makes no differences as to the rights of a man; that both the black man and the white man are at home; that the country is as much the country of one as of the other, and that both together must make it a valuable country.

∽

DEFENSE OF THE
CIVIL RIGHTS BILL

A civil rights bill meant to enforce the Civil War amendments was hotly debated in Congress in the early 1870s. South Carolina Representative Robert Brown Elliott argued that it must be passed:

These amendments, . . . have as their all-pervading design and end the security to the recently enslaved race, not only their nominal freedom, but their complete protection from those who had formerly exercised unlimited dominion over them. It is in this broad light that all these amendments must be read, the purpose to secure the perfect equality before the law of all citizens of the United States. What you give to one class you must give to all; what you deny to one class you shall deny to all, unless in the exercise of the common and

universal police power of the State you find it needful to confer exclusive privileges on certain citizens, to be held and exercised still for the common good of all. . . .

There are privileges and immunities which belong to me as a citizen of the United States, and there are other privileges and immunities which belong to me as a citizen of my State. The former are under the protection of the Constitution and laws of the United States, and the latter are under the protection of the laws of my State. . . . Are the rights which I now claim—the right to enjoy the common public conveniences of travel

Whites seize control of the Louisiana House in 1877 after the withdrawal of Federal troops.

on public highways, of rest and refreshment at public inns, of education in public schools, of burial in public cemeteries —rights which I hold as a citizen of the United States or of my State? Or, to state the question more exactly, is not the denial of such privileges to me a denial to me of the equal protection of the laws? For it is under this clause of the fourteenth amendment that we place the present bill, no State shall "deny to any person within its jurisdiction the equal protection of the laws." No matter, therefore, whether his rights are held under the United States or under his particular State, he is equally protected by this amendment. He is always and everywhere entitled to the equal protection of

the laws. All discrimination is forbidden; and while the rights of citizens of a State as such are not defined or conferred by the Constitution of the United States, yet all discrimination, all denial of the equal protection of the laws, whether State or national laws, is forbidden.

∽

BLACK RECONSTRUCTION

After Reconstruction ended in Mississippi in 1875, Senator Blanche K. Bruce, a Mississippi planter, defended his fellow blacks' role in reconstructing the state:

We began our political career under the disadvantages of the inexperience in public affairs that generations of enforced bondage had entailed upon our race. We suffered also from the vicious leadership of some of the men whom our necessities forced us temporarily to accept. Consider further that the States of the South, where we were supposed to control by our majorities, were in an impoverished and semi-revolutionary condition—society demoralized, the industries of the country prostrated, the people sore, morbid, and sometimes turbulent, and no healthy controlling public opinion either existent or possible—consider all these conditions, and it will be seen that we began our political novitiate and formed the organic and statutory laws under great embarrassments.

Despite the difficulties and drawbacks suggested, the constitutions formed under colored majorities . . . were improvements on the instruments they were designed to supersede; and the statutes framed, though necessarily defective because of the crude and varying social and industrial conditions upon which they were based, were more in harmony with the spirit of the age and the genius of our free institutions than the obsolete laws that they supplanted. Nor is there just or any sufficient grounds upon which to charge an oppressive administration of the laws.

BIBLIOGRAPHIC CREDITS: *Montgomery Daily Sentinel,* May 29, 1867; *Proceedings of the Constitutional Convention of South Carolina* I (1868); Ethel M. Christler, *Participation of Negroes in the Government 1867-1870,* unpublished master's thesis, Atlanta University, 1932; *The New National Era,* May 2, 1872; *Congressional Record* (1874); *Congressional Record* (1877).

San Francisco

*Born on the steps of the Spanish mission
San Francisco de Asis, growing to adulthood during
the California gold rush, San Francisco became the
cosmopolitan mecca of the West. Contemporary accounts allow
us to capture the spirit of this creative city.*

BOOM TOWN

With the influx of Forty-Niners, San Francisco boomed to city size almost overnight. Bayard Taylor, a correspondent for the *New York Tribune*, described the initial 1849 building of the city:

Of all the marvelous phases of the history of the Present, the growth of San Francisco is the one which will most tax belief of the Future. Its parallel was never known, and shall never be beheld again. I speak only of what I saw with my own eyes.

When I landed there, a little more than four months before, I found a scattering town of tents and canvas houses, with a show of frame buildings on one or two streets, and a population of about six thousand. Now, on my last visit, I saw around me an actual metropolis, displaying street after street of well-built edifices, filled with an active and enterprising people and exhibiting every mark of permanent commercial prosperity. Then, the town was limited to the curves of the Bay fronting the anchorage and bottom of the hills. Now, it stretched to the topmost heights, followed the shore around point after point, and sending back a long arm through a gap in the hills, took hold of the Golden Gate and was building its warehouses on the open strait and almost fronting the blue horizon of the Pacific. Then, the gold-seeking sojourner lodged in muslin rooms and canvas garrets, with a philosophic lack of furniture, and ate his simple though substantial fare from pine boards. Now, lofty hotels, gaudy with verandas and balconies, were met with in all quarters, furnished with home luxury, and aristocratic restaurants presented daily their long bills of fare, rich with the choicest technicalities of the Parisian cuisine. Then, vessels were coming in day after day, to lie deserted and useless at their anchorage. Now scarce a day passed, but some cluster of sails bound outward through the Golden Gate, took their way to all corners of the Pacific. Like the magic seed of the Indian juggler, which grew, blossomed and bore fruit before the eyes of his spectators, San Francisco seemed to have accomplished in a day the growth of half a century.

∽

VIGILANTE ACTION

With criminals on the rampage in San Francisco, citizens clamored for law and order. The actions of the 1851 Vigilance Committee are explained by early California pioneer Josiah Royce:

The committee had no sooner organized than it had undertaken work. A thief, one Jenkins, a common ruffian of a very low type had been detected Tuesday evening in the very act of burglary on Long Wharf, and, attempting to escape in a boat, was caught and brought back. At ten o'clock Tuesday night the members of the committee were called to their first appointed headquarters (near the corner of Sansome and Bush streets). For two hours the committee were engaged in examining the case, and at midnight Mr. Sam Brannan announced their verdict to the crowd assembled outside the rooms. The criminal, he said, was to be hanged in an hour or two on the Plaza. The execution took place at two. An attempt was made by the police on the Plaza to get Jenkins away from the committee, but the effort was hopeless, and the "old adobe," now so near its doom, did almost its last public service, before the June fire burned it down, in serving, through one of its projecting beams, as a gallows to hang Jenkins.

∽

EMPEROR NORTON

Only in San Francisco could Joshua A. Norton, self-proclaimed Emperor of the United States and Protector of Mexico, have ruled. His 1860-1880 reign is recollected by residents T. A. Barry and B. A. Patten:

San Francisco has rather more than its share of eccentric characters. Foremost among these is "Emperor Norton," a harmless creature, who firmly believes that he is the legitimate sovereign of the United States and Mexico; issues frequent pronunciamentos; exacts tribute from such citizens as humor his delusion; spends his days walking about the streets, his evenings at the theater, and his nights at a cheap lodging-house. He has the run of the hotel reading-rooms, appears on public occasions in tattered regalia, visits the different churches to see that heresies dangerous to the peace of the Empire are not promulgated, calls at the newspaper offices to warn the conductors against the consequences of treasonable utterances—in short, is up early and late regulating the affairs of the world in general, and the city and state in particular.

∽

BALLAD OF THE HYDE STREET GRIP

The institution of the cable car is celebrated in native San Franciscan Gelett Burgess's poem:

Throw her off at Powell street, let her
go at Post,

Watch her well at Geary and at Sutter,
when you coast,
Easy at the Power House, have a care
at Clay,
Sacramento, Washington, Jackson, all
the way!
Drop the rope at Union, never make a
slip—
The lever keeps you busy on the Hyde
Street Grip!

When the Orpheum is closing and the
crowd is on the way,
The conductor's punch is ringing and
the dummy's light and gay;
But the wait upon the table by the Beach
is dark and still—
Just the swashing of the surges on the
shore below the mill;
And the flash of Angel Island breaks
across the channel rip,
And the hush of midnight falls upon the
Hyde Street Grip!

∽

THE GREAT FIRE

**Kathryn Hulme, who as a child lived
through the terror-filled hours of fire
that followed the 1906 earthquake,
vividly remembered the dynamiting of
buildings to halt the fire's insatiable
march:**

Every now and again I looked from
the fire to us, sitting on a hill in the middle of a morning watching a city burn.
A man put out his hand, caught bits of
drifting char, and said: San Francisco,
Queen of the Golden Gate, and blew it
off his hand with a look on his face that
made me think of my father, casual
when you knew he wasn't feeling so. We
had it in our hair, bits of San Francisco,
black scraps of wallpaper, drifting ash
of business files, maybe some of it from
the stacks of gold-backs that had been
burned up in banks. It was exciting to
guess where it might have come from
but I knew I must not guess aloud. The
grown-ups were acting as though they
were at a funeral. . . .

Mother's tears dropped in her lap.
She couldn't look at the exploding buildings the way we children did. Men
around us were crying like mother, not
because they had a business down there
or money in the melting bank vaults,
they didn't mention those; but because
it was their background being blown up.

MELTING POT

**This city by the bay has always been
a melting pot for the world's people.
A Norwegian immigrant's feelings
about San Francisco in 1910 are
expressed by her daughter:**

In those days, if anyone had asked
Mama unexpectedly, "What nationality
are you?" I believe she would have answered without hesitation, "I am a San
Franciscan."

Then quickly, lest you tease her, she
would add, "I mean Norwegian. American citizen."

But her first statement would be the
true one.

Because from the moment she was to
step off the ferryboat, confused and
lonely in a strange land, San Francisco
was to become suddenly and uniquely
her own. . . .

The ingenious open-air cable car mastered
scenic San Francisco's many steep hills.

Papa would tell of the time Mama
took out her citizenship papers and
astounded the solemn court by suddenly
reciting the names of the streets. "Turk,
Eddy, Ellis, O'Farrell," Mama had said
proudly, "Geary, Post, Sutter, Bush, and
Pine."

Papa said the clerk had quite a time
making Mama understand that such
knowledge was not necessary for citizenship. . . .

And if anyone ever asked us where
we were born, Mama instructed us, we
should say "San Francisco." Didn't
copies of our birth certificates, neatly
framed and hung on the wall of Papa's
and Mama's room, testify to that proud
fact?

"After all," Papa used to tease her,
"after all, San Francisco isn't the world."

But to Mama it was just that. The
world.

"ONLY IN SAN FRANCISCO"

San Francisco Chronicle correspondent Herb Caen takes a look at his
Baghdad-by-the-Bay in 1960:

"It could only happen in San Francisco."
Is it pure conceit to think there is something so unique about the city that its
day-to-day adventures could happen nowhere else?

I think not. Surely there is a special
quality to the city, elusive as a streamer
of fog lying lightly on Twin Peaks, romantic as the muffled moan of a foghorn
somewhere in the misty Bay, insistent as
the pounding of the waves under the
windows of the Cliff House.

It is a quality built, as some insist, on
legends and fables—and yet the incredible bridges are there for all to see. San
Franciscans are no longer quite so sure
where the magic can be found, other
critics say—but there is still the patter of
invisible feet along the dark alleys of
Chinatown on a moonless midnight. The
city of today is not The City That Was,
complain the disenchanted—but Golden
Gate Park still marches, green and un-
checked, from yesterday's bay windows
to the Pacific Shores.

"Only in San Francisco . . ."

But, you protest, New York has sky-
scrapers, Pittsburgh has hills, Rio has a
harbor, Sydney has bridges.

True. But where else do you find them
all jumbled together with such artless
charm: wooden shacks nestling against
gleaming apartment houses, a financial
district dissolving suddenly into Bo-
hemia, freighters inching along at the
bottom of your own private hill, so near
you can hear the captain's commands.
All this (and more) within a few square
miles, in a city so small and personal you
can almost cup it in your hands and hold
it to your heart.

BIBLIOGRAPHIC CREDITS: Bayard Taylor, *El Dorado,
Or Adventures in the Path of Empire* (1850); Josiah
Royce, *California from Conquest in 1846 to the Second
Vigilance Committee in San Francisco* (1886); T. A.
Barry and B. A. Patten, *Men and Memories of San
Francisco in the Spring of '50* (1873); estate of Gelett
Burgess, reprinted by Joseph H. Jackson, *The Western
Gate,* Farrar, Straus & Giroux, Inc., 1952; Kathryn
Hulme, *We Lived As Children,* Alfred A. Knopf, Inc.
1938, reprinted by permission of Brandt & Brandt;
Kathryn Forbes, *Mama's Bank Account,* Harcourt Brace
Jovanovich, Inc., 1943; from *Only In San Francisco,*
copyright © 1960 by Herb Caen, reprinted by per-
mission of Doubleday & Company, Inc.

Read All About It

*With a jolt and a jar the U.S. woke up
after World War I. Change and experimentation
called the tune; sensationalism ruled the headlines
in this Age of Ballyhoo. Actual stories
from the twenties follow.*

BRANDED WITH KKK
Local Negro branded and flogged. Resurgent Ku Klux Klan continues lawless fight for white supremacy:

DALLAS, Texas, April 2 [1921]—Police today were investigating the activities of a party of well dressed white masked men who took Alex Johnson, a negro bell boy in a Dallas hotel, to a lonely spot south of Dallas late last night, flogged him and then branded with acid the letters "K.K.K." on his forehead. Johnson was brought back to Dallas in an automobile and thrown from the machine in front of the hotel where he had been employed.

Six automobiles drove to Johnson's home, and a number of masked men tied him in one of the cars. With lights out and Johnson pleading for his life, the party drove to a lonely point on Hutchins Road. Here the negro was tied to a fence post and lashed twenty-five times after being stripped to the waist.

While Johnson sagged limply against the fence a bottle of acid was produced and he was branded.

Charges were filed in County Court last week against Johnson after the police said he had been discovered in the room of a white woman patron of the hotel.

∽

WILD PARTY RAIDED
Three prominent "speaks" raided. Federal agents attempt to keep third New Year's Eve of Prohibition dry:

[New York City. Jan. 2, 1922.]
Twenty Federal prohibition agents, after a night of ceaseless activity, raided the widely known all-night rendezvous of "Jimmy" Kelley, 204 Hester Street, at 4 o'clock yesterday morning, spoiling several early morning parties scheduled to take place there. . . .

This was the third of a series of raids planned for New Year's Eve on search warrants, procured earlier in the day from Federal Judge Augustus N. Hand by United States Assistant District Attorneys Victor House and Sanford H. Cohen. The other two places raided were Reisenweber's and the Golden Eagle, in Greenwich Village. . . .

In the Golden Eagle Restaurant, in Macdougal Street, the agents said, several barrels of wine and about $1,000 worth of other liquors were found in the cellar. No liquors were found in the possession of the management at Reisenweber's at Fifty-eighth Street and Eighth Avenue, but large quantities, the agents said, were on the tables of the 2,500 diners—men and women, nearly all of whom were in evening clothes. Six diners, two women and four men, and several employes received summonses. The agents reported that the party at Reisenweber's when they entered was one of the wildest they had ever witnessed. The revelers refused to be routed by the dry agents, but continued to make merry for several hours after the sleuths had gone in search of more victims. . . .

In the daytime, the agents said, Kelley's place, which is just two blocks south of Police Headquarters, is an innocent looking spaghetti house, but after 1 A.M. the character of the place changes. At this hour the place is closed and all guests are sent away. The wise ones, the agents said, merely go out for a little fresh air, while the front doors are being closed and the curtains drawn. Then they return. . . . Outwardly the place is closed tight, while merriment goes on inside, the agents assert.

JUSTICE FAILS
The crime of Nicola Sacco and Bartolomeo Vanzetti—was it murder or political conspiracy? Analysis follows:

[April 17, 1927]
Again the attention of the country is focused on Nicola Sacco and Bartolomeo Vanzetti, sentenced to die in the electric chair next July. . . .

Sacco and Vanzetti were arrested and charged with murder at the time that the Red' raids were conducted by A. Mitchell Palmer, Federal Attorney General. After their trial and conviction at Dedham, Mass., sympathizers charged that the two men were being "railroaded" because they held radical beliefs. Sacco, a shoe worker, was a Socialist; Vanzetti, a fish peddler, was an anarchist. The local agitation in their behalf spread like a flame. It crossed the Atlantic; it went below the Equator.

The case was discussed in the Italian Chamber of Deputies. A bomb was exploded in the American Embassy at Paris. Workmen in Uruguay went on a general strike. Trade unionists, writers, intellectuals, liberals, anarchists, Socialists, Communists in every corner of the earth responded to appeals from the Boston offices of the Defense Committee. The cables were burdened with protests against the Massachusetts courts and with denunciation of Webster Thayer, the trial judge.

Seven motions for a new trial and five supplementary motions were argued before Judge Thayer in the six years that followed the conviction. All were denied. Neither the evidence on which the convictions were returned nor the new evidence was reviewed by any but the trial judge. A fortnight ago the Supreme Judicial Court of Massachusetts closed the last loophole for action in the courts of the Commonwealth by holding that the trial judge had a right to rule as he did. Retrial was refused.

s

A TUMULTUOUS WELCOME

Charles Lindbergh returns in triumph. Millions of New Yorkers wait hours to welcome hero:

[New York City. June 14, 1927]
Colonel Charles A. Lindbergh descended modestly on New York yesterday on the waves of the greatest reception the city has ever accorded a private citizen. He came as he went, out of the clouds, on the wings of a swooping plane.

Millions beheld his blond boyish head as he rode through six miles of streets and cheered from the depths of their hearts. There never was anything like it.

Arriving at 12:40 P.M. he found that the city had been awaiting him for hours. Lower Manhattan was packed at the Battery, along lower Broadway, at the City Hall. Up along the line of his procession missions were standing in line, hanging from windows, sitting in stands waiting to cheer "Lindy." The city had been drenched in bunting and in flags and ideal weather had come to add the final touch.

The pageant of his welcome was a series of pictures. There was the swoop down of his seaplane in the narrow water of the lower bay, where hundreds of vessels, dressed in a multitude of flags, closed in. Up through smoke and steam, while the harbor was rent by whistles, he came to the Battery.

He stepped ashore there. Out in the broad expanse of the Battery Park was a tumultuous mass of people. When he appeared a mighty roar of good will went up. Then he rode slowly up Broadway, in the wake of a glittering military display, and the thunder of his welcome grew more intense.

Then he was in Fifth Avenue, that thoroughfare of many parades, vivid in decorations and filled with a host. At the Public Library 10,000 children waved a welcome, while hundreds of thousands of their parents clustered near the steps shouted, waved hats, flourished sticks in happy gestures and gave cheer after

cheer. At the end of his route in the greenery of the Mall in Central Park was the greatest single group of welcomers. Upwards of 200,000 were assembled there to see Governor Alfred E. Smith place the State Medal of Valor about the flier's neck.

When "Lucky Lindy" returned from France, the popular acclaim shattered all records.

FIGHT OF THE CENTURY

Tunney retains title with seventh round disputed. Thousands watch, millions listen as fighting ex-marine repulses challenger:

RINGSIDE, SOLDIER FIELD, CHICAGO, Sept. 22 [1927].—His refusal to observe the boxing rules of the Illinois State Athletic Commission, or his ignorance of the rules, or both, cost Jack Dempsey the chance to regain the world's heavyweight championship here tonight in the ring at Soldier Field.

The bout ended with Tunney getting the decision, and the vast majority in the staggering assemblage of 150,000 people who paid, it is estimated, $2,800,000 to see this great sport spectacle, approved the verdict. . . .

. . . [In the seventh round] Dempsey . . . suddenly lashed a long, wicked left to the jaw with the power of old. This he followed with a right to the jaw, the old "iron-mike" as deadly as ever, and quickly drove another left hook to the jaw, under which Tunney toppled like a falling tree. . . .

The knockdown brought the knockdown timekeeper, Paul Beeler, to his feet automatically, watch in hand, eyes

glued to the ticking seconds and he bawled "one" before he looked upon the scene in the ring.

There he saw Dempsey in his own corner, directly above the prostrate, brain-numbed Tunney. . . .

Dempsey had no eyes for Referee Barry, who was waving frantically for the former titleholder to run to a neutral corner, even as he kept an eye on the fallen Tunney. . . .

Finally, Dempsey took cognizance of the referee's frantic motions. He was galvanized into action and sped hurriedly across the ring to a neutral corner,

But three or four, or possibly five precious seconds had elapsed before Dempsey realized at all what he should do. In that fleeting time of the watch Tunney got the advantage. No count was proceeding over him, and quickly his senses were returning. When Referee Barry started counting with Timekeeper Beeler, Tunney was in a state of mental revival. . . .

Society's bluebloods forgot decorum and yelled excitedly. Kings of finance and princes of industry were mingling their yells with those of Governors, mayors, Representatives in Congress, Senators, lawyers, doctors, theatre and movie folk and just plain ordinary people.

. . . Each punch of Tunney's to Dempsey's jaw—and there were many of them —was a thrill in itself as Dempsey recoiled under the blow for a flash, only to come charging in again. Those blows which floored Tunney were punches never to be forgotten, and the spectacle of Dempsey down squatting in the eighth round under Tunney's driving right to the jaw recalled the Dempsey-Firpo fight save that the Tunney punch had not the power behind Firpo. . . .

Tunney won on his boxing ability alone and Dempsey lost because he could not keep up with the champion. That, in a nutshell, tells the story of the fight on results. Tunney was alert, resourceful, the cool ring general, the master boxer hitting timely and accurately, and at times desperately in his own defense against the annihilating Dempsey with the revived punch.

The Rise of Organized Labor

*In the Roaring Twenties unionism fell into decline.
But under the impact of the depression and with the coming
of the New Deal, workers joined together to fight for
a better place in the national economy.*

A SOUTHERN MILLTOWN
A young woman working for $7 a week in 1925 describes the helplessness of the industrial worker in the South:

I worked eleven hours a day, five and a half days a week, for $7 a week. . . .

The sanitary conditions were ghastly. When I desired a drink of water, I had to dip my cup into a pail of water that had been brought into the mill from a spring in the fields. It tasted horrible to me. Often I saw lint from the cotton in the room floating on top of the lukewarm water. All of the men chewed tobacco, and most of the women used snuff. Little imagination is needed to judge the condition of the water which I had to drink, for working in that close, hot spinning room made me thirsty. Toilet facilities were provided three stories down in the basement of the mill in a room without any ventilation. Nowhere was there any running water; even in the houses provided by the company there was no running water. . . .

Everything in the village is company owned. The houses look like barns on stilts, and appear to have been thrown together. When I would go inside one of them, I could see outside through the cracks in the walls. The workers do all of their trading at the company store and bank, and use the company school and library for they have no means of leaving the village. The money is kept circulating from the employer to the employees to company store, store to company bank, and from the bank to the company again. The result is old torn bills in the pay envelope each week.

I worked in the South for nine months, and during that time I could not reconcile myself to the conditions of the mills and village. Therefore, I left the South

and returned to the North—back to the clock-punching, speed-up and efficiency system of the northern mills.

Five years have passed since then, and I have learned through experience that I may go North, South, East, or West in my search for work, and find miserable conditions for miserable wages. I know that the workers in any industry are in a most deplorable condition, but the workers of the South are in virtual slavery.

∽

"HELL IN PENNSYLVANIA"
**The plight of the workingman was most evident in the Pennsylvania coal fields. Unable to organize effectively, thousands of miners were left unemployed as mines closed.
A *New York Daily News* reporter portrays miner's conditions in 1925:**

I have . . . seen horrible things there; things which I almost hesitate to enumerate and describe. I can scarcely expect my story to be believed. I did not believe it myself when the situation was first outlined to me. Then I went into the coal camps of western and central Pennsylvania and saw for myself. . . .

Many times it seemed impossible to think that we were in modern civilized America. We saw thousands of women and children, literally starving to death. We found hundreds of destitute families living in crudely constructed bareboard shacks. They had been evicted from their homes by the coal companies. We unearthed a system of despotic tyranny reminiscent of Czar-ridden Siberia at its worst. We found police brutality and industrial slavery. We discovered the weirdest flock of injunctions that ever emanated from American temples of justice.

We unearthed evidence of terrorism and counter-terrorism; of mob beatings and near lynchings; of dishonesty, graft, and heartlessness. . . .

The mine fields are a bubbling cauldron of trouble. If it boils over—and it threatens to do so—blood must flow freely and many lives pay the forfeit.

∽

CHAMPION OF LABOR
When the AFL declined to organize industrial labor, John L. Lewis, president of the United Mine Workers, created the CIO. His understanding of labor's problems, as articulated in this speech, created a new spirit for the labor movement:

Labor has suffered just as our farm population has suffered from a viciously unequal distribution of the national income. In the exploitation of both classes of workers has been the source of panic and depression, and upon the economic welfare of both rests the best assurance of a sound and permanent prosperity.

Under the banner of the Committee for Industrial Organization, American labor is on the march. Its objectives today are those it had in the beginning: to strive for the unionization of our unorganized millions of workers and for the acceptance of collective bargaining as a recognized American institution.

It seeks peace with the industrial world. It seeks cooperation and mutuality of effort with the agricultural population. It would avoid strikes. It would have its rights determined under law by the peaceful negotiations and contract relationships that are supposed to characterize American commercial life.

Until an aroused public opinion demands that employers accept that rule, labor has no recourse but to surrender its rights or struggle for their realization with its own economic power.

Labor, like Israel, has many sorrows. Its women weep for their fallen and they lament for the future of the children of the race. It ill behooves one who has supped at labor's table and who has been sheltered in labor's house to curse with equal fervor and fine impartiality both labor and its adversaries when they become locked in deadly embrace.

I repeat that labor seeks peace and guarantees its own loyalty, but the voice of labor, insistent upon its rights, should not be annoying to the ears of justice nor offensive to the conscience of the American people.

ॐ

THE "SIT-DOWN"
The success of the CIO began with a rash of sit-down strikes by rubber workers in Akron, Ohio, in 1935. Author Louis Adamic described a scene in which the workers simply turned off their machines and sat down:

Sitting by their machines, cauldrons, boilers, and work benches, they talked. Some realized for the first time how important they were in the process of rubber production. Twelve men had practically stopped the works! Almost any dozen or score of them could do it! In some departments six could do it! The active rank-and-filers, scattered through the various sections of the plant, took the initiative in saying, "We've got to stick with 'em!" And they stuck with them, union and non-union men alike. Most of them were non-union. Some probably were vaguely afraid not to stick. Some were bewildered. Others amused. There was much laughter through the works. Oh boy, oh boy! Just like at the ball game, no kiddin'. There the crowd had stuck with the players and they got an umpire who was a member of a labor union. Here everybody stuck with the twelve guys who first sat down, and the factory management was beside itself. Superintendents, foremen, and straw bosses were dashing about. . . . This sudden suspension of production was costing the company many hundreds of dollars every minute. . . . In less than an hour the dispute was settled—full victory for the men!

ॐ

THE MEMORIAL DAY MASSACRE
On Memorial Day, 1937, in Chicago, 300 steelworkers made a peaceful protest march against "little steel" companies' resistance to unionization. Ten workers were killed when police opened fire. A participant in the march described the massacre:

The police "charged like a bunch of demons," Harry Harper testified. "No one had a chance in the world. I was knocked down by the impact of the officers surging forward. I received a blow that struck me in the face. I went down. I tried to get up and blood was streaming out of my left eye. It also affected the

I WILL WIN

At the end of World War I, U.S. labor stood determined to secure its rights at last.

right eye partially but I still had a little vision. I managed to run a little, covering my face with one hand. With the right eye I could see officers charging in a circle, shooting with revolvers—not up but right into the crowd—I realized the danger I was in.

"I feared I was going to be shot so I fell into a hole. Before I fell into this hole I saw people being mowed down, like with a scythe. . . . As I fell into this culvert there was a party lying there already. He said to me, 'Help me, buddy. I am shot.' And I said, 'I am helpless. I cannot help you.' I could not stay there much longer because just then a gas bomb fell into my face. It was choking to me so I made one more attempt to go into the safety zone. But then I lost all sense of reasoning."

ॐ

A COAL MINER SPEAKS
Labor reform was slow—but it did take place, and thousands of workers owed their new status to organized labor. A letter from a miner in 1938 to the *United Mine Workers Journal* reflects the new spirit of American labor:

I'd like to express my appreciation of our grand old organization—the United Mine Workers of America—for putting Logan county and southern West Virginia on the map. That is just the way it is going to be in Harlan county, Ky. I think we should be grateful to such men as Franklin D. Roosevelt, John L. Lewis, Van A. Bittner, and our district and local officers. I think it safe to say that 99 percent of Logan county miners are grateful enough that they will ever be true to the organization. I can't see how any sane coal miner could be otherwise. What a change has been wrought in this part of the country! Instead of fourteen hours we work seven hours a day. Instead of 20 cents a ton for loading we receive 52.4 cents a ton. I could name many more improvements since the coming of the union, even the dawn of free speech. Thank God for broadminded men who have brought these things about.

A. W. McClung,
Just a coal miner

BIBLIOGRAPHIC CREDITS: Andria Taylor Hourwich and Gladys L. Palmer (eds.), *I Am a Woman Worker*, Affiliated Schools for Workers, 1936; *New York Daily News*, 1925; John L. Lewis, radio speech delivered September 3, 1937; Louis Adamic, *My America*, copyright © 1938 by Louis Adamic, by permission of Harper & Row, Publishers, Inc.; M.S. Schnapper, *American Labor*, Public Affairs Press, 1972; from *United Mine Workers Journal* (January 15, 1938), reprinted with permission.

The World at War

*Twice during the first half of the twentieth century,
war swept the globe. America's young men crossed
the seas, both to the east and to the west, to fight for
freedom and democracy.*

THE DOUGHBOYS

**Fresh in mind and body, unlike their
weary European allies, the Yanks
took the hardships of W.W.I in stride.
Lieutenant H. H. Heliwell described
the experiences of the Ninth Infantry:**

After a trying and exasperating forty
days in the lines at Château-Thierry,
where we lived in the ground like go-
phers, only not so deep, and where shells
were always getting in our way to make
life a torment; where the nights were
hell and the days dragged along like
months, and where the grub was mon-
key-meat floating in grease; after all that,
we were taken back to a small town for
a rest. But, strange to say, we did not
get that rest. Before the men had bathed
or even changed . . . we received orders
to entrain for a destination to be known
when we arrived. . . .

We . . . advanced seven miles inside
of twenty-four hours, farther than we
should have gone in fact. Don't forget
that the men were doing this on empty
stomachs and tired, very tired, bodies
and legs. The men, some of them, drank
from the puddles in the roads. . . .

Will we lick the Kaiser? I'll say so,
with men like those and twenty million
more behind them just as good.

∽

AMERICA'S ACE OF ACES

**In W.W.I Captain Eddie Rickenbacker
shot down 26 German planes in
seven months. At war's end he felt a
brief regret that his days of danger
were past:**

"I've lived through the war!" I heard one
whirling Dervish of a pilot shouting to
himself as he pirouetted alone in the
center of a mud hole. . . .

Another pilot, this one an Ace of 27
Squadron, grasped me . . . by the arm
and shouted almost incredulously, *"We
won't be shot at any more!"* . . . What
sort of a new world will this be without
the excitement of danger in it? . . .

How can one enjoy life without this
highly spiced sauce of danger? What
else is left to living now that the zest and
excitement of fighting airplanes is gone?
Thoughts such as these held me entranced for the moment. . . .

It was the *"finis de la guerre!"* It was
the *finis d'aviation.* It was to us, perhaps
unconsciously, the end of that intimate
relationship that since the beginning of
the war had cemented together brothers-
in-arms into a closer fraternity than is
known to any other friendship in the
whole world.

∽

THE DEATH OF CAPTAIN WASKOW

**Death in war often seems impersonal;
yet W.W. II correspondent Ernie Pyle
caught the tragedy of every dead
soldier in his description of one
man's death:**

Dead men had been coming down the
mountain all evening, lashed onto the
backs of mules. They came lying belly-
down across the wooden packsaddles,
their heads hanging down on one side,
their stiffened legs sticking out awk-
wardly from the other, bobbing up and
down as the mules walked. . . .

. . . We went out into the road. Four
mules stood there in the moonlight, in
the road where the trail came down off
the mountain. The soldiers who led them
stood there waiting.

"This one is Captain Waskow," one of
them said quietly.

Two men unlashed his body from the
mule and lifted it off and laid it in the
shadow beside the stone wall. . . .

. . . The men in the road seemed reluctant to leave. They stood around, and
gradually I could sense them moving,
one by one, close to Captain Waskow's
body. Not so much to look, I think, as to
say something in finality to him and to
themselves. . . .

One soldier came and looked down,
and he said out loud, "God damn it!"

That's all he said, and then he walked
away.

Another one came, and he said, "God
damn it to hell anyway!" He looked
down for a few last moments and then
turned and left.

Another man came. I think he was an
officer. It was hard to tell officers from
men in the dim light, for everybody was
bearded and grimy. The man looked
down into the dead captain's face and
then spoke directly to him, as though he
were alive, "I'm sorry, old man."

Then a soldier came and stood beside
the officer and bent over, and he too
spoke to his dead captain, not in a whis-
per but awfully tenderly, and he said, "I
sure am sorry, sir."

Then the first man squatted down,
and he reached down and took the captain's hand, and he sat there for a full
five minutes holding the dead hand in
his own and looking intently into the
dead face. And he never uttered a sound
all the time he sat there.

Finally he put the hand down. He
reached over and gently straightened the
points of the captain's shirt collar, and
then he sort of rearranged the tattered
edges of the uniform around the wound,
and then he got up and walked away
down the road in the moonlight, all
alone.

PORTRAIT OF THE GI

In his cartoons and in his writing, Sergeant Bill Mauldin portrayed the toughness of the American infantryman, his ability to survive the miseries of war, and his peculiar brand of heroism:

I don't make the infantryman look noble, because he couldn't look noble even if he tried. Still there is a certain nobility and dignity in combat soldiers and medical aid men with dirt in their ears. They are rough and their language gets coarse because they live a life stripped of convention and niceties. Their nobility and dignity come from the way they live unselfishly and risk their lives to help each other. They are normal people who have been put where they are, and whose actions and feelings have been molded by their circumstances. There are gentlemen and boors; intelligent ones and stupid ones; talented ones and inefficient ones. But when they are all together and they are fighting, despite their bitching and griping and goldbricking and mortal fear, they are facing cold steel and screaming lead and hard enemies, and they are advancing and beating the hell out of the opposition.

They wish to hell they were someplace else, and they wish to hell they would get relief. They wish to hell the mud was dry, and they wish to hell their coffee was hot. They want to go home. But they stay in their wet holes and fight, and then they climb out and crawl through minefields and fight some more.

∞

WAR IN THE PACIFIC

When Japanese *kamikaze* pilots appeared, it meant a fight to the finish. Seaman James J. Fahey, who served on the cruiser *Montpelier*, recounted one such battle:

Jap planes were coming at us from all directions. . . . [One] came in on a battleship with its guns blazing away. Other Jap planes came in strafing one ship, dropping their bombs on another and crashing into another ship. . . .

Planes were falling all around us, bombs were coming too close for comfort. The Jap planes were cutting up the water with machine gun fire. All the guns on the ships were blazing away, talk about action, never a dull moment. The fellows were passing ammunition like lightning as the guns were turning in all directions spitting out hot steel. Parts of destroyed suicide planes were scattered all over the ship. During a little lull in the action the men would look around for Jap souvenirs and what souvenirs they were. I got part of the plane. The deck near my mount was covered with blood, guts, brains, tongues, scalps, hearts, arms, etc. from the Jap pilots. . . .

These suicide or kamikaze pilots wanted to destroy us, our ships and themselves. This gives you an idea what

"Joe, yestiddy ya saved my life an' I swore I'd pay ya back. Here's my last pair of dry socks."

kind of an enemy we are fighting. The air attacks in Europe are tame compared to what you run up against out here against the Japs. The Germans will come in so far, do their job and take off but not the Japs. . . . You do not discourage the Japs, they never give up, you have to kill them. It is an honor to die for the Emperor.

∞

FIGHTING FOR PIE

Correspondent John Hersey marched through the jungles with the marines, shared their hell, and wanted to ask them one question:

"What would you say you were fighting for? Today, here in this valley, what are you fighting for?"

The excited flush, which had come into their faces as they asked their questions, went out again. Their faces became pale. Their eyes wandered. They looked like men bothered by a memory. They did not answer for what seemed a very long time.

Then one of them spoke, but not to me. He spoke to the others, and for a second I thought he was changing the subject or making fun of me, but of course he was not. He was answering my question very specifically.

He whispered: "Jesus, what I'd give for a piece of blueberry pie."

Another whispered: "Personally I prefer mince."

A third whispered: "Make mine apple with a few raisins in it and lots of cinnamon: you know, Southern style."

Fighting for pie. Of course that is not exactly what they meant. Here, in a place where they had lived for several weeks mostly on captured Japanese rice, then finally had gone on to such delicacies as canned corned beef and Navy beans, where they were usually hungry and never given a treat—here pie was their symbol of home.

In other places there are other symbols. For some men, in places where there is plenty of good food but no liquor, it is a good bottle of scotch whiskey. In other places, where there's drink but no dames, they say they'd give their left arm for a blonde. For certain men, books are the thing; for others, music; for others, movies. But for all of them, these things are just badges of home. When they say they are fighting for these things, they mean that they are fighting for home—"to get the goddam thing over and get home."

Perhaps this sounds selfish. It certainly sounds less dynamic than the Axis slogans. But home seems to most marines a pretty good thing to be fighting for. Home is where the good things are—the generosity, the good pay, the comforts, the democracy, the pie.

BIBLIOGRAPHIC CREDITS: Frank Freidel, *Over There: The Story of America's First Great Overseas Crusade*, Little, Brown and Company, 1964; Eddie V. Rickenbacker, *Fighting the Flying Circus*, Doubleday and Company, Inc., 1965; Ernie Pyle, *Brave Men*, Holt, Rinehart & Winston, Inc., 1944; copyright © 1944 by United Features Syndicate, Inc., courtesy of Bill Mauldin; James J. Fahey, *Pacific War Diary, 1942-1945*, Houghton Mifflin Company, 1963; from *Into The Valley*, by John Hersey, copyright 1942, 1943 by John Hersey, reprinted by permission of Alfred A. Knopf, Inc.

The Struggle for Equality

In the most recent generation, the American people have renewed their historic ideal that "all men are created equal." In these passages representative spokesmen from several minority groups seeking recognition and equality state their goals.

THE CHICANOS' QUEST

The Mexican-American struggle for equality is largely centered in the Southwest. They struggle not only for equality with Anglos, but for preservation of Mexican culture and heritage. Rodolfo Gonzales delivered a "Plan for the Barrio" before the Poor People's March on Washington, D.C., in 1963:

We are basically a communal people . . . in the pattern of our Indian ancestors. Part of our cultural rights and cultural strengths is our communal values. We lived together for over a century and never had to fence our lands. When the gringo came, the first thing he did was to fence land. We opened our houses and hearts to him and trained him to irrigated farming, ranching, stock raising, and mining. He listened carefully and moved quickly, and when we turned around, he had driven us out and kept us out with violence, trickery, legal and court entanglements. The land for all people, the land of the brave became the land for the few and the land of the bully.

Robbed of our land, our people were driven to the migrant labor fields and the cities. Poverty and city living under the colonial system of the Anglo has castrated our people's culture, consciousness of our heritage, and language. Because of our cultural rights, which are guaranteed by treaty, and because the U.S. *says* in its constitution that all treaties are the law of the land . . .

THEREFORE WE DEMAND

HOUSING: We demand the necessary resources to plan our living accommodations so that it is possible to extend family homes to be situated in a communal style . . . around plazas or parks with plenty of space for the children. . . .

EDUCATION: We demand that our schools be built in the same communal fashion as our neighborhoods . . . that they be warm and inviting facilities and not jails. . . .

We demand that all teachers live within walking distance of the schools. We demand that from kindergarten through college, Spanish be the first language and English the second language and the textbooks to be rewritten to emphasize the heritage and the contributions of the Mexican American or Indio-Hispano in the building of the Southwest.

ECONOMIC OPPORTUNITIES: We demand that the businesses serving our community be owned by that community. Seed money is required to start cooperative grocery stores, gas stations, furniture stores, etc. Instead of our people working in big factories across the city, we want training and low-interest loans to set up small industries in our own communities.

AGRICULTURAL REFORMS: We demand that not only the land which is our ancestral right be given back to those pueblos, with restitution for mineral, natural resources, grazing and timber used.

REDISTRIBUTION OF THE WEALTH: That all citizens of this country share in the wealth of this nation by institution of economic reforms that would provide for all people, and that welfare in the form of subsidies in taxes and payoffs to corporate owners be reverted to the people who in reality are the foundation of the economy and the tax base for this society.

LAND REFORM: A complete reevaluation of the Homestead Act to provide people ownership of the natural resources that abound in this country.

Birthright should not only place responsibility on the individual but grant him ownership of the land he dies for.

∽

PEOPLE OF THE CITY

During the 1960s America rediscovered her hard-core poor. In 1967 a presidential commission summed up the goals of this minority:

The slums of virtually every American city harbor, in alarming amounts, not only physical deprivation and spiritual despair but also doubt and downright cynicism about the relevance of the outside world's institutions and the sincerity of efforts to close the gap. Far from ignoring or rejecting the goals and values espoused by more fortunate segments of society, the slum dweller wants the same material and intangible things for himself and his children as those more privileged. Indeed, the very similarity of his wishes sharpens the poignancy and frustration of felt discrepancies in opportunity for fulfillment. The slum dweller may not respect a law that he believes draws differences between his rights and another's, or a police force that applies laws so as to draw such differences; he does recognize the law's duty to deal with law-breakers, and he respects the policeman who does so with businesslike skill and impartiality. Living as he does in a neighborhood likely to be among the city's highest in rates of crime, he worries about and wants police protection even more than people living in the same city's safer regions. He may not have much formal education himself, or many books in his house, and he may hesitate to visit teachers or attend school functions, but studies show that he too, like his college-graduate counterpart, is vitally interested in his children's education. And while some inner-city residents, like some people everywhere, may not be eager to change their unemployment status, it is also true that many more of them toil day after day at the dullest and most backbreaking of society's tasks, traveling long distances for menial jobs without hope of advancement. Very likely his parents (or he himself) left home—the deep South, or Appalachia, or Mexico, or Puerto Rico—looking for a better life, only to be absorbed into the yet more binding dependency and isolation of the inner city.

∾

MAN AND WOMAN
The American woman is also searching for a new role in her society. Wilma Scott Heide, 1972 president of the National Organization for Women, advocates similar roles for both men and women by choice, not by decree:

Please know that we are not advocating unisex but unipeople. To stereotype people by sex, race, nation or religion is to polarize people. Women and men are not so opposite as we've been taught; we are more alike than different. Individual differences are far greater than sexual differences. With that understanding, women and men can come together as friends, partners and mutual lovers by choice and not by duty, exploitation, and fear. The great renewal of human kind may indeed come from the transfusions of the enormous potential and talents of women and from the liberation of men to hang up their sex hangups.

I am indeed talking about a behavioral revolution of profound implications for every woman, man and child. It is liberated women and emancipated men who are leading and welcoming the rights and liberation of women. I, for one, am delighted to welcome the participation of mature, secure, sensitive men. Nonetheless, *even* if not one man in the whole world approved and/or would benefit, women are worth it. Our liberation would be valid without *any* male blessings; it would simply take longer.

No *significant* change in the future is possible without women's human rights and liberation from centuries of blatant and subtle bondage. Only those women and men free enough from stereotyped notions of "femininity" and "masculinity" to be secure about our common humanity are as yet liberated enough to move with the level of self confidence to create an androgynous society and world. Women will demand it. Men will eventually welcome it. Our children deserve it. No woman should ever have to stand alone or be criticized for advocating and creating our own, our mothers, our sisters, our daughters personhood. It's a matter of human justice.

Eager, integrated students represent recent strides taken to achieve racial equality.

THE RED MAN'S WAY
Sioux author Vine Deloria, Jr., describes the Indian people's reactivated efforts to regain their stolen lands:

Blatant violation of [historic] treaties creates frustration among the Indian people. Many wonder exactly what their rights are, for no matter where they turn treaties are disregarded and laws are used to deprive them of what little land remains to them. . . .

Many things can immediately be done to begin to make amends for past transgressions. Passage of federal legislation acknowledging the rights of the Indian people as contained in the treaties can

make the hunting and fishing rights of the Indians a reality.

Where land has been wrongfully taken—and there are few places where it has not been wrongfully taken—it can be restored by transferring land now held by the various governmental departments within reservation boundaries to the tribes involved. Additional land in the public domain can be added to smaller reservations, providing a viable land base for those Indian communities needing more land.

Eastern tribes not now receiving federal services can be recognized in a blanket law affirming their rights as existing communities and organized under the Indian Reorganization Act. Services can be made available to these communities on a contract basis and the tribes can be made self-sufficient.

Mythical generalities of what built this country and made it great must now give way to consideration of keeping contractual obligations due to the Indian people. Morality must begin where immorality began. Karl Mundt, in commenting on the passage of the Indian Claims Commission Bill in 1946, stated:

> . . . if any Indian tribe can prove that it has been unfairly and dishonorably dealt with by the United States it is entitled to recover. This ought to be an example for all the world to follow in its treatment of minorities.

The Indian Claims Commission is, or should be, merely the first step in a general policy of restitution for past betrayals. Present policy objectives should be oriented toward restitution of Indian communities with rights they enjoyed for centuries before the coming of the white man.

∾

ANTI-SEMITISM IN HIRING
Though freedom of religion was incorporated into America's earliest governing documents, elements of religious discrimination still persist. Jewish editor Norman Podhoretz discusses this still present inequality:
Do we see an increase in discriminatory practices against Jews today? I am very much afraid that we do. The two princi-

pal areas are civil-service employment and university admissions and hiring practices, in both of which the idea of judging an individual without reference to "race, creed, or color" has lost considerable ground in favor of the idea of proportional representation according to race and, increasingly, according to sex, and very lately according also to ethnic group. But the same idea also seems to be gaining ground in areas besides the public sector and the universities. One example which comes to mind is the so-called Minority Advancement Plan. . . . By the terms of this plan all firms of a certain size would be required by law to put a stated percentage of people drawn from "minority groups" into jobs paying $15,000 per year or more. Jews, although some might consider them a minority group, since they after all add up to a mere 3 percent of the population, are not defined as such in the plan; nor are Italians or Poles or any other of the predominantly Catholic ethnic groups: only non-whites and women are minorities in this quaint and original conception. For Jews, like the other white ethnic groups, are, as [the plan's authors] put it, already in the club, which is to say that they already have more than their fair share of the better-paying jobs. Now there are substantial reasons for disagreeing with this complacent view of the economic situation of the major ethnic groups. But let us acknowledge that Jews are more than proportionately represented among those in this country who earn $15,000 or more. Are they then to be fired? . . . Or will they simply be phased out gradually by the adoption of an anti-Jewish quota in hiring and promotions? [The plan's authors] do not say. Perhaps their idea is to replace the Jews in question with their wives, thereby killing at least two birds with one stone, and maybe even one or two more. . . .

Clearly it is not the primary purpose of those who support this tendency to discriminate against Jews—though it may be that in a climate in which Jews are commonly said to be *over*represented almost everywhere they are represented at all, the idea of putting the Jews in their place is considered by some a welcome bonus—just as, conversely, the opposite development was considered a welcome bonus in the more benevolent climate of the past.

"I HAVE A DREAM"

Blacks have pressed for equality since Reconstruction. Martin Luther King, Jr., Nobel Peace Prize recipient, had a dream—expressed at the 1963 Poor People's March:

Five score years ago, a great American, in whose symbolic shadow we stand today, signed the Emancipation Proclamation. This momentous decree came as a great beacon of hope to millions of slaves, who had been seared in the flames of withering injustice. It came as a joyous daybreak to end the long night of their captivity. . . .

One hundred years later the colored American lives on a lonely island of poverty in the midst of a vast ocean of material prosperity. One hundred years later, the colored American is still languishing in the corners of American society and finds himself an exile in his own land. So we have come here today to dramatize a shameful condition. . . .

Let us not wallow in the valley of despair. I say to you, my friends, we face the difficulties of today and tomorrow.

I still have a dream. It is a dream deeply rooted in the American dream.

I have a dream that one day this nation will rise up and live out the true meaning of its creed. We hold these truths to be self-evident that all men are created equal.

I have a dream that one day out in the red hills of Georgia the sons of former slaves and the sons of former slaveowners will be able to sit down together at the table of brotherhood.

I have a dream that one day even the state of Mississippi, a state sweltering with the heat of oppression, will be transformed into an oasis of freedom and justice.

I have a dream that my four little children will one day live in a nation where they will not be judged by the color of their skin but by their character.

I have a dream today.

I have a dream that one day down in Alabama, with its vicious racists, with its governor having his lips dripping wth the words of interposition and nullification; that one day right down in Alabama little black boys and black girls will be able to join hands with little white boys and white girls as sisters and brothers.

I have a dream today.

I have a dream that one day every valley shall be ungulfed, every hill shall be exalted, and every mountain shall be made low, the rough places will be made plains, and the crooked places will be made straight, and the glory of the Lord shall be revealed and all flesh shall see it together. . . .

This will be the day when all of God's children will be able to sing with new meaning "My country 'tis of thee, sweet land of liberty, of thee I sing. Land where my fathers died, land of the Pilgrim's pride, from every mountainside, let freedom ring!"

And if America is to be a great nation, this must become true. So, let freedom ring from the hilltops of New Hampshire. Let freedom ring from the mighty mountains of New York.

Let freedom ring from the heightening Alleghenies of Pennsylvania.

Let freedom ring from the snow-capped Rockies of Colorado.

Let freedom ring from the curvacious slopes of California.

But not only that, let freedom ring from the Stone Mountain of Georgia.

Let freedom ring from every hill and molehill of Mississippi and every mountainside.

When we let freedom ring, when we let it ring from every tenement and every hamlet, from every state and every city, we will be able to speed up that day when all of God's children, black men and white men, Jews and Gentiles, Protestants and Catholics, will be able to join hands and sing in the words of the old spiritual, "Free at last, free at last. Thank God Almighty, we are free at last."

BIBLIOGRAPHIC CREDITS: Rodolfo Gonzales, speech delivered before Poor People's March, 1963; The President's Commission on Law Enforcement and Administration of Justice, *Task Force Report: Juvenile Delinquency and Youth Crime*, U.S. Government Printing Office, 1967; Wilma Scott Heide, speech delivered before the University of Nebraska, 1972; Vine Deloria, Jr., *Custer Died for Your Sins*, Macmillan Publishing Company, Inc., 1969, copyright © 1969 by Vine Deloria, Jr.; reprinted from *Commentary*, by permission, copyright © 1972 by the American Jewish Committee; Martin Luther King, Jr., speech delivered before the Poor People's March, 1963.

PICTURE CREDITS: p. 289—The Bettmann Archive, Inc.; p. 291—Library of Congress; p. 293—Johnson Publishing Co.; p. 295—Culver; p. 297—Brown Brothers; p. 299—*Solidarity*, August 4, 1917; p. 301—copyright © 1944 by United Features Syndicate, Inc., courtesy of Bill Mauldin; p. 303—Charles Moore, Black Star.

FRED MAROON

A Presidential Gallery

LINCOLN THROUGH NIXON

"I have gathered you together to hear what I have written down. I do not wish your advice about the main matter." Thus spoke Abraham Lincoln to his cabinet when presenting the Emancipation Proclamation. And thus have spoken other strong Presidents to their administrations and to their times.

Yet in the faces of the twenty Presidents who followed Lincoln—faces which stare forth from the canvasses on the following pages—restraint (and occasionally weakness) appears as well as strength. Indeed, the chronicle of the presidency since the Civil War has been a search for the proper means of controlling, balancing, and applying the tremendous power of the executive office.

To all who have held that office, the White House seems an isolated dwelling. But in this handsome photograph of "Camelot" during the Kennedy administration, the doors appear open to the people, inviting them to share in the adventure of American government.

Abraham Lincoln (1861-1865)

"A house divided against itself cannot stand," said Abraham Lincoln before his unsuccessful run for the Senate. Two years later, in 1860, he became the sixteenth President—and rose to greatness as the divided house fell apart.

There was little to earmark him for greatness in his early years. Humbly born, he was schooled for less than a year. Early employers, and even his father, often thought him lazy; he admitted no love for manual labor, though he swung an ax with legendary skill. He had ambition and utter honesty but no great business acumen, and was years paying the debts of his partnership in a country store that failed.

But always he read. Chores and customers waited unnoticed as he devoured a history, a classic, the Bible that shaped his principles, the borrowed law book that opened his future.

As a lawyer, Lincoln was popular but not gifted. As a politician, he was gifted but not always popular; he won a term in the House, was denied renomination for his stand against the Mexican War, and lost to Stephen A. Douglas in his only try for the Senate. But despite a high-pitched voice, his logic and eloquence came through with moving force as he debated with Douglas over slavery and union. By 1860 he had won the Republican nomination.

His election seemed to doom the Southern life style, and eleven states saw no choice but secession. When the guns spoke at Fort Sumter, Lincoln was swift to reply, and careful not to call into session a Congress that might thwart him. It may have been unconstitutional for him to enlarge the army and blockade Southern ports; it surely was for him to suspend the writ of habeas corpus. But he

Prophetic sadness fills this miniature of Lincoln and son Tad; of four sons, only Robert Todd lived to maturity.

Life	Born Feb. 12, 1809, Hardin County, Ky. Married Mary Todd; four children. Died April 15, 1865.
Campaigns	Ran in 1860 as a moderate, opposing both abolition and expansion of slavery. Surprised to win reelection as National Unionist in 1864.
Milestones	Named Grant to head Union armies. Issues of slavery and right to secede settled by Civil War and 13th Amendment. Proposed moderate Reconstruction policy.
Image	Self-made man of great character, fittingly memorialized on the humble penny. Amusing storyteller, yet brooding.

met the crisis with a force the presidency had not wielded in many years.

A dearth of good generals forced the gentle Lincoln to direct the war himself until 1863. By then his son Willie had died, his armies had suffered defeats, and opposition at home was growing. He was, in fact, one of the most severely criticized Presidents in history, for his initial aim was to save the Union, not decide the slavery issue, and that angered both abolitionists and anti-abolitionists.

Lincoln folds his lean length into a chair in this moody portrait by G.P.A. Healy. It was painted after the President—whose special grace was his "malice toward none"—was killed by a madman's lead ball five days after Lee's surrender. "The greatest character since Christ," said John Hay of Lincoln, who personifies the nobility of soul sought by many but attained by few.

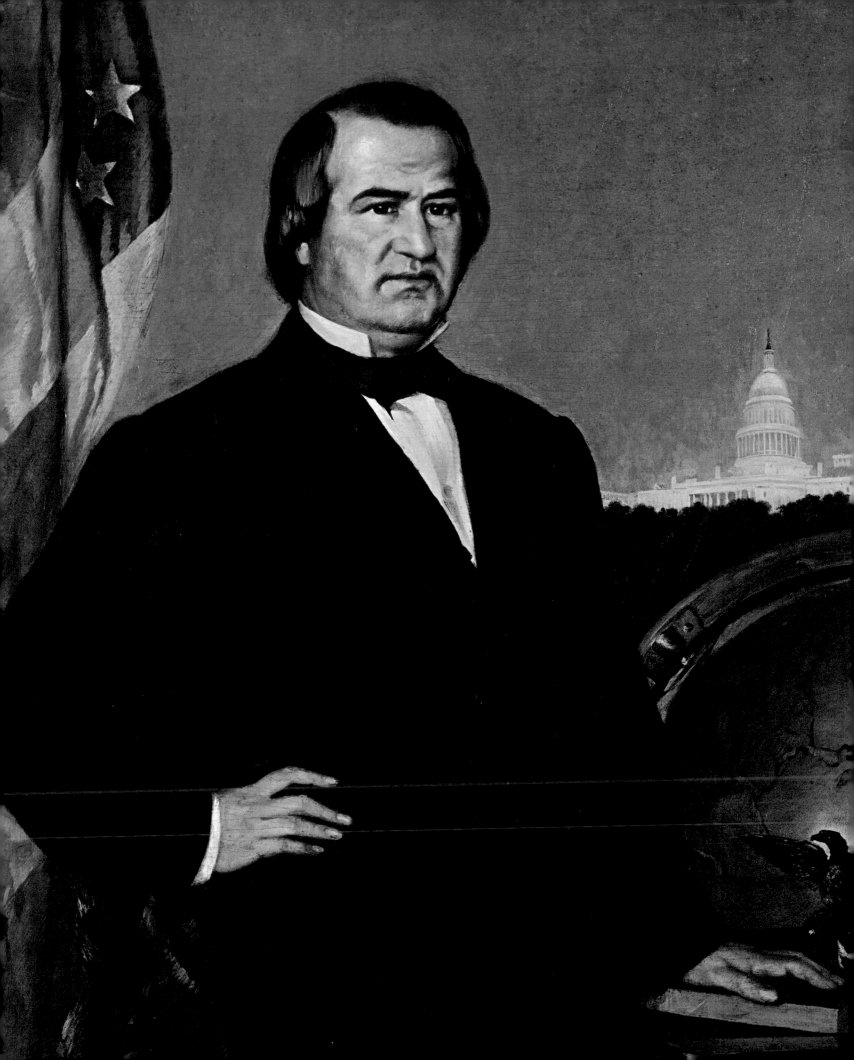

Andrew Johnson (1865-1869)

The presidency of Abraham Lincoln would have been a hard act for almost any politician to follow. It was Andrew Johnson's special misfortune to be thrust onstage, a blunt and stubborn defender of the Constitution, in times that demanded flexibility, tact, and even more political skill than perhaps the Emancipator himself had possessed.

The "little man" had a steadfast friend in Andrew Johnson, born in poverty and schooled not a day in his life. He taught himself to read in his teens and later learned to write with his wife's encouragement. He joined debating societies and his tailor's shop became a forum for the poor mountain people of Greenville, Tennessee. They elected him alderman, then mayor, and then state legislator. He went on to become a U.S. congressman, governor of Tennessee, and a U.S. senator, as he continued to champion the cause of the small farmer and mountaineer against the Northern tycoon and the Southern plantation aristocrat. But the slave-owning gentry held the reins of power, and they pulled Tennessee from the Union. Johnson, alone among Southern senators, stayed at his post in Washington—and was branded a traitor at home.

Northerners lauded Lincoln's appointment of him as governor of defeated Tennessee, supported him for Vice President. But the Radical Republicans in Congress were too much for this simple, honest man. They passed bill after bill over his veto in their drive to enfeeble the presidency, disenfranchise the former Confederates, and give the vote to the freed slaves.

When Johnson dismissed a Lincoln cabinet holdover for

Life	Born Dec. 29, 1808, Raleigh, N.C. Married Eliza McCardle; five children. Died July 31, 1875.
Campaigns	As Democrat and Southerner, drew votes to Lincoln in 1864. Not nominated in 1868.
Milestones	Issued proclamation of amnesty. Authorized purchase of Alaska. First President to have important veto overridden by Congress. Impeached by House, acquitted by Senate in what was actually a trial of the Constitution.
Image	Straightforward, frequently tactless. Self-educated, yet well-versed in the Constitution and brave in defense of it.

Ten Dollars Reward.

RAN AWAY from the Subscriber, on the night of the 15th instant, two apprentice boys, legally bound, named WILLIAM and ANDREW JOHNSON The former is of a dark complexion, black hair, eyes, and habits. They are much of a height, about 5 feet 4 or 5 inches The latter is very fleshy freckled face, light hair, and fair complexion. They went off with two other apprentices, advertised by Messrs Wm. & Chas. Fowler When they went away, they were well clad—blue cloth coats, light colored homespun coats, and new hats, the maker's name in the crown of the hats, is Theodore Clark. I will pay the above Reward to any person who

STATE DEPARTMENT OF ARCHIVES AND HISTORY, RALEIGH, NORTH CAROLINA

Fatherless at 3, a tailor's apprentice at 14, Johnson made the North Carolina *Star* in June, 1824. Years later the Radical press vilified him.

conniving with the Radicals, they said he had violated the new Tenure of Office Act. In the sorry spectacle of impeachment that followed, one senator after another leaned toward conviction under all the pressure the Radicals could apply.

Johnson stood like a lone oak in a storm, the flag of the Union by his shoulder, the Capitol looming hard by in this symbolic portrait by Swiss painter Frank Buchser. In May of 1868 the votes were cast. The President was acquitted by the vote of one senator—Edmund G. Ross of Kansas, a freshman Radical Republican who committed political suicide rather than see the office reduced to executor of the congressional mandate.

Ulysses S. Grant (1869-1877)

"Failures," said Ulysses S. Grant to the Congress as his second term ended, "have been errors of judgment, not of intent." In those nine words the eighteenth President might have summed up not only his scandal-scarred administration but the bulk of his life as well, a spotty six decades of impecunious job-hopping relieved, incredibly, by two brilliant successes. One came in the Civil War when he rocketed to the popular pantheon as the hero who gave the Union its first major victories and its final triumph. The other came as he raced against time and cancer to complete the classic memoirs that might make his family financially secure for the first time. He won, with only a week to spare.

Hiram Ulysses Grant—his name was so persistently garbled to "Ulysses S. Grant" by the army that he gave up and kept the garble—fought well in the Mexican War, but a few years later resigned his captaincy amid whispers of drunkenness that echoed ever after. For eight dreary years he failed at job after job; when war flared he was a clerk and laborer in his father's leather shop, taking orders from two younger brothers.

The Civil War turned Grant's life upside down. He began by drilling a company of volunteers and ended in muddy boots and a borrowed private's uniform, dictating terms to General Lee at Appomattox. They were generous terms, and won him the South's respect. He seemed a natural for the presidency.

He was anything but. In this 1865 portrait, artist Ole Peter Hansen Balling portends—no doubt unintentionally—the "puzzled pathos" one White House visitor later saw, "as of a man with a problem before him

Life	Born April 27, 1822, Point Pleasant, Ohio. Graduated U.S. Military Academy. Married Julia Boggs Dent; four children. Died July 23, 1885.
Campaigns	Won by small margin in 1868. Reelected by larger plurality in 1872 though Republican dissidents ran Democrat Horace Greeley against him.
Milestones	Put nation on sound fiscal basis despite Panic of 1873. Negotiated reparations from Britain. Ordered sale of gold, ruining speculators.
Image	Beloved hero surrounded by charlatans. Scant knowledge of politics.

of which he does not understand the terms."

In simple faith that good friends made good officials, he put cronies in office and defended them when they failed—or worse, when one after another bogged down in scandal. Grant emerged from his two terms a somewhat tarnished hero, but still beloved and cheered as he toured the world in honored pomp.

He died as he had lived, needing money, a victim of one more swindle. The old fighter was laid to rest in an impressive tomb in New York City. Then the memoirs he had struggled to write while he was dying became a best seller, distinguished by candor, humor, and style. Though his life had been a constant battle against poverty and failure, he did indeed leave it with colors flying.

Grant loved and understood horses, if not people; he sketched this one while a cadet at West Point.

311

Rutherford B. Hayes (1877-1881)

After eight years of the well-meaning but maneuverable Grant and the incompetence or corruption of many of those around him, there seemed little likelihood in 1876 that the voters would choose another Republican. They didn't; Democrat Samuel J. Tilden beat Republican Rutherford Birchard Hayes by almost a quarter-million votes. But on March 3, 1877, Hayes was sworn in as nineteenth President, "elected" by Republican strategists who pulled the electoral votes of South Carolina, Florida, and Louisiana away from Tilden on grounds that Democratic whites had bullied Negro voters. Republican carpetbag governments in all three states provided the evidence, a congressional panel of eight Republicans and seven Democrats endorsed it by the predictable margin of eight to seven, and Hayes squeaked in by a single electoral vote. He had taken no active part in the coup, and afterwards was convinced he had won his office fairly. But he also won a nickname: "Rutherfraud."

The charges were probably valid in Louisiana and South Carolina, and Florida was almost surely a steal. The losers raised a howl; a few firebrands threatened violent retaliation. But tempers cooled, and the nation settled down to what turned out to be a competent, forward-looking, benign, and refreshingly honorable administration.

"I shall show a *grit* that will astonish those who predict weakness," Hayes promised his diary. If the Radicals expected weakness, they were indeed astonished when he scorned the spoils system and chose a cabinet of able and dependable advisers. He pulled troops out of the long-occupied South; without them the Reconstruction regimes collapsed. He pressed for civil service

Life	Born Oct. 4, 1822, Delaware, Ohio. Graduated Kenyon College, Harvard Law School. Married Lucy Webb; eight children. Died Jan. 17, 1893.
Campaign	Factions opposing James Blaine united in nominating him. Kept out of sight during campaign. Refused renomination.
Milestones	Broke Radicals' grip on presidency; lost party support by basing appointments on ability. Forbade politicking by federal employees.
Image	Short, rumpled, unimpressive, often unimaginative, yet the epitome of respectability when it was most needed.

reforms, buttressed the shaky "greenback" money with specie payments, put down crippling rail strikes with military force.

William Carl Brown in 1878 painted this whiskery portrait of Hayes. Beyond an ordinary face, it hints perhaps at the proud bearing of the brevet major general wounded five times in the Civil War—or perhaps at the stern morality of the President who forbade liquor in the White House.

Hayes showed his greatest grit when Congress tried to bring the presidency to heel, attaching to bills a series of riders that would have pared the chief executive's power to deal with election violations. Six times the veto, and the presidency prevailed.

Withal, it was a rather dull administration. But after war, assassination, impeachment, and scandal, four quiet years made a welcome change.

HAYES
ELECTED.

TILDEN.

NUF CED.

J. DOYLE DEWITT COLLECTION

In 1876 crowing Republicans gave out victory card, celebrating what many had called a fraudulent election.

James A. Garfield (1881)

As the Republican convention of 1880 got rolling, Ohio Representative James Abram Garfield rose and, in that clear voice and eloquent style that had helped keep him in the House for eighteen years, nominated Ohioan John Sherman as the party's choice for President. Thirty-six ballots later, a weary convention unanimously nominated Garfield as a dark-horse entry in the steeplechase to the White House.

Two factions had deadlocked the convention. The "Stalwarts," hewing to the fading dogma of Radical Republicanism, had stumped for a third term for U.S. Grant, while liberals—branded "Halfbreeds" by the conservatives for diluting their Republicanism—had backed James G. Blaine. Neither owned Garfield; he had approved Grant's use of troops in the South, but opposed Grant's strategists at the convention. He fumed at the Halfbreeds' mild Reconstruction policies, but as a member of the 1877 electoral panel he voted four-square for his Halfbreed predecessor, Hayes.

Garfield struck an uneasy balance between the blocs, tipped a little toward the Stalwarts by the selection of Chester A. Arthur as running mate. A year later the balance would tip all the way by the awesome weight of a single bullet.

In naming his cabinet, Garfield locked horns with Stalwart chieftain Roscoe Conkling, who expected to dictate some of the choices. The New York senator began mustering colleagues behind him. But Garfield would not budge: "This," he growled, ". . . will settle the question whether the President is registering clerk of the Senate or the executive

Life	Born Nov. 19, 1831, Orange Township, Ohio. Graduated Williams College. Married Lucretia Rudolph; seven children. Died Sept. 19, 1881.
Campaign	Managed his own; kept silent on political issues.
Milestones	Approved investigation of star-route frauds in Post Office Department, a catalyst in reform of civil service. Chartered the Red Cross.
Image	Rags-to-riches midwesterner. Sturdy, genial scholar who could write Latin with one hand, Greek with the other. Last of the log-cabin Presidents.

of the United States." The chess game ended with Conkling out of the Senate and the power of state bosses over the federal government effectively checkmated.

Fate gave Garfield time for little else, and none for the customary presidential portrait. This posthumous likeness by Calvin Curtis ages him beyond his forty-nine years. On July 2 an office hunter, disappointed and probably deranged, drew a pistol in a Washington railroad station and shot Garfield in the spine. For eleven weeks the President clung to life while constitutional experts debated whether Vice President Arthur should be sworn in as President. Infection and an internal hemorrhage mooted the question on September 19, and ratified the edict of assassin Charles J. Guiteau as he fired the fatal shot: "I am a Stalwart. Arthur is President now."

LIBRARY OF CONGRESS

Harper's Weekly recreated moment of horror that left the nation leaderless for months.

Chester A. Arthur (1881-1885)

"Chet Arthur, President of the United States! Good God!" exclaimed an acquaintance on learning that Arthur had succeeded to the presidency. Many Americans were similarly startled to think of him as their President, since he had at times been indiscreet and tactless while Vice President and had even shown a lack of respect for that office.

If Americans were surprised to find Arthur had become their President, they were even more surprised to find that he served with dignity and integrity. In fact, according to historian Matthew Josephson, "He acted from the start with remarkable tact and grace," and impressed influential persons as "the most effective President since Lincoln."

Arthur's political advance had been by way of the spoils system. Quartermaster for the city, then for the state of New York during the Civil War, having helped the governor win reelection, he was appointed by President Grant to take over the New York Custom House. He served in these jobs with unquestioned honesty, but by 1881 the day of the spoils system was nearly over, and Arthur was under its shadow. He had been removed from the custom house by President Hayes for refusing to comply with an order forbidding government employees to engage actively in partisan politics.

To his credit, and the disgust of the Stalwart wing of the Republican party, he became a vigorous supporter of civil service reform. He signed the Pendleton Act in 1883, creating the Civil Service Commission, finally bringing a tenth of government jobs under its supervision.

Chester Alan Arthur, son of an itinerant teacher turned preacher, was born in Fairfield or Waterville,

Life	Born Oct. 5, 1830, Fairfield, Vt. (?). Graduated Union College. Married Ellen Lewis Herndon; three children. Died Nov. 18, 1886.
Campaigns	Nominated as Garfield's Vice President to satisfy Stalwart wing of Republican party in 1880. Unable to win nomination for presidency in 1884.
Milestones	Pressed case against perpetrators of mail route frauds. Signed Pendleton Act, reforming the civil service. Asked for tax relief. Proposed lower import duties. Reduced public debt.
Image	Gentlemanly, fastidious.

Vermont. There were rumors, never proved, that he was born in Canada and ineligible for the White House.

He taught to help pay for his education. In 1853 he was admitted to the bar. New acquaintances and the prestige of his position as quartermaster general were useful. A political career awaited him. In an era of unsavory politics, Arthur was an anomaly. He managed to play the role of gentleman-politician without compromising his honesty.

His short career as President was unspectacular, but not wholly unproductive. He managed to cut back the treasury surplus by reducing the public debt.

Seldom has a President so looked the part as the man in Daniel Huntington's 1885 portrait. Rarely has the cliché of "rising" to the office been more accurately applied.

LIBRARY OF CONGRESS

Arthur escaped the pressures of office out of doors, as when dining alfresco.

Grover Cleveland (1885-1889, 1893-1897)

Quite likely unique in the history of politics was Grover Cleveland's instruction to his staff: "Tell the truth." This was the directive of the 1884 Democratic candidate for the presidency when he faced a Republican attempt to embarrass him with an allegedly illegitimate son. The inflexibly honest Cleveland admitted the possibility of his paternity and took the responsibility.

The fifth of nine children, Stephen Grover Cleveland was born in a Presbyterian parsonage in Caldwell, New Jersey. After his father's death sixteen-year-old Grover went to New York City, then to Buffalo, where an uncle helped him get a job with a law firm. He read law and was admitted to the bar at the age of twenty-two.

Fiercely independent and determined, as Eastman Johnson's 1891 portrait shows him, Cleveland avoided all demanding ties, including early marriage. He planned his political life and pursued it without any of the usual "deals." Lacking "martial spirit," he followed the custom of sending a substitute to the Civil War.

His first public office, in 1870, after being defeated for district attorney, was as sheriff of Erie County. In 1881 a Buffalo reform group asked Cleveland to run for mayor. He was elected and within a year saved the city a million dollars by vetoing fraudulent sewage and street-cleaning contracts. Then came the governorship.

In 1884, with the support of reform Republicans—Mugwumps, who had bolted their party after James G. Blaine was nominated—Cleveland was elected President.

Believing his role as President required that he let Congress take the initiative in proposing laws, he waited.

Life	Born March 18, 1837, Caldwell, N.J. Admitted to bar, 1859. Married Frances Folsom; five children. Died June 24, 1908.
Campaigns	First ran as a reformer, later on his record.
Milestones	Only President to serve nonconsecutive terms. Only President married in the White House. Instituted repeal of Tenure of Office Act and of Sherman Silver Purchase Act. Accepted J.P. Morgan's offer to solve Treasury crisis. Quashed treaty for annexation of Hawaii. Sent troops to restore order during Pullman strike. Urged tariff reform.
Image	Stubborn, irritable, incorruptible.

Press gave the first presidential wedding romantic coverage and trailed couple on honeymoon trip.

In the meantime he unearthed abuses, recovering thousands of acres from the railroads, and opening them to homesteaders. He vetoed a bill allowing Civil War veterans to claim payments for any disability, even old age. He worked at civil service reform, cutting the number of patronage jobs.

In 1886 he married the twenty-one-year-old daughter of a former law partner. Just before his term ended he attacked the tariff laws, ruining, some thought, his chance of reelection. He won the popular vote; Benjamin Harrison got the electoral vote. Four years later, in a time of financial panic, Cleveland won. The ensuing economic depression and his weakened health following surgery helped deprive "His Obstinacy" of the nomination in 1896. At the time of his death in 1908 he was a much-respected "elder statesman," a man who had placed honor above expediency while President.

Benjamin Harrison (1889-1893)

President Harrison, an unreformed war hero, reacted hotly to the killing of two U.S. Navy sailors by a mob in Valparaiso and asked Congress to declare war on Chile in 1892. A clash was avoided when Chile apologized and paid a $75,000 indemnity.

Harrison's reputation as a fighter in the Civil War had been stressed during his presidential campaign in 1888. He had risen to brigadier general, receiving high praise for his "ability and manifest energy and gallantry in command."

Few were surprised to see Benjamin Harrison occupy the highest office in the land; his family's leadership in government had few equals. Great-grandson of a Signer of the Declaration of Independence, grandson of a President, Harrison began his political career as a member of the new Republican party, with election to city attorneyship of Indianapolis in 1857. In 1860 he was state supreme court reporter.

Born on his grandfather's Ohio estate, Benjamin Harrison, scholarly and athletic, had a private tutor as well as a country school education. In 1852 he graduated with distinction from Miami University in Ohio and began two years of law study in Cincinnati for admission to the bar in 1854.

Returning from the war, Harrison's memory, his ability to analyze quickly masses of facts and figures, and his impressive court presentations made him one of the most popular lawyers in Indiana. Publicly, he was aloof and cool, as he seems in this Eastman Johnson portrait done in 1895, but he was an affectionate family man, religious, and committed to humanitarian ideals.

Not until 1872 did he return to

Life Born Aug. 20, 1833, North Bend, Ohio. Graduated Miami University. Married Caroline Scott; two children. Married Mary Dimmick, one child. Died March 13, 1901.

Campaigns Ran in 1888 as General Harrison, grandson of Old Tippecanoe. Grieved by death of his wife, refused to make campaign appearances in 1892 and lost election.

Milestones Signed Sherman Antitrust Act, Sherman Silver Purchase Act. Asked for declaration of war on Chile. Sent Senate treaty annexing Hawaii.

Image Independent, honest, politically inept.

politics, to be defeated for the Indiana governorship. Eight years later he was instrumental in securing James Garfield's nomination and was offered a cabinet post, which he refused, preferring to serve the Senate term he had just won. Defeated for the Senate in 1886, he declared himself a candidate for the 1888 presidential nomination.

Civil service reform had been a campaign issue, but once elected, he could not follow through. The promise of liberal pensions for Civil War veterans had won many votes, but it had a disastrous effect on the treasury. Labor and the farmer were ignored.

Harrison's presidency succeeded in making him unpopular with almost everyone. It was doubly unfortunate, because, as Attorney General William Howard Taft remarked, "We have never had a man in the White House who was more conscientiously seeking to do his duty."

BENJAMIN HARRISON HOME

Chair of horn and leopard skin presented by a Texas rancher has "Harrison" spelled out in diamonds.

William McKinley (1897-1901)

The McKinley-Bryan race of 1896 introduced the front-porch campaign in McKinley's town of Canton, Ohio, and cross-country stumping as William Jennings Bryan traveled the U.S., enthralling audiences with his oratory.

McKinley's campaign, well financed, masterfully organized by millionaire industrialist Mark Hanna, proved more successful than Bryan's crusade for free coinage of silver. The gold standard won out, and the last Civil War veteran to occupy the White House moved in.

William McKinley was the seventh of nine children, a delicate child who liked school. After one year at Allegheny College he withdrew because of illness. Family finances did not permit his return; until he enlisted in the Union army at the age of eighteen, he taught school and clerked in a post office.

After serving as "one of the bravest and finest officers in the army" (according to his commanding officer, Rutherford B. Hayes), he studied law and went into partnership in Canton with an elderly judge.

In 1867 he campaigned for Hayes in the gubernatorial race, and two years later began his own political career as county prosecuting attorney. In 1876 McKinley was elected to his first term in Congress.

Considered a moderate, McKinley favored civil service reform, Negro suffrage, and the workingman; he opposed big business excesses. His special interest, which arose again during his presidency, was the tariff. Believing that the absence of cheap foreign goods would protect the wage scale as well as industry, he fought for a high tariff.

Defeated in his congressional bid in 1890, McKinley went home to

Life	Born Jan. 29, 1843, Niles, Ohio. Studied Allegheny College; graduated Albany Law School. Married Ida Saxton; two children. Died Sept. 14, 1901.
Campaigns	In 1896, supporting the gold standard. In 1900, continuation of prosperity.
Milestones	Declared war on Spain. Demanded cession of Philippines. Hawaii annexed; Wake Island and Guam occupied. Puerto Rico acquired. Cuba guided to self-government. Sent soldiers to help raise the siege in Peking during the Boxer Rebellion.
Image	Pillar of the community. Devoted husband. Politically moderate.

serve two terms as Ohio governor before winning the presidency.

Cuba's plight under Spain precipitated McKinley and the country into a new era when the battleship *Maine* exploded in Havana harbor in 1898. When the war ended, America had undertaken to educate and "civilize" the Filipinos, had freed Cuba, and had become a true world power.

Prosperity and popularity insured reelection for the dignified McKinley, shown in an 1899 portrait by Charles A. Whipple. Early in his second term McKinley was shot by anarchist Leon Czolgosz during a reception at the Pan American Exposition in Buffalo, New York, and died a week later. With him died the vestiges of nineteenth-century America's isolation from the rest of the world.

THEODORE ROOSEVELT ASSOCIATION

"Full dinner bucket" satisfied voters, who gave McKinley a plurality of almost a million in 1900 election.

Theodore Roosevelt (1901-1909)

"Speak softly and carry a big stick; you will go far." Theodore Roosevelt said his presidential motto was a West African proverb. Most of his contemporaries would have agreed that he carried a big stick; some may have doubted he ever spoke softly.

The man who led a company of volunteer Rough Riders into Cuba and became his country's most famous hunter and cowboy began life as a sickly, nearsighted boy. All of his father's wealth, obtained as an importer with banking interests, could not banish his asthma, but "Teedie" resolved to overcome his weakness when he found he could not hold his own in a fight with boys who jeered his New York City ways. He began a program of muscle building and achieved his goal.

He entered Harvard at eighteen, determined to be a naturalist. He began work in his senior year on *The Naval War of 1812*. At Columbia Law School he decided he did not care for law, but stuck it out.

In 1881 he joined New York City's Twenty-first District Republican Club, and at twenty-three won the district seat in the state assembly. From that podium he called Jay Gould "part of that most dangerous of all dangerous classes, the wealthy criminal class."

In 1884, after the deaths of his young wife and his mother within hours of each other, Roosevelt went to Dakota for two years of cattle ranching. Returning to New York, he placed third in a try for the mayoralty. In 1889, Benjamin Harrison appointed him to the Civil Service Commission. This was followed by the

Life	Born Oct. 27, 1858, New York, N.Y. Graduated Harvard. Married Alice Lee; one child. Married Edith Carow; five children. Died Jan. 6, 1919.
Campaigns	As McKinley's Vice President in 1900; as a reformer in 1904; as a progressive in 1912 after bolting the Republican party.
Milestones	Youngest man to become President. Enforced antitrust laws. Negotiated for Panama Canal Zone. Issued corollary to Monroe Doctrine. Settled Alaska boundary dispute. Won Nobel Peace Prize for mediating Russo-Japanese War.
Image	Vigorous, flamboyant, ebullient, liberal.

job of New York police commissioner; then assistant secretary of the navy. After Cuba he was elected governor of New York, in which job he so upset political boss Tom Platt that Platt saw to it Roosevelt got buried in the vice presidency.

But in 1901 "that damned cowboy," as Mark Hanna called him, was in the White House. It was a time of social ferment, and Roosevelt was in the thick of it. He declared war on the "criminal rich," striking at the trusts. He warned that the U.S. would "exercise an international police power" against foreign intervention in the Western Hemisphere. In 1908 he picked his successor, only to run against him four years later.

The commanding man in John Singer Sargent's 1903 portrait enjoyed the presidency; it was a "bully pulpit" from which to preach his gospel.

Refusing to shoot a bear cub, Roosevelt created a legend and "teddy bear" fad.

William H. Taft (1909-1913)

"I see a man weighing 350 pounds. There is something hanging over his head. . . . It looks like the presidency; then again it looks like the chief justiceship."

Theodore Roosevelt seemed to be offering his secretary of war a choice of two coveted offices. In reality, the choice did not exist. Chief Justice Melville Fuller was not ready to retire, and, with one exception, the Taft clan had long thought William Howard belonged in the White House. The holdout was William Howard. His cherished dream was to be chief justice of the United States.

But T.R. had decided: "Taft will carry on the work substantially as I have." So Taft took up the Republican banner.

His view of presidential prerogatives was somewhat less sweeping than Roosevelt's, and he believed the function of his administration was "to complete and perfect the machinery" of Roosevelt's programs. On occasion, he felt, his predecessor had stretched his powers a bit too much: "There is no undefined residuum of power in the presidency," he had said, and he was cautious in the use of power. Even so he initiated ninety antitrust suits, more than doubling the Great Trustbuster's seven-year record.

That William Howard Taft was uncomfortable in the presidency seems obvious in this Anders Zorn portrait painted in 1911. His was not an exciting tenure; he lacked Roosevelt's flamboyance and avoided public appearances when possible. Consequently his achievements tended to be overlooked, especially in the furor of displeasure over the firing of conservationist Gifford Pinchot, who was in charge of the Forest Service, and other evi-

Life	Born Sept. 15, 1857, Cincinnati, Ohio. Graduated Yale, Cincinnati Law School. Married Helen Herron; three children. Died March 8, 1930.
Campaigns	Elected 1908 as Theodore Roosevelt's chosen heir. Got 8 votes in 1912, trailing T.R.'s 88, Wilson's 435.
Milestones	Fought for reduced tariffs. Proposed federal income tax. Instituted "dollar diplomacy." Strengthened Interstate Commerce Commission. Broke Standard Oil and American Tobacco trusts.
Image	Genial, warmhearted, but shy in public. Scholarly love of law and courts.

dences of President Taft's loss of the Progressive faith.

The Taft promise to lower tariffs was fulfilled, but with a law so weak it had no impact. His treaties with England and France providing for arbitration of disputes were amended beyond recognition in the Senate.

He did expand the Interstate Commerce Commission's power over railroad rates; advocated an amendment authorizing income taxes; and moved 8,000 assistant postmasters from the patronage lists into the civil service. In spite of his failure to unite his party, he was renominated in 1912.

It was hopeless, and Roosevelt's Bull Moose candidacy added a touch of farce. Together they had fewer than 100 electoral votes against Woodrow Wilson's 435. Taft faced defeat with great relief.

Appointed chief justice by Warren Harding in 1921, he wrote, "I don't remember that I ever was President."

First "golfing President," Taft also threw first season's opening baseball.

Woodrow Wilson (1913-1921)

"I sometimes feel like a fire from a far from extinct volcano" was the surprising confession made by the austere Woodrow Wilson. Had any of the fire he felt been visible to the public, perhaps he would not be remembered as a President who inspired respect but not love.

His respectability stemmed from his upbringing as the son of a Presbyterian minister; the parsonage molded him into a dour young man, inclined to weigh all matters on a spiritual or intellectual basis.

Wilson achieved prominence before he was thirty with the publication of his book *Congressional Government,* which advocated the reorganization of the U.S. Congress along the lines of the British cabinet system.

By the time the Democratic party was ready to replace William Jennings Bryan as standard-bearer, Wilson had served impressively as Princeton's president and New Jersey's governor. The party and the man met. It took forty-three ballots to nominate him in 1912, and he got only 42 percent of the popular vote, but in the electoral college an overwhelming 435 out of 531 votes. His victory was due to the split in Republican ranks when Theodore Roosevelt ran as a third-party candidate.

The first term began happily and there were successes: effective tariff reform was secured; the Federal Reserve System was set up; the Clayton Antitrust Act became law. Wilson signed several social reform bills, but economic rather than social reforms were his goal.

Less than six months after his reelection as the man who "kept us out of war," Wilson failed in his final effort to

Life	Born Dec. 28, 1856, Staunton, Va. Graduated Princeton, U. of Virginia Law School, Johns Hopkins. Married Ellen Axson; three children. Married Edith Bolling Galt. Died Feb. 3, 1924.
Campaigns	Promised in 1912 to do what the "Republican party has been talking about for 16 years." Elected in 1916 as man who "kept us out of war."
Milestones	Sent troops to Mexican border. Asked declaration of war on Germany. Issued 14 Points. Helped draft Versailles Treaty. Awarded Nobel Peace Prize.
Image	Coldly intellectual, uncompromising.

bring about peace in Europe. His hopes for continued neutrality died, and in 1917 he asked Congress to declare war on Germany, primarily because American lives had been lost in the sinking of merchant ships by U-boats. After the armistice was reached in 1918, Wilson took his Fourteen Points to Paris. He bargained most away to save the vital one that embodied the League of Nations, and came home to violent opposition.

Wilson drafted his own speeches and typed them on this machine, adaptable for English or Greek.

Unable to compromise, he went to the people in an exhausting cross-country journey that broke his health. While he lay ill, shielded by his wife Edith, the Senate kept the U.S. out of his League. But his efforts earned him the Nobel Peace Prize. By 1921, when Edmund Tarbell painted his portrait, Wilson had retired to the seclusion of his home in Washington.

Warren G. Harding (1921-1923)

"To safeguard America first. . . . To live for and revere America first" were the goals set by Warren Harding, for Wilson had not made the world safe for democracy after all. Europe still had its troubles, and it was time to think of problems at home. Americans wanted a return to "normalcy."

Warren Gamaliel Harding—one-time teacher who thought farm labor easier, small-town editor and "booster"—was a popular man. When he was elected to the Senate from Ohio, he made good use of his charm and facility for remembering faces and names. When powerful Republican Senator Boies Penrose asked, "How would you like to be President?", Harding replied modestly, "Am I a big enough man for the race?"

He did poorly in the primaries, and it is often said that he really did not want to be nominated, that he wanted to withdraw. At least one biographer, Francis Russell, disagrees. Harding was "an able and astute Ohio politician (not the highest breed of that animal) who knew how to get what he wanted . . . all the while disclaiming that he wanted any such thing."

When he was asked if there was anything in his past that might embarrass the party, Harding said no. He might have added, except Nan Britton. But that liaison did not become public until later, and by then there were other scandals, involving government oil bases, to be raked over.

For Warren Harding was a good friend. He appointed his friends to office, qualified or not, saying, "God, I can't be an ingrate!" Yet there were some outstanding appointments, among them that of dedicated public servant Herbert Hoover to Commerce. William Howard Taft was appointed to the Supreme Court.

Life	Born Nov. 2, 1865, Blooming Grove, Ohio. Graduated Ohio Central College. Married Florence Kling De Wolfe; no children. Died Aug. 2, 1923.
Campaign	Won by 7 million votes with "return to normalcy" platform.
Milestones	Named former President Taft chief justice of the Supreme Court. Called international conference for naval disarmament. Pardoned Socialist Eugene V. Debs. Teapot Dome deal.
Image	In his lifetime, the personification of small-town virtues; "joiner" and "booster." Handsome, poker-playing he-man.

Because he believed in executive cooperation with Congress, Harding withdrew his advocacy of a public welfare department when congressional leaders opposed it. He could also make decisions based on moral correctness; for this reason he pardoned imprisoned Socialist leader Eugene V. Debs.

In 1921, Harding put Charles Evans Hughes in charge of an international conference on naval disarmament. Probably the administration's most successful venture, it resulted in nine treaties.

In 1922 rumors of corruption began; the next year there were two suicides (or was one murder?), but Margaret Williams's 1923 portrait reflects no lack of dignity. After his death Teapot Dome and other scandals were uncovered. That he might not have been guilty was not considered. The public, lately mourning a beloved President, turned away.

LIBRARY OF CONGRESS

Harding went traveling with Ford to prove cars were safe; bought this beauty while President.

Calvin Coolidge (1923-1929)

"It is an advantage to a President to know he is not a great man." In addition to a realistic appraisal of himself, Calvin Coolidge brought to the presidency the New England values he grew up with—self-sufficiency and community responsibility—and, most important, unquestioned honor. By the time the Harding scandals could have destroyed the dignity of the office, Coolidge had given it his own image.

Calvin Coolidge, son of a Vermont farmer and shopkeeper, graduated from college *cum laude*. Beginning his law and political education simultaneously at Northampton, Massachusetts, he rose through county and city offices to the state legislature, then governor.

Thanks to publicity from a Boston police strike which Governor Coolidge settled by calling out state guardsmen, he went to the Republican convention in 1920 with some hope of getting the presidential nomination. But the choice had already been made: Harding. The delegates refused the preselected running mate; they wanted Coolidge and they got him.

Three years later the terse New Englander looking from Ercole Cartotto's 1929 portrait was President. Calvin Coolidge had a theory about the presidency. It was his belief that the President is something of a foreman who "should not do any work that he can have done by others. Such energy as he has should be directed not so much towards doing work as making certain that the work is being well done."

This philosophy sometimes worked: when a coal strike threatened, Pennsylvania Governor Gifford Pinchot arranged the settlement. Sometimes it did not work so well: when speculation increased dangerously in the New York Stock Exchange, Coolidge, be-

Coolidge as honorary Sioux. He often posed outlandishly, saying, "It's good for people to laugh."

Life	Born July 4, 1872, Plymouth Notch, Vt. Graduated Amherst College. Married Grace Goodhue; two children. Died Jan. 5, 1933.
Campaigns	Ran in 1920 for Vice President on Harding "normalcy" platform. Elected President in 1924 on record of honesty.
Milestones	Maintained high tariffs. Lowered taxes; eliminated federal gift taxes. Relaxed regulation of business. Reduced national budget and debt. Improved relations with Latin America.
Image	Symbol of honest government. Publicly taciturn, intensely shy; privately witty.

lieving that New York should undertake any necessary regulating, refused to let the Federal Reserve Board tighten money. He left the White House sure that "there's a depression coming."

Coolidge had said, "It is the business of the President as party leader to do the best he can to see that the declared party platform purposes are translated into legislative and administrative action." Having also said the business of America is business, he moved to relax regulation of business. Federal gift taxes were eliminated, other taxes lowered; the national budget and debt reduced.

By 1928, Coolidge had had enough of the presidency. "I do not choose to run," he said. He went back to Massachusetts and wrote an autobiography. H.L. Mencken summed up Coolidge's presidency: "The country remembers only . . . that he let it alone."

Herbert C. Hoover (1929-1933)

"We in America today are nearer to the final triumph over poverty than ever before in the history of any land," Herbert Hoover said while campaigning for the presidency. Eleven months after his election came the stock market crash, depression, unemployment.

The man who had directed monumental relief works during and after World War I treated his country's illness by encouraging expanded construction and creating the Reconstruction Finance Corporation for loans to industry (jobs would be created, benefits "trickle down").

Public works, on the contrary, would be "raids upon the public treasury." The dole, he felt, would be unconstitutional and endanger the "spiritual responses" of the people. He vetoed a hydroelectric project for the Tennessee Valley because he believed government should not compete with private industry.

His were the views of a self-made man. Herbert Clark Hoover, son of an Iowa blacksmith, had lost both parents by the time he was eight. His ascetic Quaker upbringing by aunts and uncles may have fostered his reserve; it surely encouraged his life-long commitment to service.

He worked to support himself at Stanford University, then worked a seven-day week in a gold mine until it petered out. Unemployed, he learned "the bottom levels of real human despair."

Then engineering jobs in an Australian gold field in the late 1890s and later with the Chinese Bureau of Mines led in 1901 to partnership in a London mining firm, bringing him prosperity and international recognition.

With the United States in the war, the family came home and

Belgians sent thanks for war relief stitched on bags that brought food.

HERBERT HOOVER LIBRARY, WEST BRANCH, IOWA

Life	Born Aug. 10, 1874, West Branch, Iowa. Graduated Stanford U. Married Lou Henry; two children. Died Oct. 20, 1964.
Campaigns	Elected 1928 on Republican prosperity. Defeated in 1932 campaigning against "changes and so-called new deals."
Milestones	Announced tax cut. Opposed federal relief. Opposed repeal of 18th Amendment. Asked moratorium on payment of foreign debts. Urged Federal Home Loan Bank Act. Called out army to disperse bonus marchers. Opposed economic boycott of Japan.
Image	Rugged individualist. Humanitarian.

Hoover served as food administrator and then helped alleviate starvation in Europe. He was, John Maynard Keynes said, the only man to return from the Paris peace conference with an enhanced reputation.

The man in Douglas Chandor's 1931 portrait held great appeal for American voters in 1928. Yet as the Depression deepened he felt the federal government could do little. Soon hungry Americans saw his adherence to principle as a lack of concern, and refused to reelect him.

His reputation as a humanitarian rose again decades later when he accepted Truman's request to administer food distribution to Europe's displaced persons after World War II. He remained active until his death, his advice sought by Presidents from Truman through Johnson.

Franklin D. Roosevelt (1933-1945)

"If you have spent two years in bed trying to wiggle your big toe, everything else seems easy." Franklin Delano Roosevelt's triumphant battle with the disease that could have left him inactive for life matured him, gave him a new perspective and compassion.

Growing up the spoiled only child of wealthy parents, sheltered and fussed over, even as an adult, by a possessive mother, Roosevelt might have gone through life never knowing there was an "other half," but his private tutors introduced him to liberal social thought. At Groton and Harvard he espoused the cause of Boer independence. And his young wife, Eleanor, took him to slums and showed him real, grating poverty.

In 1910 he accepted an offer to run in his district for the New York senate. He had barely taken his seat as the first Democrat from his district in fifty-four years, when he fought, and won, his first battle against the Tammany machine.

From Albany to Washington was not a long step for the energetic young politician. By 1920 he was seconding Al Smith's nomination at the Democratic convention. James Cox got that nomination and chose Roosevelt as his running mate. They campaigned vigorously, but lost the election to Warren Harding.

After the election Roosevelt settled into the comfortable life of a New York lawyer until he was stricken by polio in 1921. As he recovered Eleanor encouraged his return to politics.

His smiling, spirited appearance at the 1924 convention marked the return and won him the admiration of many. In 1928 he was drafted for New York's gubernatorial race and won. Four years later he took the Democratic presidential nomination and, ignoring suggestions for a front-porch campaign, covered 27,000 miles on his way to the White House.

Murray, the Outlaw of Fala Hill, loyal companion, offered relief from the pressures of office.

Life	Born Jan. 30, 1882, Hyde Park, N.Y. Graduated Harvard, Columbia Law School. Married Anna Eleanor Roosevelt; five children. Died April 12, 1945.
Campaigns	In 1932 promised action against the Great Depression. Thereafter ran on his record.
Milestones	Declared bank holiday. Asked for New Deal legislation. Abandoned gold standard. Urged quarantine of aggressor nations. Proclaimed Four Freedoms. Asked for declaration of war against Japan. Only President elected four times.
Image	Buoyant, fearless. Consummate politician. Enemies said, a potential dictator.

Telling Americans "the only thing we have to fear is fear itself," he launched the New Deal of "bold, persistent experimentation"—a bloodless revolution. His confidence, visible in Douglas Chandor's 1945 portrait, reassured Americans as he closed banks and set up agencies to satisfy the people's wish for "discipline and direction."

Opponents called him everything from Fascist to Communist because of his strong presidency and radical programs. He had troubles with Congress and the Supreme Court, but the American people elected him again, and yet again for precedent-breaking third and fourth terms. He considered his reelections approval of his use of the presidency to move the federal government into new areas. His forceful and charismatic leadership during the Great Depression and World War II gave the presidency perhaps the strongest image it had ever had.

Harry S. Truman (1945-1953)

Fighting to prevent chaos in the midst of labor, congressional, and cabinet squabbles, Harry Truman once said, "I'd rather be anything than President."

It had been a hard job for Bob Hannegan to get him to accept the vice-presidential nomination. Finally, Roosevelt had boomed over the telephone, "You tell him if he wants to break up the Democratic party in the middle of a war, that's his responsibility." So Harry Truman became Vice President.

He had held the office only long enough to adjourn the Senate before he was summoned to the White House to hear Mrs. Roosevelt tell him, "Harry, the President is dead."

Along with his new office Truman inherited the remnants of a war. It was he who had to meet Soviet diplomats with only a few days' preparation. It was he who had to decide whether to use the atom bomb.

Harry S. Truman (nobody could agree on Solomon, for his mother's side, or Shippe, for his father's, so it was just S.) was born in Missouri. His father's financial difficulties kept him from college. He was crude sometimes, and corny — greatly different from Roosevelt.

As he tried to avoid postwar inflation with a program of controls Congress balked. Labor tried out its right to strike, and Truman acted against the strikers with mixed results. The cold war loomed, threatening to become hot when access to Berlin was blocked.

No one but Truman thought he could win a second term. He called a special session of Congress, gave it a series of proposals, which it could pass and make the President look good, or it could do nothing

Life	Born May 8, 1884, Lamar, Mo. Graduated high school. Married Elizabeth Virginia Wallace; one child. Died Dec. 26, 1972.
Campaigns	In 1944 ran as FDR's Vice President. Hit "do-nothing" Congress and "reactionaries" in government in 1948.
Milestones	Ordered A-bombs dropped on Japan. Asked statehood for Alaska, Hawaii. Proclaimed Philippine independence. Issued Truman Doctrine. Established Marshall Plan. Sent troops to fight in Korea. Relieved MacArthur of command. Seized steel mills to prevent strike.
Image	Decisive, blunt, folksy.

and make Congress look bad. Congress chose to do nothing, and Truman harangued Americans to get "reactionaries" out of office. Voters gave him the presidency's greatest surprise victory.

His new term brought the problems of McCarthy's "witch hunt" for Communists in government, and aggression in Korea. Then he had to fire MacArthur, hero of the Pacific, for disobeying orders. It was an unpopular decision, but the man looking from Greta Kempton's 1948 painting was not after popularity. That was obvious from his interpretation of the presidency: "The buck stops here."

Assessing his presidency, during which he urged liberal legislation that was not enacted until the 1960s, Truman said, "I did my damnedest, and that's all there was to it!"

Election night, 1948, Thomas E. Dewey had "won," but in the morning Harry Truman was still President.

Dwight D. Eisenhower (1953-1961)

Although he had been elected because of his fame as a warrior, peace was Dwight Eisenhower's major goal during his presidency. The biggest disappointment suffered by the most recent general to become President was that he failed to bring about international disarmament.

Dwight David Eisenhower, whose experiences left the deep-etched lines shown in Thomas Stephens's 1960 portrait, was born in a small Texas town and grew up on the wrong side of the tracks in Abilene, Kansas. He and his five brothers acquired a deep sense of honesty and justice from religious parents.

When a friend who had won an appointment to the U.S. Naval Academy suggested they enter together, young Eisenhower took the examination for both academies, but was accepted only by West Point.

In 1942, when fifty-one-year-old Major General Eisenhower was named commander for the European theater of operations, little was known of him except that he was considered a technical expert, was genial and well-liked, called Ike by friends.

With his superior administrative ability, Eisenhower welded together an efficient war machine that smashed the Axis forces in Europe. Ike emerged from the war with a Galahad image—the good man who had overcome evil.

By 1945 it was being suggested that he might become President. When he finally accepted the Republican nomination in 1952, he outran Adlai Stevenson by nearly 6 million votes. Eisenhower visited Korea, but found no immediate means of ending that war. The Communists relaxed their demands soon afterward and a cease-fire was arranged.

Life	Born Oct. 14, 1890, Denison, Tex. Graduated U.S. Military Academy. Married Mamie Doud; two children. Died March 28, 1969.
Campaigns	Elected as war hero, peacemaker.
Milestones	Visited Korea, seeking end to war. Refused to condemn Sen. Joseph McCarthy's witch hunt. Announced Eisenhower Doctrine to aid Middle East countries against communism. Proposed nuclear test ban. Sent troops to Lebanon. Signed Alaska, Hawaii into statehood. Warned of military-industrial complex.
Image	Hero. Father figure, kindly, reassuring.

Eisenhower's two terms have been referred to as dull, quiet years. In reality they were far from uneventful. While pursuing his crusade for peace, he had to contend with Senator Joseph McCarthy's Communist hunt, the Suez crisis, an integration battle in Little Rock, Arkansas, and increasing tension in the cold war.

Eisenhower also had to face criticism for filling his cabinet with businessmen, and for his habit of playing golf in the midst of crises. But even his critics could not doubt his sincerity as peacemaker: "I hate war as only a soldier who has lived it can, only as one who has . . . seen its futility, its *stupidity*."

Before he retired to his Gettysburg farm, Eisenhower warned the nation of a new power bloc— "the military-industrial complex."

> Abilene, Kansas,
> Aug. 29, 1910.
> Sen. Bristow,
> Salina, Kans.
> Dear Sir:
> I would very much like to enter either the school at Annapolis, or the one at West Point. In order to do this, I must have an appointment to

Young Dwight preferred to go to Annapolis with his friend, but was not taking chances.

John F. Kennedy (1961-1963)

The abiding memory of John Fitzgerald Kennedy's three-year presidency has been its style, its spirit of a new Camelot.

He began his term with a challenge: "Ask not what America will do for you, but what together we can do for the freedom of man."

Son of financier-ambassador Joseph P. Kennedy, John was one of nine children, almost all of whom seemed to have inherited their father's competitive spirit and ambition. Matured by a brush with war when he went to Scotland to help survivors of the torpedoed *Athenia* in 1939, the young man with the gentlemanly C average returned to Harvard to take his political science degree with honors.

After the attack on Pearl Harbor he served on a PT boat in the Pacific. He became a hero leading his men to safety when their boat was wrecked by a Japanese ship.

In 1946, the first of the Kennedy clan campaigns sent John to the House of Representatives at the age of twenty-nine. In 1952 he took Henry Cabot Lodge's Senate seat. Recuperating in 1955 from spinal surgery that nearly ended his life, Kennedy wrote *Profiles in Courage,* and apparently decided to run for the presidency.

Again the Kennedy campaign moved into action, and again he won. The thoughtful man in Aaron Shikkler's posthumous portrait was the country's first Roman Catholic President and, except for Theodore Roosevelt, its youngest.

His first crisis was the abortive attack on Cuba's Bay of Pigs; a later confrontation over Cuba, in

Life	Born May 29, 1917, Brookline, Mass. Graduated Harvard. Married Jacqueline Lee Bouvier; two children. Died Nov. 22, 1963.
Campaign	Ran on "missile gap" and youthful renewal.
Milestones	Formed Peace Corps. Established Alliance for Progress. Asked for U.S.-Soviet cooperation in space exploration. Ended Soviet missile threat in Cuba. Stopped racial discrimination in federal housing. Approved sale of wheat to Soviet Union.
Image	Sophisticated, witty, vigorous. Concerned for individual rights.

1962, resulted in the removal of Soviet missile bases.

As the New Frontier got under way, its "struggle against the common enemies of man: tyranny, poverty, disease" took shape in the Peace Corps, the Alliance for Progress, orders against racial discrimination in federal housing. Kennedy asked for an end to the arms race. He proposed civil rights legislation.

His vigor found a response among young Americans who became involved in achieving the goals of the New Frontier; a rapport was established between the people and their government that had been lacking.

His plans were left unfinished in 1963 when he was shot to death as he rode in a motorcade in Dallas, Texas. The United States and the world were stunned.

Talented Jacqueline painted an earlier-days White House to hang in her husband's office.

JOHN F. KENNEDY LIBRARY

Lyndon B. Johnson (1963-1969)

"Come now and let us reason together." This was Lyndon Johnson's favorite method of ironing out differences. He accomplished much by simply sitting and talking, giving the "Johnson treatment," described by columnist Mary McGrory as "an incredibly potent mixture of persuasion, badgering, flattery, threats, reminders of past favors and future advantages."

The tall Texan, craggy and stern in Peter Hurd's 1967 portrait, was a blend of power and subtlety. A restless, energetic politician, he accepted the vice presidency, often regarded as the most stultifying office in Washington. A southerner, he shepherded through Congress some of the most far-reaching civil rights legislation in history.

Lyndon Baines Johnson grew up knowing what hard times meant. "When I was fourteen years I decided I was not going to be the victim of a system which would allow the price of a commodity like cotton to . . . destroy the homes of people like my own family."

He worked at a number of jobs, including teaching, before he went to Washington as secretary to Representative Richard Kleberg. In 1935 Johnson returned to Texas as state director of the New Deal's National Youth Administration. In 1937, at twenty-eight, he won a seat in the House of Representatives.

Taking time out for war service, he moved from House to Senate, finally serving as majority leader. He had become, in the words of William S. White, "the most respected, the most powerful, the most activist leader of the Senate in the nearly two centuries of that institution's existence."

Life	Born Aug. 27, 1908, near Stonewall, Tex. Graduated Southwest Texas Teachers College; studied Georgetown U. Law School. Married Claudia Alta Taylor; two children. Died Jan. 22, 1973.
Campaigns	As Kennedy's Vice President in 1960. In 1964 on continuance of Kennedy programs, building of Great Society.
Milestones	Announced war on poverty. Ordered retaliatory bombing of North Vietnam. Signed Civil Rights Act, Economic Opportunity Act, Medicare Act, Voting Rights Act.
Image	Political pro. Earthy, persuasive.

On November 22, 1963, he took hold of the presidency with a sure hand. He saw Kennedy's civil rights bill through Congress, launched his own war on poverty. He soon had bills "coming out of Congress like candy bars from a slot machine."

But he was trapped in the mire of the Vietnam war. As early as 1953 he had advised against sending planes to aid the French in Indochina. By 1968 he had become highly unpopular as a war President, and announced he would not accept the Democratic nomination for another term.

For some his name will call to mind only the tragedy of the war; others will regard him as one of the most sympathetic and effective Presidents the "common man" ever had.

WIDE WORLD

Johnson's hobby was LBJ ranch. He herded cattle as easily as congressmen.

Richard M. Nixon (1969-　　)

Richard Milhous Nixon was elected in a time of turmoil, with his country deeply involved in an unpopular war and thousands of Americans feeling that their opinions were unheeded. He promised to bring American troops home from Vietnam, asked for a lowering of voices and an end to internal division.

Feeling an affinity for those he called the "silent majority," whose voices were not raised, but who were deeply disturbed by national and international conditions in the disruptive 1960s, he appealed to them especially in his campaigns, promising to hear the views of middle America, whose image Robert S. Oakes's 1971 photograph evokes.

Richard Nixon grew up in Whittier, California. He attended Duke University Law School on a scholarship, doing research at thirty-five cents an hour for spending money. In 1937 he returned to Whittier to begin practice. Nine years later he was a member of the House of Representatives after hitting at communism in his campaign. He achieved prominence as a member of the House Un-American Activities Committee and, again with an anti-Communist campaign, moved to the Senate. In 1952 he was chosen as Dwight Eisenhower's running mate.

Defeated by John Kennedy's narrow margin in 1960, he returned to California, only to lose the gubernatorial race to "Pat" Brown in 1962. He decided that he would retire from politics and return to the practice of law.

After his election to the presidency in 1968 he began a series of precedent-breaking moves in international relations. Most stunning—to liberals and conservatives alike—was his 1972 visit to mainland China.

Life	Born Jan. 9, 1913, Yorba Linda, Calif. Graduated Whittier College, Duke U. Law School. Married Thelma Catherine (Pat) Ryan; two children.
Campaigns	Promised "peace with honor" in Vietnam, representation for "silent" Americans.
Milestones	Antipollution programs set up. Began friendly relations with People's Republic of China. Achieved Vietnam cease-fire and return of POWs. All-volunteer armed forces established. Increased funding for the arts.
Image	Thoroughly political. Aloof. Affectionate in family circle.

Shortly after his reelection in 1972 he announced that an agreement to end the Vietnam involvement had been reached. Less successful at home than abroad, Nixon saw his efforts to balance the budget by cutting programs provoke strong opposition in Congress. A battle between the legislative and executive branches erupted, with Supreme Court appointments and White House proposals turned down by Congress, congressional acts vetoed, appropriations unspent. His administration was clouded in 1973 by the Watergate scandal —revelations involving his top aides in illegal activities during the 1972 campaign.

One of the most powerful Presidents the nation had ever had, Nixon's use of power made his presidency one of the most controversial.

China sent pair of giant pandas as gift to National Zoo. Peking zoo received musk oxen.

Index

*Asterisk indicates page on which illustration of subject appears.

ENDSHEET: When the Pacific stopped the westward rush of Americans, they built a beautiful city by the sea—San Francisco.

352